The

BIBLE

TOOLBOX

BRYAN H. CRIBB *and*

CHANNING L. CRISLER

ACADEMIC
NASHVILLE, TENNESSEE

We would like to dedicate this volume to our amazing,
loving, and supportive families:
Elizabeth Cribb and children, Daniel, Josiah, and Nathanael
Kelly Crisler and children, Silas, Taylee, Titus, Annalee, and Cross

CONTENTS

Part 1: The Bible Toolbox Instruction Manual   **1**

CHAPTER 1   Why Should We Use the Tools?: The Inspiration,
Authority, and Relevance of the Bible   7

CHAPTER 2   Tools for Interpreting the Story behind the Story:
The Origin of the Bible as We Know It   19

CHAPTER 3   Understanding the Tools in the Toolbox   51

Part 2: Tools for Interpreting the Old Testament   **79**

CHAPTER 4   Tools for Interpreting the Pentateuch   85

CHAPTER 5   Tools for Interpreting the Historical Books   149

CHAPTER 6   Tools for Interpreting the Poetry and Wisdom Books   227

CHAPTER 7   Tools for Interpreting the Prophetic Books   279

Part 3: Tools for Interpreting the New Testament   333

CHAPTER 8   Tools for Interpreting the Gospels   337

CHAPTER 9   Tools for Interpreting Acts and Paul's Biography   379

CHAPTER 10   Tools for Interpreting Paul's Letters   421

CHAPTER 11   Tools for Interpreting the General Epistles
and Revelation   475

Scripture Index   549

Part 1

The Bible Toolbox
Instruction Manual

Let's try an unofficial scientific experiment that I have tried with some of my classes. How many Bibles do you have? One? Two? Three or more? Five or more? Ten or more? If you possess a Bible, you join the majority in America. In fact, some 88 percent of Americans own at least one copy. And around 80 percent hold reverence for it in some manner.[1] And among students at the Christian university that employs me, we are probably talking close to 100 percent.

And yet, as ubiquitous as the Bible is, it is also perhaps the most avoided book ever printed—even by Christians. The same study cited

---

[1] Caleb Bell, Religion News Service, "Americans Love the Bible but Don't Read It Much," April 4, 2013, https://www.huffingtonpost.com/2013/04/04 /americans-love-the-bible-but-dont-read-it-much_n_3018425.html.

Someone once said that the biggest dust storm in history would be created
if Christians all took out their Bibles at once and started studying them.

above revealed only 57 percent read it more than four times per year, even though 61 percent confessed to needing to pick it up more.

Someone once said that the biggest dust storm in history would be created if Christians all took out their Bibles at once and started studying them.

Could we say that familiarity has bred not necessarily contempt but perhaps apathy among many Bible owners? Oh sure, Christians readily confess the Bible's intrinsic value, nature, and divine origins. But a distinct chasm exists between this stated belief and actual practice, between confessions of faith and expressed affections—especially compared to those who do not have such easy access.

The question is why? Why don't we have the same reaction as this people group in Indonesia,[2] weeping and dancing, when we receive or see the Scriptures? Why don't Christians study and cherish and

---

[2] United Bible Societies, "Kimyal New Testament Launch in Indonesia," 2010, https://vimeo.com/16493505.

celebrate them more? How can some be starving for the Bible itself, and yet many Christians are starving spiritually when they have spiritual food right in front of them?

The excuses are myriad. To find the excuses, I once conducted an unscientific survey of some of my students. Here are their top four excuses for not studying the Bible:

1. Chapel (and/or church) fills my quota for Bible reading.
2. I study it all the time for my classes; do I really need to study it outside of class?
3. The Bible is too hard to understand.
4. I don't see the relevance of such an ancient document.

If you boil down the excuses, you basically have two issues. Christians often don't see the value of the Bible and Bible study. And this lack of esteem is often due to the second issue: Christians often don't know how to study the Bible.

*Often, Christians don't know where to start in studying the
Bible. This book hopes to address this problem head-on.*

The following chapters seek to address this second issue head on.

If God has spoken and if he has revealed himself specially, we believe he has done so in a way that was meant to be understood. That doesn't mean that Bible interpretation is easy. Yes, it takes work, but understanding can be achieved if you have the correct tools. But you need to access the tools. Imagine attempting to put together a book-shelf or model airplane without a manual and the correct instruments.

This book purposes to provide prospective Bible readers with the proper tools to understand and interpret the Scriptures for themselves. Each chapter will describe to readers the tools to engage the Bible actively; we will even demonstrate how these tools are used with select texts. In this way, we hope not only to offer you proverbial "interpre-tive" fishes, but to give you the "exegetical"[3] poles, lines, and hooks. Ten years from now, we want you to be able to read the biblical text intuitively and naturally through this process.

The book is divided into three parts. Part 1 will serve as a manual for the process of interpretation. Chapter 1 will explain why we need the tools, examining the authority, inspiration, and relevance of the Bible. Chapter 2 will describe what we are using the tools on, looking at the nature and trustworthiness of the Bible. Chapter 3 is perhaps the most important in the book, as it will introduce the tools—what we call exe-getical principles and other topics essential to understanding the biblical text, such as geography, chronology, and other background issues.

Parts 2 and 3 will then detail and explain the tools for interpreting rightly both the Old and New Testaments. This latter discussion will proceed roughly "canonically"—that is, through the various divisions and books of the Bible in order. The Old Testament chapters cover the Pentateuch (chap. 4), the Historical Books (chap. 5), the Poetry and Wisdom Books (chap. 6), and the prophets and Prophetic Books (chap.

---

[3] Exegesis refers to the process of getting meaning "out of" the text. This idea will be explored more fully in chap. 3.

7). The New Testament chapters comprise Jesus and the Gospels (chap. 8), Acts and the life of Paul (chap. 9), the Letters of Paul (chap. 10), and the General Epistles and Revelation (chap. 11).

For each chapter in parts 2 and 3, we will have three main sections: Understanding the Tools, Putting the Tools to Use, and Applying the Results. The expansive Understanding the Tools sections will outline three categories of tools: Historical Tools (the historical context of the events themselves and the original author/audience), Literary Tools (the genre, structure, story line, message, and purpose of the books), and Theological Tools (including issues of salvation history and main theological themes). The Putting the Tools to Use sections will demonstrate how the tools might be applied to particular texts. And the Applying the Results sections will offer trajectories for personal and theological application in a way faithful to the original text. This final section will also provide discussion questions, devotional thoughts, and so forth, that will help the reader respond to the biblical message.

One final note before opening the Bible Toolbox: the goal of our discussion is not to be exhaustive but to serve as a resource. An instruction manual for a computer might tell you how to turn the computer on or how to understand some of the programs, but it won't comprehensively describe all that you might do with or find on your computer. Similarly, we will not provide all there is to know about the Bible. But our hope is that this text will open the door for future Bible study, by incorporating the discipline of Bible study into your own walk of faith.

With that stated, let's open the toolbox and see what we can find.

1

Why Should We Use the Tools?

The Inspiration, Authority, and Relevance of the Bible

Introduction

If you have your Bible within reach, pick it up and take a look at it for a moment. What you hold in your hand is an amazing book. Let's consider some Bible facts.

- The Bible is by far the most published book in history, with copies numbering in the billions, in hundreds of different languages and versions. And millions of new copies are printed every year.
- The Bible has shaped the scope and trajectory of world events and cultures. Think about what the world would be like today without it. Law and literature, architecture and art, morality and music, not to mention individual lives—hardly any area of

Western society has escaped its illuminating light and penetrating heat.

- Few books have people died to translate. Yet missionaries and Bible translators have literally given all they had—life, liberty, property, time—to ensure individuals from every tongue and tribe had access to the Scriptures. Take, for instance, Adoniram Judson, the first Baptist international missionary from the United States. Judson was imprisoned, persecuted, marginalized, and lost family members, including his wife, Ann, in an attempt to bring the gospel to the people of Burma and to translate the Bible into Burmese. Click on this link to hear a sermon from Dr. Daniel Akin, president of Southeastern Baptist Theological Seminary, about Judson's amazing life and translation efforts.[1]

- The Bible is also unlike any other so-called religious document. The sacred scripture of every other world religion—whether the Quran of Islam or the Book of Mormon of Mormonism or the Buddhavacana of Buddhism—typically originated from the spiritual claims of one man made over a relatively short period of time. Only the Bible maintains consistency and coherency of teaching and theology throughout its linear story line, despite being written over a 1,500-year period by some fifty different authors.[2]

- The Bible contains texts that accurately depict and predict events that would occur hundreds of years later. Most Christians rightly think of the amazing messianic prophecies

---

[1] Daniel Akin, Southeastern Baptist Theological Seminary chapel message, October 10, 2007, http://apps.sebts.edu/chmessages/resource_2509/10-16-07 _Dr_Daniel_L_Akin.mp3.

[2] "Is there a central message throughout all 66 unique books of the Bible?" YouTube video, 6:19, posted by Ehrman Project, September 4, 2010, https:// www.youtube.com/watch?v=DVgpkG4Ks1s.

of the Old Testament. Indeed, myriad texts look forward to both the person and work of Jesus Christ (see esp. Daniel 7; Isaiah 53; Psalms 22 and 110). But Scripture also foresees future empires (as in Daniel 2 and 7) and future kings—whether they be Jewish (Josiah in 1 Kgs 13:2) or pagan (Cyrus the Great of Persia in Isa 44:28).

- The Bible has tremendous explanatory power. For centuries, the problems of evil, purpose, being, justice, and origins, among many others, have baffled even the best minds. These are basic issues of a person's worldview or metanarrative, regardless of background or ethnicity or historical context. No other metanarrative addresses these matters as completely or consistently as that established and expressed by the Scriptures.[3]

- Finally, perhaps the most powerful testimonies to the Bible's uniqueness come from common folks like you and me. When we experience the life-changing power of the gospel as revealed in the Old and New Testaments, we join millions of others who have read the Bible and have had their hearts of stone transformed into hearts of flesh (Ezek 36:26).

Yet many people, including some Christians, would conceive the Bible as less than "amazing"—perhaps irrelevant, ancient, or at least inaccessible. Why should we study, and even base our lives on, a document written thousands of years ago to a different people in a different age from a different culture? Why should I trust the Bible over against any other ancient or modern document?

The following will seek to answer the question of relevance. It boils down to two fundamental issues: the Bible's inspiration and the Bible's authority. In other words, the Bible is relevant because it is

---

[3] For a list of 8 basic worldview questions, see https://www.christianity.com/theology/other-religions-beliefs/8-questions-every-worldview-must-answer.html.

authoritative. And it is authoritative not because I say so or because the church believes so, but because it possesses inherent divine inspiration as God's revelation.

God and Revelation

In a discussion of inspiration and authority, we should start with the topic of revelation. How do you know about God? About what he is like? About his will? About his plan of salvation? Theologians speak of God "revealing" himself in two main ways: (1) through creation and elements of the created order (general revelation or how God "generally" reveals himself to all peoples everywhere) and (2) through Scripture (special revelation or how God reveals himself through human language in a way that accommodates limited human understanding).

As the apostle Paul wrote in Rom 1:20, general revelation reveals something of God's invisible attributes, his power, and his divinity, so that all are without excuse. Creation declares "the glory of God" and "proclaims the work of his hands" (Ps 19:1). Yet without special revelation, we would lack the message of salvation. So we need special revelation, and we celebrate that God is one who has spoken in a way that can be understood.

The Nature of Special Revelation

What is this special revelation—the Bible—like? The Baptist Faith and Message,[4] the statement of faith for the Southern Baptist Convention, describes the Bible in a way with which many Christians would agree. The Bible is "a perfect treasure of divine instruction," having "God for its author, salvation for its end, and truth, without any mixture of error,

---

[4] *The Baptist Faith and Message*, 2000, http://www.sbc.net/bfm2000/bfm 2000.asp.

for its matter. Therefore, all Scripture is totally true and trustworthy. It reveals the principles by which God judges us, and therefore is, and will remain to the end of the world, the true center of Christian union, and the supreme standard by which all human conduct, creeds, and religious opinions should be tried."[5]

However, perhaps the author of Psalm 19 best describes the nature of the Scriptures: extolling them as "perfect," "trustworthy," "right," "radiant," "pure," and "reliable and altogether righteous" (vv. 7–9). The prophet Isaiah would add that the Scriptures are eternal (40:8), and the prophet Jeremiah would describe them as a "fire" (5:14).

Proof of Revelation

Can we verify that God has revealed himself in this way? If so, how? Many have tried to "prove" the Bible by using criteria from outside the Bible—archaeology, philosophy, historical proof. But these types of apologetic arguments are each limited.

---

[5] *The Baptist Faith and Message*, 2000, http://d3pi8hptl0qhh4.cloudfront .net/documents/bfm.pdf.

An archaeologist at work.

Take archaeology, for example. Imagine if you traveled to Israel on a dig and found a cave that said, "Here lies Abraham." Such a find, if authenticated, would gain you fame and demonstrate that Abraham lived. But could that "prove" that God had a covenant with Abraham, spoke to Abraham, and intervened in Abraham's life, as the Bible says he did?

There are just some things that archaeology—or any other external discipline, for that matter—cannot prove. As Australian theologian and author Graeme Goldsworthy states, "We cannot hope to prove the authority of the Bible on the basis of criteria from outside of the Bible, for that would be like shining a pocket flashlight on the sun to see if it is real."[6]

Instead, as circular as this argument seems, to establish that God has spoken, we must look at the Scriptures themselves. As Goldsworthy

---

[6] Graeme Goldsworthy, "What Is the Discipline of Biblical Theology?" IX Marks, http://sites.silaspartners.com/cc/article/0,,PTID314526_CHID 598016_CIID2031516,00.html.

says again, "God's Word is the ultimate authority and only such a word can authenticate itself." At the very least, seeing what the Bible testifies about itself is a basic starting point of any discussion of its authority. Indeed, if the Bible does not testify to its own divine origin, then we are wasting our time.

Testimony of Scripture about Scripture

So what does the Bible say about itself? The scriptural authors consistently speak of the divine origins of their writings.

In the Old Testament (OT), the authors draw a one-to-one correspondence between their words and God's words. For instance, in Exod 24:4, after describing the establishment of the covenant between God and Israel through Moses at Mount Sinai, the text says that Moses wrote down "all the words of the LORD" regarding this covenant. Notice that the text does not say "all the words of Moses."

For another example, try this experiment. Turn to any portion of the prophets—Amos or Isaiah or Ezekiel or Obadiah or Malachi. More than likely, you will find some form of prophetic formula "thus says the LORD," "the word of the LORD came to," "the declaration of the LORD," and so forth. You can find hundreds of examples of these expressions. Thus, the biblical writers display a self-conscious and universal awareness that God is speaking "through" them (Jer 37:2).

What about the New Testament (NT)? Probably the best-known text attesting to divine origins and thus inspiration comes from the apostle Paul's letter to his protégé Timothy. In 2 Tim 3:16, Paul states that all Scripture (referring to the Hebrew Scriptures or what Christians call the Old Testament) is literally "God-breathed." The clear intention of Paul's vivid word-picture is to demonstrate the divine origin of Scripture.

The apostle Peter further attests that the Scriptures were produced by "men spoke from God as they were carried along by the Holy

Spirit" (2 Pet 1:21). Thus, the text of Scripture is 100 percent the work of human authors, but also 100 percent the work of God's Holy Spirit. Jesus himself asserted his belief in the divine origin of Scripture in Matt 22:31–32, where he quoted Scripture as something "God said." Other texts that speak of or allude to the divine origins of Scripture include Matt 1:22; Acts 1:16; Heb 1:1–2; and 2 Cor 6:16.

Inspiration Clarified

This is what is meant by inspiration, then. Inspiration does not refer to the process of reading (e.g., the Bible is "inspiring" to read, even though it is), but to the process of writing. Nor does inspiration strictly refer to the authors. For example, Paul wrote other letters that are not considered to be inspired. Instead, though both the person and writings are under God's direction, "inspiration" specifically applies to the writings and in particular the autographs (the original documents, not the copies or translations).

Finally, God is not usually dictating the words to be written in some mechanical way—though this does happen at times; instead, he providentially orders the lives of the writers so that when they write they produce exactly what God would have his people to read.

> Verbal plenary inspiration refers to all the words and parts of the Bible being equally inspired.

Evangelical Christians hold to a verbal (all the words are inspired, not just the ideas), plenary (all parts are equally inspired) view of inspiration. If God is true (Rom 3:4) and the Bible is from God (2 Tim 3:16), then the Bible must be completely true. So Jesus's words in the Gospels are no more inspired than Moses's words in Exodus.

Inspiration and Authority

The scriptural authors did not believe themselves merely to be writing inspired texts "spoken from God." They also believed the texts to be authoritative. These issues are interconnected, of course. If God has indeed spoken, then those words have inherent authority.

One indication of the biblical writers' opinion of the Bible's authority is the phrase, "It is written . . . ," in reference to the OT. Some thirty-three times in the New Testament, writers ground their arguments in the authority of the OT by using this phrase. In other words, they believed that the only rationale necessary for their argument was that it was written in the authoritative OT. A popular bumper sticker when I was growing up proclaimed, "God said it, I believe it, that settles it." Today this adage does not comprise a very effective apologetic argument. But it was enough for the NT authors when it came to the Scriptures.

yodh

daleth

Finally, those who claim the name of Christ should primarily look to Jesus to see what he states about the issue of the Bible's authority. And Jesus clearly teaches a high view of Scripture. In John 10:35, Jesus states bluntly, "the Scripture cannot be broken." He also affirms the abiding authority of the OT as fulfilled in himself in Matt 5:18, where he states that

In Matt 5:18, Jesus refers to the the smallest Hebrew letter (the yodh) and the stroke of the Torah (like this tiny part of the daleth) not passing away until all is fulfilled. He speaks here of the comprehensive and abiding authority of Scripture.

not the smallest letter (Hebrew, *yodh*) and stroke (a tiny part of certain Hebrew letters) of the Torah will pass away until all has been fulfilled.

In addition, Jesus repeatedly refers to OT stories and individuals as historical. Even texts that modern scholars dismiss as mythical, Jesus affirms as actually occurring—for example, God's creation of humans (Matt 19:4), Abel's murder (Luke 11:51), Noah (Luke 17:26), and Jonah and the fish (Matt 12:40).

One final voice speaks and continues to speak to the issue of authority—the Holy Spirit, the third Person of the Trinity. Paul makes a striking statement in 1 Cor 2:14—that the things of God are foolish to natural man (unregenerate or unsaved humans without the enlivening work of God's Spirit). If this is true, then no amount of evidence and no human argumentation will convince a person of the authority/inspiration of Scripture. God is a sovereign God, and he, through his Spirit, works change in human hearts. Thus, it is he who will convict you of the truth and authority of Scripture (see John 3; 10:27).

Final Challenge

An apocryphal anecdote has been circulated for some time at my alma mater, The Southern Baptist Theological Seminary, regarding one of my former professors. The story goes that a student of this professor once questioned him as to whether he ever gave pop quizzes.

With a smile, this peculiar professor responded that he would give a pop quiz the same day that he entered the classroom through the second story window instead of the door. Of course, the threat was taken in jest. And, as is often the case, presumption precedes disaster. The next class, the professor climbed through the classroom window, quiz in hand, to the shock of all the students.

Whether or not this fable is factual, it does have a moral. If this student had truly believed that the professor would scramble through that window, a good deal of studying might have taken place beforehand. In other words, true belief is tied to action.

Unfortunately, with many Christians (myself included), a disconnect sometimes exists between our stated beliefs and our actual actions. This is especially true of Scripture, I believe.

Does it matter if God has spoken? Surely, the answer is yes. If God has, as the Bible testifies, revealed himself both specially and generally, then it makes all the difference in the world. It is not a truth that you can just take or leave. If Scripture is God-breathed, then it is authoritative, and, as Paul states, it is "profitable for teaching, for rebuking, for correcting, for training in righteousness, so that the man of God may be complete, equipped for every good work" (2 Tim 3:16–17). The Scriptures are not just perfect and pure, true and trustworthy, but they also warn and make wise, rejoice and revive, enlighten and endure (Ps 19:7–10).

As you read the rest of this book, understand that this endeavor of Bible study is not merely academic in nature. Employing the tools in the Bible toolbox can be both life changing and life challenging, because you are engaging life-penetrating revelation. Our encouragement before you read the rest of this text is that you engage in some introspection. Think about the following questions:

- Upon reading this text, what is your perception of the Bible and its authority? In other words, do you see it as an authoritative document? Why or why not?
- Would you agree that if the Bible is God's Word, then it is authoritative?
- Do you believe the Bible is God's Word? If so, how does this affirmation affect your life? Should it affect your life?

- Does the Bible contain factual errors? Does it matter if we affirm the Bible's inerrancy? Listen to this video by D. A. Carson and use it to examine your own beliefs about inerrancy.[7]
- Why do you think God reveals himself with physical manifestations of smoke, fire, and earthquakes in Exodus 19 before the giving of his revelation (in the form of the Ten Commandments) in Exodus 20? What does this say about the power of God's revelation?

---

[7] "What is 'inerrancy'?", YouTube video, 4:14, posted by Ehrman Project, September 4, 2010, https://www.youtube.com/watch?v=i6zudFtjI4U&feature=player_embedded#!.

2

Tools for Interpreting
the Story behind the Story

The Origin of the Bible
as We Know It

Although many readers are familiar with the story line of the Bible, they often lack knowledge about the story behind the Bible itself. Readers are sometimes fuzzy on questions related to the backstory of the Bible. Why are there two "testaments"? Why does it contain these books and not others? How do we connect the dots from original author to ancient manuscripts to modern-day translations? Why are there so many different translations? All of these questions and more require us to think about the "story behind the story" contained in the Bible itself.

The problem we face is that no one in ancient Israel or the early church provides a frame-by-frame account of this story. We must reconstruct it based on clues provided by the Bible itself, ancient history, and the history of the church. What follows is a brief sketch of this reconstructed story. We will track the story in four stages: (1) original production, (2) transmission, (3) canonization, and (4) translation. As we shall see, there is some chronological overlap in stages 2 through 4. Before we walk through these stages, let's take a brief tour of the Bible's contents.

Contents of the Bible

From the broadest perspective, the Bible contains two testaments, each containing various subsections.

The Two Testaments

Standing behind the English titles Old Testament and New Testament are the Latin term *testamentum*, meaning "testament," and the Greek term *diathēkē*, meaning "covenant." *Testamentum* is the Latin translation of the Greek word *diathēkē*. Therefore, early Christian references to the Old and New Testaments are actually references to Old and New "Covenants." From F. F. Bruce's perspective, Old and New Covenants are fitting titles for the two sections of the Bible, because they evoke "the ancient covenant of Sinai and the new covenant inaugurated by Jesus." These are "spiritual movements" that "gave rise to a special body of literature."[1] There is surely more to the Old Testament (OT) and New Testament (NT) than what Bruce states here, but his point is well taken. Of course, there is nothing within the biblical text itself that demands the Bible be titled Testaments/Covenants. That would, after all, be a historical impossibility, because the books of the Bible first existed as smaller collections and individual pieces of literature

---

[1] F. F. Bruce, *The Canon of Scripture* (Downers Grove, IL: InterVarsity, 1988), 21.

before they were brought together as a single volume. Only in the late second century did prominent Christian figures, such as Clement of Alexandria and Tertullian of Carthage, begin to refer to the collective books of the Bible as Old and New Covenants (Testaments). It is a reference that has endured until today.

Subsections of Testaments

Within the Old and New Testaments, we find various subsections that are delineated in a few different ways. The Hebrew Bible, or Tanak, contains three major sections: the Law, the Prophets, and the Writings. *Tanak* is an acronym built on the initial Hebrew consonant of the three parts of the Hebrew Bible: **T**orah (Law), **N**evi'im (Prophets), and **K**etuvim (Writings). This tripartite division is evident as early as 130 BC in the prologue of a Jewish apocryphal work called *Sirach* and in the first-century AD works of the Jewish philosopher Philo. Jesus seems to refer to a tripartite division of Israel's Scriptures when he explains to his disciples after his resurrection, "These are my words that I spoke to you while I was still with you—that everything written about me in the Law of Moses, the Prophets, and the Psalms must be fulfilled" (Luke 24:44). Here Jesus mentions three different parts of Israel's Scriptures. Jesus's reference to the Psalms is probably representative for all of the "Writings."

English Protestant Bibles contain the same thirty-nine books as the Tanak (though the Tanak numbers them differently), but they are often divided into the following five OT subsections: (1) Pentateuch, (2) History, (3) Poetry and Wisdom, (4) Major Prophets, and (5) Minor Prophets. This categorization is influenced by the order of the OT books as found in copies of the Septuagint (LXX—the Greek translation of the Hebrew Bible).

Hebraic Canon and Arrangement of Books

Law/Torah (תורה)

Genesis	Numbers
Exodus	Deuteronomy
Leviticus	

Prophets/Nevi'im (נביאים)

Joshua	Isaiah
Judges	Jeremiah
Samuel	Ezekiel
Kings	

The Twelve = *one of the twenty-four books of the Hebrew Canon*

Hosea	Nahum
Joel	Habakkuk
Amos	Zephaniah
Obadiah	Haggai
Jonah	Zechariah
Micah	Malachi

Writings/Ketuvim (כתובים)

Psalms	Ecclesiastes
Proverbs	Esther
Job	Daniel
Song of Songs	Ezra & Nehemiah
Ruth	Chronicles
Lamentations	

Protestant OT Canon & Arrangement of Books

Pentateuch

Genesis	Numbers
Exodus	Deuteronomy
Leviticus	

Historical Books

Joshua	2 Kings
Judges	1 Chronicles
Ruth	2 Chronicles

1 Samuel	Ezra
2 Samuel	Nehemiah
1 Kings	Esther
Poetic–Wisdom Books	
Job	
Psalms	
Proverbs	
Ecclesiastes	
Song of Songs	
Prophets	
Isaiah	Jonah
Jeremiah	Micah
Lamentations	Nahum
Ezekiel	Habakkuk
Daniel	Zephaniah
Hosea	Haggai
Joel	Zechariah
Amos	Malachi
Obadiah	

The New Testament contains twenty-seven books with five major sections: (1) Gospels, (2) Acts, (3) Pauline Epistles, (4) General Epistles, and (5) Revelation.

Stage 1: The Original Production of the Books

Writers from ancient Israel and the early church produced sixty-six books that we refer to collectively as the Holy Bible.[2] They are divided into two main parts, the Old and New Testaments. These combined testaments represent a finished product. However, to understand the

---

[2] For a discussion on the origin of the English term *Bible*, see the Online Etymology Dictionary, https://www.etymonline.com/word/bible.

origin of this finished product, we must begin by answering two basic questions: (1) Why did the biblical authors write these books in the first place? and (2) How did they write them?

Original Purposes

There are several reasons why the Old and New Testament authors produced their works. Each of these purposes is interrelated with and informs the others. There is some overlap of purposes between the testaments, but there are also purposes unique to certain historical moments.

Purposes for OT Production

Based on the internal evidence of the Bible, three main factors propelled the OT authors to produce their respective documents. First, Yahweh explicitly instructed some individuals to write. We see this in various places across the landscape of the OT:

> The LORD also said to Moses, "Write down these words, for I have made a covenant with you and with Israel based on these words." (Exod 34:27)

> The LORD answered me: Write down this vision; clearly inscribe it on tablets so one may easily read it. (Hab 2:2)

Such statements helped to set a precedent in ancient Israel for penning documents. In short, there was a divine impetus behind the production of the OT books. God commanded prophets, poets, and kings to write. So they did.

A second factor that propelled the production of the OT was the concern to teach and encourage ancient Israelites at various points in their history. We see this early in Israel's history. For example, Moses instructed future kings of Israel to *write* down a copy of the law for their own meditation and instruction: "It is to remain with him, and he is to read from it all the days of his life, so that he may learn to fear the LORD his God, to observe all the words of this instruction, and to do these statutes. Then his heart will not be exalted above his countrymen, he will not turn from this command to the right or the left, and he and his sons will continue reigning many years in Israel" (Deut 17:19–20).

Similarly, Moses commanded all Israelites to write down the words of the law as a means of instruction: "Write them on the doorposts of your house and on your city gates" (Deut 6:9). These commands indicate a correlation between the written word and instruction established by Moses. Therefore, it logically follows that subsequent OT authors wrote to teach and encourage as well. They wrote because Israel always had a need for instruction, whether it was a rebuke, a warning, or encouragement.

Third, OT writers produced their respective books to preserve and pass on to future generations what God had accomplished for Israel, what he had promised them, and what he had instructed them to do until he fulfilled those promises.

Purposes for NT Production

Multiple factors compelled NT writers to pen their documents. First, they wanted to preserve the teachings and works of Jesus to encourage the church and evangelize the lost. John makes this clear in his explicit purpose statement: "Jesus performed many other signs in the presence of his disciples that are not written in this book. But these are written so that you may believe Jesus is the Messiah, the Son of God, and that by believing you may have life in his name" (John 20:30–31).

Second, they wrote to respond to suffering and various crises in the church. Early Christians faced internal and external afflictions that prompted the production of various documents. Internally churches

faced ongoing problems with sin, factions, false teachers, and challenges, such as blending together Jews and Gentiles into one believing
community. Externally early Christians faced social, political, and religious pressures. These kinds of afflictions had to be addressed in person
and sometimes in writing. The latter resulted in many of the canonized
NT books.

Third, some NT writers indicate that God prompted them to
write. John's Apocalypse is a prime example. In the opening lines of
Revelation, John hears a divine voice with the following command
"Write on a scroll what you see and send it to the seven churches"
(Rev 1:11).[3] Similarly, as Paul answers the Corinthians' question about
marriage, he notes that the Spirit has directed what he wrote: "And
I think that I also have the Spirit of God" (1 Cor 7:40). Additionally,
Peter briefly mentions Paul's Letters and elevates them to the level
of Israel's Scriptures, which Jews held to be inspired by God (2 Pet
3:15–16). In other words, Peter tacitly acknowledges that God led Paul
to write.

Original Manner of Production

Clearly, the biblical authors produced their writings for various purposes. But what did the actual process of writing look like? Let's consider the biblical authors' sources, writing surfaces, instruments, and
practices.

Manner of OT Production

Some *sources* that OT writers used to produce their respective works
include (1) divine testimony, (2) oral tradition, and (3) copies of Torah

---

[3] See similar commands to write in Rev 1:19; 2:1, 8, 12, 18; 3:1, 7, 14;
10:4; 14:13; 19:9; 21:5.

(for post-Pentateuchal writers, ca. 1406 BC–433 BC).[4] In some instances, God explicitly told an OT author what to write. The classic example is Moses's reception of the law and instructions for the tabernacle (Exodus 20–31; 35–40).

Moses's reception of the law is a classic example within Israel's history of the importance placed on a written word.

OT authors also employed oral tradition. Before certain events were written down, they were preserved and passed on by word of mouth. Although some scholars question the stability and reliability of the oral period, it is reasonable to assume that ancient Israelite

---

[4] The range of dates 1406 BC–433 BC is based on the assumption that the first post-Pentateuchal book, Joshua, was written in 1406 BC, and the last post-Pentateuchal book, Malachi, was written in 433 BC. See John Walton, *Chronological and Background Charts of the Old Testament* (Grand Rapids: Zondervan, 1994), 12.

communities employed checks and balances to preserve faithfully the testimony. Moreover, from a theological perspective, it is logical to believe that God oversaw the preservation of the material prior to its inscripturation.

Finally, post–Pentateuchal authors often used the Torah (i.e., Genesis, Exodus, Leviticus, Numbers, Deuteronomy) as a source for their own writings. For example, the psalmist gushes over Torah (Law/instruction), exclaiming, "The instruction of the LORD is perfect, renewing one's life; the testimony of the LORD is trustworthy, making the inexperienced wise. The precepts of the LORD are right, making the heart glad; the command of the LORD is radiant, making the eyes light up" (19:7–8).

The *writing surfaces* used by the OT writers included (1) stone, (2) stone tablets, (3) wooden tablets, and (4) papyrus.[5] The OT mentions these various writing surfaces.

> Stone: I wish that my words were written down, that they were recorded on a scroll or were inscribe in stone forever by an iron stylus and lead! (Job 19:23–24)

> Stone Tablet: The LORD said to Moses, "Cut two stone tablets like the first ones, and I will write on them the words that were on the first tablets, which you broke." (Exod 34:1)

> Wooden Tablet: Go now, write it on a tablet in their presence and inscribe it on a scroll; it will be for the future, forever and ever. (Isa 30:8)

> Papyrus: Take a scroll, and write on it all the words I have spoken to you concerning Israel, Judah, and all the nations from

---

[5] I am helped here by Ernst Würthwein, *The Text of the Old Testament*, 2nd ed. (Grand Rapids: Eerdmans, 1988), 4–7.

the time I first spoke to you during Josiah's reign until today. (Jer 36:2)

OT authors or the scribes who assisted them (e.g., Jer 36:18) used *writing instruments* that included (1) a stylus, (2) reed pen of a professional scribe, and (3) ink. The OT mentions these various writing instruments.

> Stylus: The sin of Judah is written with an iron stylus. With a diamond point it is engraved on the tablet of their hearts and on the horns of their altars. (Jer 17:1)

> Reed Pen: My heart is moved by a noble theme as I recite my verses to the king; my tongue is the pen of a skillful writer. (Ps 45:1)

> Ink: Baruch said to them, "At his dictation. He recited all these words to me while I was writing on the scroll in ink." (Jer 36:18)

For a demonstration of the *writing practices* used by ancient biblical scribes, see Ancient Scribal Practices.[6]

Manner of NT Production

The *sources* used by the NT authors include (1) eyewitness testimony, (2) oral tradition, (3) the Greek OT, (4) written sources, and (5) other NT writings.

The Gospel writers and the writer of Acts (Luke) used eyewitness testimony as a source for their depictions of Jesus and the mission of the early church. For example, the author of John notes, "This is the

---

[6] "The Work of a Scribe," YouTube video, 1:35, posted by Josh McDowell, December 22, 2015, https://www.youtube.com/watch?v=e6IGj42UX_Y& feature=youtu.be.

disciple who testifies to these things and who wrote them down. We know that his testimony is true" (John 21:24).

Prior to the writing of the Gospels, *oral tradition* helped in preserving the teaching and deeds of Jesus. Once again, despite the objections of some, the early church had a series of checks and balances to preserve the accuracy of the tradition.[7]

As we will discuss in later chapters, the NT writers made judicious use of the OT. They usually employed a Greek version of the OT. Additionally, some scholars have suggested that the NT writers used no-longer-extant written sources that contained items such as sayings of Jesus, early Christian hymns, and collections of messianic OT passages.

Finally, in the case of the Gospels, Matthew and Luke used Mark as a resource for writing their own Gospels.

The *writing surfaces* used by the NT writers included papyrus and parchment. Papyrus is a surface produced from the papyrus plant found in the Nile Delta.[8] Parchment is made of animal skins, particularly from a sheep or goat. Both of these writing surfaces are explicitly mentioned in the NT.

Parchment: When you come, bring the cloak I left in Troas with Carpus, as well as the scrolls, especially the parchments. (2 Tim 4:13).

Papyrus: Though I have many things to write to you, I don't want to use paper [papyrus] and ink. (2 John 1:12)

---

[7] E.g., Paul mentions in 1 Cor 15:6 that many of those who saw the risen Jesus were still living at the time that he wrote his letter. The insinuation is that if the Corinthians had doubts about the resurrection of Jesus there were witnesses who could and did verify it.

[8] Kurt Aland and Barbara Aland, *The Text of the New Testament* (Grand Rapids: Eerdmans, 1987), 75.

To see part of P[46], an ancient NT papyrus manuscript, see P[46].[9]

The reed pen and ink are the *writing instruments* used by NT writers. John refers to both: "I have many things to write you, but I don't want to write you with pen and ink" (3 John 13).

Among the *writing practices* employed by NT authors, it should be noted that they often used an amanuensis or secretary. For example, toward the end of Romans, we find "I Tertius, who wrote this letter, greet you in the Lord" (16:22).[10] Paul provided the content of the letter, but Tertius performed the physical writing process.

Stage 2: The Transmission of the Books

We can label the next stage in the story of the Bible's origin as "transmission." Transmission refers to the events that occurred after the original production of the documents. The events span several centuries and include (1) preservation and collection, (2) copying, (3) early translations/versions, and (4) the multiplication of manuscripts.

OT Transmission

Preservation and Collection

The OT provides some clues about the way ancient Israelites preserved these documents through the centuries. For example, we know that Moses gave instructions about making copies of the law to future kings (Deut 17:18). When Joshua entered Canaan, he wrote a copy of the law on stones (Josh 8:32). Although Josiah's rediscovery of the law during the seventh century BC paints a bleak picture of Judah's spiritual condition at that time, it indicates that Scripture was preserved from the

---

[9] "P[46]," The Center for the Study of New Testament Manuscripts, http://www.csntm.org/manuscript/View/GA_P46_Mich.

[10] See also 1 Pet 5:12.

1400s BC to the 600s BC (2 Kgs 22:1–11). In the postexilic era (538 BC–430 BC), the writer of Nehemiah recounted how Ezra the scribe read the law before the assembly of Israel. His description includes "Ezra opened the book [*sepher*] in full view of all the people, since he was elevated above everyone. As he opened it, all the people stood up" (Neh 8:5). So there are indications that for almost 1,000 years Israelites preserved copies of what we now call the OT. Various groups likely contributed to the preservation and collection of texts, such as disciples of prophets, priests, and scribes.[11] Additionally, it should be kept in mind that after the Babylonian exile (538 BC), Jewish people lived in Palestine, Babylon (Persia/Mesopotamian region), and Egypt where different text types developed (Proto-Masoretic; Proto-Samaritan; Proto-Septuagint). By 100 BC–AD 100, a standardized text emerged based on all three text types.

Copying

The copying of OT manuscripts is also a key step in stage 2. The most important evidence that we have for this step begins with materials from around 300 BC and runs through the tenth century AD. The 1947 discovery of the so-called Dead Sea Scrolls at Qumran in Israel provided the oldest manuscript evidence of the Hebrew Bible. The caves of Qumran preserved a rich cache of manuscripts, which collectively contained fragments from every OT book except Esther.[12] Prior to this discovery, the oldest complete copies of the OT books were from

---

[11] Eugene Ulrich, "The Old Testament Text and Its Transmission," in *The New Cambridge History of the Bible, Vol. 1: From the Beginnings to 600*, ed. James Carleton Paget and Joachim Schaper (Cambridge: Cambridge University Press, 2013), 86.

[12] The caves of Qumran also contained sectarian literature produced by members of the Qumran community that reflected their distinct beliefs and practices.

around the tenth century BC. The tenth-century text is known as the Masoretic Text, named after a group of Jewish scholars from the sixth to tenth centuries AD who established a stable and recognized text of the Hebrew Bible. When scholars compared the OT text of the Dead Sea Scrolls to the Masoretic Text, they concluded that there were very few differences between them. As Ellis Brotzman puts it, "While there are small differences between the Masoretic text and various Qumran documents, the overall agreement between them is striking."[13] It provided evidence that the OT text had been faithfully preserved from the second century BC to the tenth century AD.

This is part of a papyrus manuscript labeled P⁴⁶. The section shown here is from 1 Cor 2:3-3:5.

Early Translations

In addition to scribes making copies of the OT, stage 2 is marked by the production of early translations and versions of the OT. The Septuagint (LXX) is the first known translation of the Hebrew Bible into another language, namely Greek. Production of the LXX began in the third

---

[13] Ellis R. Brotzman, *Old Testament Textual Criticism: A Practical Introduction* (Grand Rapids: Baker, 1994), 95.

century BC. Other ancient translations/versions of the OT include the Aramaic Targums and the Peshitta (the earliest Syriac version of the OT).

This is the beginning of the scroll referred to as Pesher or Commentary on Habakkuk (1QpHab). It is one of the many scrolls discovered at Qumran.

Multiplication of Manuscripts

The copying and translation of the OT resulted in the multiplication of manuscripts. Today OT textual critics compare these manuscripts to establish the original reading of the OT text.

NT Transmission

The transmission of the NT likewise involves (1) preservation and collection, (2) copying, (3) early translations/versions, and (4) the multiplication of manuscripts.

Preservation and Collection

The preservation and collection of NT writings began as early as the first century AD. In fact, some of the original authors helped orchestrate this process. For example, at the end of his letter to the Colossians, Paul gives the following instructions: "After this letter has been read at your gathering, have it read also in the church of the Laodiceans; and see that you also read the letter from Laodicea" (4:16). Notice that Paul wants the letter originally written for the Colossians to be passed on to another congregation. The Colossians most likely made a copy of the letter and sent it to the Laodiceans. Once the letter arrived in Laodicea, before sending it to another church, the Laodiceans most likely made a copy. And this process would churn on. What we also gather from the NT is that the various documents were being copied and gathered into collections. For example, at the close of his second letter, Peter mentions Paul's "letters"—plural (2 Pet 3:14–16). This reference indicates an early collection of Paul's Letters. Additionally, we can infer a process of preservation and collection in the writings of the apostolic fathers and early church fathers (second-third centuries AD). Many of these writers reference a variety of NT documents in their own writings, which indicates they had a collection of documents with which to work.

Copying

As noted already, the copying of NT documents took place early and often. Beyond the copying of texts that began in the first-century era, extant manuscripts from as early as the second century AD indicate the regularity of this practice. From the second to fifteenth centuries AD, scribes produced thousands of copies by hand. *See Wordsearch video for an example of textual variants that arose due to hand copying of manuscripts.*

Early Translations

The original authors and subsequent scribes wrote in Koine Greek and various translations of the NT appeared as early as AD 180. The oldest translations of the NT include the Old Latin version as well as translations written in Syriac and Coptic. As Christianity spread, so did the need for translations of the NT in various languages.

Multiplication of Manuscripts

The papyrus fragment known as P[52] is from the 2nd century AD. It contains John 18:31-34, 37-38.

All of this literary industry resulted in the multiplication of manuscripts. If we consider only manuscripts written in Greek, the current total stands at approximately 5,800. Just to give you a sense of how significant that number is, let's compare the textual evidence for the NT to two other ancient writings.[14] There are currently 643 copies of Homer's *Iliad*, which was originally produced in the eighth century BC. The oldest extant and full copy of the *Iliad* dates to the tenth century AD. Similarly, there are currently ten copies of Caesar's *Gallic Wars*, originally produced in the first century BC. The oldest extant copy dates to around the ninth century AD. Compare this to the 5,800 manuscripts of the NT. The earliest fragment of the NT dates to the second century AD, and the earliest complete copies of individual books from the NT date to the second century AD as well. Codex Sinaiticus (ca. 4th century AD) contains the oldest complete copy of the NT. Clearly the age and sheer volume of NT manuscripts

---

[14] I am helped here by Andreas Köstenberger, L. Scott Kellum, and Charles L. Quarles, *The Cradle, the Cross, and the Crown* (Nashville: Broadman & Holman, 2009), 34.

dwarfs its ancient competitors. NT textual critics sort through these manuscripts to establish the original reading of the NT. To learn more about this fascinating work, see Overview of NT Textual Criticism.[15]

Codex Sinaiticus is from the 4th century AD. It contains the oldest complete collection of NT documents.

Stage 3: The Canonization of the Books

One of the most pressing questions in the story of the Bible's origin involves how the early church came to recognize some writings as

---

[15] Michael Bernard YouTube channel, "What is New Testament Textual Criticism," YouTube video, 9:05, posted by Michael Bernard, December 24, 2016, https://www.youtube.com/watch?v=gK1O4VHtD9I.

authoritative while excluding others. This whole discussion is often called canonization. In antiquity, the term *canon* referred to a rod used for measuring purposes. Its figurative use in the early church referred to an authoritative list or group of writings. Athanasius, bishop of Alexandria, first applied the term to the books of the Bible in AD 367.[16] However, as well shall see, the idea of canon preceded Athanasius's reference by several centuries.

Canonization of the OT

Hypotheses abound when it comes to the formation of the Old Testament canon. It has often been popular to think of the formation of the OT canon as a three-stage theory that corresponded to the three divisions of the Hebrew Bible. In this hypothesis, the Law was canonized in the late sixth century BC; the Prophets were canonized in the third century BC; the Writings were finally canonized in the late first century AD. However, there is no hard evidence that the process unfolded in this exact manner.

Early "Canonical" References

One of the first explicit references within Jewish history to a collection of texts is found in the second-century BC apocryphal work, 2 Maccabees. The writer recalls that Nehemiah "founded a library and collected the books about the kings and prophets, and the writings of David, and letters of kings about votive offers." Whether or not Nehemiah actually founded a library is beside the point. What is important for our purposes is that here we have an explicit reference to a collection of scriptural books. The narrator continues, that Judas Maccabeus "collected all the books that had been lost on account of

---

[16] Bruce, *Canon of Scripture*, 17.

the war that had come upon us, and they are in our possession" (2 Macc 2:13–14 NRSV). Again, this is a reference to a collection of books. The fact that these works had been "collected" implies that they were viewed as authoritative. All of this points to at least the conception of a "canon" in the second century BC of early Judaism.

Other Sources for an OT Canon

Our understanding of the OT canon is also informed by evidence from four other sources: Qumran, Jesus, the New Testament writers, and Josephus. As noted already, in 1947, approximately 850 ancient scrolls were discovered in eleven caves northwest of the Dead Sea. The scrolls contained some works unique to the community. More important for our current purposes is that the entire Hebrew Bible is represented among these scrolls except for the book of Esther. In addition to copies of OT books such as Isaiah and the Psalms, the Dead Sea Scrolls contain commentaries on various OT books such as Habakkuk. In light of this textual evidence, Bruce concludes "We may confidently say, therefore, that the 'canon' of the Qumran community included the Pentateuch, the Prophets, and the Psalms."[17]

Second, Jesus's teaching in the NT indicates that Jews in the first century had a fairly clear sense of "canon." In Luke 24:44, Jesus explains his death and resurrection to his disciples, noting, "These are my words that I spoke to you while I was still with you—that everything written about me in the Law of Moses, the Prophets, and the Psalms must be fulfilled." Jesus mentions the tripartite division of the Hebrew Bible, because his reference to the Psalms probably represents all of the Writings.

Third, the various OT citations by the New Testament writers also inform us about the existence of an OT canon among Second

---

[17] Bruce, 39.

Temple Jews and the early church. The NT writers cite verses from all three parts of the Hebrew canon. Conversely, with the exception of Jude 14, the NT writers do not cite any other extant Jewish writings. Other Jewish works referred to as OT Pseudepigrapha were available to the NT writers, but they did not cite them authoritatively in the way they did the OT.[18] Therefore, we can safely infer that, at least for the NT writers, the Law, the Prophets, and the Writings stood alone as an authoritative body of literature during the Second Temple era and their own day.

Finally, the works of the first-century AD Jewish historian Josephus also indicate familiarity with some kind of tripartite canon of Scripture. For a brief bio on Josephus, see the Josephus Bio.[19] In his work *Against Apion*, Josephus defends the reliability of the OT sources for writing about Jewish history:

> We have not a myriad of books, disagreeing and conflicting with one another, but only twenty-two, containing the record of all time, and justly accredited. Of these, five are *the books of Moses,* containing the laws and the history handed down from the creation of the human race right to his own death. This period falls a little short of three thousand years. From the death of Moses to the time Artaxerxes, who was king of Persia after Xerxes, *the prophets* who followed Moses have written

---

[18] Jude 14–15 contains a quotation from *1 Enoch* 1:9 and reads, "It was about these that Enoch, in the seventh generation from Adam, prophesied: "Look! The Lord comes with tens of thousands of his holy ones to execute judgment on all and to convict all the ungodly concerning all the ungodly acts that they have done in an ungodly way, and concerning all the harsh things ungodly sinners have said against him."" Jude most likely cites this pseudepigraphal text due to the audience's familiarity with it and for illustrative purposes.

[19] "Flavius Josephus: Jewish priest, soldier, and scholar," Christian Classics Ethereal Library, http://www.ccel.org/ccel/josephus.

down in the thirteen books the things that were done in their days. The remaining four books contain *hymns to God and principles of life* for human beings.[20]

Josephus's reference to "twenty books" does not mean that his own "canon" is missing other works that are now contained in our OT. Instead, like many who numbered the Hebraic books in his day, he has most likely combined books that the English Protestant Bible counts separately (e.g., Ruth counted as an appendix to Judges rather than a separate book). In any case, Josephus is helpful at this point, because he again reinforces the historical reality of an authoritative body of literature in the first century AD.

The Role of the LXX

Another factor to consider in discussing the OT canon is the Septuagint (LXX). As mentioned earlier, the Septuagint is the Greek translation of the Hebrew Bible. The translation began with the first five books around 250 BC in Alexandria, Egypt. Within the next two centuries, the rest of the books were translated into Greek as well.

The LXX does present one problem for understanding the canonization of the OT within Second Temple Judaism and Christianity. Specifically, it contains books that are not in the Hebrew or Protestant Bible. Many of these books, referred to by some as the Apocrypha, are recognized in Catholic and Orthodox traditions as canonical. For a comparison of Hebrew, Protestant, Catholic, and Orthodox canons, see the List of Canonical Works.[21] However, these particular books are not Greek translations of prior Hebrew works. They are Jewish writings written in Greek; they were not originally part of the Hebrew

---

[20] Josephus, *Against Apion* 1.38–41, emphasis added.

[21] "The Old Testament Canon and Apocrypha," http://www.bible -researcher.com/canon2.html.

Bible. Their inclusion in the Catholic Bible stems in large part from their prior inclusion in the Latin Vulgate (the fourth-century AD Latin translation of the Bible). During the Reformation, the canon of the Latin Vulgate faced challenges by Protestants who translated the OT afresh from the Hebrew text, which did not contain this apocryphal material. Consequently, these additional books were not included. Since the Council of Trent (AD 1545–1563) the Catholic Church has continued to recognize these additional Jewish Greek works as canonical, while Protestants do not. For a brief discussion about Protestant views in comparison to Trent, see the Protestant Views of Canon.[22]

Canonical Criteria for the OT

We have established that an OT canon existed as early as the second century BC and possibly prior to that. However, we must also consider how OT books came to be recognized as authoritative within the ancient Jewish community and early Christian church. What kind of criteria did a book have to meet in order to be recognized as "canonical"? To reiterate, we do not have records of ancient discussions about these matters. Yet we can infer some criteria based upon Scripture itself, as well as Jewish and early Christian practices.

1.   Some OT texts explicitly mention their own inherent authoritative status (see Deut 4:2).
2.   A book's authorship needed to have a clear connection to an authoritative figure within Israel, such as a prophet or king.
3.   From an early Christian perspective, OT books cited by Jesus or the NT writers could be considered authoritative.

---

[22] Joe Carter, "9 Things You Should Know about the Council of Trent," The Gospel Coalition, December 5, 2013, https://www.thegospelcoalition .org/article/9-things-you-should-know-about-the-council-of-trent/.

Canonization of the NT

We now turn our attention to the canonization of the New Testament. As a reminder, we are exploring the concept of *canon* even though the term does not appear in Christianity until AD 367. There are some key pieces of evidence that indicate the concept of canon was alive and well long before Athanasius penned his festal letter in 367.

Internal Evidence for a NT Canon

The evidence for a canon of NT works in the early church begins within the pages of the NT itself. For example, in his closing exhortations,

Athanasius is often considered the first Christian figure to use the word "canon" as a reference to the authoritative nature of the biblical books. However, as noted in this chapter, the idea of "canon" existed within the early church long before Athanasius coined the term.

Peter writes: "Also, regard the patience of our Lord as salvation, just as our dear brother *Paul* has written to you according to the wisdom given to him. He speaks about these things in all his *letters*. There are some matters that are hard to understand. The untaught and unstable will twist them to their own destruction, as they also do with the *rest of the Scriptures*" (2 Pet 3:15–16, emphasis added).

Two phrases stand out here. Peter refers to Paul's Letters in the plural. As I noted previously, this implies that first-century Christians were already circulating and collecting Paul's Letters. Other communities besides Paul's original addressees were reading what Paul had written to the Corinthians, Romans, and so forth. Paul himself encouraged this kind of sharing of his letters (Col 4:16). We should also pay close attention to Peter's comparison between Paul's Letters and "the rest of the Scriptures." This is a clear reference to Israel's Scriptures (OT). Peter essentially elevates Paul's Letters to the same kind of authoritative, eventually canonical, status as the OT.

"Patristic" Evidence for a NT Canon

After the first century AD, we find evidence for the concept of a NT canon in two sources: patristic writers and authoritative lists of books.[23] For example, the second-century martyr Polycarp mentions a kind of authoritative collection of Paul's works: "For neither I nor anyone like me can keep pace with the wisdom of the blessed and glorious Paul. When he was with you in the presence of the people of that time, he accurately and reliably taught the word concerning the truth. And when he was absent he wrote you letters" (*Polycarp to the Philippians* 3:2).

---

[23] Patristic writers, or "church fathers," is shorthand for Christian leaders in the period of AD 100–750.

In their own works, patristic writers often allude to and quote NT documents, which indicates that they recognized the NT's authoritative nature.

In the case of the Gospels, Tatian's second-century attempt to "harmonize" Matthew, Mark, Luke, and John into one Gospel, though an ill-conceived idea, points to the collection and "canonical" status of these four works. Tatian does not attempt to harmonize apocryphal Gospels such as the Gospels of Thomas or Judas. Instead, he tries to bring together the four Gospels that we recognize as canonical today, which implies that they were recognized as authoritative in Tatian's day as well.

Ancient Lists of NT Books

F. F. Bruce notes that in 1740 a theologian named Ludovico Antonio Muratori published a Latin list of NT books, the list had been found in "a codex copied in the seventh or eighth century at the monastery of Bobbio, in Lombardy, but later lodged in the Ambrosian Library, Milan (of which Muratori had at one time been keeper)."[24] Many scholars have argued that the Latin text is a translation of a Greek original that has been lost. However, Bruce believes that the original language of the text was probably Latin. Scholars are uncertain of the list's original date, going back to the second or fourth century AD. The beginning of the list is lost. The first complete sentence of the remaining fragment mentions Luke. The books not mentioned are Matthew, Mark, 1 Peter, Hebrews, and perhaps 2 & 3 John. The fragment includes the apocryphal documents Wisdom of Solomon and *Shepherd of Hermas*, but the former seems not to be canonical according to the original author of

---

[24] Bruce, *Canon of Scripture*, 158.

the fragment. For a brief description of the Muratorian Fragment, see the Muratorian Fragment.[25]

The so-called "Muratorian Fragment" (ca. 2nd-4th century AD) is further evidence that early Christians operated with the idea of an authoritative list of writings.

Eusebius (fourth century) also provides an authoritative list of NT books. As Paul L. Maier puts it, "If Herodotus is the father of history, then Eusebius of Caesarea (ca. A.D. 260–339) is certainly the father of church history."[26] Eusebius traced the history of Christianity from its rise in the first century to Emperor Constantine in the fourth century.

---

[25] "The Muratorian Fragment," http://www.bible-researcher.com/muratorian.html.

[26] Paul L. Maier, *Eusebius—The Church History* (Grand Rapids: Kregel, 2007), 9.

In his most significant work, titled *Ecclesiastical History*, Eusebius listed the writings of the NT.[27] His list puts early Christian writings into three categories: (1) universally acknowledged, (2) disputed, and (3) spurious.[28] The books he placed in each category are as follows:

> Acknowledged: Four Gospels; Acts; Paul's Letters; 1 John; 1 Peter
>
> Disputed: Jude; 2 Peter; 2 & 3 John
>
> Spurious: Revelation; *Gospel of Peter*; *Gospel of Thomas*; *Gospel of Matthias*, etc.

Eusebius included Revelation in the spurious (i.e., noncanonical) books. Bruce explains that Eusebius probably felt torn between churches he valued that saw Revelation as canonical and his own distaste for Revelation's apparent millenarian teaching.[29]

In any case, Eusebius's catalog indicates that in the third to fourth centuries, there was some debate surrounding books that today rest securely in the NT canon. However, the debate surrounding these books should not be exaggerated.

Canonical Criteria for the NT

We do not possess an early Christian work that lists the criteria used by the early church to assess various writings. Nevertheless, given the emphasis they placed on the NT documents, it is safe to assume that they did not simply take a straw vote. They most likely vetted these books according to the following criteria:

1. *Conformity to the rule of faith.* The writing had to conform to orthodox teaching held by the early churches. Already in the

---

[27] Eusebius, *Ecclesiastical History* 3.25.1–6 (Loeb).

[28] Bruce, *Canon of Scripture*, 198.

[29] Bruce, 199.

NT, we see the germ of heresy (Gal 1:8–9; Col 2:8; 1 Tim 6:3–10; 1 & 2 John). In the second century, Ignatius's writings reveal a concern to distinguish truth from falsehood. False teaching spilled over into writings as well. Therefore, a "canonical" book had to conform to the established truth of the church.

2. *Apostolicity.* The writing needed a clear apostolic connection. That means it was written by an apostle or someone closely associated with an apostle.

3. *Widespread acceptance and usage in churches.* A document not used widely in various churches probably raised red flags. In the second century AD, Origen traveled around the Mediterranean world visiting churches in different geographical locations. What he discovered is that almost all churches had a major corpus of works, many of which were the same books that make up the NT today.

Stage 4: Translations of the Bible

Although the authors of the Bible originally wrote in Hebrew, Aramaic, and Greek, today the Bible has been translated into more than 670 different languages.[30] That is a story in itself. For some quick facts and statistics on translations, see the Overview of Translations.[31]

Of course, that translation process began as early as the third century BC for the OT and as early as the second century AD for the NT. Part of the story behind the Bible is that people have felt compelled

---

[30] "FAQ #19: How Many Different Languages Has the Bible Been Translated Into?," Biblica, The International Bible Society, October 2017, https://www.biblica.com/resources/bible-faqs/how-many-different-languages-has-the-bible-been-translated-into/.

[31] "How Many Different Languages Has the Bible Been Translated Into?" https://www.biblica.com/resources/bible-faqs/how-many-different-languages-has-the-bible-been-translated-into/.

to translate it. They have felt a need to make it available in a form that people can understand and read. Some have even seen it as a divine calling, a call to make the Word of God more accessible.

Martin Luther (1483–1546) is one example. He felt compelled to translate the Bible into his native German tongue. The Catholic Church of his day looked askance at his translation. But Luther was undeterred. He endeavored to produce a translation that was both faithful to the original text and accessible to the German layperson. In this way, Luther had a sincere motivation for his translation works:

> This I can testify with a good conscience—I gave it my utmost in care and effort, and I never had any ulterior motives. I have neither taken nor sought a single penny for it, nor made one by it. Neither have I sought my own honor by it; God, my Lord, knows this. Rather, I have done it as a service to the dear Christians and to the honor of One who sits above, who blesses me so much every hour of my life that if I had translated a thousand times as much or as diligently, I should not for a single hour have deserved to live or to have a sound eye. All that I am and have is of his grace and mercy, indeed, of his precious blood and bitter sweat.[32]

Clearly Luther saw translation work as a service to the church, the world, and God himself. It is one of the most important stages in the story behind the Bible. It is a stage of the story that actually continues until today. There are almost 7,000 languages in the world but only 670 full translations of the Bible into different languages.

---

[32] Martin Luther, "On Translation: An Open Letter," in *The Annotated Luther: The Interpretation of Scripture*, vol. 6, ed. Euan K. Cameron (Minneapolis: Fortress, 2017), 33.

Luther worked diligently to translate the Bible into his native German tongue to make God's Word available to people from all walks of life.

Putting the Tools to Use

1. Why did OT and NT writers produce their respective writings in the first place?
2. What is textual criticism?
3. How (by what manner) did the biblical authors originally produce their works?
4. What did the discovery of the Dead Sea Scrolls tell us about the transmission history of the OT?
5. How did the early church view the canonization of the OT and NT?

3

Understanding the Tools in the Toolbox

Introduction

Every now and then, I come across a stark reminder of why it is important to interpret the Bible correctly. Sometimes it is in the form of a book or a blog or conversation. Recently the reminder was a somewhat frightening, but not altogether surprising, Christianity Today article titled "New Poll Finds Evangelicals' Favorite Heresies."[1] The LifeWay Research poll reported that many modern evangelicals hold to theological beliefs that, at one time or another, have been considered heretical by the church.

---

[1] Kevin P. Emmert, "New Poll Finds Evangelicals' Favorite Heresies," CTOnline, October 28, 2014, https://www.christianitytoday.com/ct/2014 /october-web-only/new-poll-finds-evangelicals-favorite-heresies.html.

So, for instance, some 22 percent (nearly a quarter!) of evangelicals surveyed believe that God the Father is more divine than Jesus. Nine percent said that they did not know. Scary.

Some 16 percent believe that Jesus was the first creature created by God. I think the infamous early church heretic Arias would agree, but orthodox Christians should not. Perhaps influenced by the Star Wars generation, a whopping 51 percent believe that the Holy Spirit is a "force" and not a personal being.[2] And some 56 percent think they contribute their own effort to achieve personal salvation.

Upon reading this article, my first reaction was to be challenged—challenged about the need to teach correctly "the word of truth" (2 Tim 2:15) and to interpret the Bible correctly. If God has spoken in his Scriptures, we want to be sure we hear him correctly.

This chapter focuses on helping the reader achieve this goal by providing the tools for your Bible toolbox that will help you to exegete rightly the biblical text for yourself.

Barriers to Bible Interpretation

Nobody will argue that the Bible is easy to interpret. In fact, many barriers stand in the way of understanding the Bible correctly.

Consider this sampling of obstacles:

- **Language.** The Bible was obviously not originally written in English or Spanish or any other contemporary language. The original Old Testament (OT) is written in classical Hebrew with a little Aramaic. The New Testament (NT) is written in Koine Greek. And whenever literature is translated from one language to another, something is always lost in the translation.

---

[2] "Arius," *Wikipedia*, last modified March 6, 2019, https://en.wikipedia.org/wiki/Arius.

(This, by the way, is a good reason to study the biblical languages for yourself!) In addition, the Bible uses terms that rarely appear in modern conversations. When was the last time you heard someone use the term *covenant* or *justification* or *sanctification* or *propitiation*? Yet, all of these are crucial theological terms found in the Scriptures. Also, other terms, such as *love* or *holy*, have different connotations in modern parlance than they did several thousand years ago in the ancient world

The Great Isaiah Scroll found among the Dead Sea Scrolls. Like this Scroll, the OT as a whole was originally written in Hebrew.

- **Culture.** The ancient Near Eastern world of the Bronze and Iron Age covenant people of God and the Greco-Roman world of the first-century church are very different from today's modern world. Foreign to us are things like the cosmologies (how you understand the universe), anthropologies (how you understand humanity), philosophies, rituals, political situations, and even daily lives of the ancient world. None of us perform sacrifices today? Right?
- **Literature.** Each culture has its own types of literature (genres). If you belong to that culture, you intuitively understand how to interpret these genres. So today the average American can tell the difference between the comic strips and the obituaries in a newspaper. We naturally know "rules" for interpreting

them. One leads you to laugh; one to cry. But how are we to read genres that aren't common today: the prophetic literature of the OT, the apocalyptic messages of Revelation, the Gospels of the NT? Even literature types that have the same titles as today—history, law, poetry—operate by different interpretive rules.

- **Personal frame of reference.** Anytime you read any literature, you bring to your reading numerous presuppositions, biases, and preconceived notions shaped by your culture, upbringing, church experience, and even geographical context. When we read the Scriptures through our limited frame of reference, we can end up misreading them. For example, when I was growing up, I possessed a mental picture of the Jordan River based on my personal understanding of rivers—the rather wide Chattahoochee in Atlanta. When I finally saw pictures of the Jordan as it flows today, I was disappointed. It seems like more of a creek than a mighty river like the Mississippi or Ohio.

The "wide" Jordan River.

Ultimately, because of these barriers, the mistake many people make is to read the Bible as if it were written yesterday—using our frame of reference, our genre rules, and our language—and as if it addresses only us.

The task of Bible interpretation is to bridge the context between today and the biblical world. To do this, you must immerse yourself in and understand ancient culture, literature, history, and worldviews.

Such a grounding will bring the ancient message into today in a way that is faithful to the original text.

Exegesis and Original Intent

The process of obtaining the original meaning from a biblical passage is called *exegesis*, a term derived from the Greek that refers to extracting meaning "out of" (Greek, *exe*) the text. In fact, many Bible readers today do the opposite. They take their preconceived notions of what they think the Bible says or should say, and they insert that "into" the biblical text (eisegesis; *eis* or into).

The best method of exegesis is called grammatical-historical exegesis. Simply put, this process involves searching for the original meaning based on the grammar/syntax and the historical context of a passage.

The branch of theology that examines the how and why of biblical exegesis and interpretation is called hermeneutics. The following tools for your Bible toolbox, then, are technically exegetical tools for proper interpretation.

> Biblical exegesis is the process of finding the original meaning of a biblical text.

As mentioned earlier, the first goal of exegesis is to discover the author's intended meaning. In other words, we do not treat the Bible as we might artwork or a poem, where we stand in front of it and say, this is what this work means to me. Instead, the meaning is what the author intended. Indeed, meaning cannot be ascertained if it is disconnected from the original author.

All communication assumes this. If I give a study guide for a test, the students will certainly want to find out what I intended, not what they hope or think I meant.

Take a last will and testament, for example. Whom do you want to determine to whom your worldly possessions go? Do you want someone to read your will and say, I know what the deceased wrote, but the document means something different to me?

If our goal is to find the original meaning, we must be committed to hearing the text as the original author wants it to be heard. Avoid bringing systems, presuppositions, and biases to the text. Try looking at each text anew, not necessarily ignoring your own traditions and preconceived notions or the history of interpretation, but at least acknowledging these things. And be willing to have those traditions and preconceived notions adjusted or even rebuilt by the text.

So how do you find that original meaning? The following will outline three principal tools: (1) historical tools (the historical, cultural, and geographical context of the events themselves and of the original author/audience), (2) literary tools (literary structure, storyline, purpose, genre, and syntax/structure/semantics), and (3) theological tools (including the issues of salvation history and main theological themes). Each of these will be described and even employed in subsequent chapters to train you, the reader, in this method. We will also discuss some means and methods of applying texts personally and theologically in a way faithful to the original text.

Historical Tools

The first tool employed to find the original meaning is the historical tool. The basic goal with this tool is to understand that each text was written for a particular situation and describing a particular situation.

Importance of Historical Context

Imagine attempting to determine and appreciate the original meaning of Abraham Lincoln in the Gettysburg Address without understanding the context of the Civil War. Imagine trying to feel the rhetorical force of Charles Dickens's novels without knowing the context of the Industrial Revolution in Europe.

Now imagine trying to understand the book of Revelation apart from the context of persecution in the first-century church or the book of Kings apart from the context of the Jewish spiritual and national crisis of the Babylonian exile.

Placing the text in context can help you determine the original meaning but also can help you feel—to use a technical term—the *oomph* of the passage and even identify with the author/audience.

Let's say I find an old love letter—worn with time, riddled with holes, but obviously full of the passionate prose of a man expressing undying devotion to his wife. If I try to explain that letter to you, I could obviously describe its contents. I could even give you some personal examples and modern illustrations of what it means to love someone as deeply as this letter relates.

Does context matter with a love letter?

However, would you feel the impact of the letter and its words? Perhaps.

But let's say I then tell you in dramatic detail about the original context of the letter—about how a naval midshipman in World War II had penned this hurried note to his new wife before an impending battle in the Pacific; about how he had written her daily of his love despite the distance, in the face of fear, and uncertain of their future; about how he had died in that Pacific battle, never to see his love again; and about how she had clung to this letter to her dying day many years later.

Knowing this story, would the words in the letter mean more to you? Wouldn't you sense more of its pathos? Its importance? Its implications?

In the same way, we can read a text of Scripture. We can understand at times the meaning of the words on the surface. But in my experience, the way to make a text really come alive is to live in the text.

Levels of Historical Context

There are two levels of historical context: that of the events described in the text itself (e.g., the events of Joseph's life as related in Genesis 37–50) and that of the original author/audience (the context of the exodus and wilderness wanderings—events that shaped the telling of the Joseph story by its original author, Moses).

Sometimes these contextual levels are the same—that is, the text is written at the same general time as the events described, as with many of the prophetic OT books or the Letters of Paul. Sometimes these levels are quite different, as with the Gospels or with books such as Kings and Chronicles. For both levels, seek to answer the question: What is going on historically or culturally that makes an impact on our understanding of the events themselves or the reporting of the events?

Example of Historical Context

Take a scriptural passage such as Lam 3:19–24. Go ahead and look it up. The text is the basis of the hymn "Great Is Thy Faithfulness" and contains a powerful message about hope in the midst of hopelessness.[3] The words of this passage and the message are not hard to understand: have hope in God. But what truly makes the text and the message live in the minds and hearts of the hearers is the original context of the book.

Imagine being in the shoes of the author, Jeremiah. After years of prophesying of the coming doom of Jerusalem, after years of witnessing spiritual infidelity on the part of the people, God's judgment in the form of the Babylonian exile had finally come in 586 BC.

The Babylonian exile was the greatest spiritual crisis faced by Old Testament Israel and provided the historical backdrop for the book of Lamentations.

---

[3] "Great is Thy Faithfulness—Chris Rice," YouTube video, 4:39, posted by borisimmo1, January 3, 2009, https://www.youtube.com/watch?v=0k1W hFtVp0o.

Babylon laid siege to the holy city of Jerusalem for eighteen months. People were starving. The hands of compassionate women even boiled their own children, being reduced by their desperate hunger to cannibalism (Lam 4:9–10). Finally, the invading nation breached Jerusalem's walls. The Babylonians slaughtered many. Other Israelites they removed from their beloved Promised Land, dragging them across the desert with bronze hooks in their noses to a pagan land, never to see their homeland again. The temple of God's presence—Solomon's grandiose temple—was razed. And Zedekiah, the Davidic king, the source of messianic hope, had his sons killed before his eyes before having his own eyes gouged out. Read 2 Kings 24–25 for a blunt description of these events.

Jeremiah's response to the devastation of the exile was
the book of Lamentations.

Only the prophet Jeremiah and the poorest of the poor remained in the ruined city, devoid of provision, protection, and prospects. Visualize yourself walking through the streets with him—seeing the death, the destruction, seeing families ripped apart, seeing the rubble, the ruin. What would be your response?

Jeremiah's response to the devastation was the book of Lamentations—a series of five laments composed as alphabetic acrostics (where each verse begins with a word that begins with a subsequent letter of the Hebrew alphabet—twenty-two in all). He used all the letters of the alphabet to express his complete and profound grief over the events.

Yet in the center of the book, in the longest of the laments (sixty-six verses, in acrostic triads), surrounded by bitter expressions of despair and despondency, Jeremiah found hope—a sure and certain hope. It was a hope based not in his circumstances, but upon the firm foundation of God's unchanging character. When all Judah believed that God had abandoned them to the hopelessness of the exile, Jeremiah confessed his resolute faith in the enduring faithfulness and lovingkindness of God. When even the most compassionate earthly mothers failed, resorting to cannibalism, Jeremiah confessed that God's compassions never fail.

To me, such a historical account makes those words of Lamentations 3 and its message of hope come alive much more than any modern illustration or anecdote ever could.

So, again, if you really want to make the text live, live in the text. Use the historical tool.

Excursus on Geography

An overlooked aspect of historical and cultural context is geography—a topic that can glaze the eyes of Bible readers unlike any other. But a general knowledge of the geography of Bible lands is essential to attaining an informed understanding of many biblical texts. We do not

have the space in the present volume to give a full description of the
geography of the ancient world. For that, check out the accessible and
detailed *Holman Bible Atlas*.[4] Instead, note the following two examples
of the exegetical importance of geography.

Geography Can Help Clarify the Intended Message of Specific Texts

Amos 1:2 is a great example. Here the eighth-century BC prophet
Amos declares poetically, "The LORD roars from Zion and makes his
voice heard from Jerusalem; the pastures of the shepherds mourn, and
the summit of Carmel withers." In this one verse, four geographical
locations are mentioned: Zion, Jerusalem, pastures, and Mount Carmel.
The first two designate the same general location—Jerusalem, the Holy
City and the location of God's temple and God's king. *Pastures* refers to

From the Top of Carmel

---

[4] Thomas V. Brisco, *Holman Bible Atlas* (Nashville: B&H Publishing Group,
2014).

the abundant, albeit rocky, pastoral expanses south of Jerusalem, including Bethlehem and Amos's own hometown of Tekoa. Importantly, Amos is most likely talking about locations in the southern kingdom of Judah. The final place mentioned is Mount Carmel on the Mediterranean coast in the northern kingdom of Israel. This prominent promontory defined the landscape in this region with its lush vineyards and farmland.

How do these locations communicate Amos's message? To understand this, we need a little historical context. Amos's ministry occurs about 170 years after the division of the kingdom of Israel in 931 BC. Since that split, shortly after Solomon's reign, the two kingdoms (Judah in the south and Israel, comprising the remaining ten tribes, in the north) had followed different spiritual paths. Judah had maintained the Davidic dynastic line, the temple of Israel's God, and the rightful capital in Jerusalem. Israel in the north had rejected all three and, in doing so, had forsaken their faith in their covenant with the LORD.

Tekoa, Amos's hometown

By stating that the LORD was roaring from Jerusalem in Judah, God, through Amos, affirmed his abiding commitment to both the Davidic kings and the capital city of Jerusalem. But the geography also affirmed that God's authority and authoritative message were not confined to the borders of the south. Instead, by citing the pastures of the south and Mount Carmel in the north, Amos declared that God's sovereign rule extended to all the land, from meadows to the mountains, including the land of the wayward northern kingdom of Israel. But without a knowledge of geography, the reader will most likely overlook the intent and impact of Amos's pronouncement.

See link in Wordsearch for another example of how geography helps to determine the meaning of a text.

Geography Can Clarify Some Big-Picture Issues

In addition to its exegetical utility, geography helps the reader to grasp God's missional purposes, particularly in the OT.

Many people misperceive God in the OT as the God of only Israel, with little connection to or concern for nations such as Egypt, Babylon, Philistia, Phoenicia, or Persia—the rest of the world outside the Promised Land. As long as Israel existed in some monastic manner among the nations and did not contract their pagan propensities, God would be pleased. Right? Geography says otherwise.

If God truly wanted his people completely cloistered, there are more appropriate locations. When God called Abraham out of Ur, he could have guided the father of the Hebrew people to Madagascar or Siberia or lower Alabama or some other out-of-the-way destination. Instead, God promised the Hebrew patriarchs the land of Palestine.

Why? God wanted his people to be a missional people—a blessing (Gen 12:3) and a kingdom of priests to the nations (Exod 19:4–6). A quick look at the location of the Promised Land shows how this evangelistic objective would be accomplished. Israel lies on a land bridge of sorts—as my grandmother used to say, "smack dab" in the middle of all the nations of the Fertile Crescent.[5] To go anywhere in the ancient Near East via land, one most likely would pass through Israel. So whenever peoples traded or traveled, combatted or communicated in the ancient world, they would have to encounter the eccentric and exceptional monotheistic Israelites. And maybe, just maybe, these nations would start to understand something of this worldwide God, worshiped by this seemingly insignificant international stepping stone.

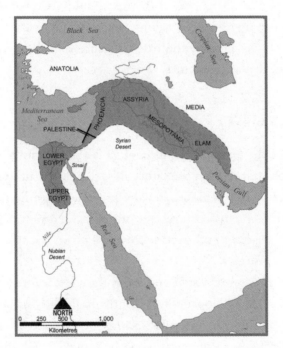

Israel, located in the land of Palestine, lay on a land bridge between the nations. It was among the nations to be a light to the nations.

So there is a theology of geography. Israel is placed purposefully to be a light to the nations. By the way, so is the church. The apostle

---

[5] Joshua J. Mark, "Fertile Crescent," Ancient History Encyclopedia, https://www.ancient.eu/Fertile_Crescent/.

Peter quotes from Exodus 19 when he tells the first-century church that God positioned them providentially as a "holy nation" and "royal priesthood," so that the church might "proclaim the praises of the one who called you out of darkness into his marvelous light" (1 Pet 2:9–10).

Literary Tools

Once the historical context of a passage is established, the interpreter can then move to an analysis of the text itself. This analysis is accomplished by accessing what we call literary tools. We will examine three of these tools: (1) literary context, (2) genre, and (3) structure/story line/purpose/syntax/semantics.

Literary Context

"Interpreting the text without its context is a pretext for a proof text."[6] This oft-cited quote from the father of well-known author and theologian D. A. Carson demonstrates the importance of literary context. In other words, if you take a passage out of its literary context, you can make it say whatever you want it to say to prove whatever point you are trying to prove.

For instance, what would you say is the most quoted verse in the Bible? John 3:16? Philippians 4:13? Both are finalists, to be sure. But I suspect that the winner in today's postmodern world would be Matt 7:1: "Do not judge, so that you won't be judged." Like Phil 4:13 in a football locker room, Matt 7:1 has become a rallying cry—in this case, for our modern era of moral relativism and the lack of moral absolutes. "Don't judge me!" people exclaim. After all, doesn't this text show that Jesus was a relativist?

---

[6] D. A. Carson, "Take Up Your Cross and Follow Me," *Themelios* 37, no. 1 (2012): 2.

But is Jesus really saying in the context of Matthew 7 that no moral judgments are ever to be made? If you look at the context, the answer is clearly no. He *is* speaking against hypocrisy. He *is not* speaking against moral fortitude and moral judgment. In fact, in the same text, Jesus states that we should beware of wolves in sheep's clothing. Well, how do you discern a wolf, if not by making a moral judgment?

See link in Wordsearch for another example of taking something out of context.

So how do you determine literary context? The goal is to understand the part in light of the whole. Just as contact lenses allow one to have greater peripheral vision, viewing a text through a "context lens" allows the interpreter to see outside the borders of the chosen text and orient the text to its surroundings.

Start with the level of the biblical book itself. Attempt to gain a basic understanding of the purpose of the book. Most times, you can find this type of information explained in your study Bibles (or this book!), but sometimes the biblical author himself will tell you. See, for instance, Luke 1:1–4 and John 20:31. After you discover the author's purpose, examine how that purpose is furthered through the structure and argument of the book. Then you can place your passage in the context of that purpose and structure. You can also perform this process on the level of the section or even the immediately surrounding verses of your text.

Let's look at one example. A few years ago, I was asked to preach at a Good Friday service at an AME (African Methodist Episcopal) church in south Georgia. The pastor tasked me and six other preachers to preach on one of the last seven sayings of Christ from the cross. My assigned text was "I'm thirsty," from John 19:28. Now, how do you preach on "I'm thirsty"?

I did so based on literary context. In John 20:31, John states that Jesus did a lot of amazing things while he was here on earth. But John contends that he chose to write about the events in his Gospel so that we "may believe that Jesus is the Messiah, the Son of God, and that by believing you may have life in his name." There is the author's purpose. And if that was John's purpose, the inclusion of the declaration "I'm thirsty" from the cross must also contribute to that purpose in some way. And it does. It shows that Jesus suffered as fully man and fully God and that he fulfilled the OT. And so, with every major point I made in the sermon, I asked the congregation, "Do you believe that Jesus is the Christ? Do you have life in his name?" Thus, I derived my sermon's purpose and application from John's for his entire book.

John's inclusion of Jesus's statement, "I'm thirsty," helped fulfill the overall purpose of the Gospel of John, articulated in John 20:31.

This previous example points to another important aspect of literary context: canonical context and intertextuality. Texts do not just occur in a book, such as John or Luke or Deuteronomy, but in a canon—a fixed, authoritative collection of books (see chap. 2). This biblical canon has a purposeful order and specific intent as well, and there is a reason why the books are located where they are. So we must consider how texts in the larger canon relate to one another. In the case of John 19:28, John purposefully quotes from Psalm 22 or perhaps Psalm 69 to show Jesus purposefully fulfilling Scripture. When studying a passage, always check cross-references to other Scriptures (sometimes footnoted in your Bibles) to see if the author is quoting or alluding to other texts. For me, it's like a puzzle. It's fun to make these connections, especially between the NT and the OT.

Also look at the role the text plays in the canon. For example, if you are analyzing Gen 1:1, you should consider the role the verse plays not only in Gen 1:1–2:3 (the creation account), but also as an introduction to the Primeval History (Genesis 1–11), the book of Genesis as a whole, the Pentateuch as a whole, and indeed, the entire Bible.

In addition, allow Scripture to interpret Scripture. You need the whole to understand the parts. Don't base huge doctrines on obscure passages. Allow clear texts to explain more equivocal ones.

Genre

A crucial and often overlooked tool in the exegetical process is that of genre identification. Simply, a genre is a type of literature—such as narrative or poetry or prophetic oracle—that is defined and delimited by distinct traits.

Genre also dictates what the reader *expects* out of a passage. If you read a straight news article in a newspaper, you expect an unbiased reporting of actual events. If you read an editorial, you expect someone's opinion. If you read the advertisements, you expect someone to try to persuade you to part with some of your money.

*As modern readers, we intuitively know how to interpret the
genres in a newspaper.*

But, as mentioned earlier, our understanding of genre is derived
from our own culture and time and frame of reference. When dealing
with other cultures, especially ancient ones, we need to operate by the
rules that they establish for their own genres. Biblical genres are no
different. Do we read narrative the same today as then? Are prophecies
strictly future predictions, or is something else entailed by the biblical
genre of prophecy? Are the Gospels biographies, or are they in their
own unique category? What do we do with the apocalyptic imagery of
Revelation? Do we interpret it literally or figuratively? How would an
original reader "hear" it?

The following chapters will examine more thoroughly the common genres found in each of the Bible's canonical divisions.

Structure/Story Line/Purpose/Syntax/Semantics

Once the literary and historical context is established as much as possible, the next step is to determine how the words, phrases, clauses, and sentences in the text relate. Context is like a funnel. We start broad with context, but then we eventually narrow to the text itself.

The questions to explore in analyzing the text itself are myriad:

- How does the author use repetition of a *leitwort* (key or leading word) or *leitmotif* (leading motif) in the passage? Usually, someone who repeats something is trying to emphasize it in some way.
- How does the author use figures of speech and metaphors, which may occur in both narrative and poetry in the biblical text? Always ask why an author chooses to express something a specific way.
- How does the author use patterning? Patterns include parallelism, chiasms, and acrostics (all to be explained later). Biblical writers love patterns, and texts are replete with them.
- How does the author structure his narrative or poem or argument? Does he deviate from the expected norm? To use a modern example, what happens when a fairy tale does not end happily ever after? Does that shocking shift not communicate some of the author's original intent?
- Does the author employ any key theological terms? Sometimes the meaning of a passage can be keyed to one particular word or phrase. For example, words such as *righteousness* or *fear* or *loving-kindness* or *love* are laden with a theological weight. But remember, always determine the meaning of a word based on

context not on a dictionary meaning, especially not a modern dictionary meaning.

Here are a few suggestions regarding how to analyze a text on this grammatical and syntactical level:

- Use a good translation that attempts to tie the text as close to the order, structure, and word choices of the original Greek and Hebrew as possible (e.g., the New American Standard, English Standard, or Christian Standard). These translations allow you to follow the flow of the original texts.

- Find the main idea and then diagram the passage, tracing the flow and argument of the author. Look for grammatical features, such as transitional words, repetition, cause-effect, emphasis, and so forth.

- Write observations and questions; mark up the text. And follow up on those questions. Don't leave them unanswered. Using your own curiosity is one of the best ways of Bible study.

- Look up cross-references and find key words. As mentioned above, cross-references help you to see intertextual anticipations and echoes.

- Read the passage out loud, emphasizing different words. Approach the text like a prism. See its many dimensions by shining different exegetical "lights" on it.

- Pray through the text and meditate on it. The Spirit of God is a source of illumination for the Christian, often granting understanding and also application where none previously existed (1 Cor 2:12–14).

- Identify people and places. Keep your map, Bible dictionary, and study Bible handy for this.

- Don't be afraid to consult other sources, but consult the right ones. The internet is particularly cratered with dubious resources. So have a discerning and critical eye.

Above all, sllooowwww down! In our fast-paced world and with our legalistic tendencies, the temptation in Bible study is often to read it just so we can say we did it. This error is especially tempting if you are attempting to read the Bible through in a year. Instead, try to take smaller bites and chew slowly on the text, like a cow with its cud, getting as much spiritual nutrition out of the passage as possible.

Avoid the temptation in Bible study of reading the text quickly just to say you did it. Instead, slow down.

Theological Tools

The Bible by nature is a theological document. In other words, it is a book about God from God to save and create a people unto God. God and his Christ are at the center of the Bible. And theology is the study of God. To study a passage of Scripture, then, is to study God and all the things concerning him theologically. So it is not enough to examine context, genre, words, and syntax. You must take the next step and examine the theology of the text.

Theological Examination

My mentor and biblical scholar Daniel I. Block suggests five helpful questions to use in discerning the theology of a text.[7]

- What does this passage tell us about God?
- What does it tell us about the world and society in general?
- What does it tell us about the human condition, the nature of sin, the destiny of humankind?
- What does it tell us about the way God relates to human beings?
- What does it tell us about an appropriate ethical and spiritual response to the work of God in one's life?

I would add one more: always ask how the Scripture passage presents Christ (typology and prophecy of Christ in the OT and proclamation of and reflection on Christ in the NT). It is not necessarily the case that every passage overtly points to Christ. Don't force the text to say something it doesn't. However, the overarching story of the Bible is driving forward to a point and is all about Jesus. God is working out his plan of salvation through history, and this salvation history culminates at the cross.

Salvation Historical Examination

This previous paragraph points us to a second theological tool for understanding the text: fitting the text into the overarching story line

---

[7] Daniel I. Block, "Tell Me the Old, Old Story: Preaching the Message of Old Testament Narrative," in *Giving the Sense: Understanding and Using Old Testament Historical Texts*, ed. David M. Howard Jr. and Michael A. Grisanti (Grand Rapids: Kregel, 2003), 434.

of salvation history. One could almost devote an entire chapter (or even book!) to this topic. And understanding the full scope of salvation history will be emphasized over and over in the following chapters.

When most people study the Bible, they do so in a piecemeal fashion. They'll study individual books or characters or stories. In other words, they study the parts, but rarely do they try to fit the parts into the whole. Perhaps it is because the whole—sixty-six books, 1,189 chapters, 31,102 verses—is so intimidating.

My encouragement is not to get caught up in the minutia—memorizing the names of kings or Jacob's twelve sons, the dates of certain minor events, and so forth. Instead, the key is to get the big picture.

I suggest learning about fifteen major events in salvation history, and then you can get the overall flow. Imagine a coatrack with pegs on which to hang coats. These major events are the pegs. You can hang other events on them as you grow in your knowledge of Scripture. But even without knowing these other events, these fifteen will help you to get a pretty good idea of the salvation historical context of most every biblical text.

These fifteen events include:

- Creation/fall/flood (prehistorical)
- The call of Abraham (2100 BC)
- The exodus and conquest (1446 and 1405 BC respectively)
- The reign of King David (1011 BC)
- The dedication of the First Temple (966 BC)
- The kingdom of Israel divides between the northern and southern kingdoms (931 BC)
- The Assyrian exile and end of the northern kingdom (722 BC)
- The Babylonian exile of the southern kingdom of Judah (586 BC)
- The return of Judah from exile and the rebuilding of the temple (539 BC and 515 BC respectively)

- The end of the Old Testament period with Ezra and Nehemiah (mid-400s BC)
- The intertestamental period (400–6 BC)
- The birth of Jesus in fulfillment of prophecy (6/4 BC)
- John the Baptist's ministry and Jesus's ministry begin (AD 26)
- Jesus's death, burial, resurrection, and ascension (AD 30)
- Saul's conversion and the early church (AD 35)

These events will be expounded upon in much greater detail later, but learn them now.

A Note on Application

Scripture is not meant merely to be studied in an academic sense. If the Bible is true, then that changes everything. And Bible study is not just for the classroom, but also for the dorm room, coffee shop, grocery store, cubicle, car seat, and all of life.

In other words, biblical study should not be merely descriptive but also normative—meaning that it establishes norms for life and it demands response. As a Bible interpreter, you are not being true to the intended purpose of the text if the message of the text does not transform you. If we are going to be true to the text, if we are going to be true to authorial intent, if we are truly going to recognize the inspiration of Scripture, then we must never approach the task of Bible interpretation with aloof detachment. It always has personal implications.

As Paul exhorted the church in Rome, "For whatever was written in the past was written for our instruction, so that we may have hope through endurance and through the encouragement from the Scriptures" (Rom 15:4). Second Timothy 3:16–17, cited earlier, reiterates this sentiment: "All Scripture is inspired by God *and is profitable* for teaching, for rebuking, for correcting, for training in righteousness, so that the man of God may be complete, equipped for every good work" (emphasis added).

So we are never to leave the Bible in the academic and hypothetical and theoretical realm—disconnected from our own personal experience.

How do we apply the text? Three simple steps:

Step 1. Understand the original meaning of the text. Application should always stem from and be based in the authoritative original meaning and intent of the text. Otherwise, the application is not authoritative.

Step 2. Understand yourself. What are your strengths, weaknesses, presuppositions, traditions, struggles, triumphs? Be honest.

Step 3. Respond and take action. Allow the Spirit to use the Scripture to permeate and penetrate, conform and convict, renew and restore, direct and defend.

Conclusion

In the following chapters, you will learn about the three tools from the discussion above—historical, literary, and theological—and how they apply to the texts in the canon of Scripture. On your own, you can then get plenty of practice with the tools. Our hope is that you will not become merely Bible readers but Bible interpreters and also Bible appliers.

Questions for Thought

1. What have been some barriers for your own personal study of the Bible?

2. Do you agree that the meaning of a text should be determined by the original author? Why or why not?

3. Which of the Bible study principles discussed is most helpful to you?

4. In your opinion, why is it important to know and understand the biblical story line?

Activity

Choose your favorite passage and try to apply to it the tools presented above. If you don't have a preference, try John 3:16 or Psalm 23. Write out the titles—Historical Tools, Literary Tools, and Theological Tools—with some blanks underneath. Then sketch out some observations. Once you have an understanding of the original meaning, explore some modern applications. Make sure these applications are based in the original meaning.

Part 2

Tools for Interpreting the Old Testament

A staple of public broadcasting is a series called *Antiques Roadshow*.[1] The basic premise for this long-standing popular PBS program is that people bring discarded, forgotten "antiques" for an expert to appraise. Some of these vintage items are deemed to be of little value. But most of the air-time is given to men and women who are shocked and over-joyed when appraisers tell them that what they perceived to be worth a couple of bucks is actually worth exponentially more.

Like the antiques in the roadshow, the Old Testament (OT) is often overlooked by many Christians and, if we are honest, by many pastors and Bible teachers. I think many evangelicals would be baffled if someone told them that these ancient Scriptures, which they've treated

---

[1] Public Broadcasting Service, "Antiques Roadshow," PBS.org, http://www.pbs.org/wgbh/roadshow/.

as obsolete, outmoded, and otherwise fulfilled in Christ, were actually valuable and profitable and authoritative for life and ministry.

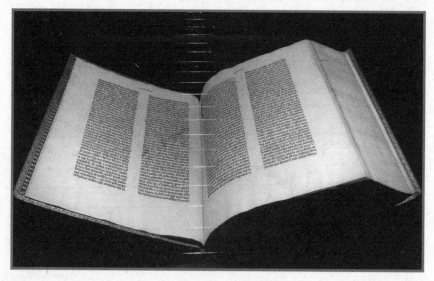

The Gutenberg Bible

Good evangelicals will readily confess a belief in the OT to be true and trustworthy, inspired and inerrant, and all those nice descriptive words. They would confidently assert this part of the Bible to be "inspired by God" or God-breathed, as Paul does in 2 Tim 3:16. But do they actually take the next step, using it "for teaching, for rebuking, for correcting, for training in righteousness"?

The sad truth is that most either avoid the OT or use it only for illustrations or for examples of faithful living or for proof-texting or for moralistic tales, kind of like Aesop's Fables.[2] Maybe we use Samson as a paradigm for a good marriage or Jephthah, a man who sacrificed his one and only daughter, as an example of a man who keeps his word.

---

[2] "Aesop's Fables," *Wikipedia*, last modified January 31, 2019, https://en.wikipedia.org/wiki/Aesop%27s_Fables.

Well, maybe we don't go that far, but you get the point. In essence, we ignore or misapply three-quarters of the Bible we allegedly consider as God's special revelation.

My experience has been that when Christians understand the OT the way the NT authors (and Jesus himself!) understood it, they get excited about God's Word, and they start to see it in all its fullness and beauty. Moreover, they gain a better grasp of the arguments, imagery, and worldview of the NT.

One example will suffice. People always struggle with the book of Revelation, perhaps because it is so steeped in OT imagery. In fact, John's Apocalypse has more OT allusions than any other NT book, even though it rarely quotes directly from the OT.

We see this use of OT imagery from the start, in the opening vision of Revelation 1. Go ahead and read that first chapter. There the apostle John paints us a picture—one of the resurrected, reigning, and sovereign Christ.

But he does not do it with brushes or film. He paints Jesus with words, telling of the vision of Christ that he has received from God. But these aren't just any words. God gives John a picture that is painted with Old Testament brushes. He uses a little Ezekiel 1 here, a little Daniel 7 and 10 there. . . . Each word and phrase in this picture in Revelation 1 harkens back to a previous text in the OT. So you cannot understand the message without understanding the OT background.

The central figure in this passage is, of course, Jesus himself, the "Son of Man." Undoubtedly John gives this title to the "Voice speaking" to him to allude to Daniel's vision of the messianic "Son of Man" who in Daniel 7, comes up to the Ancient of Days (God the Father) and receives "dominion, and glory, and a kingdom; so that those of every people, nation, and language should serve him" (7:13–14).

So by describing his vision in this manner, John is inviting his readers—the persecuted first-century church—to cast their eyes back to Daniel's shocking vision. In doing so, he would remind the first century

*The apostle John filled his Apocalypse with more OT allusions
than any other book in the NT.*

martyrs (lit., witnesses) of Christ's sovereignty over all nations. Just as
Daniel's message comforted the Jews in exile within mighty Babylon,
John's Apocalypse comforted those believers under the yoke of the
seemingly insuperable Roman Empire.

But the same message still rings true for Christians today. No matter what our life situation, nothing will comfort us, nothing will give
more hope, nothing will enable us to live radically Christian lives more
than keeping a picture of the powerful and victorious Christ before us.

But we will not grasp the depth, breadth, and height of this message from Revelation 1 if we do not investigate and appreciate the OT
background.

So let us commit to doing a little work and dust off that antique portion of our Bible.

This is what part 2 of this book is all about. Each chapter will describe the tools of chapter 3 as they apply to specific OT books according to their canonical divisions. Again, the goal is not just to teach you what the proper interpretation of the books is, but how to interpret the books rightly for yourself. And as you do so, we think you will discover the immeasurable worth of the OT.

4

Tools for Interpreting the Pentateuch

Picture the Bible as a skyscraper, with sixty-six floors (books), complete with rooms (individual stories) and occupants (characters). Now allow your eyes to drift to the base of this towering structure. There, in the first five books of the Bible, you will find the foundation of the canonical Scriptures—the Pentateuch (Greek, *penta*, five; *teuchos*, scrolls) or the Torah, as it is called in Jewish tradition. It supports the entire structure of the Bible.

In these books—Genesis, Exodus, Leviticus, Numbers, and Deuteronomy—the Bible's story line begins. Here the main setting (creation and specifically the Promised Land) and the main characters (God and humanity and his covenant people) are revealed. The main plot complications of sin, death, and evil are also introduced. And the author even hints at the resolution to these complications—God's redemption through his chosen Messiah (see Gen 3:15; Num 24:17).

The Pentateuch also functions as the fountainhead for every foundational theme in the Scriptures. Think of the major theological themes of the Bible: sacrifice, redemption, law, grace, creation, justification, covenant, promise, atonement, holiness, and so forth. Every one of these themes begins in these five books.

Here also God reveals clearly his essential nature and character—one that does not change in the next sixty-one books of the Bible. Want to know what God is like in Revelation? Look at Genesis. Want to know what Jesus's mission was and is? It's the same as God's mission in the Pentateuch. Want to know how God relates or redeems or re-creates in the rest of Scripture? Look in these five scrolls.

In this way, the Pentateuch is extremely practical, relevant, and even essential to the Christian faith. According to Matt 5:18, Jesus agrees:

In the biblical skyscraper, the Pentateuch is the foundation.

"For truly I tell you, until heaven and earth pass away, not the smallest letter or one stroke of a letter will pass away from the law [Torah/ Pentateuch] until all things are accomplished."

But Genesis, Exodus, Leviticus, Numbers, and Deuteronomy also have their challenges. According to the Bible timeline, some of these Pentateuchal events happened 4,000-plus years ago. The Hebrews lived and walked amid temples, altars, priests, prophets, and polytheistic pagan neighbors. They spoke a different language, used different literary genres, and possessed different conceptions of the cosmos. Yet, as mentioned in chapter 3, the tendency among many Bible readers is to interpret these texts as if these differences, stemming from the 4000-year time gap, do not exist at all.

The result is that we either avoid the Pentateuch or we misuse it. Tell me, when is the last time you heard a sermon on sacrifice? Or a devotional from Deuteronomy? Or a homily on the Holiness Code of Leviticus?

The most common abuse of the text is to interpret the stories allegorically or moralistically. So when we read of Abraham's willingness to sacrifice Isaac in Genesis 22, we talk about what we need to sacrifice to God. Or maybe we hear a sermon on the story of the Tower of Babel in Genesis 11, and the pastor asks, "What is your Tower of Babel in your life?" Or the exodus becomes a symbol of God's deliverance from your oppressive Bible professor!

The fundamental error for each above abuse is that the essential exegetical questions—What did the author originally intend? How did the original author want his audience to respond?—are never answered. As argued in chapter 3, we must keep our application tied to these. But how do we unearth that original meaning and purpose?

Understanding the Tools

To access these materials and to understand the authorial intent and authoritative meaning, we need to bridge the contexts—from ancient and original to modern and applied. Again, to make the text come alive, you need to live in the text. The following tools will assist us in this exegetical examination of the Pentateuch.

Historical Tools

The first tool to grab when analyzing a biblical text is that of historical context. Remember that historical context operates on two levels—the context of the events themselves and of the author/audience. Sometimes, as with the prophets, these are the same. With the Pentateuch, they are different.

Level-2 Historical Context: Author and Audience

Let's first deal with the second-level context—that of the author and audience. To address this issue, one has to delve into one of the thornier Old Testament (OT) questions that scholars like to debate—the authorship and composition of the Pentateuch. In other words, if we want to establish the context of the author/audience, we should find out who that author is, correct?

At this point in my classes, students' eyes start to glaze. Do we really need to discuss a topic as unexciting and esoteric as authorship? How important could this issue be? The short answer is "very." The authorship of the Pentateuch is one of those hot-button topics that reveals a lot about your view of Scripture and your presuppositions regarding its inspiration and authority.

A little history is in order. For centuries, Jews and Christians alike ascribed the Torah to Moses. And rightly so. Yes, the Pentateuch is officially anonymous. Moses does not say, "I, Moses, am writing this," as Paul does, for instance, at the beginning of his letters.

But the scriptural and traditional and internal evidence attesting to Mosaic authorship is overwhelming. Several times within the Pentateuch itself, the text speaks of Moses "writing down" parts of this tome (see Exod 17:14; 24:4; 34:27; Num 33:2; Deut 31:9). Many more references in the OT and NT speak of the "Torah of Moses" or some similar title. (A sampling can be found in Josh 8:31–32; 1 Kgs 2:3; 2 Kgs 14:6; Ezra 6:18; Neh 13:1; Dan 9:11; Mal 4:4; Matt 19:8; John 7:19; Acts 3:22; Rom 10:5.)

More convincingly, Jesus himself saw Moses as the recognized authority behind these texts. In John 5:46, he states, "If you believed Moses, you would believe me, for he wrote about me." Well, where did Moses write about the Messiah? It could be in only one place—the Torah. So if Moses was not a principal author of the Torah, then we have some problems not only with the Bible, but also with Jesus himself.

Affirming Mosaic authorship does not mean that Moses had to write down everything himself—for instance, the account of his own death in Deuteronomy 34. And it does not mean that he did not use preexisting materials, such as the traditions behind much of Genesis or the genealogies and law codes. And it does not mean that materials haven't been updated over time. But it *does* mean Moses is the primary authority behind the text. The Torah in the OT is the Torah of Moses.

So why doubt Mosaic authorship? Both the history of the issue and the issue itself are complex. Throughout most of church history until the 1700s, most generally assumed the Pentateuch to be a unified and datable Mosaic composition. But in the eighteenth century, scholars for the first time began to reject Mosaic authorship openly and regularly.

The impetus was the advent of the intellectual and cultural movement known as the Enlightenment,[1] with its accompanying emphasis on rationalism,[2] evolutionary development, progress, and antisupernaturalism.

---

[1] "Age of Enlightenment," *Wikipedia*, last modified March 6, 2019, https://en.wikipedia.org/wiki/Age_of_Enlightenment.

[2] "Rationalism," *Wikipedia*, last modified February 27, 2019, https://en.wikipedia.org/wiki/Rationalism.

These provided the fertilizer for the sprouting and spread of new critical theories about the Bible—initially in Europe but eventually in the United States. With rationalism, the highest determiner of truth became human reason and natural explanations, accessed via the scientific method.[3] And scholars attempted to cast off what they saw as the oppressive authority of the church and its emphasis on "simplistic" supernatural explanations.

Rationalists argued for a closed universe of cause and effect. So if you have an effect in this world—say, dropping a powdered donut and having it fall tragically to the ground—you also have a natural cause, in this case, gravity. The same goes for human beings, the existence of whom is an "effect" in this world. And the "rational" cause of "us" would be evolutionary naturalism.

Rationalists argued for a closed universe of cause and effect. So if you have an effect in this world—say, dropping a powdered donut and having it fall tragically to the ground—you also have a natural cause, in this case, gravity.

---

[3] "Scientific method," *Wikipedia*, last modified March 4, 2019, https://en.wikipedia.org/wiki/Scientific_method.

What about the Pentateuch? Gone must be the supernatural explanation for its development—that God inspired a Hebrew prophet named Moses to write down texts while on a mountain, after that same God had supernaturally redeemed a people through this prophet from Egypt. In its place, critical scholars needed a natural explanation.

That explanation, which is still held in many variant forms by critical scholars today, was something called the Documentary Hypothesis, popularly known as JEDP. The basic theory goes that, rather than being the product of one hand, the Pentateuch developed over time as a compilation of four distinct sources—with the first (J, or the Yahwist source, so-called based on its preference for Yahweh[4] as the name of God) being written around the time of the Israelite monarchy, more than 400 years after Moses, and the last (P, or the Priestly source, so-called based on supposed additions to the text made by the priestly caste) adding its content in the postexilic period, right before the end of the OT era (late 400s BC). The composition history of the Pentateuch, critical scholars argue, was thus later and longer than previously held, and definitely not Mosaic.

Each hypothesized source—J, E (or the Elohist source, written in the 800s BC and so-called because of its preference for Elohim[5] as the name of God), D (the Deuteronomist source, mostly the book of Deuteronomy, believed to be written in the 600s BC), and P—was originally composed independently. But later editors merged the sources into the complete Pentateuch we have today. And by using a method called source criticism, scholars today still isolate and identify those original sources. This theory was first popularized by a German

---

[4] Yahweh, or YHWH in Hebrew, is God's covenant and personal name. It is often translated as Lord or LORD in the English text.

[5] Elohim is the generic name for God in the Hebrew language.

scholar named Julius Wellhausen, so the hypothesis is often titled after its founder.[6]

A critique and thorough treatment of this theory is beyond the scope of this book. See the article on the Pentateuch in the *Holman Bible Dictionary*[7] for more details. For now, let's just examine three main problems with the theory.

First, those who hold to the Documentary Hypothesis engage in circular reasoning, assuming what they are trying to prove. In other words, if you look for "sources" behind any one writing, you will probably find anything you want, including multiple sources. And if you do find evi-

The Documentary Hypothesis was first popularized by Julius Wellhausen.

dence for Mosaic authorship for the Torah in the Pentateuch, such as the texts I listed above, then, well, those are just retrojections by later authors to give the writings credibility.

But seeing the Bible as a "pious fraud" and ignoring internal scriptural evidence is problematic. What does this do to your view of the inspiration of the Bible?

Second, those who hold to the Documentary Hypothesis tend to force modern expectations onto ancient genres. For instance, one of

---

[6] "Julius Wellhausen," *Wikipedia*, last modified January 6, 2019, https://en.wikipedia.org/wiki/Julius_Wellhausen.

[7] Chad Brand, Eric Mitchell, and Holman Reference Editorial Staff, *Holman Illustrated Bible Dictionary* (Nashville: B&H Publishing Group, 2015).

the common arguments for JEDP is the existence of so-called dupli-cate narratives in the text. For example, see Genesis 12, 20, and 26, in which the main characters, Abraham and Isaac, pass off their wives, Sarah and Rebekah respectively, as their sisters. To source critics, these repetitions represent evidence of several sources behind the texts. Their rationale: modern historians do not repeat the same stories. But if you look at ancient sources, Semitic narrators used a technique called reca-pitulation, where similar stories are told in similar ways to make rhe-torical points. Compare Judges 19 and Genesis 19 for a good example. Ancient writers don't have to abide by our rules of writing.

Third, source critics can become so consumed with the hypothet-ical process of excavating sources that they miss out on the overall meaning, teaching, and rhetorical fervor of the final form of the text. The final form of the Scriptures—what we have today in its totality—is always most important in determining meaning and application.

In sum, to go back to a point made at the beginning of this section, your position on this authorship issue is not as important to me as the rationale that led you to your position. In other words, if you doubt that Moses wrote the Torah, let's explore why you do so. Is it because you doubt what the Scriptures themselves assert? Is it because you doubt the text's supernatural origins? In both of these cases, the presup-positions are more problematic than the resulting position.

Thus, for now, this book will assume traditional Mosaic authority behind the Pentateuch. And if Moses wrote the Pentateuch substan-tially and his audience was the exodus generation leaving Egypt, how does that affect the way one reads the text?

Again, the goal is to put yourself in the shoes of the audience as you read it. So what would it mean to one rescued from Egyptian slavery that God had promised Abraham and Jacob a nation and a place to dwell? How would one on the cusp of the Promised Land "hear" the stories in the book of Numbers of the failures of her recent forefathers? How would someone who grew up in polytheistic Egypt and is about to enter polytheistic Canaan hear Moses's exhortation, "Listen, Israel: The LORD our God, the LORD is one" (Deut 6:4)?

In each case, such a reading, based in the level-2 context, makes the text more personal and poignant and persuasive. Context gives the text, as mentioned in chapter 3, "oomph." So when exploring any Pentateuchal text, always explore the significance of the level-2 context.

Level-1 Historical Context: The Events Themselves

A second important historical tool is the level-1 context of the events themselves. We will explore these same events more closely in the literary section below. But here let's take a big-picture look.

Broadly speaking, the Pentateuch details many centuries of history, and even more depending on when one dates creation itself. But upon closer examination, the events are unequally covered. This fact aids in determining the focus and interest of the author.

How do you establish an author's emphasis? The most obvious way is by examining the amount of space allotted to the description of the events. If I wrote your biography in a hundred pages and ninety of those pages dealt with your freshman year of high school, that might say something about the importance of that "awkward year" in your life.

What about the Pentateuch? Starting with Exodus 1 and going through Numbers 14, almost half of the Torah deals with a single year of Israel's history—just one out of all those centuries covered in the Pentateuchal books. What happened in that year? The exodus and the Sinai covenant. And if you expand out to Exodus through Deuteronomy, some 80 percent of the Torah deals with a mere forty years of Israelite history.

This should not surprise us; as argued above, Moses, who experienced the events in Exodus through Deuteronomy, is the author. But the space allotted also should tell us something about the overall significance of these happenings in the story of Israel and in the story of

Half of the Torah deals with just one year of Israel's history—the exodus and events at Mt. Sinai.

God's salvation. If you were to ask most Christians to identify the most important events in the OT Torah, they might say the creation, the Noahic flood, and so forth. Although these are definitely important, for the author, his eyes are drawn to the formation and constitution of Israel as a covenant people at Sinai.

Literary Tools

The second set of tools to use are literary—literary genre and structure/story line/message/purpose. Let's consider them.

Genre

What is the genre of the Pentateuch? Obviously, as with any document this size, you will find a diversity among the types of literature in the books—including poetry, prescriptive material, narrative stories and reports, genealogies, blessings, among many others.

But is there a designation that fits the whole of the Pentateuch? Modern scholars have labeled it as a treaty or biography or even national history. The Jewish designation for the books is *Torah*, a term rendered in the English most often as "law."

But is the Pentateuch law?

Again, genre affects what we expect to "get out of" the text. What do you anticipate "getting" in reading law? Probably nothing compelling or vital. When is the last time you longed to go down to the local court house and pull down some legal books of records or codes?

Instead, a better way of understanding the Torah comes from the original Hebrew. The noun *torah* in Hebrew derives from the verbal root *ytr*, "to instruct." So the Torah is "instruction"—about God, about his history with his people, about his creation and redemption, about the way he relates to his people in covenant, about the proper response to God in covenant relationship, about the people's responsibilities in covenant relationship, and so forth.

But it is not just instruction for the purpose of communicating facts. This narrative—as will be discussed more in the next chapter—is prophetic. In other words, it communicates a revelation from God to his people of all ages in order to change mind-sets and behaviors and to form a covenant people for himself. These narratives purpose to transform the reader—to bring them and the entire community into right covenant relationship with God and one another (Deut 6:5; Lev 19:18).

So as you read the Pentateuch, don't just read it for facts. Read it and be exhorted. Be encouraged. Be challenged. And through the Holy Spirit, be changed.

With the genre established, let's now consider the literary structure/story line/message/purpose of each book. With each of the following, we will consider the purpose and outline and overall flow of the books.

Literary Structure/Story Line/Message/Purpose—Genesis

One can hardly overstate the importance of the first book of the Bible. Indeed, Genesis provides the foundation for the whole Bible and biblical story line.

As Ken Mathews writes,

> If we possessed a Bible without Genesis, we would have a "house of cards" without foundation or mortar. . . . The first verse declares the metaphysical assumption, that is, a transcendent Creator-God, that acts as the philosophical cornerstone of the entire biblical revelation. Just as we have no gospel without the cross, we would have no salvation story without the sacred events of Moses' first book.[8]

In fact, the book's titles in the English (Genesis or "origin") and in the Hebrew (*Bereshith*, "in the beginning," from the first word in the Hebrew text) both speak of its nature as a foundational document. It is a book of "origins"—of the world, of humanity, of the nations, of the human predicament and the major complication of the story line of Scripture (sin, evil, and death), and of God's program of salvation (God's promise). In addition, so much of what comprises a Christian worldview is introduced here. Who are we? How did we get here? What is our purpose? What is wrong with us? Is there a God? What is he like? Is there a way to fix this sad old world? . . .

A good starting point for understanding the book is its structure. If you look up commentaries on Genesis in the library, likely you will find the book covered in two volumes, divided based on subject matter. These divisions include the so-called Primeval History (chaps. 1–11, detailing more universal and prerecorded historical events, such as the

---

[8] Kenneth A. Mathews, *Genesis 1–11:26*, The New American Commentary, vol. 1a (Nashville: Broadman & Holman, 1996), 22.

creation, fall, flood, and the Tower of Babel) and the Patriarchal History (chaps. 12–50, recounting God's specific and localized dealings with the fathers or "patriarchs" of the Jewish people—Abraham, Isaac, and Jacob). Although this two-part structure is thematically convenient, one must remember that such a division does not arise from Genesis itself.

Instead, scholars have rightly identified an internal clue to Genesis's structure—the so-called *toledoth* formulae. This Hebrew word, *toledoth*, which means "generation" or "family history," often introduces genealogies and is repeated eleven times in the book (2:4; 5:1; 6:9; 10:1; 11:10, 27; 25:12, 19; 36:1, 9; 37:2). The phrase serves as a hinge—both revisiting and anticipating certain themes and persons. Conveniently and appropriately, it divides the book into twelve sections—mirroring the number of sons of Jacob and the number of the eventual tribes of Israel.

The effect is to make Genesis into an expanded "family history." I liken it to old VHS tape players. The genealogies "fast forward" between generations in the story, and the narratives "pause" to expand on major figures in the story line. But even more important, with these connecting *toledoth*, the story of creation at the beginning of the book becomes intimately linked to the stories of God's covenant people in the middle and end. In other words, when God created, he had his covenant people in mind. Even "in the beginning," God's people have always been prized, promised, and planned.

The first *toledoth* comes after Gen 1:1–2:3—a section of Scripture that ranks perhaps as the most theologically weighty and debated in the entire OT. What makes it controversial is that people often use it solely as an instrument of battle in the perceived science/faith schism.

Although we don't have the time to unpack this text in its entirety, one truth is obvious: God did not intend Genesis 1 to be a science textbook. Remember the genre. Genesis 1 is an ancient document written in an ancient style that ancient people would understand.

But it has a resilient and enduring purpose; that is, it is a highly structured, almost liturgical doxological narrative, written to give glory

Like an old VHS tape player, the genealogies of Genesis "fast forward" between generations in the story, and the narratives "pause" to expand on major figures in the story line.

to God.[9] By emphasizing poetically and rhythmically things such as the power of God's words ("then God said") and the goodness of God's work ("it was good"), the author demonstrates God's creation to be an orderly, wise, and beautiful product of divine decree. And if you read it and you do not respond by praising God as did the psalmist in Psalm 8, then you have misread it. "LORD, our Lord, how magnificent is your name throughout the earth!" (vv. 1, 9). See the Putting the Tools to Use section in chapter 6.

---

[9] Merriam-Webster Dictionary, s.v., "doxological," accessed March 4, 2019, https://www.merriam-webster.com/dictionary/doxological. I first heard this category used of Genesis 1 by my mentor, Daniel I. Block, in one of my classes I had with him.

Genesis 1 details an ancient story written
in an ancient style that ancient people would understand.

Besides these repeated themes or phrases, the key to this first section in the book is found in Gen 1:2. Here the writer tells of three circumstances or even complications in the initial creation: it is formless, void, and dark. I can comprehend what darkness is. But what does it mean to be formless and void? A good way of understanding these ideas is as uninhabitable and uninhabited (see Jer 4:23, where Jeremiah uses the same words to describe the effects of the Babylonian exile).

The subsequent text in Genesis 1 explains how the sovereign Creator addresses these issues; that is, he creates an inhabitable kingdom and inhabits it with occupants. Each day corresponds in this process—day 1 to day 4, day 2 to day 5, and day 3 to day 6. On days 1–3, God forms something (heavens, light; sky, sea; land, plants) making it livable and functional, and on days 4–6, God fills the now inhabitable spaces with appropriate functionaries (sun, moon, stars; fish, birds; animals, humans). This structure is something scholars have called the form-fill pattern in the text.

Day 1: Heavens, Earth	Day 4: Sun, Moon, Stars
Day 2: Sea, Sky	Day 5: Fish, Birds
Day 3: Land, Plants	Day 6: Animals, Humans

The climax of this orderly creative work occurs on day 7. Often ignored in the creation story, the Sabbath is not just a day of rest, where God is tuckered out from a long week of work. John Walton has done some key research in this area.[10] He has demonstrated how Gen 1:1–2:3 mirrors ancient Near Eastern documents that describe the dedication of ancient temples. How does this work? After the completion of a temple, often ancient Near Easterners would hold a seven-day inauguration ceremony for the temple's god. These temples were not primarily places of worship, but instead were the palaces for the gods—places of their rule. In these ceremonies, when the gods "rested" on the seventh day, they took their thrones like a king in his castle or like the president on Inauguration Day. The king was ready to rule.

If this parallel is accurate, then God's rest at the end of creation in Genesis 1 symbolizes the completion of his kingdom and the inauguration of his reign over it. For the Hebrews, their literal rest on the Sabbath recognized and celebrated God's sovereign control and rule. God's people could "rest" (literal ceasing from work) because God continues to "rest" (rule) on his throne.

Conceiving of God as a sovereign king was not a foreign concept in the ancient Near East. What is unique in the Bible is the role humans play in his kingdom. In most ancient religions, gods created people to

---

[10] See John Walton's groundbreaking work, *The Lost World of Genesis 1: Ancient Cosmology and the Origins Debate* (Downers Grove, IL: IVP Academic, 2009).

Genesis 1 portrays creation as the temple of the Creator. Above is a photo of the most well-preserved Yahwistic Temple from Tell Arad in Israel.

serve their needs, basically as slaves. The gods couldn't care less about most human life and involved themselves in human activity only when their minions became toilsome or irritating or when the divine counsel needed something.

Not so with the true, biblical God. Genesis 1:26–31 shows humanity to be the pinnacle of God's productive work and to be central in God's purposes in glorifying himself through his kingdom. God created humans to be his image-bearers. To be an image-bearer is not taking the form of God or possessing some ontological characteristic of God (e.g., having a rational or relationship capability).[11] Instead, the text tells us that image-bearing is a status—designating the ones who serve creation and God's kingdom as God's vice-regents, perhaps like

---

[11] Merriam-Webster Dictionary, s.v., "ontological," accessed March 4, 2019, https://www.merriam-webster.com/dictionary/ontological.

a prince to a king. "Then God said, 'Let us make man in our image, according to our likeness. *They will rule . . . the whole earth*" (Gen 1:26, emphasis added).[12]

And this imageness does not extend only to one person or one class or one gender or one race. In the Bible, all share in the *imago Dei* (v. 27). This high status enjoyed by all people has tremendous ethical and practical applications for believers today. See the Applying the Results section below.

The next *toledoth* section of Genesis (2:4–4:26) describes the unfortunate fate of God's image-bearers. God placed Adam and Eve in a pristine sacred space resembling a garden-like temple—a sphere of God's rule.[13] There the original couple had the opportunity to "fill and subdue" the earth and expand the place of God's presence and "rest" to all of creation.

Though they had the capacity to rule for God, their rule was one under God. God established his sovereignty over them by prohibiting them from eating from the Tree of the Knowledge of Good and Evil. But this happy existence did not last. In a bold act of rebellion against the divine Sovereign, God's vice-regents transgressed (lit., crossed over) this divine boundary marker. The humans listened to the deceitful serpent and took from the forbidden fruit.

This original sin found in Genesis 3 is something known as the fall. And the fall's effects were catastrophic. The garden, which had been

---

[12] See also Col 1:15, where Jesus is described as the true image of God and the firstborn over creation. In ancient culture, the firstborn child is one who would inherit the rights, privileges, and rule of the father.

[13] Interestingly, Adam is charged with serving and keeping the garden of Eden (Gen 2:15). In the same way, the Levitical priests were to serve and keep the tabernacle (Num 3:7–8; 8:25–26; 18:5–6). This connection shows the temple-like nature of the garden. Other connections between the garden and the temple/tabernacle include the presence of God in both; the entrance facing the east with both; the abundant life found in both; among others.

a place of God's blessing, order, rule, and presence, had now become cursed. And God forcibly dismissed humanity from his presence. Most tragically, through Adam, sin had entered into the world (Rom 5:12). Since Adam is our representative and head, it can now be said that we inherit a sin nature—"For all have sinned and fall short of the glory of God" (Rom 3:23). Also as a consequence, death entered creation, as the just "wages of sin" (Rom 6:23).

Thus, the complications for the rest of Scripture—sin, death, and evil—enter the biblical story line in Genesis 3. Other tragic effects of the fall ensued. As image-bearers, Adam and Eve had been instructed to "be fruitful and multiply" and "fill and subdue" the earth. In response to the fall, God increases pain in childbirth and toil in working the soil—in essence, making the tasks of image-bearing burdensome and cursed. Creation—including us as image-bearers—now groans, waiting for redemption (Rom 8:22).

Of course, Christians believe this image-ness and creation itself will be and is being redeemed through the true *imago Dei*—the God-man Jesus Christ (Col 1:15). Indeed, in Gen 3:15, even in the midst of the curse, God promises a "Seed" of the woman that would one day crush the head of the serpent and all that he represents—sin, evil, death, and rebellion against God. This promise is something known in Greek as the *protoeuangelion*—the first gospel. Even from the beginning of the Bible, the hope of the gospel is revealed.

The remainder of Primeval History relates the immediate effects of the fall—the quick

The complications to be resolved in the rest of Scripture—sin, death, and evil— enter the biblical story line with the fall in Genesis 3.

and tragic work of sin and a sin nature. For instance, in Genesis 4, the unthinkable happens. Adam's son Cain in a jealous rage takes the life of his brother, another image-bearer. In Genesis 5, we see a long genealogy bringing the reader to the time of Noah. But even as we note the gracious continuation of life in the generations following Adam, we read over and over in the genealogy, "then he died . . . then he died . . . then he died." Death reigns in creation because of sin.

The downward spiral continues in Genesis 6, where we find that the intent of the heart of humankind had become "nothing but evil all the time" (6:5). In response, God proclaims a devastating judgment, known as the Noahic flood.

The narrative here brings the Primeval History to its climax. Will a holy God allow humanity to self-destruct and sin to reign? The answer clearly is no. But in the midst of his judgment, God does something surprising—or not so surprising based on the character of God. He redeems humanity, by acting to save the righteous Noah and his family.

Through the ark, God rescues Noah and by extension all of humanity. Noah becomes a new Adam in a newly cleansed creation, with the same role and responsibilities and blessing as the previous image-bearers: "Be fruitful and multiply and fill the earth" (Gen 9:1). God also makes a redemptive covenant with Noah, showing his commitment to creation as a whole and promising never to flood the earth to that extent again. The sign of this covenant, of course, is the rainbow.

Yet, as with the original creation, a sin nature remains as the chief characteristic of humanity. Immediately upon exiting the ark, an inebriated and naked Noah knowingly sins again. Humanity is still fallen.

And as with the initial Edenic fall, sin spreads quickly and catastrophically. This time, in Genesis 11, humanity gathers as one on the plains of Shinar—directly rejecting God's dispersal mandate, in order to "make a name" for themselves (v. 4). They decide to build a tower—perhaps an ancient ziggurat—in order to bring God down to the level of fallen humanity.[14] God responds by confusing their languages and scattering them himself across the globe.

Many scholars believe that the Tower of Babel was an ancient ziggurat, like this one found in the ancient ruins of Ur.

What will happen now? Here the author shocks the reader. Consider the progression of events from chapters 1–6: creation out of water, the blessing of Adam's line, the Edenic fall, the spread of Adam's line, the corruption of Adam's line (6:1–5). Now consider the order of events in Genesis 6–11: re-creation out of water, the blessing of Noah's line (9:1), the "fall" of Noah, the spread of Noah's line (chap. 10), and the corruption of Noah's line (the Tower of Babylon/Babel). Based on

---

[14] "Ziggurat," *Wikipedia*, last modified March 5, 2019, https://en .wikipedia.org/wiki/Ziggurat.

that parallel order, one might expect in Genesis 12 that God would send another devastating judgment as with the flood.

But God had promised not to do so. Instead of another re-creation and expression of extreme justice, God responds redemptively. He does the unexpected and perhaps what the world would consider foolish. He decides to bring redemption by working through one unremarkable Mesopotamian from a pagan family in Ur. A man named Abraham.

Through Abraham and his "seed," God would create a nation that would bring blessing to the other nations (Gen 12:3). And through Abraham and his seed, God would begin his program of redemption in earnest. With the benefit of hindsight, we see that this blessing of the nations would come through the true seed of Abraham, the Son of David, and the Son of God—Jesus Christ (Matt 1:1).

One problem existed with this promise, however. Abraham and his wife Sarah were childless and far past childbearing years. How could God's promises of land, seed (Gen 3:15), and blessing be fulfilled in the face of insuperable barrenness? Yet when it comes to God fulfilling his promises, all things are possible.[15]

But even as Abraham journeys to the Promised Land, he begins to doubt God's promises. Still, God is gracious to reiterate and reinforce his covenantal commitment—most poignantly in Genesis 15. Following a confession of Abraham, in which the patriarch is described as believing in God's covenant promises and as being credited with righteousness (v. 6), God affirms his commitment to Abraham. In a covenant ceremony that mirrors ancient Near Eastern treaties, God restates his promise to Abraham that he will be the father of many. God also looks forward

---

[15] As mentioned above, the tendency is to see these patriarchal stories as mere moralistic fables—with characters presented as examples to follow, either positively or negatively. But the story of the patriarchs is much more. It is a story about God, about his covenant faithfulness, and about his commitment to redeem humanity and to create a people for himself.

to the exodus and pledges his commitment to bring the children of Abraham out of a foreign nation, in which they will be sojourners (vv. 13–15).[16] *See Wordsearch video for more details on the significance of this covenant ceremony.*

Eventually, the promised child—Isaac—is born. But before Abraham dies, his faith is tested once more. This time, in Genesis 22, God calls on Abraham to sacrifice that which is most precious to him—the son of the promise—on Mount Moriah. Obedient even while facing the possibility of losing his child, Abraham treks up the mountain and prepares for the deed. What will happen to salvation history if Abraham follows through?

At the last moment, though, God provides a substitute—a ram caught in a thicket (vv. 12–14). Not for the first or last time, the concept of substitution—a life given for a life—enters the story line of Scripture. This time, the ram clearly foreshadows the Passover Lamb of the exodus and eventually the Passover Lamb of the cross.

After the death of Abraham, the story becomes focused not on Isaac, who remains a passive figure in the text, but on Jacob. Even the narrative between Isaac's succession in Genesis 25 and his death in Genesis 35 seems to center on his son Jacob. There is a reason for this. Jacob is Israel.

Isaac has twin sons, Jacob and Esau, with the latter being the firstborn. But the promises pass not through the expected firstborn son. Instead, God continues to work through the unexpected—in this case, the deceitful, second-born momma's boy, Jacob. He swindles his older brother and steals Esau's birthright (25:27–34) and blessing (chap. 27). Yet Jacob—this uninspiring character—becomes the father of the

---

[16] Note again the level-2 historical context. How would this promise be "heard" by the exodus generation? Think about how significant the inclusion of this promise is.

The sacrificial ram of Genesis 22 clearly foreshadows the Passover Lamb of the exodus and eventually the Passover Lamb of the cross.

twelve tribes of Israel, almost as if to prove that only God could accomplish something like this.

Later God's program of salvation is further imperiled because of Jacob's many misdeeds. But at key moments, God continues to reassure Jacob of his presence and promises. The most poignant of these events occurs when Jacob wrestles with an angelic figure and is renamed Israel ("he strives with God" or "God strives"; see Gen 32:22–32). Henceforth, the narrative alternates names for Jacob/Israel, demonstrating that Jacob the man is becoming Israel the nation. And indeed, by the beginning of the book of Exodus, that nation has come into being, becoming numerous and fulfilling God's word to Abraham (Exod 1:7).

But before the story ends, the author narrates one final story—the extended story of Joseph (Genesis 37–50). This well-known account relates how this favored and spoiled son of Jacob is sold into Egyptian

*Jacob wrestles with an angelic figure and is renamed Israel
("he strives with God" or "God strives") in Gen 32:22–32.*

slavery by his resentful brothers. While enslaved, Joseph rises to power; through God's providential workings in Joseph's life, he saves Egypt and surrounding populations from a devastating famine.

The irony of this story is that if Joseph is never sold into slavery by his siblings, many peoples—including Joseph himself, Joseph's brothers, and thus the entire promised people—would have died. This fact is not lost on the lead character, who proclaims that what his brothers intended for evil, God meant for good—to preserve his people, his "seed" (Gen 50:20).

The move of Jacob and his family to Egypt leaves the reader wondering what will become of God's program of salvation—kind of a cliff-hanger. Will the Israelites be swallowed up in the general population of Egypt like so many others? But God's hand is in it all. God is placing the seed of his nation in the womb of Egypt—ready to be birthed after a 400-year gestation period.

Literary Structure / Story Line / Message / Purpose—Exodus

No Old Testament book has captured the imagination of Westerners more than Exodus. It has inspired political movements and popular movies, such as Charlton Heston's *The Ten Commandments*[17] and Dreamworks' animated *Prince of Egypt*.[18] And one can easily see why. The story is action-packed and compelling.

Charlton Heston as Moses in Cecile B. DeMille's movie re-telling of the Exodus, titled The Ten Commandments.

---

[17] "The Ten Commandments (1956)—Trailer," YouTube video, 1:43, posted by YouTube Movies, May 17, 2013, https://www.youtube.com/watch?v=EiLmKxiTT3g.

[18] "'The Prince of Egypt' Trailer," YouTube video, 2:00, posted by B.B.R., June 14, 2007, https://www.youtube.com/watch?v=yWs81poMgiM.

But Exodus is more than just a thrilling and inspiring tale. For Israel, the events of the book represented perhaps the most important historical happenings in its history. Like the Revolutionary War period for the United States, the exodus and the encounter with God at Mount Sinai defined Israel as a nation. These narratives laid the groundwork for Israel's national and theological self-understanding—as a promised people redeemed by and in covenant relationship with God.

The narratives also lay the groundwork for Israel's ethics, worship rituals, festivals, daily life, and so forth. Every generation is called on to identify with the original redeemed population and to renew the Lord's covenant.

Future biblical authors also use the exodus deliverance as a paradigm for how God will restore his people in the future—especially in difficult times like the Babylonian exile (Jer 16:14–15). New Testament authors even make use of exodus imagery (see Matthew 2–7; John 6–8; 1 Corinthians 10; and 2 Corinthians 5; 6:14–18; among many) in describing Christ's person and work. *See Wordsearch video for a brief discussion of a few of these.*

The structure of the book of Exodus focuses on three major events: the exodus itself (the redemption of God's covenant people in chaps. 1–18); the covenant at Mount Sinai (the constitution of God's covenant people in chaps. 19–24); and the tabernacle narratives (God's presence with his covenant people in chaps. 25–40).

Exodus begins with a narrative describing the peril of the Israelite nation. When we last left the story in Genesis, the family of Jacob/Israel boasted only seventy men. Now they number in the thousands. They had "increased rapidly, multiplied, and became extremely numerous so that the land was filled with them" (1:7). This obvious reference to the Abrahamic promise begins the book with anticipation; the reader already sees God's hand of blessing on his people.

But at this point, the Egyptian hand also oppresses them. A new pharaoh has arisen, and in an attempt to prevent a Hebrew insurrection, he enslaves them. He attempts to stem the population growth by working the men to death and killing the male children. But powerful peoples and potentates cannot prevent God from pursuing his purposes. He "remembers" his promises (2:23–25), and he promises deliverance to his people.

In fact, early in the text, we see one of the main points of the entire book, and we also encounter perhaps one of the main misconceptions of the book. Movies and popular portrayals focus on who they believe to be the "hero" of the text—Moses. But in these first chapters and in every subsequent one, the reader understands that the protagonist is not Moses, but God himself.

For instance God uses humble midwives to frustrate the plans of the powerful pharaoh. And God raises up a deliverer; but even then, God delivers the deliverer as a baby. Moses is spared ironically and providentially by the daughter of the pharaoh himself.

The next story in the text is the call of Moses, in Exodus 3. Many might see this as a call of Moses as a deliverer. But think about the progression of the story. God appears to Moses in a theophany—a physical manifestation of his glory (the burning bush). God commissions Moses to speak a message—to go and tell Pharaoh to "let my people go." Moses expresses reluctance—he has a speech impediment. God gives Moses assurance—the miracles of the staff and the leprous hand. Finally, Moses goes to his people as God commands.

This progression actually mirrors later calls of the prophets (see, e.g., Isaiah 6; Jeremiah 1; Ezekiel 1–3; Amos 7). In other words, Moses's main role was not as a deliverer of a people, but a deliverer of a message to the Hebrews and to Pharaoh. Moses is a prophet (Deut 18:15).

And as with the prophets, when Moses does convey God's communication, it meets stiff resistance. So begins the battle for the deliverance of "my people" in Exodus 5–11. Through Moses, God threatens Pharaoh with devastating physical judgments if he does not relent. And each time, a hardened heart causes Pharaoh to resist allowing the Hebrews to leave.

Many scholars have noted parallels between these ten plagues and the so-called "gods" of Egypt. Such a connection is probably overemphasized, but at least the first (the turning of the Nile to blood) and the last (the death of the firstborn child, including the pharaoh's) have the feel of a divine confrontation. Indeed, the Egyptians deified both the Nile and the pharaoh.

What is definite is the purpose of the narrative—establishing the identity of God. The plagues are sent ten times to reinforce to the Israelites and Egyptians what God told Moses in his call (Exod 3:14–15; 6:1–8)—that God is Yahweh, their covenant God, "I AM," who causes things (worlds and covenant peoples) to come into existence (Exod 7:17; 10:2). And the Israelites must understand the identity of Yahweh to become Yahweh's covenant people (Exod 15:11). *See Wordsearch video for an explanation of this name.*

The last plague proclaims something else about God. Like the flood, the Passover represents a supreme act of judgment and also deliverance. As a judgment, it is an appropriate reaction to the enslavement of Yahweh's firstborn, Israel. As an act of deliverance, it demonstrates God's fulfillment of his promises to the patriarchs (Exod 6:2, 8; cf. Gen 15:13–16).

In addition, the Passover once again highlights the biblical theological concept of substitution. By slaughtering the lamb and placing the lamb's blood over the doors for deliverance from death, we see that God accepts a life for a life. And one day, he will send the "Lamb of God" to be slaughtered as a substitute for the sins of the world (John 1:29).

With the death of his firstborn, the pharaoh finally relents. But the battle is not yet complete. The spurned ruler pursues his fleeing captives toward the Red Sea (Hebrew, "Sea of Reeds"). Once again, God, the hero in the text, intervenes, splitting the sea and leading his people across. And famously, the returning sea inundates the Egyptian pursuers. Note that Israel has nothing to do with this victory; they merely witness it.

All of this story of redemption is important and to be celebrated (see Exodus 15). But its main purpose is to set the stage for the book's main event—the formation of God's people into his covenant people at Mount Sinai. Chapters 1–18 are like the narrative of the courtship before the marriage or the story of the Revolutionary War before the ratifying of the Constitution. Chapters 1–18 tells a story that is going somewhere. And that somewhere is the covenant at Mount Sinai.

Chapters 19–24 tell the story of that climactic moment in Israel's history. Here God reveals himself on the mountain with fire, smoke, and earthquakes (see chap. 19). This revelation is what I call "divine accommodation." God condescends to reveal himself in a way humans understand (overwhelming physical means) so that we might scratch the surface of the ultimate reality (the overwhelming power of his glory and imminent revelation). Only, like the proverbial "tip of the iceberg," the infinity of God's glory and revelation lies below the surface of these finite physical demonstrations.

After God brings his people to himself, he then reveals his covenant stipulations to the people—the famous Ten Commandments.

Perhaps no text in the Old Testament is misunderstood more than the Ten Commandments. Christians use them as evangelistic battering rams to show nonbelievers their missteps. Non-Christians believe they are the check-boxes for achieving divine approval.

But these "Commandments" are not even called commandments in Exodus 20. They are labeled the "Ten Words"—the Decalogue. Words about what?

To understand them, we need to see them for what they are—a covenant document. They follow the form of an ancient treaty (see the discussion below on Deuteronomy). They are written on two tablets—not five commandments on each, mind you, but all ten on each, with one tablet for each covenant party. And the tablets are kept in the—yes—ark of the "covenant." *For more on this covenant nature, see the great*

Perhaps no text in the Old Testament is misunderstood
more than the Ten Commandments.

discussion on the Ten Commandments in the entry on "Law" in the Holman Bible Dictionary.[19]

In other words, these commandments are really principles for living out covenant relationship. Or perhaps a better way is to see them as vows of one covenant party to another—like the vows in a marriage. In this way, they represent the people's appropriate response to God's salvation, not a way of achieving it. And obedience to them is not a rote, burdensome activity, but a joyful expression of worship that arises

---

[19] Daniel Block, "Law" in *Holman Illustrated Bible Dictionary* ed. Brand, Mitchel, and Holman Reference Editorial Staff (Nashville: B&H Publishing Group, 2015).

from love. In the same way, my vows in my marriage are not out of a sense of legalism, but of covenant love for my wife.

So, by Exodus 24, God has rescued, redeemed, and constituted his covenant people.

The rest of Exodus (chaps. 25–40) celebrates how Yahweh will dwell with his covenant people. The chapters relate first the plans for (25–31) and then the building of (35–40) the tabernacle.

This structure was a tent pitched in the midst of the Israelite camp. It represented the residence of God and God's gracious presence in the midst of his covenant people without compromising his holiness.

Based solely on the amount of literary space given to it—about a third of the book!—we see its importance. How vital is it for a husband and wife to be near each other? So also, God provides for his covenant partner to be with him. This desire to be with his people is one demonstrated by God from the garden of Eden to the new creation in Revelation.

The tabernacle also represented a microcosm of the cosmos, which of course was also God's kingdom. It was a physical reminder to the people of God's grace and justice, holiness and righteousness, and immanence and transcendence. See the *Holman Bible Dictionary*[20] for an excellent description of it.

Before turning to Leviticus, however, one more story should be discussed. In Exodus 32–33, in response to these three great acts of grace of God in the book—God's deliverance of his people, God's revelation of the Torah to his people, and God's presence among his people—his people turn their backs on God. With Moses on the mountain, the people decide to offer allegiance to a more tangible representation of deity—a golden calf. Ironically led by Aaron, Moses's brother and the high priest, the Hebrews engage in a raucous religious orgy.

---

[20] Brand, Mitchell, and Holman Reference Editorial Staff, *Holman Illustrated Bible Dictionary* (Nashville: B&H Publishing Group, 2015).

Upon descending from the mountain and witnessing the people's debauchery, Moses breaks the newly minted covenant tablets, symbolically demonstrating how Israel had broken their covenant with Yahweh. And Yahweh almost destroys the people. But in response to Moses's intercession, God graciously allows the nation to survive.

In doing so, God also reveals his character audibly in Exodus 34:6–7—a rich theological text that I believe to be one of the most important in all the OT. Moses had asked that God proclaim his name. And he does so.

Do you want to know who God is? Ask him. These verses establish the character of God for the entire OT—as a covenant Lord who is gracious, patient, and just (see Neh 1:5; Dan 9:4; Joel 2:13; Jonah 4:2; among many other examples, especially in the Psalms).

Indeed, the entire book of Exodus is a book about a faithful, gracious, just, covenant-keeping God. He is the hero of the book.

Literary Structure / Message / Purpose—Leviticus

Every January, many Christians resolve to read the Bible in one year. And every year, one prominent biblical roadblock stops them in their tracks—the book of Leviticus. This book represents perhaps the most avoided and misunderstood of all OT books.

Yet, in reality, its message and theology are central to that of the entire Bible. When introducing this book, I often ask my students to define the essential elements of the Christian gospel. And they rightly point to biblical themes like sin and separation from a holy God, substitutionary sacrifice and salvation by grace, sanctification (growing in holiness), and suitable worship in a covenant community. Guess what you find in Leviticus?

Yes, each of these themes finds fulfillment in Christ in the NT. But Christ's salvific and sanctifying work is understood by the NT authors in light of this Levitical framework and foundation.

That doesn't mean the book is not difficult, because of its cultural and literary distance. But it is relevant and accessible—with the right tools.

The message of the book is best understood in light of what just happened in the biblical story line. In fact, the Hebrew title ("And He Called," from the first word in the Hebrew text) demonstrates that it is intimately connected to what just happened in Exodus—namely, God's covenant redemption (the exodus), God's covenant revelation (at Mount Sinai), and God's covenant presence (in the tabernacle). More precisely, that which is found in Leviticus—whether the sacrificial system, the priesthood, the Holiness Code, the covenantal blessings and cursings, and the prescriptions for holy days—teaches the Israelites how to respond to the new exodus realities. Like the Ten Commandments, Leviticus teaches God's people how to live in covenant with their God.

In this way, the Levitical laws were not to be seen as burdensome, but gracious. It was a Torah to be celebrated (see Psalm 119). Indeed, among the ancient Near Easterners, Israel was considered great—not because of prodigious prosperity, power, or population, but because they had a "near" God who had revealed his righteous Torah (Deut 4:6–8).

Each text in Leviticus should be viewed in this covenantal context. For instance, the first seven chapters detail the different types of sacrifices to be offered to God, as an expression of that covenant relationship.

As a practice, sacrifice seems quite foreign and unpalatable to modern readers. Yet for the Israelites it was a crucial worship ritual. To understand sacrifice, the practice must be grounded in the ancient Near Eastern worldview.

For Canaanites, for instance, sacrifice provided nourishment for the gods, so that the gods could do "god-things," like holding the cosmos together. Destroying, pouring out, and burning sacrificial materials—animals, grains, liquids, and so forth—allowed these items to pass through this world and sustain the gods in their own world. Notice that this ancient Near Eastern conception of sacrifice has nothing to do with sin or substitution. Instead, sacrifices served almost as magical acts to get the numerous, capricious, manipulative, and often violent gods on the sacrificer's side. The greater the need, the greater the sacrifice required—even human sacrifice (see 2 Kgs 3:26–27).

*Other cultures practiced sacrifice, as this altar found in
the ancient Canaanite city of Meggido illustrates. But the
Hebrew view of sacrifice was uniquely covenantal.*

For the Hebrews, however, sacrifice was at its heart a worship ritual and expression of covenant relationship. As Allen Ross states, "It was a divinely instituted drama that enacted God's way of sanctifying those who desired communion with him."[21] Or, as Daniel Block defines it,

---

[21] Allen P. Ross, *Holiness to the Lord: A Guide to the Exposition of the Book of Leviticus* (Grand Rapids: Baker Academic, 2002), 73.

sacrifice was one of many "reverential human acts of submission and homage before the divine Sovereign, in response to his gracious revelation of himself and in accordance with his will."[22]

Sacrifice also symbolized the doctrine of substitution (life for a life) for atonement (covering) and propitiation (appeasement of God's wrath)—for remission of sin. When people in the OT made sacrifices from the heart, they recognized the gravity of sin, as well as the unfathomable grace of God to forgive this sin. God, being rich in mercy (Eph 2:4), accepts this substitute looking to Christ's death, whose sacrifice was sufficient for all. There is no magic; this is the real thing.

Yes, at times some Israelites adopted a "magical" or "mechanical" view of sacrifice, like their pagan neighbors. But, as the prophets assert, sacrifices without the heart and covenant obedience were worthless and even an abomination to God (Isa 1:10–17; Amos 5:21–25; Mic 6:6–8; Ps 40:6–8).

Of course, OT sacrifice was just a shadow and type of the real thing (Isaiah 53). Christ offered a once-for-all, effective sacrifice that paid for the sins of the redeemed (see Heb 10:1–18). Jesus is confessed in the NT as the Lamb who takes away the sins of the world (John 1:29; 1 Pet 1:18–20). Thus, the OT sacrifices provide the backdrop by which we understand Christ's substitutionary work of atonement.

One of the most important Hebrew sacrifices took place on Yom Kippur (the Day of Atonement), described in Leviticus 16.[23] Observed after the autumnal new-year celebration, Yom Kippur provided a time for the entire covenant community to celebrate how their sins (embodied in the high priest) are "covered" or atoned for and removed from the community.

---

[22] See Daniel I. Block, *For the Glory of God: Recovering a Biblical Theology of Worship* (Grand Rapids: Baker Academic, 2016).

[23] "Yom Kippur," *Wikipedia,* last modified March 5, 2019, https://en .wikipedia.org/wiki/Yom_Kippur.

OT sacrifices provide the backdrop by which we understand Christ's substitutionary work of atonement.

Other important sections in Leviticus include the consecration of the high priesthood in chapters 8–10. The high priests must be descendants of Aaron, Moses's brother. The basic function of the priesthood was to do for the nation what the nation was to do for the world—to sanctify them and make them wholly devoted to God (Exod 19:4–6). They were to keep Israel holy by communicating Torah, keeping the community from defilement, and providing atonement for the sins of the covenant community when defilement did occur.

Leviticus 11–15 details laws of purity, demonstrating to the Israelites what is ceremonially clean and unclean. Though quite strange to modern readers, these laws are physical representations of what the covenant community ought to strive for spiritually—that is, being holy and separate like God himself (19:2). The NT offers a similar ethical motivation to the church (1 Pet 1:16).

The central part of Leviticus is the Holiness Code in chapters 17–26. The idea of holiness in the Torah is being separated but also dedicated to God (Lev 20:26). This code taught the people how they were to be separated from the cultures surrounding them and devoted to their covenant and holy Lord (19:2). This context, plus the context of the ancient Near East, is crucial for seeing the modern and enduring applicability of these laws.

For instance, consider the prescription not to reap the edges of your field. How many of you are farmers? Probably not many. So can we non-agrarians even apply this? For the Israelites, such a prescription allowed the covenant community to provide for the poorest among them—the widow, the orphan, the alien—by setting aside some of God's provisions for them. Such concern for outcasts not only set the Israelites apart from other nations, who did not often practice such things, but it also exhibited the heart of God, who cares for the "least of these" (Matt 25:35–46), to a watching world. In the same way, the church should provide for those who cannot provide for themselves. And the world will notice.

So holiness also fulfilled the purpose of God for Israel and for the church—that they become a missional people. Interestingly, this same "strangeness" led to the spread of the early church (1 Pet 1:15–16). As the church devoted itself to the apostles' teaching and lived out that teaching through their life together, "every day the Lord added to their number those who were being saved" (Acts 2:47).

See the Putting the Tools to Use section below for another example from the Holiness Code.

Literary Structure/Story Line/Message/Purpose—Numbers

I saw recently a rather embarrassing news article asserting, "We Hate Math, Say 4 in 10—A Majority of Americans." Whether or not you can do or even like math, a book titled "Numbers" probably doesn't inspire enthusiastic reading. But this fourth Pentateuchal book does occupy a crucial place in the story line and the canon.

If Genesis provides the background of the formation of the covenant people; if Exodus provides the account of the building of this nation as a covenant people saved by a revelatory God; if Leviticus expands on the stipulations of the covenant; and if Deuteronomy reconstitutes the nation before entering the Promised Land . . . Numbers bridges the gap between the first three books and last book, recording Israel's initial covenant failure, resulting in God's judgment for forty years. During these forty dark years, Israel is prohibited from entering the Promised Land and flounders and falters in a forbidding desert.

In the book of Numbers, Israel spent 40 years
floundering in the forbidding Sinai Wilderness.

But Numbers is more than a diary of dreary wilderness wanderings. Keep in mind the context of the initial readers, who are on the plains of Moab ready finally to enter into the Promised Land. It warns those Hebrew readers of the dangers of disobedience and encourages them with the prospects of blessing and life as a result of Yahweh's faithfulness and love. But with these warnings and encouragements, the book also speaks with much relevance to God's covenant people today—the church.

In the Hebrew, Numbers is titled *Be-midbar* (the fifth word in the Hebrew text, meaning "in the wilderness") to reflect the aforementioned geographical setting of the book. The English title refers to two censuses or "numberings" that occur in chapters 1 and 26. Appropriately, the book of Numbers may be structured based on these numbers in the book. The two numberings tell a tale of two Israels, two generations, with two vastly different destinies—the first dies in the wilderness, the second enters the Promised Land.

The first census, in chapter 1, takes place as Israel makes initial preparations for entering the Promised Land. A census in that day would occur for one express purpose—to count the men of fighting age (twenty and above). For a military conquest, this enumerating endeavor would represent an important first step. *For a discussion of the problem of the large numbers found in Numbers, see Wordsearch content.*

Soon after this first census, Israel, under Moses, makes other preparations: organizing the camp, charging the Levitical priests, consecrating the tabernacle, celebrating the Passover, and purifying the people. Notice that all of these arrangements share one commonality. They are all spiritual. Israel's success in the conquest depended not on military might or savvy strategy, but on covenantal fidelity and God's empowering presence.

With the fulfillment of the patriarchal promises in sight, the Israelites finally leave Sinai (Num 10:11). They find themselves at a place called Kadesh-Barnea—nearly directly south of their intended target of the Promised Land.[24] Entering and conquering seemed a foregone conclusion for God's people—a simple expression of faith in

---

[24] "Kadesh (biblical)," *Wikipedia*, last modified December 16, 2018, https://en.wikipedia.org/wiki/Kadesh_(biblical).

God's promise that they would possess it. It was a journey they could easily complete in weeks.

To scout out the land, Moses sends twelve spies, representing the twelve tribes. These scouts discover the Promised Land to be all that was promised—a land flowing with milk and honey. They also find Canaan to be filled with scary Canaanites. And the Israelites' fear leads to unbelief.

Although two of the spies (Joshua and Caleb) maintain their faith in God's conquering provision and ability, the other ten express fearful hesitation. The majority of the people side with and agree with the majority report of the spies. Ultimately the people's doubt was not in themselves, but in God himself (14:11). This explains the serious and harsh reaction on God's part. The Hebrews' skepticism represented rebellion against the covenant Lord.

So God condemns that entire generation, except for Joshua and Caleb, to forty years of wilderness wanderings and desert death.

But the rebellion was only just starting. Beginning in chapter 10, the next fifteen chapters of Numbers deal with nearly forty years of Israel's history. In these chapters, the author chooses to include only select negative, "revolting" events. For example, in chapter 12, Aaron and Miriam, Moses's own siblings, engage in a seditious family mutiny. In chapters 16–17, the sons of Korah engage in a priestly uprising, and Dathan and Abiram participate in a civil rebellion that brings a plague.

Most shockingly, in chapter 20, Moses himself exhibits unbelief, striking a rock to provide water, when God had clearly commanded him to speak to the stone. This public disobedience by Israel's covenant mediator is punished severely by Yahweh. And Moses himself is prohibited from entering the Promised Land.

One more rebellion is to come. Numbers 22–25 relates a series of curious stories surrounding Balaam, a pagan prophet, whom Balak, the king of Moab, hires to curse Israel, as the Hebrews attempted to pass through Moabite territory. In a rather humorous account in which Balaam's donkey speaks, Yahweh prohibits Balaam from cursing his people.

In a rather humorous account in which the donkey of the pagan prophet Balaam speaks, Yahweh prohibits Balaam from cursing his people.

But what Balaam could not do with his words, he accomplishes through other means. In chapter 25, Balaam tempts Israel to engage in Baal worship and pagan orgies. This rebellion results once again in God's judgment in the form of a plague. When the priest Phineas intervenes by killing the Hebrew offenders, God's vengeance is placated and the plague abates.

Indeed, after this event, things change for the better for God's people. Another census is taken in chapter 26, signaling that the preparations to enter the Promised Land are beginning anew. The curse seems to be over.

In this section of the book after this second numbering, as mentioned above, we meet a new Israel—a new generation that will finally be allowed into the Promised Land. Amazingly, after this census, death is not mentioned again in the text, even in a battle with the Midianites (chap. 31). God's grace has preserved his people, his seed, even in the face of their murmuring and mutinous behavior.

But the damage is done. Comparing the numbers from the two censuses, we see that the population has actually diminished over forty years. Even while enslaved in Egypt, the people had multiplied and filled the land (Exod 1:7), but in the wilderness, they shrank. The only explanation for the ebbing totals is the total application of the justice of God in response to Israel's unbelief. God may pardon the sinner, but the consequences of sin often remain.

God takes rebellion seriously—a fact not lost on later scriptural authors. Indeed, for this reason, this "exodus generation" is held up as a negative example for the early church (Heb 3:7–19). Don't be like them. And such an admonition undoubtedly reverberated in the ears of the conquest generation as they read the book of Numbers for the first time. And it should for the modern church as well.

Literary Structure / Message / Purpose—Deuteronomy

At the close of the Pentateuch, one finds what may be the most theologically significant OT book. Indeed, I would argue, Deuteronomy is similar to Romans in the NT, providing the most comprehensive description of the theology of the OT. Authors in the OT, such as the former and latter prophets, and authors in the NT use Deuteronomy's contents to explain who God is, who we are as his people, and how we are to live in covenant with him. Jesus himself often quoted from the book—most notably in response to Satan's three temptations in the desert (Matt 4:4, 7, and 10), but also in summarizing the entire Torah (Matt 22:37–38).

The biblical and theological significance of Deuteronomy is due to several factors; first among these is a historical one: these are the last words of Moses.

I remember seeing a YouTube video titled "Randy Pausch Last Lecture," delivered by Carnegie Mellon professor Randy Pausch before he died of cancer.[25] It got me thinking. What would I say if I had one last lecture to give? My guess is that, regardless of the content, it would be memorable to my students. The book of Deuteronomy houses Moses's "last lectures"—an elaborate series of valedictory sermons by the dying leader.

And what an important leader he was. From the land of Egypt to the plains of Moab, from the early chapters of Exodus to the last verse of Numbers, Moses has taken center stage in the emancipation, establishment, and exhortation of the nation of Israel. As the Pentateuch draws to a close, this great leader has reached the point of death.

If that fact alone does not add to the pathos of the book, the situation in the life of Israel should. Deuteronomy provides a vivid picture of the historical context for Moses's final addresses. An entire generation of God's chosen people has perished in the wilderness, but their progeny is now poised on the edge of God's Promised Land on the plains of Moab. Though prohibited from crossing the Jordan River himself, Moses desires to lead this new generation vicariously through his last words.

---

[25] Randy Pausch, "Randy Pausch Last Lecture: Achieving Your Childhood Dreams," YouTube video, posted by Carnegie Mellon University, December 20, 2007, https://www.youtube.com/watch?v=ji5_MqicxSo.

Mt. Nebo in Jordan, where Moses was granted a view of the Promised Land.

Do you feel the immediacy and tension?

In addition to a final, impassioned sermon, the book can also be viewed another way. The last half of the twentieth century provided several helpful comparisons of Deuteronomy to extant ancient suzerain-vassal treaties. These treaties between unequal parties are attested from the ancient Hittites and Assyrians and date to 1200–600 BC. Very similar in many ways to OT covenants, the treaties speak of the rights and responsibilities of a sovereign king (the suzerain) and lesser entities (the vassals) in a political and/or military relationship.

Amazingly, if you compare the structure of these treaties to that of Deuteronomy, you find some striking parallels. Both share component parts such as a preamble to the treaty, a historical prologue describing the preexisting relationship of the parties in the treaty, stipulations governing the treaty relationship, blessings and cursings for keeping the stipulations, divine witnesses to the treaty, and so forth. Remarkably, in these treaties, the vassals are even called upon to "love" the suzerain, just as Israel is called upon to "love" God (Deut 6:5).

Many believe that Moses or a final editor of Deuteronomy used this treaty form as a kind of sermon illustration. In other words, Moses believed God's relationship with Israel to be like this well-known treaty bond—but as a covenant relationship (see below). Eugene Merrill perhaps labels Deuteronomy best as a "covenant expressed in narrative and exhortation, the whole thing comprising a farewell address."[26]

In summary, whenever you read a text from Deuteronomy, ask the following question: How does this text passionately exhort God's people (then and now) to live in right covenant relationship with him in a cultural context that imperils that relationship? See the Applying the Results section below for a discussion of the most significant text in the book.

Theological Tools

Salvation History

Of the theological tools to employ in understanding these texts, we need to first and foremost consider the place of these events in salvation history. Remember that one tends to read stories isolated from their context. But the events in Genesis–Deuteronomy are part of a larger narrative of God's saving work. And what a narrative it is!

Genesis tells the story of the creation and fall. It tells how God intends to redeem fallen creation through the promised seed (Gen 3:15). That seed becomes specified as the Seed of Abraham, through whom the nations will be blessed (Gen 12:3). That seed then grows into a multiplied people in Egypt (Exod 1:7).

God redeems that seed out of bondage and then forms the seed into a covenant nation in the book of Exodus. Leviticus then provides covenant ordinances to help that seed to become a holy people

---

[26] Eugene Merrill, *Deuteronomy*, The New American Commentary, vol. 4 (Nashville: Broadman & Holman, 1994), 29.

dedicated to God. Numbers tells of the crisis and near extermination of the seed in the wilderness. Yet God preserves them and then reconstitutes them as a covenant nation in Deuteronomy.

As you read these stories, always ask how that story furthers the greater narrative—a narrative that ultimately culminates in the ultimate promised Seed, Christ himself. Indeed, throughout the narrative, the reader finds hints or prophecies of this coming Christ. *For instance, see Wordsearch content for a look at how the book of Numbers anticipates Christ.*

In this great story of salvation, the Israelites also had a role to play.

As John Collins writes, "This over-arching story serves as a grand narrative or worldview story for Israel: each member of the people was to see himself or herself as an *heir* of this story, with all its glory and shame; as a *steward* of the story, responsible to pass it on to the next generation; and as a *participant*, whose faithfulness could play a role, in God's mysterious wisdom, in the story's progress."[27]

We can say the same about the church today. Israel's story in the Pentateuch is our story. And that story continues even today in and through the church, God's new covenant people.

Theological Themes

As mentioned above, the Pentateuch is the foundation for the rest of the Bible; this is especially true of the theological themes found in the Bible. Doctrines like creation, covenant, law, sacrifice, redemption, kingdom, and even God himself find their first exposition here. Among these, most prominent are law, covenant, and God himself. For the first, see the great discussion of the theme of law by Daniel Block in the

---

[27] C. John Collins, "Always Alleluia: Reclaiming the True Purpose of the Psalms in the Old Testament Context," in *Forgotten Songs: Reclaiming the Psalms for Christian Worship*, ed. C. Richard Wells and Ray Van Neste (Nashville: Broadman & Holman, 2012), 27.

Holman Bible Dictionary.[28] The following will expand on the all-important theme of covenant—a concept that we've mentioned many times already in our discussions above.

Covenant

In the Bible, you will not find a more crucial or central theological theme than covenant. Students joke in my classes that if you ever forget the right answer to an in-class question, just answer "covenant."

It explains so much of what we find in the Scriptures. In fact, covenant helps us to put our Bibles together. Our Bibles are composed of two sections, correct? An Old Testament and a New Testament. What is another word for "testament"? Covenant. So the Old "Testament" tells of a covenant God's dealings with his covenant people Israel under the old covenant document, the Torah. And the New "Testament" proclaims a new covenant relationship and a new covenant people of God through a new covenant Mediator in the person of Jesus Christ.

Covenant as a theme also helps us to understand the nature of God and his dealings with us. God is a relational God. He desires to form unto himself a covenant people. So we relate to him not just as individuals, but also (and perhaps primarily) as corporate covenant bodies. Today this is the church.

Most important, through these covenant relationships, God chooses to bring about redemption to the world—in the Old Testament and in the New. Mission was the purpose of the OT covenant people, Israel (Gen 12:3; Exod 19:5–6), and is the purpose of the NT covenant people, the church (1 Pet 2:9).

---

[28] Daniel Block, "Law" in *Holman Illustrated Bible Dictionary* ed. Brand, Mitchel, and Holman Reference Editorial Staff (Nashville: B&H Publishing Group, 2015).

Despite its importance, covenant is not a term found in everyday parlance, and its meaning is largely lost on many modern Christians. "So how's your covenant relationship with your spouse today?" It's not something you hear.

My definition is as follows: a covenant is a solemn union between two individuals or groups, grounded in loyalty, love, promise, and commitment.

But I have found the best way to understand a covenant is by looking at analogous relationships, whether ancient or modern. One of these is the suzerain-vassal treaties cited in the Deuteronomy discussion above. But a better, more accessible parallel for today is that of a marriage. In fact, this analogy is not foreign to the biblical text. God often describes his covenant relationship with his people in both the OT and the NT as a marriage (see Hosea 1–2; Jeremiah 2; Eph 5:22–32).

Comparison of Abrahamic Covenant with Marriage

Covenant Characteristics	Marriage	Abrahamic Covenant
Covenant Parties	Two individuals—husband and wife	Two individuals—God and Abraham
Covenant History	A preexisting relationship—the courtship of the couple	A preexisting relationship—the calling of Abraham out of Ur (Genesis 12)
Covenant Ceremony	The wedding of the couple	Cutting the animals in half in Genesis 15 (aren't you glad this is not part of a marriage ceremony today?)
Covenant Symbols	The ring	Circumcision (Genesis 17)
Covenant Promises	Marriage vows	Faith and belief (Gen 15:6)
Covenant Basis	Loyalty and love	Loyalty and love
Covenant Purpose	To mirror Christ and the church	To bring blessing to the nations (Gen 12:3)

Of course, no analogy is perfect. For example, a marriage is a relationship of equals. The biblical covenants between God and his people are not. But I believe the marriage comparison helps us to understand many things about covenants (and marriages!)—in particular the depth, weightiness, and purposefulness of the relationships.

Most scholars see six major covenants in the Scriptures—though some see more and some fewer. The covenants include the covenant with creation through Adam (Genesis 1–3), the covenant with creation through Noah (Genesis 6–9), the covenant with Abraham (Genesis 12, 15, 17), the covenant with Israel at Sinai (Exodus 19–24), the covenant with David (2 Samuel 7; Psalm 89), and the new covenant (Jer 31:27–34). One will note that four of these occur in the Pentateuch.

The major characteristic to note about the covenant history of the OT is that with each covenant, God's plans for redemption become more specific. He begins with a single man, Adam, in Genesis 1–3. Though the word *covenant* is not used in Genesis 1–3, God clearly is establishing a relationship through Adam with his entire creation. Indeed, as discussed above, creation itself is likened to a kingdom, in which God grants his image-bearers the authority to rule (1:26–31). Part of this role of vice-regent is to expand the sphere of God's sanctuary rest to all of creation. However, when Adam fell, the covenant was breached. All subsequent covenants are meant to restore this original promise.

The next covenant is the covenant with Noah (Genesis 6–9). In this passage (6:18), the word *covenant* is first used. The goal of the covenant is to reestablish the covenant with creation. It is a new start. Similar to Adam in the creation covenant, Noah was to multiply and rule over the earth (9:1–2). In this covenant, God also promised never again to destroy the earth with a flood—symbolized by a physical sign, the rainbow. God will preserve the world until his saving purposes can be fulfilled.

With the Abrahamic covenant, God's redemptive purposes become even clearer. As mentioned above, things seemed to be falling apart in God's purposes with the Tower of Babel in Genesis 11, but God calls a new Adam in Genesis 12. Abraham would receive land, blessing, and seed, and all nations would be blessed in him. Abraham's role was to "go" (obedient faith; Gen 15:6). The covenant begins in Genesis 12 and is formalized in Genesis 15 and 17. The sign of the covenant was circumcision, a physical reminder to Abraham of the promise of many offspring.

The Israelite covenant (fourth covenant) is formalized after the redemption of God's people in the exodus from Egypt. Notice that the goal of this covenant is the same as from the beginning—to restore creation and for God's people to be a blessing (see Exod 19:4–6). The terms/vows of this covenant are the stipulations and laws found in the Torah. As the covenant people lived out this Torah covenant, they would proclaim to a watching world the identity and salvation of Yahweh. The Israelite covenant was conditional, but only in the sense of blessing/cursing on individual generations. In other words, God's people are now formalized as a covenant people, but individual generations could lose the covenant blessings and incur cursings.

The fifth covenant, the Davidic covenant, comes in response to David's desire to build God a temple. Yahweh promised to give David an eternal kingdom, seed, and throne (2 Sam 7:8–16)—an amazing assurance to this budding king of a rather inconsequential nation, politically speaking. The goal in the covenant was for the Davidic king (as a covenant mediator) to lead God's people to be a blessing, through Torah obedience. David is a new Abraham in the sense that Davidic kingship is now the means by which nations are blessed. God's promise is being crystallized in one person. This covenant will be explored more in the next chapter.

A new covenant is outlined in Jeremiah 31, where Jeremiah anticipates a reunification of Judah and Israel. How is the "new" covenant
new? There is a temporal and also a qualitative newness. The form
passes away, but the substance remains the same. The basis (grace) and
purpose (bless the nations; 1 Pet 2:9–10) of this covenant are the same.
The commands are similar—if anything, the expectations are higher in
the new covenant. But with the new, there is a better sacrifice (Jesus
once for all) and provision (the Spirit, enabling covenant keeping) and
promise (a new heart; Ezek 36:24). This new covenant will be unpacked
in more detail in the NT chapters.

Putting the Tools to Use

The following will offer one example showing how the use of tools
can be helpful in interpreting a biblical text from the Pentateuchal
books. Before reading the following, try it for yourself. Work through
the following questions and then see if you can discern the original
meaning.

Example: Leviticus 19:28 and the Question of Tattoos

Historical Tools

What is the level-1 or level-2 historical context and how does that
affect my reading of the text?

Literary Tools

What is the genre of the text? What is the book/section/chapter's purpose and structure? How does this text fit that purpose?

Theological Tools

Are there any key theological terms or concepts in the text? How do I understand the text in light of Christ and the full testimony of the Bible?

Application

What does this text tell me about God? About myself? About the world? About how I relate to God?

Interpretation

As an experienced OT professor, occasionally I'll receive random emails asking for the translation of certain English phrases into Hebrew. When I do, I can typically predict a reason for the request: "I'm thinking about getting a tattoo."

Tattoos are becoming increasingly common among the younger generation of believers. In response, some well-intentioned Christians have attempted to buck the trend by mustering biblical texts that seemingly prohibit the practice. The most commonly cited of these is Lev 19:28.

The text itself seems unambiguous. It reads, "Incisions for the dead you shall not make on your flesh; and tattoo marks you shall not make on yourselves. I am YHWH" (Cribb translation).

If read in a woodenly literal manner, the application seems rather straightforward: No tattoos! But in interpreting the Bible, "straightforward" literal readings of the text are not always the right readings. For instance, what would happen if we took Jesus's statements in Matt 5:29–30 literally? Our churches would be filled with sightless, handless Christians.

As we have stated repeatedly in this book, to interpret any biblical text correctly, one must interpret it according to its original context by using the tools. Hear it the way the original Hebrew hearer would have heard it. This original meaning is the authoritative meaning. And interpreters must ground any application in this original meaning.

So what is the original meaning of Lev 19:28? First, we must understand the historical context. Moses delivers these principles found in Leviticus at Mount Sinai in the first year after the exodus. Here, at this holy mountain, God is forming a holy covenant people unto himself. Thus, in essence, the Levitical code is an exposition of the covenantal principles given to God's covenant people.

What about literary context? As argued above, I liken the code to vows taken in a marriage commitment. Just as a husband honors his wife and keeps his marital vows as an expression of his abiding and abundant love for her, so also the Israelites kept the code as an outflow of their exclusive commitment to Yahweh—perhaps best summarized in Deut 6:4–9. This is not legalism. It is an expression of covenantal love and devotion.

The essence of the Israelites' expression of covenant commitment is found in the so-called Holiness Code of Leviticus 17–26. And the central chapter of that code is Leviticus 19. Here, God exhorts his people to live holy lives, telling them that they should be holy, "because I, the LORD your God, am holy" (19:2). The code concerns all aspects of life, demonstrating that all of life—family life, work life, communal life, cultic life—falls under the authority of the divine Sovereign.

Reading the text, one soon discovers that God grounds these admonitions on one fact—he is Yahweh (as in 19:28). Since he is the sole covenant Lord, he deserves exclusive covenant loyalty, just as my wife deserves my exclusive love, simply and profoundly because she is my wife.

So this admonition against tattoos in verse 28 must be understood first and foremost as a way of expressing covenant fidelity to God by living holy lives—primarily because God is our covenant Lord.

But what does it mean to be holy? Leviticus 20:26 clarifies: "Thus, you shall be holy to me for I, YHWH, am holy, and I have separated you from the peoples so that you would be mine" (Cribb translation). Here holiness is equated with two ideas: separation and dedication.

What does this definition mean for Lev 19:28? Well, whatever the text itself admonishes, keeping the admonition must result in both separation from the peoples and dedication to Yahweh, as an expression of covenant relationship.

But how does not getting tattoos accomplish this goal for the ancient Israelites? Here one must understand a little cultural context. Scholars disagree here, but most believe that the prohibited practices were either Canaanite mourning rituals or aspects of the cult of the dead (a form of ancestor worship) or perhaps both. Regardless, for an Israelite to participate in bodily mutilation (like receiving tattoos) would identify them with the surrounding peoples and their pagan deities. In other words, they would be not separated and not dedicated—"unholy."

What is the application here for modern Christians? Simply, God's people are not to portray themselves outwardly in a way that identifies with or promotes pagan elements of society. This principle is clearly articulated in the NT as well (1 Cor 6:19–20)—as are virtually all of the principles found in Leviticus 19, rightly understood in their ancient context.

The question is, in modern Western culture, does a tattoo identify the Christian with pagan elements of society? I'm not sure the answer is clear. Surely, if you have a Charles Manson-like swastika tattooed on your forehead, you have seriously compromised your holiness! But what about a "forearm-tat" of a Hebrew word celebrating God's grace? Probably not.

Do not hear me as saying that everyone should go visit the closest ink-shop. I do think that other texts influence such a decision—for example, 1 Cor 10:31.

But using the tools, we see that Lev 19:28 should not be used as an exclusive prohibition against tattoos.

Applying the Results

The following will offer two possible trajectories for application using what we have learned from the Pentateuchal books.

The Shema and Church Health

In America, the "forever young" industry is thriving. Surgical procedures, Botox, hormones, vitamins, exercise facilities, health food stores, natural supplements—all are used in a "Ponce de Leon"-like quest to find an antiaging magic bullet.

Nothing is necessarily wrong with desiring good health. But are we just as passionate about church health? What if Christians put the same amount of effort into keeping churches healthy as we do our bodies? How do we even maintain a healthy church?

Popular Christian culture says the answer is obvious: build bigger buildings, grow bigger budgets, pack bigger numbers of behinds in the pews. But in all those B's, the one "B"-word you don't see is "biblical."

One oft-ignored biblical book may provide a better answer to church health—the book of Deuteronomy. Why Deuteronomy? Isn't it just some boring book of laws? After all, doesn't the name mean "Second Law"? I mean, who wants to study that?

But Deuteronomy actually has a lot to say about maintaining healthy churches—new covenant bodies of Christ. Remember that Deuteronomy was Moses's last chance to influence the Israelites, and so it is filled with practical and passionate preaching on how to sustain a holy and healthy covenant community in the face of the perils of a pagan Canaanite culture.

The heart of Moses's zealous missive is found in one text—Deut 6:4. You could argue that this text is the heart of the entire OT.

This text is known as the Shema. The title comes from the first word in the Hebrew text, *shema*, meaning "hear." Today, the Shema is the centerpiece of Jewish daily worship, and it is still recited every morning and evening by Orthodox Jews.

Here, you find the motivation for the rest of Deuteronomy and indeed all of the covenant. It is the sum of the relationship between God and his people. Simply stated, the Shema expresses loyalty.

A Knesset Menorah Shema inscription. The Shema is recited every morning and evening by Orthodox Jews.

Traditionally the Shema has been considered an affirmation of monotheism—the belief in one God. In this way, it is translated, "Listen, Israel: the LORD our God, the LORD is one." Although monotheism was no doubt a belief of Moses and many Israelites, I don't think "oneness" is the main focus here. On this count, I'm indebted to my mentor Daniel Block, who argues that the traditional translation (based on the ancient Greek translation of the OT, the Septuagint)—"The LORD our God, the LORD is one"—is better translated in context as "Yahweh is our God, Yahweh alone."[29]

The Israelites were not questioning, how many is God? Instead, Moses wanted to ensure and encourage the Israelites' commitment and exclusive allegiance to God alone. By reciting the Shema, the Israelites were declaring their complete, undivided, and unqualified devotion to Yahweh.

Yes, Moses wanted the people to have proper theology. But he was more concerned that they have practical theology. As a husband, I'm sure my wife wants me to acknowledge her intellectually and verbally as the only true "wife of Cribb"; but I think she is more concerned that I show her exclusive loyalty and treat her as that one true wife.

So here is the Israelite confession. But it was also their rallying cry as they entered the Promised Land. Think of the great rallying cries in history. Patrick Henry's "Give me liberty or give me death!" Mel Gibson's cry of "Freedom!" in *Braveheart*.[30] Inigo Montoya's cry in the *The Princess Bride*, "My name is Inigo Montoya. You killed my father. Prepare to die."[31]

---

[29] Daniel I. Block, *Deuteronomy*, The NIV Application Commentary, vol. 4 (Grand Rapids: Zondervan, 2012), 180–82.

[30] "Mel Gibson yelling FREEDOM in 'Braveheart' (1995)," YouTube video, 1:04, posted by Best Movies By Farr, June 13, 2016, https://www.youtube.com/watch?v=k7rPOaoPL4I.

[31] "Hello, My name is Inigo Montoya. . . . ," YouTube video, 0:10, posted by Clare Elaine, November 13, 2010, https://www.youtube.com/watch?v=6JGp7Meg42U.

Like these, the Shema united the Israelites, gave them purpose, gave them focus, gave them motivation. Indeed, it gave them the foundation of their covenant community.

What about Christians today? What is our common confession? What gives us purpose, focus, and a foundation?

We can ask the apostle Paul. In 1 Cor 8:5–6, Paul adapts the Shema in arguing against the existence of idols. Paul states, "For even if there are so-called gods, whether in heaven or on earth—as there are many 'gods' and many 'lords'—yet for us there is one God, the Father. All things are from him, and we exist for him. And there is one Lord, Jesus Christ. All things are through him, and we exist through him." Paul clearly identifies Jesus as Yahweh, the one and only God to whom true Israelites (today, the church) declare allegiance.

In other words, the confession of every Christian, the confession of the new covenant church, the rallying cry, must be simply, profoundly, and foundationally, "Jesus is Lord." This is the key to healthy churches as covenant communities today.

When people come to my church, my prayer is that people don't go home thinking something like, "Man, they have a great building," or "They have a great preacher." I want them to say, "That is a church that exalts Jesus as Lord and lives it out."

If you get "Jesus is Lord" right, everything else falls into place.

Humans as Image-Bearers

The Bible has always been countercultural. Nowhere is this truth more evident than in the Bible's portrayal of human beings.

In the ancient Near East, literature from the cultures surrounding Israel consistently portrayed humans as nothing more than divine conscripts. Those well-placed and divinely connected—i.e., priests, prophets, and potentates—perhaps possessed some privilege. But the common folks existed at the whim of the gods, having little to no value.

In modern culture, human life is also diminished in significance. Evolutionary naturalism and utilitarianism portray humans as merely more sophisticated animals.[32]

And when our uniqueness as humans is removed, ethics tend to dissolve. From an ethical perspective, a utilitarian would argue that we all stand on equal footing whether it be two feet or four feet or none at all.

The results of this worldview have been disastrous. The abortion blight is a clear example. As of this writing, America has witnessed some 60 million abortions since *Roe v. Wade* in 1973 legalized the practice. Worldwide, millions more abortions occur each year. Allow those numbers to sink in.

Even 1 million deaths (approximately the number of annual US abortions) is still more than the populations of San Francisco, Indianapolis, Charlotte, and Detroit, to name a few cities. Imagine a natural disaster or terror attack destroying the city of San Francisco, killing a million people.

A culture of diminished personhood has created this tragedy.

But the Bible presents a countercultural anthropology—whether those cultures be ancient or modern. As argued earlier, the Bible presents humanity as the crown of creation, possessing a singular and special status as God's image-bearers.

Thus, according to Genesis, all have equal dignity in the eyes of God—Jew or Greek, slave or free, male or female (Gal 3:28), born or unborn, regardless of mental or physical or social or economic capacity. And we should treat all with dignity and respect.

---

[32] "Utilitarianism," *Wikipedia*, last modified March 3, 2019, https://en.wikipedia.org/wiki/Utilitarianism.

In this way, imageness also ups the stakes for a believer's ethics. If all humans are status-holders, no matter how much sin may have tainted that status, any malicious act directed against another image-bearer is an act directed toward God.

Think of King David. David infamously committed adultery with Bathsheba and subsequently murdered her husband, Uriah, to cover it up. Against whom did David sin? Bathsheba? Yes. Uriah? Yes. His people? Yes? His family? Yes. Himself? Yes. But when David confesses his sin in Ps 51:4, he states, "Against you (Yahweh)—you alone—I have sinned and done this evil in your sight."

So as we contemplate our theology of humanity, contemplate also the implications. And consider how countercultural the biblical views are.

Application Questions

1. Do you think it is important to discuss the issue of Mosaic authorship? How does this illustrate the aphorism "ideas have consequences"?

2. What do you think of Dr. Cribb's comparison of the biblical covenant and marriage? Does this change your perception of the marriage relationship? Does this change your perception of the church's relationship with God? What does it mean to be a "new covenant Christian"?

3. How does Genesis 1 conflict with the modern, naturalistic, evolutionary view of the world? What is your position on this issue? How has that belief affected your life?

4. Do you believe that the flood story is literal? Does it bother you that we lack archaeological evidence for these early biblical accounts?

5. When the apostle Paul says that we are children of Abraham and children of the promise, what do you think he means (see Galatians 4)?

6. How have you seen the exodus portrayed in modern media? How does the biblical portrayal of the event differ?

7. Are the Ten Commandments still applicable today? If so, how?

8. How do you see concepts found in Leviticus (sacrifice, priesthood, holiness) fulfilled in Christ?

9. What is your position on the numbers of Numbers? Of the options given by Dr. Cribb in his video, which do you think makes the most sense?

10. The Shema (Deut 6:4) is still viewed by Jews as the great confession of their faith. Why do you think it was important for the Israelites entering the Promised Land to heed this charge? Is it still important for Christians today for similar reasons?

5

Tools for Interpreting the Historical Books

Students often ask me, what are the most difficult books of the Bible to interpret correctly? The exegetically impenetrable prophets? The future-oriented apocalyptic material? The subtle and elusive poetic books? The perplexing rhetoric of Paul? The seemingly superseded and archaic Torah? My answer is the narrative texts of the Historical Books of the Old Testament (OT).

These twelve books—Joshua through Esther in the English canon—cover nearly a thousand years of Jewish history from the conquest of the Promised Land (ca. 1400 BC) to the Jewish restoration after the Babylonian exile (400s BC). They are filled with wonderful and compelling and often frustrating accounts of real individuals and nations, who lived, fought, ruled, and worshiped centuries before the time of Christ.

And we simply don't know what to do with them. Do the characters—the kings and commoners and even countries in the stories—provide examples for us? Are the stories allegories like John Bunyan's The Pilgrim's Progress?[1] Are they moralistic tales like Aesop's Fables? Are they in reality anecdotes about us?

A basic problem with these approaches is that they ignore the fundamental question outlined in chapter 3. What did the original authors intend? And when you move away from authorial intent, you move away from authority. You place the meaning outside of the text, with the reader.

Let's take one well-known example: the story of David and Goliath from 1 Samuel 17. One of the best-known stories in the Bible, this account of "facing the giant" has inspired stirring movies and moving speeches, football teams, and fearless leaders—and sometimes all four at once, as in the Christian film *Facing the Giants*.[2] Most take it as a story meant to motivate valor against adversaries, whether they be physical, emotional, economic, or spiritual—the so-called "giants in your life." With this allegorical approach, we are David—the underdog, the unlikely, the overlooked, the oppressed. Goliath represents any in a myriad of enemies. And God is God, who enables us to slay our Goliaths. Some even imagine the slingshot stone to represent the "smooth rock of faith" or the like.

It is true that God gives us strength in our struggles. This is not theologically wrong. But is that what "this" author—the author of 1 Samuel—is communicating? What is the original authorial intent?

---

[1] "The Pilgrim's Progress," *Wikipedia*, last modified March 3, 2019, https://en.wikipedia.org/wiki/The_Pilgrim%27s_Progress.

[2] "Facing The Giants—Trailer," YouTube video, 2:06, posted by YouTube Movies, August 19, 2013, https://www.youtube.com/watch?v=py5ogs YFUU8.

Is the story of David and Goliath really meant to encourage
us to "slay our giants" in the strength of God?

To answer this question, we need to use a "tool" that will be detailed more fully below: the literary tool of message and purpose.

The books of Samuel in which we find this story have a singular purpose—to highlight King David. Around half of 1 Samuel and all of 2 Samuel deal with this renowned ruler, the king "after God's own heart." The reason is that for the author, the fate and spiritual health of the nation are—for better or worse—inextricably tied to that of the Davidic king. This truth is borne out throughout the Historical Books. As these Davidic kings go, so goes the nation. And so the author has his eyes fixed on David.

As will be explained in the sections below, in the story of God's redemption found in the Scriptures, we know why the biblical authors focus so much on David. King Jesus is from David's line. Christ is the fulfillment of the promises given to David in 2 Sam 7:8–17. Even for a Jewish person, the term *Messiah* connotes the anointed king in the line of David who fulfills these promises. See the Applying the Results section below.

How does the author highlight David in the story of Goliath? The emphasis is clear even on the surface, but let's dive in a little.

The story possesses three main characters—David and Goliath, of course, but also King Saul. Goliath is described as tall, strong, and fearsome, a champion of his people, the Philistines. Saul, the first Jewish king, is described similarly—a head taller than most; as king, he should have been the people's champion. Indeed, in the ancient Near East, the king was always the one to lead the people into battle, like William Wallace in *Braveheart* or Aragorn in *The Lord of the Rings*.[3] The king was the one to inspire victory. The king was the one to model faith in God's enablement.

And yet where is "King" Saul? Cowering in his tent, in no wise acting the part of king. Enter David—the opposite of Saul in many ways. He possesses no distinguishing physical or familial traits. Taken from his task of following after the sheep (2 Sam 7:8), he's definitely not of royal stock. He's just a lad and a small one at that. But as demonstrated over and over in Scripture, God uses the weak things of the world to shame the strong (1 Cor 1:27–28). What separates this son of Jesse from Saul? David is on the front lines. He is acting as the people's true champion. The author's point? David is the true king, not Saul.

So who is David in the story? Definitely not us. David is God's true king, brought into the story line of Scripture to pave the way for the true and coming Messiah, Jesus. In other words, the story is not about

---

[3] "Famous Speeches: Aragorn at the Black Gate," YouTube video, 1:08, posted by Luke Bolduan, April 28, 2008, https://www.youtube.com /watch?v=EXGUNvIFTQw.

us and about our struggles with giants; rather, by using our toolbox, we see it is about what God is doing through his king and about Christ, who has overcome the world for us.

As you can see, allegory and other such Bible study methods make the text self-centered, when it is really God-centered and Christ-centered. *To see another example of the dangers of allegorical interpretation, see Wordsearch content.*

So to avoid authority-less allegory, we need to use our tools. Let's see how our tools apply to the Historical Books.

Understanding the Tools

Historical Tools

Once again, the first tool to grab when analyzing these historical texts is appropriately that of historical context. Remember that historical context operates on two levels—the context of the events themselves (level 1) and of the author/audience (level 2).

Level-1 Historical Context: The Events Themselves

We start with the context of the events themselves. We will explore these same events more closely in the literary section. As with the Pentateuch, let's take a big-picture look. As mentioned above, the books of Joshua–Esther detail the rise and fall and partial restoration of Israel as a nation—events spanning nearly a thousand years. The books themselves are necessarily expansive. And events are treated, once again as expected, unevenly.

The authors focus on events that carry the story of salvation forward and make their rhetorical/theological/prophetic points. So just because something is important to secular historians doesn't mean that it will find its way into these "history" books.

For instance, one of the most important kings in the history of the northern kingdom of Israel was Omri. This king had a short reign (twelve years), but he successfully expanded the kingdom and moved the capital of the north to Samaria. Secular historians would pay much attention to him. But the biblical author grants Omri's account a scant eight verses. Meanwhile, this same author devotes multiple chapters to Omri's historically unimportant (relatively speaking) son—a king named Ahab. Do you know anyone outside of Melville's *Moby Dick* named Ahab?[4] The biblical author famously highlights this evil king— not because Ahab is all that important historically—but because he is representative of all the failures of the Israelite kingship.

As readers, we should follow the lead of the authors in constructing the level-1 context. Know the main events, yes. But also pay attention to what the writers emphasize.

And what do they emphasize?

Again, one could divide this historical period in a number of ways. Based on chapter 3, I think the best way is to imagine a series of historical pegs—those primary salvation historical events on which you can "drape" other events.

The pegs we will outline below include the conquest of Joshua (covered in the book of Joshua); the period of the judges (covered in Judges and Ruth); the united monarchy under Saul, David, and Solomon (covered in 1 & 2 Samuel, 1 Kings 1–11, and 1 Chronicles–2 Chronicles 9); the divided monarchy, including the exile of the north kingdom and the exile of the southern kingdom (covered in 1 Kings 12–2 Kings and 2 Chronicles 9–36); and the return from exile and the rebuilding of the nation (Ezra, Nehemiah, and Esther).

The events of the Historical Books begin with the *conquest of the Promised Land in 1405 BC*. After Moses (Deuteronomy 34) and the

---

[4] "Captain Ahab," *Wikipedia*, last modified March 5, 2019, https://en .wikipedia.org/wiki/Captain_Ahab.

exodus generation die (except for Joshua and Caleb), the next generation of Hebrew people prepares to take their inheritance under the leadership of Moses's successor, Joshua. The conquest begins famously with the destruction of Jericho, as the walls of one of the oldest walled cities[5] in the world come "atumblin' down."[6] God then delivers several other cities into Israelite hands, and the land is subsequently apportioned among the twelve tribes of Israel (stemming from the twelve sons of Jacob).

However, though this period is one of conquest, the Israelite tribes actually do not fully conquer the land. Judges 1 tells of the continued failure of the Israelite tribes to drive out the Canaanites, and they end up living among them in many cases.

Joshua dies at the beginning of *the period of the judges.* And with a dearth of godly leaders, the Israelites progressively spiral downward—with everyone doing what is right in their own eyes (Judges 21:25). For more than 300 years, the Israelites repeat a cycle of rebellion, judgment, deliverance, rest, and then worse rebellion. In the end, they become indistinguishable from the Canaanite tribes around them (Judges 19–21).

Thankfully, with God's anointing of Samuel as a priest and prophet and last judge in Israel, this dark period draws to a close. Samuel institutes religious reforms, but the people want more. They desire a king like the nations (1 Samuel 8). God grants this desire, and Saul is crowned the first king of Israel. This period—beginning around 1050 BC—is known as *the united monarchy.*

---

[5] "Tower of Jericho," *Wikipedia,* last modified December 16, 2018, https://en.wikipedia.org/wiki/Tower_of_Jericho.

[6] "The Martins—Joshua Fit the Battle of Jericho [Live]," YouTube video, 2:22, posted by GaitherVEVO, https://www.youtube.com/watch?v=FoeSdDcS1LA.

Saul's failures, though, prompt his rejection as king, and God subsequently anoints David, a man after God's own heart, who becomes king in 1011 BC. God makes a covenant with David, who represents a new Abraham (2 Sam 7:8–17). David is promised an eternal dynasty, one that would eventually be fulfilled in the coming of the Davidic Messiah. This covenant represents the climax of OT history. See below for more details.

David, however, is an imperfect and at times unrighteous king, as the narrative of 2 Samuel bluntly details, and so his desired temple for Yahweh must wait until his son Solomon builds it.

In 971 BC, Solomon becomes Israel's king, and he begins well. He expands the kingdom, rules with his legendary wisdom, and builds the promised temple (ca. 966 BC). However, in his later years, Solomon engages in excess politically and economically and, most infamously, relationally—having some 700 wives and 300 concubines.

Solomon's overindulgence and oppression continue in the reign of his son Rehoboam, and his unrelenting heavy-handedness in the first year of his reign results in the division of the kingdom into the northern kingdom, which is called Israel in the text, and the southern kingdom, which is called Judah, in 931 BC. God's people are, for the present and for many years after, divided, thus entering a period known as *the divided monarchy*.

Both of the respective kingdoms have their successes and failures. However, while Judah and the southern kingdom experience brief periods of revival during the reigns of some good kings (such as Hezekiah and Josiah), the northern kingdom of Israel never regains its focus on God.

Israelite history is a story of lost opportunities. And the insufficiencies of both kingdoms are pointed out repeatedly by the prophets (see chap. 7). Indeed, the divided monarchy is the golden age of prophecy in Israel.

The prophetic message is simple. Because of the people's abandonment of the covenant, covenant curses and judgment (see Leviticus 26)—including exile—are coming from God. But the prophets also look forward to a day of the Lord for restoration (Hos 2:14–23), the promise of a new covenant (Jer 31:31–34), and a new exodus (Isa 11:11–15). In these intervening years, the faithful remnant of Israel and the true prophets of Yahweh also begin to look for the promised new David—the Messiah (Isa 9:6–7; Jer 23:5–6; Ezek 34:23–24; 37:24–25; among many others).

Because of the failures of the northern kingdom, the predicted judgment finally occurs. The brutal Assyrian Empire invades the northern kingdom and takes its people into exile, scattering them, in 722 BC. Samaria is repopulated with pagans, and the northern kingdom virtually disappears—the "lost ten tribes" of Israel.

The southern kingdom of Judah, however, is initially spared. Judah, with its kings in the line of David, remains temporarily, but it continues to rebel under various monarchs. After the death of good king Josiah in 609 BC, the kingdom begins to fall apart politically and spiritually. The nation eventually falls, enduring three successive invasions by Babylon in 605 BC, 597 BC, and finally 586 BC.

In the final attack after a one-and-a-half-year siege, Babylon destroys Jerusalem, and many of the Jewish people are *taken into exile*. The last of the Davidic kings, Zedekiah, is hunted down, and his sons are slain before his eyes (before they are gouged out). A month after demolishing Jerusalem's walls, the Babylonians raze the entire city to the ground, including the temple. The people not slaughtered (2 Kgs 25:18–21) are taken captive. Only the poorest of the poor are left in Judea. The judgment of God had finally occurred.

After a period of fifty years, Persia takes over a weakened Babylon in 539 BC, and the powerful Persian emperor, Cyrus the Great, allows some of the *exiled peoples to return* to their native lands—including the

Jews (Ezra 1:1–2). With Persian blessing and money, the Jews begin to rebuild the temple in 536 BC. Obstruction from the native population initially delays this second temple. But through the preaching of Haggai and Zechariah in 520 BC, the temple construction restarts and is completed in 516 BC.

Some sixty years later in 459 BC, a scribe named Ezra leads more returning Jews. And through an emphasis on Torah, he inspires a spiritual revival among the people. Several years after Ezra's return (445 BC), the Persian emperor's cupbearer, a Jew named Nehemiah, returns to rebuild the walls of Jerusalem—an amazing 140 years after the initial destruction of the walls.

The restored nation, though, remains recalcitrant. Many of the people continue in covenant rebellion, as pointed out in the books of Ezra and Nehemiah as well as the prophetic book of Malachi. The OT period ends with expectancy—a cliff-hanger of sorts. Will the people return? Will God keep his promises—to the people, to the land, to the king? When will the Messiah come and restore all things?

Level-2 Historical Context: Author and Audience

Just as important as the level-1 context in properly interpreting the Historical Books is the level-2 context—that of the original author or audience. Immediately, however, a difficult issue confronts the interpreter. All of the Historical Books are officially anonymous. Although some of the ascriptions have valid traditions, most of the books possess an uncertain provenance.[7] How can we know the author's context if we don't know the identity of the author?

For example, possibly some of the book of Joshua comes from the stylus of Joshua himself (see Josh 24:26). But references in the book to

---

[7] Merriam-Webster Dictionary, s.v., "provenance," accessed March 4, 2019, https://www.merriam-webster.com/dictionary/provenance.

"to this day" or "still today" (4:9; 5:9) suggest a later author. And even later hands may have contributed to the book of Joshua before the final form took shape.

Other Historical Books with ambiguous level-2 contexts include Judges, Ruth, and to a certain extent Samuel. Jewish tradition has often ascribed the books of Samuel to Samuel, but Samuel the character dies in 1 Samuel 25. And though he makes a postmortem appearance in chapter 28, I doubt if it is Samuel's ghost who writes the rest of 2 Samuel.

Some critical scholars claim to have a definitive answer on authorship. If you go down to the library and read a commentary on Joshua or Judges or Samuel or Kings, you may read of a so-called Deuteronomistic historian.[8] Based in the same Enlightenment rationalism that produced JEDP (see chap. 4), this theory was first popularized by the mid-twentieth-century German scholar Martin Noth (pronounced "Note").[9]

The theory goes something like this: Deuteronomy is not part of the Pentateuch, but the book was instead composed in the seventh century BC (during King Josiah's reign and reforms) as a theological prologue to Joshua, Judges, Samuel, and Kings—known to the Jews as the Former Prophets.[10] The Deuteronomistic historian then compiled and thoroughly edited those "histories" using Deuteronomy to reflect his theological emphases. Supposedly, this pseudepigraphal composition had a "pious" motive—to inspire covenant renewal and revival among the people.[11]

---

[8] "Deuteronomist," *Wikipedia*, last modified February 13, 2019, https://en.wikipedia.org/wiki/Deuteronomist.

[9] "Martin Noth," *Wikipedia*, last modified November 16, 2018, https://en.wikipedia.org/wiki/Martin_Noth.

[10] See the genre discussion below.

[11] "Pseudepigrapha," *Wikipedia*, last modified January 28, 2019, https://en.wikipedia.org/wiki/Pseudepigrapha.

Today, most scholars outside of the evangelical world hold this the-orized origin of Joshua–Kings to be established fact, with some modifi-cations. But affirming this hypothesized historian has many hitches. The first of these is that dating Deuteronomy 800 years after Moses goes against the biblical testimony to Mosaic authorship cited in the previ-ous chapter. In addition, to label Deuteronomy as a "pious fraud"—a book attributed to Moses with good motives just to give it rhetorical "oomph" during Josiah's reign—casts some real doubt as to the veracity and inerrancy of Scripture.

The fact that Deuteronomy has influenced the telling of the his-tory in the OT Historical Books is irrefutable. See the Theological Tools section below for examples. But wouldn't it be more logical to say that Deuteronomy was written many years prior and then influ-enced the retelling of Israel's history—not vice versa?

In sum, we will leave the authorship of these books anony-mous. However, while the authorship issue remains murky for all the Historical Books, some of them do have clear audiences. These especially include Kings–Esther. And the context of the respective audiences greatly influences the final shaping and message of these books.

Take Kings, for instance. We know that the last event reported in the books of Kings occurred in 561 BC—the freeing of King Jehoiachin from prison in Babylon. Thus, the final composition of the books nec-essarily took place after 561 BC, but probably before the return from exile in 539 BC.

Imagine experiencing a faith-shaking event such as the Babylonian exile—seeing the temple destroyed, the Promised Land vacated, the covenant shattered, thousands killed or enslaved, the Davidic dynasty in tatters. How would you describe the history leading up to this event—in this case, the last 300-plus years before the exile?

As the author of Kings, you would undoubtedly remind the people why they are experiencing the current judgment. You would want to inspire change so that they might avoid future judgment. You would also probably desire to proclaim to them the hope that they still have—in a restored Davidic monarchy and in a reestablished covenant. So this exilic context colors the message and content of Kings in its final form. The Literary Tools section below will explain more clearly how this is accomplished in Kings.

In the same way, the postexilic period provides the history-shaping backdrop of the books of Chronicles, Ezra, Nehemiah, and Esther. The impact this audience has on the final product is especially evident with Chronicles. These books relate the same history as Samuel and Kings (i.e., they have the same level-1 historical context). But Chronicles has a different level-2 context—postexilic, rather than exilic. Comparing how each author "tells" and selects the included history allows one to see clearly how that level-2 context affects the message.

As noted above, in the postexile, the Israelites faced different issues than those of the people experiencing the immediate trauma of exile in Babylon. The postexilic community was attempting to rebuild from the ruins, but they also battled the complacency brought about by other pressing concerns and spiritual or political opposition. See the Literary Tools and the Putting the Tools to Use sections below for examples of how this impacts Chronicles' specific message.

So when studying the Historical Books, always ask yourself: if I experienced what the audience experienced, how would I read and react to the retold history?

Literary Tools

Remember that our literary tools focus on the issues of literary structure/story line/message/purpose and literary genre. As with the Pentateuch, let's start with genre—which just so happens to be the key to interpreting these "historical" books correctly.

Genre

How should we understand the genre of the Historical Books? Of course, we label them "history." But what do you expect to get out of history books?

Since the mid-1700s and the Enlightenment, history has been approached as a just-the-facts, objective, comprehensive portrayal of "what really happened." Causation is secular—meaning that any events are explained as having causes in this world. For instance, the spark that started World War I was the assassination of Archduke Franz Ferdinand. And the purpose of history is typically to communicate factual information.

But what happens when Christians call the book of Joshua "history"? They expect to "get out of it" a bunch of facts about how the nation of Israel began by means of the conquest of the Promised Land—something like you might read in a Rand McNally History of Israel.

But that is definitely not the purpose of the OT Historical Books. Yes, they communicate true facts about Israel's history. But their purpose and means of achieving that purpose are different.

Rather than being objective, the books are *subjective*. The authors couldn't care less about the Moabite or Edomite perspective or even the unorthodox Israelite perspective. They are communicating God's perspective. Instead of comprehensively reporting all events, the authors are *selective*—including only events that further their points. We will see several instances of this selectivity below. It is perhaps the major distinguishing feature of OT narrative.

In addition, the Historical Books are *theological*. Everything that occurs in the books does so via divine causation. God is the main character, moving the events and stories along in order to achieve his purpose—the fulfillment of all things in the person of Christ.

Finally, the purpose of these books is *prophetic*. In fact, the Jews recognized this, labeling Joshua, Judges, Samuel, and Kings as the "Former

Prophets." And what does a prophet do? He communicates a word from God to reprove, rebuke, and exhort God's people (2 Tim 3:16).[12]

To use a modern analogy, what we find in these books is "historical preaching"—appealing to and exhorting God's people using real historical events.[13] So, when you read Joshua–Esther, don't just do it for information, but for transformation. Ask, how does the author tell his story in such a way to inspire faithfulness to God and his Word and his covenant?

So a better genre label for these books is prophetic narrative, not history.

Let's now move to an examination of the literary structure, story line, message, and purpose of each of the Historical Books. Out of necessity, these discussions will seem cursory. But I will focus on the most significant aspects of the books.

> What we find in the Historical Books is "historical preaching"— appealing to and exhorting God's people using real historical events.

Literary Structure / Story Line / Message / Purpose—Joshua

If you ranked the Bible books that present the biggest stumbling blocks—the books that cause the most faith struggles among believers and nonbelievers alike—at the top might be Joshua. Why? Joshua is a book of conquest and a violent one at that. And such a bloody and intense story does not jibe with many people's conception of God or Christianity or love or grace, causing some to discard the book and even the Bible as a whole.

---

[12] See chap. 7 for more details on the role of a prophet.

[13] I was taught these characteristics of Hebrew narrative by my mentor Daniel I. Block. For a great summary of his method, see his article, "Tell Me the Old, Old Story," in *Giving the Sense,* ed. Howard and Grisanti. (see chap. 3, n. 3).

To deal with this issue and indeed any other text in the book, however, requires a thorough and contextual examination of the book—in other words, using the tools.

In the canon, Joshua functions as an important hinge book—looking backward and forward. Looking backward at the Pentateuch, Joshua completes the incomplete story of the Torah, showing how God fulfills his promises to the patriarchs of land, seed, rest, covenant, blessing, and nationhood. In fact, by the end of Joshua, the author can proclaim, "None of the good promises the LORD had made to the house of Israel failed. Everything was fulfilled" (21:45).

Jericho is one of the oldest walled cities in the world. The tower pictured above dates to approximately 8000 BC. Jericho was the first city conquered in the Promised Land.

Another connection to the Torah is the lead human character in the book. Joshua appears several times in the Pentateuchal narratives. Most notably, he served as one of the two faithful spies whom Moses sent into the Promised Land. These two—Joshua and Caleb—did not doubt God's ability in conquest (Numbers 13–14).[14] And Joshua's faithfulness in the book of Numbers is the reason why he survives to lead the people in the battle for the land in the book of Joshua.

However, the book not only looks backward, but forward, paving the way for the rest of the Former Prophets. In particular, Joshua emphasizes the theme of the Promised Land—a theme that dominates and frames all the Historical Books. In the book of Joshua, the people enter the land, and then they reenter the land after the exile at the end of the Historical Books in Ezra–Nehemiah.

The conquering of the land also takes a central place in any outline of the book of Joshua. Chapters 1–5 speak of the preparations to conquer the Promised Land. Chapters 6–12 deal with the actual attempts at the conquest of the land. Chapters 13–22 explain how the land is divided after the conquest. And in chapters 23–24, the author explains the covenant renewal ceremony that Joshua leads as the people prepare to live in the conquered land. The following will examine each of these sections briefly.

Joshua 1 provides the prologue for the book, introducing the dominant themes, such as rest, Torah, land, covenant, holy war, and inheritance. Most famous in chapter 1 is Yahweh's commissioning of Joshua. Three times, Yahweh charges Joshua to approach his task with courage (recalling Moses's similar charge to Joshua in Deut 31:1–8).

But the courage required is not so much for battle and war. Joshua needed courage to lead the people in Torah obedience (Josh 1:7–8).

---

[14] Joshua is identified as Moses' assistant (Josh 1:1), and he plays a prominent role in several other narratives, including the covenant ceremony (Exod 24:13) and the golden calf incident (Exod 32:17).

Success in conquest lay not in military might, but covenant fidelity. And the principal threat to Israel would not be the fighting force of the Canaanites but their hedonistic idolatry. The Canaanites attributed their prosperity to false fertility gods; because of this, the Israelites would be tempted to adopt these same pagan practices (see Moses's warnings in Deuteronomy 8).

Preparations for the conquest continue in chapter 2. With the Israelites positioned across the Jordan River opposite Jericho on the plains of Moab, once again, spies are sent. This time, Joshua sends two instead of twelve—perhaps because two corresponds to the number of faithful spies in Numbers 13–14. And this time, the spies succeed. They see the land as ripe for the taking, and the Canaanites know their own vulnerability. The success of the spies provides a literary clue from the author that the conquest itself would succeed.

Central to the Israelite espionage narrative is a Canaanite prostitute named Rahab. If you read the story, this harlot provides refuge for the spies, by hiding the men from the Canaanite authorities, who had discovered the infiltrators' presence in the city. Her reason for supporting the Israelite cause: her faith in Yahweh.

Rahab's confession (2:9–13) of Yahweh is one of the most profound and clearest statements of faith in the entire OT.

Rahab's confession (2:9–13) of Yahweh is one of the most profound and clearest statements of faith in the entire OT. Amazingly, the confession comes from the lips of a base sinner—a Canaanite harlot, perhaps even a cult prostitute. But because of her faith and her faithfulness (her intervention on behalf of Israel), the Canaanite is not only saved physically, but she is brought into the line of Jewish Messiah (Matt 1:5). God's kingdom is larger than just Israel. Even the most pagan Canaanite may be included in God's great story of redemption.

After the spies return, the people cross the Jordan River in chapter 3. This river is usually not a very imposing barrier. But at the time of the crossing, it was at flood stage (3:15). Undoubtedly the Canaanites saw the overflowing waters as a sign of their gods' protection—gods who supposedly ruled the waters. Instead, God gathers the Jordan's waters in a heap (3:16). And in an almost liturgical march, with the ark of the covenant and the priests of Yahweh in the lead, the Israelites cross the divinely divided river. Readers will note the purposeful connection to the previous generation's crossing of the Red Sea. Just as God delivered the Israelites *from* the Egyptians, he would deliver the Canaanites *unto* the Israelites.

Joshua 6 begins with the story of the actual conquest. The first target is Jericho. Strategically and spiritually, Jericho is the "Normandy Beach" of Israel's D-Day. If Israel takes Jericho, the victory grants them access to the rest of Canaan to the north and south and also gives assurance of a future full conquest.

The battle proceeds almost as an act of worship, rather than a military action—complete with trumpets, the ark of the covenant, and seven-day marches. The reason for this display is simple. God is the victor and the warrior. His presence guarantees success. And all the spoils and glory go to him.

After Jericho falls, subsequent cities also fall (chaps. 8–12). The only thing that stands in Israel's way is Israel itself. For instance, in attempting to take the next city, Ai (lit., the "ruin"), Israel fails miserably for one reason. A member of the Hebrew army, a man named Achan, had stolen spoils from Jericho against the specific instructions of Yahweh. I liken this failure to Clemson (Israel) trouncing Alabama (Jericho) in college football and then failing to defeat a Division 3 school (Ai) the

Ancient Jericho, Tell es-Sultan.

next week. This failure once again demonstrates that ultimate victory was tied to faithfulness not military force.

The conquest brings up an interesting historical debate. For the first time in our discussion of Israel's history, we encounter events with available archaeological evidence, and the evidence demonstrates the Bible's veracity.[15] *Watch the video in Wordsearch to hear about some archaeological discoveries that substantiate the biblical conquest.*

As mentioned above, the conquest also brings up the thorny theological question raised above. How can a loving God command such

---

[15] See Bryant G. Wood, "From Ramesses to Shiloh: Archaoelogical Discoveries Bearing on the Exodus-Judges Period," in Giving the Sense: Understanding and Using Old Testament Historical Texts (Grand Rapids: Kregel, 2003), 256-282.

a destruction? This debate is book-length in complexity. Let me point you to some excellent books and videos on this topic.

One of the best resources is a book by OT scholar Christopher Wright called *The God I Don't Understand*.[16] He explores some "dead-end" responses to the Canaanite question that don't work. [17] And he points to some necessary considerations that help to frame the issue.[18]

Another helpful resource is John and J. Harvey Walton's book *The Lost World of the Israelite Conquest*.[19] In it, this father-son team attempts to understand the conquest in its ancient Near Eastern context.

If you prefer a more philosophical answer, check out these videos of Christian philosophers Paul Copan[20] and William Lane Craig.[21] Copan has a well-known book on the issue called *Is God a Moral Monster?*[22] *Finally, see link in Wordsearch for my own thoughts on this issue.*

---

[16] Christopher Wright, *The God I Don't Understand* (Grand Rapids: Zondervan, 2008). See esp. chaps. 4–5.

[17] Wright, "The God I Dont Understand, Chp 4," YouTube video, 1:46, posted by zondervan, March 12, 2012, https://www.youtube.com/watch?v=xmjJOq4lJo4.

[18] Wright, "The God I Dont Understand, Chp 5," YouTube video, 2:27, posted by zondervan, March 12, 2012, https://www.youtube.com/watch?v=oHDsj-cUwdo.

[19] John Walton and J. Harvey Walton, *The Lost World of the Israelite Conquest* (Downers Grove, IL: IVP Academic, 2017). See also "'The Lost World of the Israelite Conquest' by John H. Walton and J. Harvey Walton," YouTube video, 2:56, posted by InterVarsity Press, August 22, 2017, https://www.youtube.com/watch?v=-sVeax0tUH8.

[20] Paul Copan, "Dr. Paul Copan—Is God a Moral Monster?" YouTube video, 1:03:06, posted by Apologetics Canada, August 29, 2012, https://www.youtube.com/watch?v=1C3q3Zr_R8E.

[21] William Lane Craig, "Did God Command Genocide in the Bible?" YouTube video, 9:48, posted by drcraigvideos, April 30, 2013, https://www.youtube.com/watch?v=9FGv9aOCcyU.

[22] Paul Copan, *Is God a Moral Monster?* (Grand Rapids: Baker Books, 2011).

After the conquest, Joshua describes the division of the land among the tribes (chaps. 13–22). While this section undoubtedly will bore the modern reader, remember that just because a text isn't entertaining doesn't mean it lacks significance. The fact that nearly half the book is devoted to the tribal allotments shows how important that event was in the eyes of the author. Step by step, tribe by tribe, in glorious detail, the author shows God faithfully fulfilling his promises to his people.

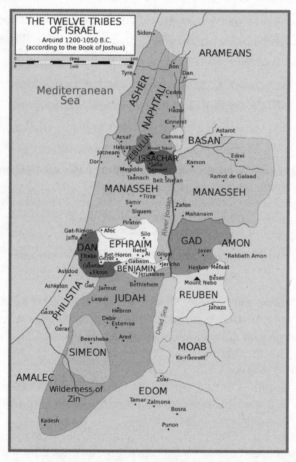

The fact that nearly half the book of Joshua is devoted to the tribal allotments shows how important that event was in the eyes of the author.

Of course, the divided lands still needed to be possessed, and ultimately Israel will be unable to seize these Canaanite lands (see Judges 1). But this does not diminish the promise and demonstrated faithfulness of God.

By the end of the book of Joshua, the primary issue facing the people has changed from one of conquest to one of settlement. The promise of land is no longer a future prediction but a present reality. Still, the principal threat to the people's well-being and continued success in the conquest remains the same—their own faithlessness.

The death story of Joshua ends the book with a prophetic challenge to the people to renounce the religion and riches and practices of the pagan inhabitants of Palestine and to reaffirm and embrace a covenant relationship with Yahweh.

Like Deuteronomy, the book of Joshua closes with inspiring and prophetic farewell speeches by a dying leader (chaps. 23–24). In this way, Joshua orders his house. Both speeches recount Yahweh's faithfulness and call for the Israelites to choose a life of covenant obedience. The importance of these instructions becomes evident in light of the destructive "Canaanization" of the next book, Judges (see below).

The last of Joshua's speeches occurs in chapter 24 in the context of a covenant renewal ceremony. Joshua reviews with the people in detail salvation history until that point, and then he asks the people three times, "Will you serve Yahweh?" In response, the people declare three times (vv. 18, 21, 24) their commitment and devotion to Yahweh exclusively. They assent to the charge despite Joshua's doubts (v. 19) and warnings (v. 20). They will be witnesses against themselves (v. 22) in the covenant—an ominous commitment, considering the future history of Israel.

Finally, in verses 25–28, the covenant is reaffirmed. This account of covenant renewal is not just an amusing history lecture. The narrative itself encourages future readers to make the same decision that the Israelites make in the chapter.

We must read it the same way. Choose this day whom you will serve. May we, like Joshua, say: "As for me and my family, we will worship the LORD" (24:15).

Literary Structure/Story Line/Message/Purpose—Judges

For many reasons, Judges is my favorite OT book. Practically, Judges speaks to the dangers facing the modern church in a postmodern culture—perhaps more clearly than any other OT book. Theologically, the book proclaims plainly God's faithfulness, patience, and grace, even in the face of rank rebellion. Literarily, one will not find a more carefully crafted and creatively rhetorical book in the OT. With Judges, the reader witnesses the artistry of the inspired biblical author on full display.

The judges of Judges didn't judge in the modern sense. Instead, they "saved" Israel from the power of their enemies (Judg 2:16–18).

Let's begin by clearing up one misconception. What is the first thing that comes to your mind when you think of a judge? Black robes, a gavel, and a grim dignitary rendering legal decisions? Maybe TV judges like Judge Wapner[23] in my generation or Judge Judy[24] today?

---

[23] "Joseph Wapner," *Wikipedia*, last modified February 5, 2019, https://en.wikipedia.org/wiki/Joseph_Wapner.

[24] "Judge Judy," *Wikipedia,* last modified March 5, 2019, https://en.wikipedia.org/wiki/Judge_Judy.

On the contrary, the judges of Judges didn't judge in the modern sense. Instead, they "saved" Israel from the power of their enemies (Judg 2:16–18). So they function more as warriors than lawyers. As Block suggests, we should perhaps call the book the "Book of Deliverers."[25]

Historically, the book deals with a complex and dark time for Israel. As mentioned above, the level-1 historical context of Judges begins with the death of Joshua shortly after the conquest and ends with the coronation of Saul (1380s–1050s BC). This period spans the late Bronze Age and early Iron Age in the ancient Near East. During this time, the nations of the Fertile Crescent saw widespread disruption and destruction at the hands of the Sea Peoples, who migrated down the coast of Syria-Palestine from the upper Mediterranean.

Israel was not immune from this turmoil. Though unified initially in the conquest, the twelve tribes quickly became scattered. And without a Joshua-like leader, they continued bickering and even warring with one another. But Israel's issues were more spiritual than political and familial. The author targets one chief "sin" for Israel during this time: they committed "the" evil. See the summary statement in Judg 2:11.

Most Bible translations render this text as, "The Israelites did what was evil in the LORD's sight." But the original Hebrew has the definite article *the* on the front of the word for evil. If I said, sit in "a" chair, it

---

[25] Daniel I. Block, *Judges, Ruth*, The New American Commentary, vol. 6 (Nashville: Broadman & Holman, 1999), 23. Early in my seminary training, I took my first Hebrew exegesis class with Dr. Block at The Southern Baptist Theological Seminary in Louisville, Ky. The topic? The book of Judges. The class was life changing and ministry shaping. His understanding and explanation of the book showed me the beauty of the OT and of this book in a way that I had never seen before. His teaching and example ultimately inspired me to teach the OT as well. Dr. Block became my PhD supervisor, and I still consider him my mentor. The Literary Tools concerning the book of Judges are inspired by and adapted from his groundbreaking work in this commentary and from the class I had with him so long ago.

could be any chair in the room. But if I said sit in "the" chair, I'm indicating a specific seat. Here the author has an explicit evil in mind. And "the" evil is idolatry. See Judg 2:11–13: "They worshiped the Baals and abandoned the LORD, the God of their fathers, who had brought them out of Egypt. They followed other gods from the surrounding peoples and bowed down to them. They angered the LORD, for they abandoned him and worshiped Baal and the Ashtoreths."

Baal Stele. A stele depicting the image of Baal,
a Canaanite fertility deity.

This idolatry points to the overarching point of the author. As Block states, "The theme of the book is the Canaanization of Israelite society during the period of settlement. The author's goal in exposing this problem is to wake up his own generation. This is an appeal to the covenant people to abandon all forms of paganism and return to Yahweh."[26]

The warning against the dangers of Canaanization is a prophetic message. And the author communicates this exhortation through the means of a carefully shaped "history."

Structurally, the book divides clearly into three principal sections—the prologue (1:1–3:6), the "Book of Deliverers" (3:7–16:31), and the epilogue (chaps. 17–21).[27]

In the prologue, the author begins by outlining why Israel was floundering in a moral and spiritual morass. Namely, the nation failed in driving out the Canaanites. Bluntly and without significant elaboration, in chapter 1, the author details the sundry tribes and their relative successes and mostly failures in conquest.

In the end, the majority of the tribes end up living among the Canaanites (1:21–36), rather than expelling them. And what did your mom always say, "If you hang out with the wrong people, you don't influence them; they influence you"? Predictably, the Israelites start to become like the Canaanites. God's people become "Canaanized," until at the end of the book, they are virtually indistinguishable from their neighbors.

In the remainder of the prologue, the author uses several sections to evaluate the present state of the Israelites (2:1–5; 3:1–6) and to sketch out the future misdeeds of the nation and judges (2:6–23).

The bulk of the book then details the narratives revolving around the individual judges. Once again, this is a rhetorically structured section. The author includes twelve judges. Obviously, this choice of number is deliberate, given the significance of the number twelve for the

---

[26] Block, 58.

[27] See David Dorsey, *The Literary Structure of the Old Testament: A Commentary on Genesis–Malachi* (Grand Rapids: Baker Books, 1999), 104n, for an excellent discussion on the rhetorical advantages of the tripartite structure.

twelve-tribed nation. Six judges are what we might consider "major," in that the author includes more extensive narratives about them. The other six deliverers are mentioned only briefly.

The narratives of the six major judges all follow a well-known pattern or "cycle." The people begin with rebellion and idolatry (2:11). God responds with judgment in the form of a foreign oppressor (2:14–15). When the people cry out to God in their suffering (2:15), God graciously raises up judges or "deliverers" who "saved them from the power of their marauders" (2:16). The nation then experiences some respite for a few years. But after a while, the Israelites always begin to rebel again, and "act even more corruptly than their fathers" (2:19).

Notice, however, that the nation is not just doing the same thing over again. They are caught in a downward spiral—with each cycle being worse than the previous. Indeed, with every judge, the same pattern hammers home over (Othniel) and over (Ehud) and over (Barak) and over (Gideon) and over (Jephthah) and over (Samson) a prophetic point: Israel is on a death-spiral toward Canaanization.

But it is not just the Israelites themselves who get worse and worse. They are led by judges who also act more corruptly with each cycle. Let's examine each judge briefly.

The cycles start with the first major judge—Othniel (3:7–11). Othniel's narrative is easily the most concise of the major cycles. Read through the text and see if you can spot the elements of the cycle.

Notice anything wrong here? Probably not. Othniel achieves a great victory—over the king of Mesopotamia, no less! In fact, Othniel perhaps gains the most significant triumph in all the book. And yet the story of his success receives only a scant five verses from the author. This shows that the author is not concerned to spend much time on Israel's high points.

A descendant of the faithful spy, Caleb, Othniel seemingly does nothing wrong. But one thing is curious about him. He is not Hebrew.

He is a Kenazite (3:9). So the greatest victory in the book is achieved by a nonnative Israelite. And it goes down from here.

The next judge is Ehud (3:12–30). *This is my favorite story, so please see the Wordsearch video to allow me to tell it.* The major point of this text is that Ehud as a judge possesses a questionable character, and the Israelites are continuing their downward spiral.

Following a minor deliverer named Shamgar (3:31), the author in Judges 4 tells of the third major judge, Barak. This judge does deliver Israel, but he keeps losing his glory to female characters in the story. In that patricentric cultural context, such a character would not have been esteemed highly. He first will not go into battle until the prophetess Deborah goes with him. And when Barak does conquer the Canaanites at Hazor, the Canaanite army commander, Sisera, flees and is subsequently killed by another female character, Jael. She does so with . . . a tent peg. Read the account if you have the stomach for it! The story is subsequently recapitulated in poetic form in Judges 5.

The next judge, Gideon, is a transitional one (chaps. 6–8). At times, he acts the part of a great and godly deliverer. At times, he takes the role of a reluctant warrior and degenerate despot. In fact, in the narrative, he goes by two names—Gideon and Jerubbaal. Like Israel itself, he seems caught in the "in between" in the journey toward Canaanization.

Yes, he does deliver Israel. *But* when the author first introduces Gideon, he explains that the future judge's father has an altar to Baal in their house. Yes, Gideon does hack down the shrine (hence, the name Gideon or "Hacker"). *But* when it comes to delivering Israel, Gideon insists on testing God for a sign—the infamous "sign of the fleece"— even though Yahweh has already assured him of his ultimate victory (6:36–40). Yes, after defeating the oppressing Midianites, Gideon states his desire for God to be king over Israel. *But* when Gideon names one of his sons, he calls him Abimelech—"My father is king" (8:22–31).

So with Gideon, the reader wonders which direction Israel will go—up or down.

*Gideon is a transitional character (chaps. 6–8). At times, he
acts the part of a great and godly deliverer. At times, he takes
the role of a reluctant warrior and degenerate despot.*

The next cycle answers this question definitively. God raises up a
very "Canaanitish" deliverer named Jephthah in Judges 11. The son of
a prostitute, Jephthah is most known for an infamous and tragic vow.

He promises God that, if Yahweh grants him victory, he will sacrifice the first thing that comes out of his house when he returns.
God allows Jephthah to deliver Israel. And when Jephthah returns, he
is greeted with tambourines and dancing by his only child—his virgin
daughter. See the story in 11:29–40. At the end, the text bluntly states
that Jephthah "kept the vow he had made about her" (v. 39).

Question: Who practiced child sacrifice in the ancient Near
East? The Canaanites. Do you see the author's point? Israel is rapidly
approaching full Canaanization.

And with the last major judge, Samson, Canaanization is achieved. Samson is known, of course, for three things: his legendary strength, his long hair, and his love of the ladies. The way the story is told, the reader might expect Samson to be the one to bring a reprieve from the dark period of the judges. His mother is barren, and God grants a miraculous birth—perhaps evoking memories of Sarah for the reader.

Samson, like Israel, squandered away his holiness and opportunity to be a light to the nations.

Samson possesses extraordinary physical power. And the Spirit of God rests upon him. His power is derived from his "set-apartness." At his birth, his mother dedicates him as a Nazirite—individuals within the community who demonstrate holiness by refraining from anything "grapish" (like wine), by not cutting their hair, and by not touching anything dead (see Num 6:1–21).

If anyone should be different from the Canaanites and be holy, it should have been Samson. If anyone could help the Israelites fulfill their destiny as a holy nation and kingdom of priests (Exod 19:4–6), it should have been Samson.

Yet Samson's life becomes a sad parable for the nation. Samson is the embodiment of Israel's problems. Chosen and blessed and set apart by God, Samson, like Israel, should have been a light to the world. But like the nation itself, Samson squanders this missional opportunity.

When we first meet Samson, we find him breaking two of his Nazirite vows—touching and even consuming honey from a dead lion carcass (14:9), spending time in some vineyards (14:5), and hosting a drinking festival (14:10–18). He flippantly breaks these vows because he is pursuing a Philistine woman, and she is "the right one" in his eyes (14:3). He chooses his own urges over Yahweh.

Like the Israelites, Samson goes after illicit lovers; for the Israelites, these are foreign nations and gods. For Samson, these are foreign women, against the prescriptions of the Torah. Most famously, one woman causes this strongman's ultimate demise—Delilah. Because of his own folly, Samson allows Delilah to know the secret of his strength—his Nazirite hair. When she cuts it in his sleep, Samson breaks his last vow, and he loses his hair and Yahweh's blessing. Like Samson, when God's covenant people compromise and become Canaanized, they too lose their blessing and strength.

The Philistines capture Samson, gouge out his eyes, and make him a laughingstock. Of course, he does get revenge in the end. Regaining his hair and his strength, Samson pushes down posts holding up a roof full of partying Philistines. In the collapse, all the carousing Canaanites die, including Samson. Yet even as Samson brings the house down, he cries out not, "Avenge Yahweh," but "Avenge me!" Samson is self-centered to the end. Like Israel, he is doing what is right in his own eyes.

Two stories (chaps. 17–18 and 19–21) comprise the last section of Judges. Both stories involve corrupt Levites—the tribe of the priests, the supposed religious leaders of Israel. Both stories are temporally (but not thematically) out of order from the rest of the book. And both portray the decay of Israel—morally and spiritually.

The first account relates the Levite-enabled idolatry of Micah, a man from the tribe of Ephraim. Micah has stolen some silver from his mom. But when he returns it to her, she gives it back to him, and he makes for himself an idol. False god in hand, Micah decides he needs a priest. It just so happens that an unnamed Levite is passing by. Micah then hires him as his own personal priest. Soon after, the wandering tribe of Dan wanders past Micah's house, and they steal his priest and his idol.

That a priest of Yahweh would facilitate such idolatry is shocking enough. But the author actually withholds the most shocking element of the story until the end: the identity of this Levite. Look up Judg 18:30. Your text may say that the priest's name was Jonathan, son of Gershom, son of Manasseh. But the actual identity is "Jonathan, son of Gershom, son of Moses." In other words, this idolatrous priest is the very grandson of Moses!

At this point, the reader realizes that the stories in chapters 17–21 are out of order chronologically. But the author places them at the end of the book to show how Israel is hitting "rock-bottom" Canaanization.

It gets even worse. The second story in the epilogue (chaps. 19–21) relates an even more distressing example of Canaanization. I believe it is one of the most grotesque accounts in all of Scripture. And the author means it to be so, to shock the reader.

Another lewd Levite is the central character. He has a concubine—or mistress. She runs away from him, and he finally retrieves her at her father's house.

On the way back to their home in Ephraim, the two decide to stay the night in Gibeah, a city of Benjamin—Israelite territory. Taken in by an old man for safety, the two males start to "make merry" and have a party. But during the night, ruffians from the city pound on the door, demanding that the old man send out the Levite so that they might "have sex with him" (19:22).

The perceptive reader will see that this is a story told in a way that recalls the story of Sodom and Gomorrah (see Genesis 19). Except in this case, the story is worse. Instead of sending out the Levite, the two men toss out the concubine, and the local Benjaminites proceed to violate her all night. Israel had become a nation that is worse than the worst of the Canaanites—the infamous people of Sodom and Gomorrah.

But just as bad as the Benjaminites is this Levite. In the morning, the Levite almost trips over his unconscious concubine as he leaves. She is lying with her hands at the threshold of the door. She had been trying desperately to find help. Unsympathetically, the Levite orders her to get up, but she does not arise. He places her on his donkey and returns to his home. The reader doesn't know if she is actually dead.

When the Levite gets to his house, he cuts his concubine into twelve pieces and sends these remains throughout the tribes of Israel. The narrator then includes this note: "Everyone who saw it said, 'Nothing like this has ever happened or has been seen since the day the Israelites came out of the land of Egypt until now. Think it over, discuss it, and speak up!'" (19:30) The author includes this statement as a prophetic plea to his own generation. Think it over! Speak up! Do something to cease your own Canaanization!

In the end, the other tribes come to fight against their fellow tribe, Benjamin, and almost wipe it out. In other words, God's people end up trying to destroy their own tribe, instead of the Canaanites. Why? Because they had become the Canaanites.

The refrain that resounds in these last two accounts is, "in those days, there was no king in Israel; everyone did whatever seemed right to him" (21:25). This is the attitude of the Canaanites that the Israelites had adopted. Yet that same danger—that of becoming Canaanized—is still a danger for the church today.

*At the end of Judges, the other tribes come to fight against
their fellow tribe, Benjamin, and almost wipe it out.*

The church must be, rather, the kingdom of priests that God has
called us to be. Think it over. Discuss it. But most of all, speak up.

Literary Structure / Story Line / Purpose / Message—*Ruth*

One of my favorite radio personalities of all time is the late Paul
Harvey. With an unforgettable voice and an uncanny ability to spin
yarns, Harvey captivated audiences for years with his news of the day
and his popular syndicated segment, *The Rest of the Story*.[28]

---

[28] Paul Harvey, "Paul Harvey, The Rest of the Story Radio Show—
Abraham Lincoln 1," YouTube video, 3:22, posted by American Radio Classics,
January 26, 2018, https://www.youtube.com/watch?v=5KblX7HMIDw.

Harvey would often fashion a fascinating story about a famous figure from history. But the genius of Harvey is that he would withhold the name of that historical person or some other significant detail until the end. Only at the end—when Harvey revealed this "rest of the story"—would you figure out how significant the entire story was.

The late radio personality, Paul Harvey.

The book of Ruth functions in this way. The enchanting tale details the travails and tragedies of a rather obscure family from an obscure city of Judah, the little town of Bethlehem. The author deliberately draws the reader into this family's lives and loves, mishaps and misfortunes. It is a carefully conceived and entirely enthralling narrative. But by the end of the book, one is struck by what was truly at stake in all that this family endured—the fate of salvation history, of the line of David, and eventually of God's Messiah.

The author begins the story by providing the historical setting—in the days in which the judges judged (Ruth 1:1). Many readers might gloss over this contextual note. But we just learned about the darkness of that period in the previous canonical book, Judges. Indeed, such a context fails to inspire confidence in a happily-ever-after outcome to this story.

But the news gets worse. A famine afflicts the land. This "cleanness of teeth" is not due to Mother Nature, but because the nation is violating its covenant with Yahweh (Lev 26:19–20). See chapter 7, Theological Tools. In other words, the events of Ruth occur not just in the darkness of the period of the judges, but in the darkest of times within that dark period.

The famine is so severe that it causes this humble family—a man named Elimelech, his wife, Naomi, and their two sons—to flee the Promised Land to Moab, a nation that had often oppressed Israel (see Judges 3). Their situation is truly desperate.

As the entire people experience a national trial, this family endures another very personal tragedy. Elimelech dies. Then the sons take for themselves Moabite wives, Orpah and Ruth, seemingly against the instructions of God, who desired his people not to intermarry among the nations (Deut 7:3). But then these sons die (1:5). So three women remain—one Israelite and two Moabites. Without means of support in a patricentric society, these women faced an uncertain, if not frightening, future.

But something happens. God acts. In Ruth 1:6, the author tells us that God has removed the covenant curse, has provided food to the land, and has "visited" his people. Although this word may not mean much to nonnative readers, a Hebrew would immediately associate "visit" with a dramatic salvific action by God's own hand, as in the exodus event (see Gen 50:24; Exod 4:31; 13:19). Could God be doing something in and through this obscure family that is on par with the exodus in salvation history?

The book is actually framed with God's dramatic actions. Twice in the book, God is said to act—here in 1:6 and again in 4:13, where God enables Ruth's conception. So while God's actions are noticeably absent in the middle of the book, this frame tells us that everything that happens throughout the book is due to God's providential dealings with his people and for his people.

Because of God's provision of food, the three women decide to return to Bethlehem. Naomi urges both her daughters-in-law to stay in Moab, their homeland. And Orpah remains there. But in one of the greatest statements of faith in the Historical Books, Ruth asserts her commitment to both Naomi and her God (1:16). Ruth "clings to" Naomi (v. 14)—an expression that recalls the covenant commitment of the first couple in Gen 2:24. It is truly surprising that this model of faith and faithfulness is not even a native Israelite. In fact, five times in the text, the author uses the title "Ruth the Moabitess" almost as a purposeful emphasis. So, as with Rahab, one of the greatest expressions of faith in the Bible is made by a Gentile woman.

Dire circumstances still endanger Ruth and Naomi. Where will they find regular provision? True, the Torah mandated that Israelites provide for the poor and widow and orphan, by allowing them to glean from the excess of the harvest (Lev 19:9–10). But how many people in the period of the judges were following Torah? In fact, the extreme opposite was more likely—that Ruth would be violated in the fields, as the Levite's concubine in Judges 19.

But she goes to the pastures anyway. And her "chance chances" upon the field of a Yahweh-fearing, wealthy man named Boaz (2:3). This man not only provides for her and Naomi's immediate needs, but he agrees to allow Ruth to glean for the entire season, gathering as much as needed.

The story takes a turn at the end of chapter 2, however. It becomes, well, a love story.

It "just so happens" that Boaz is a "kinsman redeemer." Here cultural context helps. In the Torah, in order to provide for widows and to carry on the father's name, if a man died without a son, his widowed wife could marry the closest kin—typically a brother. This strange law is called the law of levirate marriage (Deut 25:5–10). Since Naomi was past childbearing years, it appears that this law could apply to the daughter-in-law as well. In other words, the Torah allowed and even encouraged the marriage of Boaz and Ruth.

*Ruth's "chance chanced" upon the field of a Yahweh-
fearing, wealthy man named Boaz (2:3).*

Naomi realizes this and arranges, for lack of a better phrase, a "set up." She instructs Ruth to approach Boaz at night, when he would not be "put on the spot" in front of his workers and others. Ruth does this, asking Boaz, "Take me under your wing, for you are a family redeemer" (3:9). Basically and boldly, she is asking Boaz to marry her. Boaz could have misconstrued such an intrepid and nocturnal request. But instead, he recognizes Ruth as a "woman of noble character" (3:11).

Boaz amazingly and providentially agrees to Ruth's proposal, but there is one last impediment to this movie-worthy marriage. Another redeemer is a closer relative. But after a brief conversation in chapter 4, the other redeemer agrees to cede Ruth to Boaz. God has brought this couple together, to preserve the line of Elimelech. Upon their marriage, as mentioned above, God enables Ruth to conceive, and she and Boaz name their son Obed.

The book ends with a genealogy. And in this ostensibly dull and disregarded genre we have our "Paul Harvey" moment. The author tells the reader that Boaz is the great-grandfather of David—the most significant character in all the OT (4:17). And of course, David is the ancestor and forerunner of Jesus (Matt 1:1).

All the tension. All the "chance" events. The love story. In all of it, God was working. Even in the dark days of the judges, God was working. God used, of all people, a faithful Moabite woman and an ordinary farmer from Bethlehem to continue the messianic line in Scripture.

And now you know the "rest of the story."

Literary Structure/Story Line/Message/Purpose—Samuel

Sometimes book titles in the Bible can be head scratchers. Reading the books of 1 & 2 Samuel, one might think that the books would focus on Samuel. But while Samuel does play a prominent role in the first half of the first book, he is not *the* major figure in the books.

Instead, 1 & 2 Samuel have an alternate and singular emphasis. In fact, as discussed in the introduction above, the author arranges and selects the material in these books for one purpose—to highlight the rise and fall, the significance and salvation-historical centrality of David as king.

Indeed, one could argue—and be correct—that David is the main character, other than God himself, in the entire OT. No other biblical figure, except Jesus himself, is both anticipated[29] and revisited in Scripture to this extent.[30]

---

[29] See Gen 49:8–10; Num 24:17; Deut 17:14–20; Ruth 4:18–22; and 1 Sam 2:10.

[30] See Isa 9:7; 11:1–2; 53; Jer 23:5–6; 33:14–17; Ezek 34:20–24; 37:24–28; Amos 9:11; Zech 3:8; Matt 1:1; Mark 10:47; Rom 1:3; Rev 5:5; 22:16; among

In the books of Samuel, the author is completely captivated by David. In fact, in outlining the two books, we see David as the primary focus of each section. We'll explore the reasons for this emphasis below. But for now, let's show how this emphasis works itself out in the structure of the books.

First, in chapters 1–7, the author details religious preparations for King David. Why do we need these preparations? Remember that when the story concludes in Judges, the people are dwelling in deep spiritual darkness. And that blackness still hovers over 1 Samuel 1. The judges still control the land. The people are still struggling spiritually.

But in 1 Samuel 1, the reader meets a barren woman—a pious and humble woman named Hannah. In reading the Bible, if you ever come across a woman who cannot have children, exegetical bells should sound. Think of Sarah and the other patriarchal wives. Think of Samson's mom. Think of Elizabeth, the mother of John the Baptist, in the Gospel of Luke. In each case, God overcomes the physically impossible to demonstrate that he is doing something miraculous in salvation history. With Hannah, one gets the sense that something on this same level is about to happen.

Rewarded for her fervent prayer, Hannah is granted a child, whom she names Samuel and whom she dedicates to God's service (1 Sam 1:22). This dedication should remind readers of Samson and John the Baptist.

In response to God's gift of a son, Hannah praises Yahweh in a song in 1 Sam 2:1–10. Note the last verse: "The LORD will judge the ends of the earth. He will give power to his king; he will lift up the horn of his anointed [lit., "Messiah"]." Wait. This is the time of the judges. "In those days there was no king in Israel" (Judg 21:25). But through

---

many others. Of course, there is a biblical theological reason for this focus on David: Jesus is the promised King in the line of David. So, the promises of David and to David are ultimately fulfilled in Christ.

the words of this humble mother, God hails the arrival of his promised King—both in history and in 1 & 2 Samuel.[31]

The young Samuel proceeds to serve as a literary and theological break with the book of Judges. God has been silent in this historical period. But through Samuel—the last of the judges and the first of the prophets in the monarchic period—God begins to speak to his people once again. Why? To prepare the way for his king.[32] And when Samuel grows up, he continues to lead the people back to God, in preparation for the king's arrival (1 Sam 7:3–4).

In chapter 8, the story shifts significantly. God's people demand a king. This sets up the next section in 1 Samuel—one that establishes the kingly office for David (chaps. 8–15). For Israel to desire to have a king is not wrong. As mentioned, Moses even foresaw the monarchy's eventuality (Deut 17:14–20). But the people wanted a king like those of the nations. And that is exactly what they receive—King Saul, who mirrors the character and persona of many of the surrounding ancient Near Eastern despots.

Saul functions as a foil for David in the narrative.[33] He's the anti-David. Saul is tall, handsome, magnetic, self-willed, mercurial, with a strained relationship with Yahweh. David is slight, young, lesser, but a man after God's own heart. The contrast between David and Saul reaches a climax in 1 Samuel 17—the story of David and Goliath (more appropriately, the story of David and Saul). As mentioned in the introduction to this chapter, the author shows David, not Saul, to be the obvious king in this battle.

---

[31] See Luke 1:46–55, where Luke uses Mary's song, known as the Magnificat, with the same effect.

[32] Again, we see a parallel with Luke. After a long period of revelatory silence from God in the intertestamental period, God speaks again through John the Baptist to hail God's new Davidic King.

[33] "Foil (literature)," *Wikipedia*, last modified January 10, 2019, https://en .wikipedia.org/wiki/Foil_(literature).

This inscription, found on the remains of a stele at Tel Dan in northern Israel dating to the 9th century BC, contains one of the earliest references to King David. Line 8 refers to the "king of Israel" and line 9 refers to the "house of David."

Throughout the remainder of 1 Samuel and into 2 Samuel (1 Samuel 16–2 Samuel 8), David is shown to be the true and chosen "anointed one," even though he does not accept that role at first. David, to his credit, patiently waits for God to remove Saul from the throne. At the end of 1 Samuel, that ejection finally occurs. Saul dies an ignominious death, insane and rejected by God. This sets up David's acceptance by God and the people—and the author and reader.

Soon after Saul's death, David begins to consolidate power. He moves the capital from Hebron to Jerusalem. He returns the ark of the covenant to Jerusalem as well (2 Samuel 6). And in what is perhaps the climax of the entire OT, he receives covenant promises from God (2 Samuel 7). See the Theological Tools section below for an explanation of this text.

However, soon after this climactic event, the author details David's fall. This narrative of his decline, sometimes called the Succession

Narrative, covers the last chapters of 2 Samuel. The king's faltering begins with his infamous adultery with Bathsheba, and his subsequent murder of this woman's husband, Uriah.

David's failings extend to his family, with several of his sons rebelling against their father. The book ends with David rebelling against God himself by ordering a census against God's will—an event that leads to a plague on the people. Yet all is not lost. As David repents, the plague stops. David chooses the place where the plague breaks as the location for the future temple.

In sum, the OT presents no character more conflicted or complicated than David. The books of Samuel honestly reveal David's flaws and even present these imperfections as a foretaste of future royal (mis) behavior. Still, the biblical authors believe David to be God's anointed, who had been anticipated since Israel's beginnings (Deut 17:14–20). They understand him to be the nation's covenantal representative, dynastic head, and the symbol of the people's messianic hope.

In this way, the character of David possesses a prophetic purpose. The characterization of David in the books of Samuel prophetically foreshadows the weaknesses of Solomon and other Davidic kings, who would give lip service to orthodox Yahwism but also dabble in political intrigue and violence. The author's characterization of David also prophetically foreshadows the future history of Israel, which began with such great promise but falters in the end, experiencing God's judgment.

Literary Structure / Story Line / Message / Purpose—Kings

Have you ever heard the expression "rose-colored glasses"? These are "lenses" that makes one's perspective of every event—whether positive or negative—well, rosy. As mentioned in the Historical Tools above, the author of Kings relates a large swathe of Israel's history—some 400 years of it (971–561 BC)—through "exile-colored" lenses. From the beginning of the book, all the stories seem to spiral downward toward this ultimate traumatic event for God's people.

Also, remember that 1 and 2 Kings are part of the "Former Prophets." The author does not write just to communicate history, but prophetically to exhort his audience based on that history. And so the collapse of the nation is presented theologically—showing the dangerous results of covenant disobedience (particularly on the part of the Davidic kings) to warn future generations.

The two books of Kings cover three of the historical periods outlined above in the Historical Tools—the united monarchy (1 Kings 1–11); the divided monarchy (1 Kings 12–2 Kings 23), including the exile of the northern kingdom at the hands of the Assyrians; and the exile of the southern kingdom (2 Kings 24–25).

I won't restate this level-1 context, as it was discussed in the Historical Tools section. But allow me to use two events to illustrate the exilic lens of the author.

First, the books begin with a death—and not just any death. King David is dying. Isn't that an odd and ominous way to begin a book? Not only is David dying; he is dying poorly. Here a genre tool can help us.

The books of Kings begin with David's death. This ominous beginning to the books points forward to the future exile.

The story of David's death is a "death story"—a particular and common genre in the Old Testament.[34] Many of the major characters in the OT have death stories, including Sarah, Abraham, Jacob, Joseph, Aaron, Moses, and Joshua. Each of these stories follows a recognizable and well-known (to the original reader) pattern. In each, the death is announced, usually by the narrator, and then the author shows how the lead character attempts to order his or her house before death. Finally, and often anticlimactically, the author reports the actual death and response to the death (burial, mourning, etc.).

The book of 1 Kings begins with David's death story. Interestingly, the narrative begins exactly how Abraham's death account does—with the exact same announcement of impending death (Abraham and David are both "old and advanced in age"; Gen 24:1; 1 Kgs 1:1). Immediately following Abraham's announcement, though, one learns that Yahweh had "blessed him [Abraham] in everything" (Gen 24:1). But after David's announcement, the author tells us that David's courtiers covered him with clothes, and he couldn't keep warm (1 Kgs 1:1)—i.e., he's sick and dying. David does not seem to be blessed like Abraham in death. And it appears that the author of Kings is deliberately comparing the two characters—to show that David was no Abraham in his old age.

After these announcements of impending death, both Abraham and David attempt to put their respective houses in order. These attempts or lack thereof confirm David's problems. In Abraham's death account, we see this patriarch put his house in order excellently—finding a wife for his son Isaac and ensuring the passing on of the patriarchal covenant promises (Genesis 24). But in David's death account, David's son Adonijah stages a coup. David is not even aware of this seditious and blatant takeover. His house is not in order. Only when his son Solomon

---

[34] For a fuller discussion of this genre, see Bryan Cribb, *Speaking on the Brink of Sheol: Form and Message of Old Testament Death Stories* (Piscataway, NJ: Gorgias Press, 2009).

reminds him of his promise to make him king does David finally act to prepare for death.

So it seems that David's death story hints of the troubles to come in the book—particularly among the Davidic kings. David's inability to put his house in order properly prophetically foreshadows a disordered house of Israel.

The disarray in the nation and kingship seems to dissipate initially with Solomon. Indeed, this famously wise king's reign is the time in Israel's history when the nation almost achieved God's purposes for itself. The borders expanded. Peace is enjoyed. Solomon has become renowned for his understanding, so that world leaders come to him to

Because of temple entry restrictions, the Western Wall (Wailing Wall) encasing the Temple Mount (where Solomon built the first Temple) is one of the holiest places where Jews can pray. The wall is part of the remains of Herod's Temple from Jesus's day.

witness the wisdom of God. Most importantly, the temple—the permanent dwelling for God's glory—is built.

But in the end, Solomon becomes enthralled with the world and involved in idolatry. For the author, this failure establishes an all-too-predictable pattern for future kings and generations, even in the face of rebukes from prophets such as Elijah and Elisha. Solomon's primary sin, like Israel's, is allowing his heart to turn to foreign women and their gods in "love" (covenant faithfulness). Israel itself will fall because of these same things, though the foreign "women" for Israel are other nations and other gods (see, among many examples, Jer 3:1).

Hezekiah's Tunnel brought water from the Gihon Spring inside Jerusalem's defenses. King Hezekiah used it to ensure water during the expected long Assyrian siege. The construction—which started from both ends—is considered one of the marvels of early engineering.

As detailed above, Solomon's excess and idolatry leads to the division of the kingdom under his son Rehoboam in 931 BC. And from this point onward, there are two kingdoms—Israel in the north and Judah in the south. The subsequent history for both is basically one of failure—particularly and predictably led by the kings.

The northern kingdom, the worst offender, experiences God's devastating judgment before Judah in the form of the Assyrian exile in 722 BC (2 Kings 17).

This brings us to the second event that illustrates the exilic lens of the author—his narrative of the death of Hezekiah in 2 Kings 20. First, some context: In 2 Kings 18, we read that the southern kingdom of Judah is initially spared from the Assyrian onslaught that had led to the exile of the north. In fact, it appears that even as the northern kingdom is failing and falling, the southern kingdom—under the charge of good King Hezekiah—is charting a course toward ultimate restoration and revival. The account of Hezekiah's reforms and of his subsequent leadership of Judah during the Assyrian crisis in 2 Kings 18–19 represents one of the high points in the Former Prophets.

Hezekiah's Tunnel inscription commemorates and describes the moment when the excavators from both sides of the digging operation met underground.

But by 2 Kings 21, the optimism of these two chapters has disappeared, and the southern kingdom of Judah has begun again the inevitable slide to exile. Indeed, with the reign of King Manasseh in 2 Kings 21, the historian bluntly predicts that Jerusalem will be wiped clean like a dish.

However, this sudden shift is not without warning. The author expertly signals the coming exile with his story of Hezekiah's death in 2 Kings 20. How? With another manipulated death story.

In 2 Kings 20, the author begins Hezekiah's death story with another announcement of impending death. In fact, Hezekiah's demise is predicted twice—by the narrator and by Isaiah the prophet. In other words, death is assured. What should this dying king do? Based on the other death stories in the OT, he should put his house in order. Instead, Hezekiah begs for more time.

God grants him fifteen more years, but one can't help but wonder if the typical order of events has been disordered. This is a disordered death story—a story that veers from what one expects, in order to show the author's point.

Two things happen in Hezekiah's extra years: a tragic diplomatic visit from Babylonian envoys, which is condemned by the prophet Isaiah; and Hezekiah's son and future rebellious king, Manasseh, is born. Both of these events are used by the author to hail the future exile.

In a way, Hezekiah's last days mirror those of Judah found in the remainder of Kings. Despite the pleas of the faithful to extend life, God would withhold death only so long. God grants salvation for a period of time so that Judah might order its house. But both Judah and Hezekiah commit serious errors during these "extra years." Despite God rescuing the nation from death many times over, Judah, like Hezekiah, would ultimately die.

So with 2 Kings 20, the ultimate fate of Judah seems inevitable. This is confirmed in 2 Kings 21 with the reign of Manasseh—the worst king in Jewish history and the "last straw" with God. Even good king Josiah (640–609 BC) cannot stave off the coming exile. After Josiah's untimely death, the kingdom rapidly degenerates politically and spiritually under the brief reigns of four subsequent kings. And in 586 BC, under King Zedekiah, the exile finally happens. The nation seems to have become a valley of dry bones (Ezekiel 37).

But hope remains. The restoration of deposed Davidic king Jehoiachin at the end of the book points to a hope for future restoration of the king and kingdom. But that hope would have to wait for realization for another 500-plus years.

Literary Structure / Story Line / Message / Purpose—Chronicles

Along with Leviticus and the Minor Prophets, 1 & 2 Chronicles rank as perhaps the most avoided OT books. Not only do these books ostensibly relate old and seemingly irrelevant history, but the author also

Ezekiel has a vision of a valley of dry bones in Ezekiel 37.
This deadness represents the wayward nation of Israel in the exile.

retells history. Readers of Chronicles often have that déjà vu feeling, especially if they have just read Samuel and Kings. In fact, more than 50 percent of Samuel and Kings is also in Chronicles.

So why read it? For starters, since so few access it, perusing its pages is like mining for gold in uncharted lands. Indeed, Chronicles contains practical and spiritual treasures that have gone virtually unnoticed by many interpreters throughout the centuries. For a great example, see the Putting the Tools to Use section below.

I also love Chronicles because it impressively illustrates how the Hebrew authors use "selection" as a tool for making their points. In other words, the author picks and chooses and shapes his sources theologically to make his divinely-inspired rhetorical points.

What are those points in Chronicles? To understand this, let's revisit the level-2 historical context above. Remember that the author—scholars call him the Chronicler—writes at the end of the OT period in the postexile (possibly late 400s BC). He is writing to a shell-shocked and dangerously apathetic people. Doubt and disinterest in the faith was rampant. Is God still working? Is he still in charge? Are his promises still believable?

The Chronicler prophetically retells his history to reprove, rebuke, and exhort this audience, but also to encourage them with hope. In fact, the book ends with a hopeful narrative—the story of King Cyrus of Persia allowing God's people to return from exile in 539 BC.[35] For the Chronicler, the object of his hope is focused on the restoration of two institutions in Israel's faith: the temple and the Davidic king. As the author tells Israel's history from kingdom to exile to return, those two entities take center stage.

---

[35] Interestingly, Chronicles is the last book in the Hebrew Scriptures—unlike our Bibles, which end the OT with Malachi. So the Jews end their Scriptures with a message of hope, whereas the Christian Old Testament ends with a warning of a coming day of the Lord.

Regarding the former, since Solomon, the Jewish people had based their confidence in God's presence and protection on the temple. Its ruin in 586 BC represented something of the ruins of the people's own faith. In turn, the second temple of the postexile, rebuilt before the Chronicler writes, continued to serve as a symbol of their rebuilt covenant community. The second temple gave hope for God's abiding presence, even as that presence had come into doubt in the exile. And it linked pre- and postexilic Israel as God's people.

How does the author emphasize the temple in the books? The Chronicler devotes nearly 14 percent of his chapters (1 Chronicles 21–29) to describing how David made preparations for the temple. Similarly, some six chapters show how Solomon builds and celebrates it (2 Chronicles 2–7). The author also evaluates kings based on their esteem for and care of the temple (2 Chr 13:10–12).

But it is the figure of the Davidic king who dominates Chronicles and who is the principal source of hope for the author. The Chronicler

A panorama of the Temple Mount in Jerusalem. The second temple gave hope for God's abiding presence, even as that presence had come into doubt in the exile.

highlights the Davidic line in the genealogies that begin the books (1 Chronicles 2–3). Then nearly 60 percent of the rest of the books focuses on David and Solomon—with the entire first book of Chronicles centered on the former.

And the Chronicler does not just talk about David; he does so glowingly, presenting David as an ideal king. David is the chief covenant representative. David is the chief champion of the temple.

In fact, he does little wrong in the Chronicles account. Omitted from the David narratives in Chronicles are key missteps presented in 2 Samuel and 1 Kings, such as his adultery with Bathsheba and his failures as a father.

The Chronicler's idealistic presentation of David is most apparent when we compare the accounts of David's death in Chronicles and Kings (1 Chronicles 23–29 and 1 Kgs 1:1–2:12). Reading the two narratives, one notes that both accounts begin with a similar statement: David was old and advanced in years and about to die. But after that statement, the two Davids could not be more different.

As mentioned above, in the Kings account, David is described as weak politically. He is a poor father, who does not even know that his son Adonijah is rebelling against him. He struggles to order a disordered house. And he barely survives a well-orchestrated coup attempt.

But the author of Chronicles summarizes that whole succession narrative of 1 Kings 1–2 in a half verse: "he installed his son Solomon as king over Israel" (1 Chr 23:1). The Chronicler glosses over David's frailty at the end of life, his loss of control over his kingdom, and the entire succession controversy.

On the contrary, the Chronicler describes David as a king who, despite his old age, orders his kingdom rightly. Indeed, each element in 1 Chronicles 23–29 reinforces this impression. In particular, the Chronicler's inclusion of various "orderings" of Levites, priests, temple musicians, gatekeepers, treasurers, and the tribes and military (23:2–27:34) makes a clear statement regarding the orderly nature of David's departure. The king ensures that the temple is well provisioned. He offers encouragement to his successor, Solomon, with words reminiscent of Moses's charges to Joshua (1 Chr 28:10, 20; cf. Deut 31:2–8). By contrast, the 1 Kings account depicts chaos and infighting in David's dying days.

Most important for an ordered house, in Chronicles David ensures an orderly succession. The Chronicler summarizes Solomon's succession by portraying him as sitting and prospering on the "throne of Yahweh," with the devoted obedience of the officials, the mighty men, and also all the sons of King David (1 Chr 29:23–25). The author is silent about Solomon's seditious sibling Adonijah and the rebellious army commander Joab, as well as any of the other mutineers against Solomon's reign as found in 1 Kings 1.

Is the author trying to fool the reader? No, he knows his readers realize David's failures. The author of Chronicles just chooses to select other events to include, to establish one point: David is the ideal king.

Why? Like the prophets, the Chronicler and the faithful of Israel awaited an ideal Davidic king who would restore all things. That was their hope. The new David. The true David. The righteous David. The Messiah. But unlike the prophets, the Chronicler communicates his hope through the medium of

Like the prophets, the Chronicler and the faithful of Israel awaited an ideal Davidic king who would restore all things.

history. And he does so beautifully. And in several centuries that new king would come, born in a humble stable in David's city, Bethlehem.

Literary Structure/Story Line/Message/Purpose—Ezra and Nehemiah

Two of the more obscure books among the Historical Books are Ezra and Nehemiah. I group them together because that is how they appear in the Hebrew Bible, and they both deal with the same time period and issues.

Chronologically, the books take up Israel's history where Chronicles leaves it. In fact, the last two verses in Chronicles are the same as the first two in Ezra. The history told in Ezra–Nehemiah begins with the return from exile, commissioned by Cyrus the Great of Persia in 539 BC. Archaeologists have found a copy of the general decree of Cyrus—called the Cyrus Cylinder, which allowed all peoples conquered by the Babylonians to return to their native lands.[36]

The Cyrus Cylinder, courtesy of the British Museum.

---

[36] The British Museum, "The Cyrus Cylinder," www.britishmuseum.org, accessed March 4, 2019, https://www.britishmuseum.org/research/collection _online/collection_object_details.aspx?objectId=327188&partId=1.

The books then continue to detail the events outlined above in the Historical Tools—the rebuilding of the temple, the return of Ezra and the subsequent Ezrian revival, the rebuilding of the walls under Nehemiah, and the continued rebellion on the part of the people.

Because of the focus on the namesakes of the books, the most common application derived from Ezra and Nehemiah is to use these lead characters as examples. In fact, I sometimes joke that I have never heard a sermon on Nehemiah that wasn't on the topic of leadership. Undoubtedly, these towering postexilic figures do model righteous and commendable attitudes and actions (see the Applying the Results section below). But is that the chief purpose of the author(s)?

I would argue that the main purpose of Ezra–Nehemiah is to teach something about what God is doing. Again, our temptation is to make the text all about us or even the human character, when it is much more about the Divine. In this case, the books demonstrate how God rebuilds and renews, purifies and protects his covenant community of faith.

In this way, the return from exile is presented as a divinely orchestrated second exodus, returning the people to the Promised Land, so that they can fulfill their missional purpose. Ezra functions as a new Moses, skilled in communicating and exhorting based on Torah (Ezra 7:10; Neh 8:1–8). He even intercedes for the people as Moses did (Ezra 9:6–15). And the people end up renewing their covenant with Yahweh (Neh 9:38).

Nehemiah shows a similar passion for the rebuilt covenant community—a passion that inspires his return to Jerusalem from Persia in the first place (Neh 1:4–11). His desire to rebuild the walls has a larger and more spiritual purpose—to show God rebuilding his covenant people. Indeed, throughout the narrative, Nehemiah and the narrator note the providential "gracious hand of God" being directly involved in key events (Neh 2:8, 18; see 4:15; 6:16).

The books also sound a more ominous tone. As with the initial exodus, God's people in the second exodus have much to learn. Remember that in the first exodus, the people respond to God's grace in deliverance, covenant, revelation, and divine presence, with the golden calf (Exodus 32–33). Similarly, in Nehemiah, despite the people's affirmation of Torah (8:1–12), despite their celebrating the Feast of Tabernacles (8:13–18), and despite their initial repentance (9:1–37), they continue to show covenant infidelity.

In the last chapter of Nehemiah, the people intermarry with foreigners (13:23–24), profane the Sabbath (13:15–17), and fail to provide for the temple (13:10–11). Though Nehemiah works to bring reform (13:31), the reader gets the sense that old patterns will remain. But the faithful continue to anticipate a great "day of the Lord," in which God "will turn the hearts of fathers to their children and the hearts of children to their fathers" (Mal 4:6). That day would come several hundred years later, with a man named John the Baptist.

Literary Structure/Story Line/Message/Purpose—Esther

The last of the Historical Books, Esther represents one of the most curious and polarizing books in the canon. In fact, while Jewish tradition places it on the level of the Pentateuch,[37] some interpreters throughout its history have doubted its canonicity. Reformer Martin Luther once even wrote of his hostility toward the book.

Such negative reactions are undoubtedly due to its seemingly secular story line and subject matter. Famously, the book does not mention

---

[37] The reason for this esteem is due to Esther providing the historical background of the annual Jewish Feast of Purim ("lots"). This festival is the only one commended in the canon of Scripture that is not commended first in the Pentateuch.

the name of God at all. The "why" of this omission will be explored later; for now, one can perhaps understand the opposition to Esther.

Yet the story itself is riveting. Set in postexilic Persia, the narrative begins with a scene in the palace of the Persian King Ahasuerus (probably Xerxes, 486–465 BC). This ambitious ruler has staged a feast to display his glory. However, when his queen, Vashti, refuses to appear before the merrymakers, the enraged king deposes her. To replace Vashti, the king's advisers suggest a nationwide beauty contest of sorts. Among those chosen to join the king's harem, seemingly by chance, is a young Jewish girl named Hadassah or Esther. She quickly becomes the king's favorite.

Readers of Scripture will see a pattern here, similar to that of the stories of Joseph and Daniel—a Hebrew raised to prominence in a foreign government, for the ultimate purpose of saving God's people. And in the story of Esther, the need for salvation is soon revealed.

Ahasuerus's second-in-command, Haman, takes exception to Esther's uncle Mordecai, who has refused to bow to him. Because of this, Haman has plotted the extermination of the Jews in the kingdom. The date for the massacre is determined by the casting of *purim* (lots)— something like dice.

Again, seemingly by chance, Mordecai learns of the plot and enlists Esther to intercede with Ahasuerus. To come before the most powerful man in the world unbidden—even as the queen—was prohibited, and to do so imperiled one's life. But in the climax of the book, Mordecai reasons that Esther has been raised up—the "by whom" is not stated— to intervene for "such a time as this" (Esth 4:14).

Esther ends up being accepted by the king. Through several more "chance" events, the tables are turned (9:1). Haman is deposed, after his plot is discovered. Mordecai replaces him. And the Jews are allowed to defend themselves. The Feast of Purim is instituted to commemorate the deliverance. You'll need to read the story to get the details.

Esther was raised up—the "by whom" is not stated—to intervene before the Persion King for "such a time as this" (Esth 4:14).

What is fascinating is that through all of these "chance occurrences," God remains hidden. No divine intervention is mentioned. But for a Jewish person, God's involvement would never be doubted. Jews believed that even when the lot is cast in the lap, "its every decision is from the LORD" (Prov 16:33).

But if God indeed saves his people in Esther, why does the author keep God's hand hidden? Two reasons. First, God may be involved in our lives, but his providential control is not always evident to those experiencing the event. Second, in life, human responsibility is necessary. Believers should not necessarily "wait" for something to happen; instead, God usually works through the faithful to accomplish his purposes.

Esther is a commentary on the nature of faith and faithfulness.

Theological Tools

Several theological tools could be considered for interpreting the Historical Books. For instance, readers will want to be aware of important and recurring theological themes, such as land, covenant, kingdom, and exclusive loyalty to Yahweh. But we will consider two principal theological tools—one that gazes backward and one that prophetically peers forward.

Deuteronomy and History

First, the retrospective theological tool is the book of Deuteronomy. As mentioned above, some scholars have wrongly argued that Deuteronomy was written many years after Moses by a hypothetical Deuteronomistic historian as a prologue to the Former Prophets. Despite this incorrect conclusion, one cannot deny that Deuteronomy does provide a theological backdrop to the Historical Books, especially Joshua, Judges, Samuel, and Kings. Indeed, Deuteronomy provided the criteria by which the biblical writers examined and judged the nation and her kings.

In addition, theological themes from Deuteronomy appear throughout the Historical Books. For instance, both Deuteronomy and the Former Prophets implore the people to demonstrate complete covenantal fidelity to Yahweh (Deut 6:4–15; 9:7–12; 30:15–20). Failure to do so will result in covenantal curses and death (Deut 11:26–28, 28:15–68; 30:15–20). But obedience would also bring blessing. This cycle of blessing and curse is the history of Israel.

Both Deuteronomy and the Historical Books also show concern for justice, especially on behalf of the poor, outcast, and alien (Deut 10:18–19; 14:28–29; 15:1–18; 24:14–15). And both highlight the central role of the king in the nation (Deut 17:14–20).

In other words, if you are reading the Historical Books, be sure to check the cross-references—notes in many study Bibles that point you to other Scriptures related to the one at hand. If these references refer to Deuteronomy, look it up. The cross-reference may lead you to understand better your historical text.

If you are reading the Historical Books, be sure to check
the cross-references—notes in many study Bibles that point
you to other Scriptures related to the one at hand.

One example will suffice. Turn to 1 Kings 10–11. This passage brings the story of King Solomon to a close and evaluates his reign. In chapter 10, the author seems to extol the king's great accomplishments. Solomon had accumulated great wealth—with visible and ostentatious gold and ivory and exotic pets adorning his palace and capital city (vv. 14–22). Indeed, the author states that the king "surpassed all the kings of the world" in wisdom and wealth (v. 23).

Reading this passage on its own, you are left with one conclusion: King Solomon was the man! But try reading it in light of Deut 17:14–20. In this text, Moses outlines the qualifications for a future king of

Israel. Of course, this future king would not arrive for several centuries; nevertheless, Moses tells the reader some things the king should and should not do. The king *should* order his kingdom by reading and keeping Torah (vv. 18–19). He *should* possess humility and model obedience to and fear of Yahweh (vv. 19–20). And if he does, he *will* maintain his throne.

Just as important, this future king *should not* accumulate excessive gold and wealth (v. 17). He *should not* multiply wives for himself, lest they lead his heart astray (v. 17). And tellingly, he *should not* acquire many horses for himself from Egypt (v. 16).

As the author of 1 Kings seemingly praises Solomon for all his deeds, he includes in his description this little detail: "Solomon accumulated 1,400 chariots and 12,000 horsemen and stationed them in the chariot cities and with the king in Jerusalem. . . . Solomon's horses were imported from Egypt and Kue" (17:26, 28). Do you see it? Solomon's action may not seem bad on the surface, until you read it in light of Deuteronomy 17. By including this detail, the author subtly shows that all is not well with Israel or the king.

Of course, what is subtle in chapter 10 becomes explicit in 1 Kings 11. There the author describes how Solomon obtains his 700 wives and 300 concubines; predictably they turn "his heart away" (11:3), just as Moses said they would in Deut 17:17. Indeed, it is almost as if the author of 1 Kings has Deuteronomy in one hand and his stylus in the other.

And that is the way we should read the Historical Books as well— with Deuteronomy in one hand and the Historical Books in the other.

The Davidic Covenant

As mentioned above, the climax and central text for perhaps the entire OT is 2 Samuel 7. The context of this text is David expressing a desire to build God a "house"—the temple. God responds by stating that he will build David a house as well—amazingly, an eternal dynasty. In addition, God promises a father-son relationship with his chosen "servant." This term *servant* in turn becomes almost inseparable from David and the Davidic Messiah in future texts.

After David returns the ark of the covenant to Jerusalem and expresses a desire to build a house for God, God responds by promising David an eternal dynasty—a promise that is the seed of Israel's messianic hope.

Think about the amazing nature of these promises. In the grand scheme of world history, David is a pretty minor king. At the time, Israel was just an inconsequential and relatively puny nation among the "big boys" on the political playground of the ancient Near East. At any moment, these powers could invade and wipe Israel off the map.

But God promises the king of this fragile state an eternal throne? How can this be?

Of course, the kings had responsibilities as well. Within this covenant, as explained in chapter 4, the Davidic king would lead the people in covenant obedience as a mediator. In this role, the king would be disciplined by God himself. And the nation would be evaluated through the king. As the king went, so went the nation. So individual generations and kings could experience the covenant curses.

But God's promises would never depart from the Davidic line. So when all seemed lost in Israel; when, for instance, the exile removed the people from the land; when the Babylonians razed the temple to the ground; when all other promises seemed unfulfilled, the people still remembered God's covenantal promises to David. The prophets over and over again would revisit and draw hope from these promises. See, among many others, Isa 9:7; 11:1–2; 53; Jer 23:5–6; 33:14–17; Ezek 34:20–24; 37:24–28; Amos 9:11; and Zech 3:8.

Then one day, a Man from Galilee came proclaiming that the kingdom of God was on earth again. And it was present in himself. This Man, of course, is Jesus, the "anointed One," the promised King in the line of David. See the Applying the Results section below for more details.

Putting the Tools to Use

The following will offer an example of how the use of tools can be helpful in interpreting a biblical text from the OT Historical Books. Before reading the following, try it for yourself. Work through the following questions; then see if you can discern the original meaning.

Example: Judgment, Forgiveness, and Tale of Two Kings in 2 Kings 21:1–18 and 2 Chronicles 33:1–20

Historical Tools

What is the level-1 and level-2 historical context, and how does that context affect my reading of the text (hint: this is most important for these texts)?

Literary Tools

What is the genre of the text? How does the author use narrative tools?

Theological Tools

Are there any key theological terms or concepts in the text? How do I understand the text in light of Christ and the full testimony of the Bible?

Application

What does this text tell me about God? About myself? About the world? About how I relate to God?

Interpretation

Have you ever met people who thought themselves to be "too far gone" to be forgiven? Perhaps they think they've sinned too grievously or maybe rebelled against God too willingly. Second, third, and fourth chances have been sought and squandered.

If so, show them the story of the King Manasseh of Judah in 2 Chronicles 33.

To see the significance of this text, you must compare it with 2 Kings 21. By comparing the two texts, one can see how the author has "selected" the material to make his point. Remember that both the respective authors of Kings and Chronicles are writing about the same events, but during different time periods, from different perspectives, and to different populations.

Let's start with 2 Kings 21. Go ahead and read the account.

As detailed in the Historical Tools section, the author of 2 Kings is writing from the exile. Having experienced the devastation and the despair, his account of the nation's history explains the theological

*The story of King Manasseh in 2 Chronicles 33 demonstrates
the great forgiveness of God and also shows how the Hebrew
authors used selection to further their points.*

"why" of the exile. For what reason are the Israelites now experiencing their greatest crisis of faith in Babylon?

This author places the blame squarely at the feet of the Davidic kings. These kings should have led the people in right covenant relationship. These kings should have modeled righteousness and Torah obedience (Deut 17:14–20). These kings should have maintained the singular allegiance to Yahweh (Deut 6:4–5). Instead, monarch after monarch manifestly failed both God and the people.

Exhibit A for the author of the book of Kings was Manasseh. As outlined above, this son of the godly King Hezekiah had squandered every benefit, every promise, and every opportunity to lead the Israelites in a faithful manner. Instead, he had participated in the extreme opposite of everything righteous. According to the author, Manasseh reigned for fifty-five years in Jerusalem, and his sole occupation was idolatry. He constructed idols in the temple (2 Kgs 21:3–5). He sacrificed his own son through fire (v. 6). He filled Jerusalem from one end to the other with innocent blood (v. 16). He was even worse than the Canaanites (v. 9)

For these reasons, God would wipe Jerusalem as one wipes a dish (v. 13). The entire nation, and especially the capital of Jerusalem, would be held to account for the sins of this wayward Davidic king.

We get to the end of the story, and the author, in 21:17–18, simply states, "The rest of the events of Manasseh's reign, along with all his accomplishments and the sin that he committed, are written in the Historical Record of Judah's Kings. Manasseh rested with his fathers and was buried in the garden of his own house, the garden of Uzza. His son Amon became king in his place."

So according to the author of Kings, Manasseh did a bunch of evil junk and then died. And because of him, exile came, and nothing—not even the righteous King Josiah who reigned shortly after Manasseh—could stop the inevitable. No repentance. No forgiveness. No hope.

Now consider the account in 2 Chronicles 33. Notice any differences.

Before we point these out, let's recall the purpose and context of Chronicles. This author—the Chronicler—is "chronicling" the same history (level-1 historical context) as the historian behind Samuel–Kings. But he is writing from the postexile, rather than the exile, to a despondent and apathetic and hopeless people—so he has a different level-2 context. The Israelites were out of Babylon but still under Persian rule. They had a temple, but not like Solomon's. They were back in the land, but the people continued to disobey Torah. The Davidic line remained, but those descendants did not sit on any throne. Could God forgive the nation after so much sin and apostasy? Will God's kingdom and God's covenant ever be restored?

The Chronicler writes his history in a way to encourage hope in God's restoration. As mentioned above, this hope is focused primarily on the Davidic king. But the author brings hope in other ways as well. One way is to show the possibility of repentance and forgiveness through his retelling of the history.

Now, what about 2 Chronicles 33? Well, the author begins the account the same way as the author of 2 Kings 21, telling of all the evil of Manasseh. Indeed, it seems even worse here. For instance, the Chronicler clarifies that Manasseh actually sacrificed his "sons" through fire to pagan gods (v. 6).

But then we get to verses 10–13:

> The LORD spoke to Manasseh and his people, but they didn't listen. So he brought against them the military commanders of the king of Assyria. They captured Manasseh with hooks, bound him with bronze shackles, and took him to Babylon. When he was in distress, he sought the favor of the LORD his God and earnestly humbled himself before the God of his ancestors. He prayed to him, and the LORD was receptive to his prayer. He granted his request and brought him back to Jerusalem, to his kingdom. So Manasseh came to know that the LORD is God.

What? Manasseh repented? God restored him? This idolatrous king even removed the idols (v. 15)? Why didn't the author of Kings tell us this? Simple: That wasn't his purpose. That author had "selected" his material to show the "why" of the exile.

On the contrary, the Chronicler selects his material to show the possibility of restoration and forgiveness after the exile. Are these stories contradictory? No. They are told for different purposes. Think about it. You could probably do the same thing in retelling the events of your life. You could select happenings from your life to show you to be the most righteous person ever. Alternatively, you might also select events that reveal you to be a pretty rank pagan.

But notice the way the author of Chronicles tells of what happened to Manasseh. He failed to listen to God. He was punished by being taken to "Babylon"—not Assyria, even though he was captured by the Assyrians. He was dragged away with bronze hooks in his nose. These are the very things that happened to the Jews in the exile. In a way, Manasseh becomes paradigmatic for the nation itself.

But Manasseh, one of the kings responsible for the exile, repents. And God "was receptive to his prayer" (v. 13), so that Manasseh knew his God—a sign of restored covenant relationship.

What is the author's point? If Manasseh, the most reprehensible person any Jew can remember and the one responsible for the nation's exile, can be forgiven, so can the Jews as a whole. God can restore and forgive the Jews in the postexile; they were not "too far gone." But the only way to see that message is by comparing the texts and examining the selection and context of the authors—in other words, by using the tools.

By the way, if God can forgive Manasseh, he can also forgive any of us who believe that we are "too far gone."

Applying the Results

The following will offer two possible trajectories for application using what we have learned from the Historical Books.

Jesus as Messiah, the Anointed Davidic King

A single word can be crammed with meaning.

For instance, the mere mention of Christmas can evoke images of sparkling lights, smiling children, joyful carols, and jovial Santas. As we have seen, biblical words are no different. Terms like covenant, law, loving-kindness, and even the word *word* itself overflow with scriptural significance.

In the well-known story of the magi's visit to Jesus found in Matthew 2, we find one of most important and loaded scriptural words,

Messiah (v. 4). Modern-day Christians often gloss over this term as just another name for Jesus, without fully appreciating its depth and import.

But to Matthew's audience of Jewish Christians, that title brought to mind hopes, images, and promises, steeped in OT tradition, particularly as found in the Historical Books. The word also induced strong responses among the characters in Matthew's account—King Herod and the magi.

Appreciating the background of Jesus's messiahship from the Historical Books can help us to grasp the significance of our Lord more fully and can inspire us to do what the magi did—bow before the Savior. The following will explore the OT word *Messiah* and examine the proper response to the One who held that designation.

First, some initial clues to the Old Testament understanding of the Messiah are found in the text of Matthew 2 itself.

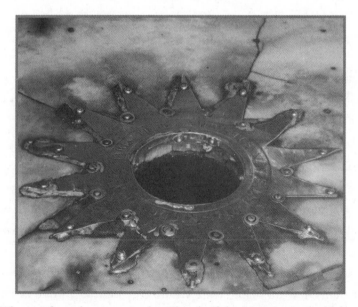

The star from the grotto in the Church of the Nativity in Bethlehem.
The star supposedly marks the place where Jesus was born.

Matthew indicates that the Messiah will "rule" (v. 6) as king. As the magi state, the Messiah will be "king of the Jews" (v. 2). Indeed, the Hebrew term *Messiah* ("anointed one") is clearly a royal title.

But the messianic ruler Matthew references is not just any king. As we have seen in this chapter, the Messiah in the OT is inseparable from King David (1 Sam 2:10; 2 Samuel 7; Pss 2:2; 89:20; 132:17). And Matthew makes this connection very clear. In quoting Mic 5:2, Matthew indicates that the Messiah would hail from David's home-town—Bethlehem (1 Samuel 16). So too, in using the verb *shepherd*, Matthew makes another allusion to David.

Why is it significant that Jesus is a King from the line of David? Like David (Deut 17:15), Jesus would be the King whom Yahweh has chosen. Like David (1 Kgs 11:33–38; 14:8), Jesus would keep Yahweh's Torah and commandments and possess exceptional spiritual quality. Like David (2 Sam 7:14–15), Jesus would have a father-son relationship with God and be the object of God's loving-kindness.

But though David served as the example against whom all subsequent Israelite kings were measured (1 Kgs 15:3; 2 Kgs 18:3), he was still flawed—and dead. Thus, later biblical writers would refer to and anticipate another "anointed one" in David's line who would surpass David in every way.

By citing Mic 5:2, Matthew unmistakably demonstrates the Messiah's superiority to his predecessor. Though he, like David, would be born in Bethlehem, the Messiah's "origin is from antiquity, from ancient times." And the greatness of the messianic kingdom would extend "to the ends of the earth" (Mic 5:4)—unlike David's provincial realm.

Other verses in the OT also prophesy of the Messiah's incomparability. This new messianic King would rule on the "throne of David" eternally in fulfillment of the Davidic covenant (2 Samuel 7) and would even be called Mighty God (Isa 9:6–7). His reign would be universal (Isa 49:6), and ultimately, all the nations will resort to this Root of Jesse

(Isa 11:10). Perhaps this is the reason Matthew included the account of the magi in the first place. Matthew shows that the Messiah will receive worship not merely from Jews, but from all peoples.

This messianic King would also outshine his ancestor, David, spiritually. God's Spirit would rest on him (Isa 11:2; 42:1) and righteousness and faithfulness would be as his belt (Isa 11:5). In fact, the very name of this "righteous Branch" of David would be "The LORD Is Our Righteousness" (Jer 23:5–6). How important is this righteousness for us? Remember that God viewed (and views) his people through the lens of the king. But our King Jesus is perfectly righteous. And we are included into his covenant people not because of our righteousness, but because of that of our King's.

And all this is packed into one word, *Messiah*. Is this how we think of the Messiah, Jesus Christ? It is easy to allow the world to define who Jesus was and is. We should strive to make our conceptions of the Messiah scripturally based.

But how should we react to such a Messiah? As we noted above, the term *Christmas* for many induces warm imagery and emotions. However, some do not react to the term as positively. The same is true with the word *Messiah*. In Matthew 2, the news that the Messiah had come inspired contrasting responses from Herod and the magi.

Having governed Judea for almost forty years, Herod felt threatened by the Messiah. Herod acted as "king" (Matt 2:1), and he took drastic measures to preserve his dominion, often killing those who opposed him. The Messiah's advent did not please him at all; because of his fear and suspicion, "he was deeply disturbed, and all Jerusalem with him" (v. 3). Though he espoused a desire to worship the Messiah, in actuality he hated him.

Similar reactions are seen today. An orthodox, scriptural presentation of Jesus Christ as Messiah, Lord, and only Savior often evokes hatred of the message, the messenger, and especially Christ himself. The gospel is an offense (1 Cor 1:18–25). As Christians, we should expect opposition to our message (2 Tim 3:12). But like the apostles and Jesus himself, such antagonism should not discourage us from sharing the Good News; nor should it deter our worship of Christ.

Herod's rage did not daunt the magi from the east, who model for us the second type of reaction to the Messiah—worship. Foreigners and strangers to the covenant, the magi traveled great distances, followed an evasive star, and sacrificed much—all for the opportunity of seeing and worshiping a promised King.

Many Christians are dissuaded from worship of this same Messiah by persecution and worldly pleasures. Let us commit to be like the magi. Despite "Herodian" opposition, let us bow in worship before our Savior.

A Teacher like Ezra

At the institution where I teach, professors are required to outline their "philosophy of teaching." Mine is based on my "life verse" from the Historical Books: Ezra 7:10.[38]

This text states that Ezra "had determined in his heart to study the law of the LORD, obey it, and teach its statutes and ordinances in Israel."

Yes, I know few biblical texts and characters exist for the purpose of providing examples. And I know the primary goal of this text is to show God rebuilding his covenant community in the postexile. But I can't help but suspect that Ezra also intended this text to set an example for the spiritual leadership of God's people—the teachers of the Holy Scriptures, for his time and for subsequent generations.

---

[38] My choice of this verse as a "life verse" is again influenced by my mentor and PhD supervisor, Daniel I. Block. Dr. Block keeps this verse as his own life verse and models it daily in his life and ministry. I am indebted to him for much of the knowledge imparted in these chapters. More than that, I am indebted to him for his example. He wrote on this verse in "Training Scribes and Pastors in the Tradition of Ezra," *Southern Seminary Magazine* 67, no. 2 (June 1999): 3–6.

Thus, I take the text as a personal challenge and paradigmatic pattern for pedagogy. In the same way, many of the readers of this book will be Bible teachers—possibly in the church, but definitely in the home. The verse can provide a healthy model for your own biblical instruction.

How so?

This verse explains how Ezra first committed himself to the study of God's Word with all his being, intellect, and passion. Teachers—especially Bible teachers—should also begin with this commitment. The Hebrew verb *to teach* used in this verse is an intensive/factitive form of the verb that usually means "to learn."

Ezra "had determined in his heart to study the law of the Lord, obey it, and teach its statutes and ordinances in Israel."

So scriptural teaching should engage in *intensive* study alongside the students as an example to them, resulting in their learning *in fact*.

The subject matter of Ezra's study is also crucial. He studied the Torah—which was his Scripture. What about Bible teachers? Obviously, they should study the Bible. Only in the Scriptures does one find the words of life. Only in the Scriptures does one find God's authoritative and definitive will revealed. And only in the Scriptures does one find Jesus Christ revealed, as Savior and Sovereign.

But Ezra did not merely study, as is the temptation for so many teachers in academia. He applied. For him, the study of Scripture was not just academic; it was driven by a desire to integrate the timeless truths of Scripture into all of life.

For modern Bible teachers, including you, the Scriptures are the basis and guide for each aspect of your life—whether that is in the church, home, or place of ministry. If you are a Bible teacher, pray that your students will see that scriptural faith actually exhibited in your life—whether in the home, church, or classroom. And commit to open your life to your students so that they will have opportunity to witness this demonstration.

Finally, Ezra dedicated himself to teaching God's Word. The importance of this instruction for Ezra is obvious, based on the discussion of the book above. The reestablishment of fidelity to Torah was essential to avoiding another potential judgment from God. It was essential to a healthy covenant community of faith. So too is the faithful teaching of God's Word essential to healthy churches, healthy families, and healthy Christians.

Notice also the order of Ezra's qualifications: study, practice, then teach. Only when Bible teachers have studied and practiced should they consider themselves viable teachers. Far too many teachers of the Bible confuse the order and may appear pridefully unprepared, scripturally vacuous, and grossly hypocritical.

To summarize, like Ezra, every Bible teacher should seek to engender within their students a love and passion to study God's inspired, inerrant Word; to enter into and invest in the lives of the students, for through them future generations and the church itself can be influenced for Christ; and to teach and encourage the students in not only intellectual achievement, but also in Christian discipleship, discipline, and humility, so that the entire person is trained.

Application Questions

1. How have you heard 1 Samuel 17 (David and Goliath) preached in the past? What things can we learn from this passage? How does the previous chapter change your view?

2. How would you tell the history of the United States if you approached it like a Hebrew historian?

3. How should Christians handle the issue of the destruction of the Canaanites? Is this a difficult issue for you personally?

4. What would you have done in Rahab's situation? Do you think it is wrong to lie if it preserves someone else's life?

5. What aspects of the book of Judges do you see in today's society or in today's church? Would you agree with the statement that many in the church have become "Canaanized"?

6. How have you observed God's hidden providence (as seen in the books of Ruth and Esther) in your own life?

7. How are the promises given to David in 2 Samuel 7 fulfilled in Jesus? Does this change your perception of Jesus as Messiah?

8. What ultimately led to Solomon's failure as described in 1 Kings 11–12? How could a king who was responsible for the Proverbs and known for wisdom fall into this type of sin? What can we learn from his negative example?

9. Why does the author attribute the fall of Israel to idolatry in 2 Kings 17? Why does he not cite political or military issues? What would comprise idolatry today? Why do you think God takes this sin so seriously?

10. Read Ezra 1:1–4 in light of Isa 44:24–45:7 (written some 200 years earlier). What does the return from exile by the hand of the Persian king Cyrus say about the sovereignty of God?

11. What is important about the order of Ezra's qualifications in Ezra 7:10? That is, if you want to teach, why should you study and practice first?

12. Can you identify with Nehemiah's passion for the things of God? What other aspects of Nehemiah's character are to be emulated?

13. What does the book of Esther say about the providence of God? Do you find it odd that a book in the canon would not even mention the name of God? Why do you think this is so?

6

Tools for Interpreting the Poetry and Wisdom Books

When my wife and I honeymooned in Plymouth, Massachusetts, we chose to drive the entire way. I know a twenty-hour car ride on your honeymoon sounds like a bad idea, but it was really quite nice. On the way, we visited places like Hershey, Pennsylvania, as well as Amish Country and New York City.

One place that I especially wanted to tour was Princeton University—a theological promised land of sorts in the United States and the producer of great theologians from church history such as B. B. Warfield, Charles Hodge, Jonathan Edwards, J. Greshem Machen, Gerhardus Vos, and Cornelius Van Til.

We pulled onto campus only to find it full of activity. Apparently, some big event was going on. Students everywhere. Cars everywhere. We finally found a place to park—right near a rather ostentatious Porsche.

The chapel at Princeton University.

A security guard informed us that the hustle and bustle was due to Jerry Seinfeld being on campus. Imagine my disappointment that a school with such history had reduced itself to having a comedian speak.

My disappointment changed to curiosity when the security guard pointed out that the car we had parked beside was actually one of Seinfeld's many Porsches. I thought, "No one back home will ever believe this."

So I did what anyone would do. I had my bride take my picture in front of it. Some people have selfies with celebrities. I have a selfie with a celebrity car.

To be honest, I took the picture so that folks back home might do two things—*see* and *appreciate*, but then also *respond*. "Yes, I see and appreciate you were standing beside Seinfeld's car, and I confess that you are the coolest college professor ever."

The Poetry and Wisdom Books of the Old Testament (OT) have this same provocative purpose. Sure, these beloved books present beautiful pictures of God in all his glory and of the anticipated Messiah. They contain practical wisdom, striking poetry, probing proverbs. However, like my picture, these books exist not only to inform the intellect and captivate the eyes, as some piece of ordinary literature or artwork; but the Spirit also works through the books of Job, Psalms, Proverbs, Ecclesiastes, and Song of Songs to change us *and* elicit a response.

As Paul states, these books are not only "inspired" or God-breathed, but also "profitable" (2 Tim 3:16). Indeed, what famous Baptist preacher C. H. Spurgeon[1] said about the Psalms[2] can also be said of all the Poetry and Wisdom Books: "The delightful study of the Psalms has yielded me boundless profit and ever-growing pleasure."

Understanding the Tools

But as with the other Old Testament books, we need to use the tools to profit from these texts.

Historical Tools

As always, the first tool to grab when analyzing a biblical text is that of historical context. For the first time, however, we find books in which the historical context is beneficial but not exegetically essential. The primary reason is that for these five books, the historical context tends to be ambiguous.

---

[1] "Charles Spurgeon," *Wikipedia*, last modified March 5, 2019, https://en.wikipedia.org/wiki/Charles_Spurgeon.

[2] AZ Quotes, https://www.azquotes.com/quote/1369306.

Historical Context of Psalms

Take the book of Psalms, for example. The psalms were composed and collected over a thousand-year period—nearly the time span of the entire OT itself. The earliest psalm is attributed to Moses (Psalm 90) and the last psalms date to at least the postexile (e.g., Psalm 126). Yet the specific historical situation of most is unclear.

Of the 150 individual compositions in the book, some 116 contain a type of heading, which in English shows up in the text as a super-scription.[3] These headings contain information on the person or group connected to the psalm (see Psalms 3, 72, 90) or musical/liturgical[4] notes (see Psalms 38, 70, 92, 100). Many of these superscriptions also provide some historical traditions behind the individual psalms—particularly from the life of David. In fact, numerous psalms are ascribed to David as the author. And some in Jewish history have attributed all 150 to him.

Although these traditions have a rich history and the book of Psalms is undoubtedly a "Davidic" document (i.e., focused on the Davidic king), the superscriptions are not part of the original text and thus do not rise to the level of inerrancy. So although the historical headings may help us to appreciate the way the Jews traditionally have read them (e.g., Psalm 51, which expresses David's repentance after his adultery with Bathsheba) and they give us an important clue on how to view them (through the eyes of the king), most psalm superscriptions do not provide enough firm details for us to be confident about their historical background.

---

[3] In the Hebrew text, the headings often are verse 1 and are not separated out.

[4] "Liturgy," *Wikipedia*, last modified February 17, 2019, https://en.wikipedia.org/wiki/Liturgy.

The Poetry and Wisdom books exist not only to inform the intellect and captivate the eyes, but the Spirit also works through the books of Job, Psalms, Proverbs, Ecclesiastes, and Song of Songs to change us and elicit a response.

Historical Context of Proverbs

Like the Psalms, Proverbs also has a traditional ascription—this time to David's son, Solomon. This ascription is more probable—with chapters 1–24 likely written by this famously wise king. However, other parts of the book are written or commissioned by others—such as the good King Hezekiah (chaps. 25–29) and the mysterious King Lemuel (chap. 31). Nevertheless, such ascriptions add little to our understanding of the meaning and significance of the original text. Although knowing the author here is interesting and adds color to the text, identifying the actual historical circumstance of the writing would be more helpful. Yet this original setting in life is unclear with Proverbs.

Here, Solomon is pictured acting as a wise arbiter between two women claiming a baby (1 Kgs 3:16-28). Proverbs 1-24 are attributed to this famously wise king.

Historical Context of Song of Songs and Ecclesiastes

Song of Songs (traditionally called Song of Solomon) and Ecclesiastes are also historically attributed to Solomon. Both of these determinations are based on the first verses of the respective books. In Song of Songs, however, the opening phrase "which is Solomon's" could mean in the original Hebrew "dedicated to Solomon" or "about Solomon." And in Ecclesiastes, although the author—the "Preacher" or "Qoheleth" in the Hebrew—is described as a "son of David" and "king in Jerusalem," he is never definitively identified as Solomon. Surely the excesses described in the book as enjoyed by Qoheleth would match those of the legendarily opulent king. But this context is not absolutely certain.

Thus, many scholars more cautiously label Ecclesiastes and Song of Songs as anonymous.

Historical Context of Job

The historicity of Job perhaps ranks as the most controversial among these books. Also officially anonymous, Job has been variously identified as the earliest OT book (even before the Pentateuch) and as one of the latest—a postexilic document (at the end of the OT period).

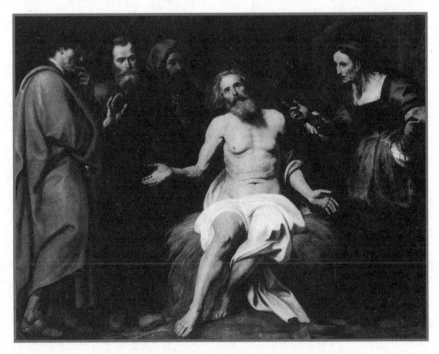

Job is definitely a historical figure, but not much is known about the level-2 context of the book.

Certainly, the original narrative bookends of the book (chaps. 1–2 and 42) seem to arise out of a patriarchal period (i.e., the time of Genesis 12–50), thus making the story itself seem early. And Job is definitely a historical figure (see Ezek 14:14; James 5:11).

Less confidence exists concerning the poetic discourses, which comprise the bulk of the book. Undoubtedly, these soliloquys are accurate portrayals of the substance of the events, but the author has certainly shaped them theologically and rhetorically to make his points. In other words, in all likelihood, some years separate the level-1 and level-2 historical contexts of the book, and the level-2 context is uncertain.

Literary Tools

Given the historical ambiguity of these books, the literary tools of structure, genre, and other literary/theological features become essential to a proper understanding. As with the other chapters, one of the most important literary tools is that of genre.

Each of the books—Job, Psalms, Proverbs, Ecclesiastes, and Song of Songs—possesses its own unique and specialized genre, which will be detailed below. But primarily, they all, save perhaps Ecclesiastes, make profuse use of poetic verse. After all, they are the *Poetry* and Wisdom Books. And this poetry communicates the message in powerful ways.

Genre—Poetry

Every now and then, I like "jamming" to some older folk music. One of my favorites in this genre is Jim Croce, a singer-songwriter who died in a plane crash in 1973, the year after I was born. Croce is perhaps most famous for his Billboard chart-topper, "Bad, Bad, Leroy Brown," which I won't sing for you.[5] Of Croce's ditties, though, I best love "I'll

---

[5] "Jim Croce—Bad Bad Leroy Brown," YouTube video, 3:04, posted by deathbybulletsmg42, March 13, 2010, https://www.youtube.com/watch?v

Have to Say I Love You in a Song." Question: Why did Jim have to say "I love you" in that way—in a song? Couldn't he just say it through a text or email or tweet?

No, Croce said "I love you" in poetic verse because the form of expression communicates as much as the words themselves. The same is true for the poetry of the Poetry and Wisdom Books.

As biblical scholar Robert Alter notes, the scriptural author's  "delight in the suppleness and serendipities of poetic form is not a distraction from the seriousness of the poems but his chief means of realizing his spiritual vision, and it is one source of the power these poems continue to have not only to excite our imaginations but also to engage our lives."[6]

So to access these texts, one must possess a basic knowledge of Hebraic poetic techniques.

For most English readers, poetry is characterized by rhyme and rhythm—or what we might character-

Why did singer Jim Croce have to say I love you in a song?

ize as correspondences in sound between lyrical lines. So for example, "Mary had a little lamb, whose fleece was white as snow. Everywhere

---

=QvwDohEEQ1E.

   [6] Robert Alter, *The Art of Biblical Poetry*, rev. ed. (New York: Basic Books, 2011), 170.

that Mary went, the lamb was sure to go." Here, "snow" and "go" rhyme, and the meter, or pattern of beat, of the two lines match.

On the contrary, Hebrew poetry rarely employs these techniques. And even if it did use rhyme and meter, these would not translate from one language to another. Try translating "Mary had a little lamb" into Russian, and see if it still rhymes.[7]

Instead, ancient Hebrew writers exploited poetic techniques that are much more conceptual—a correspondence in ideas: "Mary had a little lamb; the young girl one from the flock." The advantage of this style, in God's providence, is that conceptual correspondence translates well from one language (Hebrew) to another (English or Russian or any other).

The defining linguistic characteristic of Hebrew poetry is called "parallelism." If I said you and I have "parallel" lives, I might point to our corresponding backgrounds or experiences. With parallelism in poetry as well, we are looking at lines of poetry that correspond in some way—whether that is in vocabulary, syntactical structure, meaning, or thought. The purpose of parallelism can be for intensification or specification or further explanation.

Old Testament scholar Robert Lowth first categorized the types of parallelism seen in the Hebrew text in 1753. He suggested three primary types:

- Synonymous: repetition of the same thought (Pss 15:1; 19:1; 24:1; Prov 9:10)
- Antithetic: joining of two contrasting thoughts (Ps 1:6; Prov 10:2, 4, 7)
- Synthetic: the second line completes the thought of the first in some way (Pss 1:3; 2:6; Eccl 11:1)

---

[7] Google Translate, "mary had a little lamb," https://translate.google.com/?oe=utf-8&client=firefox-b-1-ab&um=1&ie=UTF-8&hl=en&client=tw-ob#auto/ru/mary%20had%20a%20little%20lamb.

While helpful, limitations and low points exist with Lowth's method. For instance, the synthetic category is too broad and becomes a catch-all category. In my class on the Poetry and Wisdom Books, I introduce about twenty different categories. But Lowth's method does at least teach the concept. And parallelism is definitely something to note as you read and study biblical poetic texts.

Another dominant feature of Hebrew poetry is one also found in English poetry: a concentration of figurative language. One finds figures of speech involving comparison (metaphors,[8] similes,[9] personification,[10] anthropomorphism,[11] anthropopathism,[12] hypocatastasis,[13] zoomorphism,[14] etc.), figures of speech involving substitution (metonymy,[15] synecdoche,[16] merisms,[17] euphemism,[18]

---

[8] "Metaphors," *Wikipedia*, last modified March 5, 2019, https://en.wikipedia.org/wiki/Metaphor.

[9] "Simile," *Wikipedia*, last modified February 13, 2019, https://en.wikipedia.org/wiki/Simile.

[10] "Personification in the Bible," *Wikipedia*, last modified March 14, 2018, https://en.wikipedia.org/wiki/Personification_in_the_Bible.

[11] "Anthropomorphism," *Wikipedia*, last modified March 6, 2019, https://en.wikipedia.org/wiki/Anthropomorphism.

[12] "Anthropopathism," *Wikipedia*, last modified May 16, 2018, https://en.wikipedia.org/wiki/Anthropopathism.

[13] "Hypocatastasis," *Wikipedia*, last modified October 19, 2017, https://en.wikipedia.org/wiki/Hypocatastasis.

[14] "Zoomorphism," *Wikipedia*, last modified January 30, 2019, https://en.wikipedia.org/wiki/Zoomorphism.

[15] "Metonymy," *Wikipedia*, last modified February 17, 2019, https://en.wikipedia.org/wiki/Metonymy.

[16] "Synechdoche," *Wikipedia*, last modified March 6, 2019, https://en.wikipedia.org/wiki/Synecdoche.

[17] "Merisms," *Wikipedia*, last modified October 29, 2018, https://en.wikipedia.org/wiki/Merism.

[18] "Euphemism," *Wikipedia*, last modified February 28, 2019, https://en.wikipedia.org/wiki/Euphemism.

hendiadys,[19] etc.), and figures of speech involving addition (hyperbole[20] and repetition in its many forms such as anadiplosis, anaphora, epistrophe,[21] etc.).

Finally, other prominent characteristics of Hebrew poetry include

- Unusual word order: Hebrew prose usually follows a verb–subject–object order, but Hebrew poetry (as with English) defies grammatical conventions.
- Unusual vocabulary: Hebrew poems tend to be transmitted as received and orally recited, and thus preserve archaic words (like modern hymnals, with their "thee"s and "thou"s).
- Terseness: If the Hebrew poet can say it with fewer and more powerful words, he usually does.
- Intense emotion: Compare the news-article-like narrative of Judg 4:17–22 with the celebratory and poetic rendering of the same event in Judg 5:24–27.
- The use of word pairs: Hebrew poets often make word associations between parallel lines, such as man/woman, earth/heaven, left/right, and steadfast love/faithfulness.

There's delight in noticing all of these poetic techniques. But, as with English poetry, you always want to ask the "why" question. Why does the author express his thoughts this way? Why does Jim Croce say "I love you" in a song?

---

[19] "Hendiadys," *Wikipedia*, last modified October 29, 2018, https://en.wikipedia.org/wiki/Hendiadys.

[20] "Hyperbole," *Wikipedia*, last modified March 5, 2019, https://en.wikipedia.org/wiki/Hyperbole.

[21] "Repitition (rhetorical)," *Wikipedia*, last modified February 19, 2019, https://en.wikipedia.org/wiki/Repetition_(rhetorical_device).

Other Genres

Although poetry is the main medium in these books, other, more specific, genres are found in Job, Psalms, Proverbs, Ecclesiastes, and Song of Songs. These genre identifications are just as crucial to understanding the books. Three examples will suffice: the genres of Proverbs, Psalms, and Song of Songs.

Genre—Proverbs. While Proverbs contains longer discourses (chaps. 1–9), a good majority of this book (chaps. 10–24) contains what we would typically consider a proverb—short (often two-line), pithy, practical, and parallel maxims, urging wisdom over folly, righteousness over wickedness, industry over sloth, and purity over indulgence. But misunderstanding this genre can lead to unfortunate results.

Let's consider one example. Proverbs 22:6 states, "Start a youth out on his way; even when he grows old he will not depart from it." How should we interpret this? As a universal truth that always occurs? That's what many might expect to "get out of" a proverb like this.

But are proverbs universal truths that are always applicable? In our example, what happens if parents do all they can, raise the child rightly in the nurture and admonition of Christ, and the child still goes astray? Did they do something wrong? Should they feel guilty?

No. Though the proverbs often contain absolutes, in many cases, they are simply general observations on life that are true most of the time. So, generally speaking, if you raise a child in the proper manner, she will not stray. But not always.

For another great example of the proverbs as general truths, see Prov 26:4–5: "Don't answer a fool according to his foolishness or you'll be like him yourself. Answer a fool according to his foolishness or he'll become wise in his own eyes." In this text, which is it? Should you answer a fool or not? It depends on the situation, correct? It depends on someone rightly applying wisdom to know how to act with regard to the fool.

Proverbs 22:6 states, "Start a youth out on his way; even when he grows old he will not depart from it." How should we interpret this? As a universal truth that always occurs?

So with a proverb, as with other genres, the most important rule is: do not force ancient types of literature to conform to modern ways of interpreting them.

Genre—Psalms. For the book of Psalms, genre identification also is a crucial tool in proper interpretation. As stated above, all the psalms are poetic. But scholars have long identified more specific genres among the compositions. These are often called psalm "types." What governs these types is not so much the content of the psalm, but the form, structure, and original situation in life of the song.

The three basic categories include praise psalms, lament psalms, and thanksgiving psalms. Praise psalms typically include exhortations to praise God along with the rationale for this praise. Psalm 117, the shortest "chapter" in the Bible, is a great example, but many more praise psalms inhabit the Psalter—a fact that shouldn't surprise us, since the Hebrew title of the book, *Tehillim,* means "praises." See Psalms 8, 29, 33, and 146–150 for other examples.

Lament psalms—which surprisingly comprise almost a third of the Psalter—contain honest and often raw appeals to God concerning crisis situations. Most often, they begin with a question or protest directed at God, but then they typically move from hurt and darkness to hope and light (but see Psalm 88). For examples, see Psalms 3, 12, 13, 22, 74, and 130. The inclusion of these laments in the Bible is important and instructive to our life of faith. God provides in his revelation opportunities for his people to voice grief and mourning and questions directly to him. So it is okay to express such raw emotion in your personal devotion and in corporate services of worship.

The last major type is the thanksgiving psalm. These psalms express awareness of pain, but that pain passes as one professes gratitude for God's demonstrated saving power and grace. See Psalms 104, 107, 116, and 136.

Other minor psalm types include penitential psalms, in which the psalmist appeals for forgiveness (Psalms 6, 32, 38, 51, 102, 130, and 143); imprecatory psalms, in which the psalmist petitions for justice to be meted out on his enemies (Psalms 35, 69, 109, and 137); and Torah psalms, in which the psalmist praises God for his covenantal revelation (Psalms 1, 19, and 119). Many others have been identified as well.

Most important for biblical theology are the royal and messianic psalms. These focus on God's rule in his kingdom as realized primarily in his Davidic king and his future Messiah (Psalms 18, 20, 21, 45, 72, 89, 93, and 95–99; see esp. Psalms 2, 22, and 110 as examples of specifically messianic psalms). These will be explored more in the Theological Tools section below.

With all of these types, one should realize that not every psalm will have a discernible genre. And some will have characteristics of multiple types—for example, Psalm 1 is both a Torah and a wisdom psalm. But by comparing and contrasting psalms of the same type, one can often discern the point being made by the author. *See video in Wordsearch for an example.*

Genre—Song of Songs. None of the Poetry and Wisdom Books has divided interpreters on the issue of genre more than Song of Songs. Just read the first chapter and see how quickly you blush. Undoubtedly, the sexual subject matter and the "adult" content creates a certain awkwardness for the reader—especially in corporate settings. Because of this, throughout the early history of the church, many preferred to view the book allegorically. That is, the love relationship celebrated by the Song pointed to and expressed the love of Christ for his church (or God for his people in the OT).

Some of the allegorical reaches were quite creative: the woman's skin represented sin (1:5); the lovers' kisses represented the Word of God; and so forth. Indeed, there were other, more "imaginative" connections that will remain unstated here.

Yes, the Bible does compare the relationship of God/Christ and his covenant people to a marriage relationship (see Jeremiah 2; Hosea 1–3; Eph 5:22–32, among many). But is that the original intent of this author—to explain God's relationship to his people in sexual terms? Probably not.

I believe a more natural reading is that the Song is what it appears to be at first glance—a genuine, wholesome, beautiful, and sensual love poem between a husband and bride. The Song's close resemblance to ancient Near Eastern love poetry seconds this assessment. With its delicate, lyrical, and unsullied celebration of the God-ordained sexual union, the Song provides a properly oriented sexually charged book for a promiscuously oriented sexually charged culture. See below for more on this purpose.

Literary Context

Our final literary tool to use with the Poetry and Wisdom Books is that of the structure, message, and purpose of the individual books. Remember that literary context is about determining where a passage occurs in the course of the book and why. So these big-picture depictions of the books (e.g., their structure, message, and purpose) are indispensable tools in discerning the literary context of individual texts.

Literary Structure/Message/Purpose—Job. The best-known narrative of the Poetry and Wisdom Books is undoubtedly that of Job. But for most readers, the narrative is all that is known.

And indeed, the story is powerful. A blameless, affluent God-fearer has his wealth, health, and progeny stripped from him by Satan, after this "accuser" gains God's permission to take them. Job struggles to comprehend his misfortune, asking for an audience with God to obtain an explanation. Meanwhile, Job's "friends" urge him to repent of sins that in their mind brought on this curse. At the end of the story, Job has his prosperity restored, his friends are rebuked by God, and "then Job died, old and full of days" (42:17).

What does this text teach? Many believe that the text is about the issue of why bad things happen to good people or the problem of evil (theodicy).[22] The problem with those assertions is that, though bad things are definitely happening to a good Job, the question of "why" they happen is never really answered for the lead human character.

Instead, the author seems to emphasize two principal messages.

The first is the rejection of a mechanical application of divine retribution—the idea that good deeds always bring blessing and bad deeds

---

[22] "Theodicy," *Wikipedia*, last modified February 18, 2019, https://en .wikipedia.org/wiki/Theodicy.

always bring cursing from God. Job is described as one who fears God and turns away from evil (1:1). According to Proverbs, these should result in "healing for your body and strengthening for your bones" (3:7–8). At the same time, those whose house is cursed must be wicked (3:33), correct? At least, this is what Job's friends maintain.

However, besides being poor counselors, Job's friends are bad at logic. Yes, Proverbs asserts that in general (see the discussion on genre above), evil produces cursing and righteousness produces blessing. But just because you suffer doesn't necessarily mean that you are a sinner in need of repentance. In other words, "if X then Y" does not imply "if Y then X." For example, if I am a car, then I have an engine. But just because I have an engine doesn't necessarily imply that I am a car. I could be a lawn mower or motorcycle.

In addition, God cannot be placed in a box where something "has to happen" as if God is some cosmic gumball machine. Put in your righteousness coin and get blessing out. Put in your naughtiness nickel and get a curse. But God is free. God is sovereign. And God is at times mysterious and definitely not mechanical.

A second issue, and I believe the main message of the book, deals with the question of faith. In the narrative in chapter 1, Satan asks a good question of God. In verse 9, he queries, "Does Job fear God for nothing?" In other words, is Job's faith merely based on his circumstances (in this case, his blessed life) that can change at any point, or is it based in the unchanging character of God?

Throughout the important and often ignored poetic discourse between Job and his friends, Job's faith is tested. Indeed, he questions repeatedly why bad things have happened to him. Interestingly, though, his question is never answered. Instead, God responds in a different manner with a different answer to a different question. God finally grants Job's request for an audience and reveals the fullness of his fearful sovereignty (chaps. 38–41).

The message of Job is this: the kind of faith that endures the changing tides of fortune in this life is not one based on mutable circumstances, but upon a powerful and providential and immutable God.

Remarkably, this revelation of God's unchanging character satisfies Job. In fact, he regains a healthy fear of Yahweh—a faith in an unchanging covenant Lord. So the message of the book is this: the kind of faith that endures the changing tides of fortune in this life is not one based on mutable circumstances, but upon a powerful and providential and immutable God.

Literary Structure/Message/Purpose—Psalms. Perhaps no OT book is read and cherished more than the Psalms. And rightly so. The main reason is that they are readily relatable. The psalms speak of every conceivable human emotion—doubt and devotion, praise and pain, thanksgiving and trust, sorrow and shame.

As the early church father Athanasius wrote, while most of Scripture speaks to us, the psalms speak for us.[23] C. S. Lewis adds, in the Psalter "I find an experience fully God-centred, asking of God no gift more urgently than His presence, the gift of Himself, joyous to the highest degree, and unmistakably real."[24]

For all of these reasons, most modern Bible readers conceive of the Psalter solely as a tool for personal piety, as a kind of private prayer diary. On the contrary, most probably the psalms possess an original corporate setting in life. In other words, as the psalm headings demonstrate, the majority of the psalms were originally intended for the believers gathered rather than scattered.

Famous author C. S. Lewis once stated in the Psalter, "I find an experience fully God-centred, asking of God no gift more urgently than His presence, the gift of Himself, joyous to the highest degree, and unmistakably real."

---

[23] Quoted in Ernest C. Lucas, *Exploring the Old Testament: A Guide to the Psalms and Wisdom Literature* (Downers Grove, IL: InterVarsity, 2003), 1.

[24] C. S. Lewis, *Reflections on the Psalms*, in *The Inspirational Writings of C. S. Lewis* (1958; reprt., New York: Inspirational Press, 1994), 158. See also GoodReads, "Reflections on the Psalms Quotes," https://www.goodreads.com/work/quotes/558664-reflections-on-the-psalms.

The psalms' corporate nature does not negate their utility in personal devotion. But it does mean that we should not neglect the Psalter's power on a more communal level.[25]

What is that communal purpose? The structure of the Psalter actually gives us some insight here. As mentioned above, the book of Psalms was collected over a long span of time and thus has always had a fluid structure, with the final version perhaps dating to the New Testament (NT) era. But as it stands today, the book has a clear framework.

Turn to Psalm 41 and read the last verse. It ends very "Baptistly" with an "Amen and Amen." Then above Psalm 42, your Bible probably has the title "Book Two." At the beginning of Psalm 73, you will see "Book Three." In fact, the Jews have traditionally and purposely divided the Psalter into five books (1–41; 42–72; 73–89; 90–106; and 107–150). Can you think of another section of Scripture that has five books? If you said "the Torah," you are correct.

The question is why. Is it just to mirror the number of Pentateuchal books? I think something deeper is afoot. The structure is reflective of the Jewish view of the message and purpose of the books. Remember that "Torah" means "instruction"—the kind of instruction that exhorts the corporate covenant community of faith to faithfulness to their covenant Lord.

So the purpose of Psalms, to use the words of the "thesis" psalm, Psalm 1, is to encourage members of the covenant community to place their "delight in the Torah of the Yahweh" so that the entire assembly will be like trees "planted beside flowing streams" that are fruitful and prosper. In fact, the reason the book begins with Psalm 1 is to establish the nature and the function of the entire book.

Even in the early NT church, this "Torah" purpose for the book of Psalms was recognized. As the apostle Paul states, "Let the word of

---

[25] For a great discussion of the corporate nature of the Psalter, see C. John Collins, "Always Alleluia," in *Forgotten Songs*, ed. Wells and Van Neste, 17–34.

Christ dwell richly among you, in all wisdom teaching and admonishing one another *through* psalms, hymns, and spiritual songs, singing to God with gratitude in your hearts" (Col 3:16, emphasis mine).

There is a pedagogical power in song. Can you remember a sermon from a year ago? Six weeks ago? Last week? Now, can you remember the words of a song that you sang ten years ago? Songs take hold of us and can transform our way of thinking. And the psalms do the same thing.

So as you read the book of Psalms, allow them to warm your heart, express your emotions, and draw you close to God. But also allow them to "instruct" you and the church in covenant faithfulness.

Literary Structure/Message/Purpose—Proverbs. More than any other OT book, people identify Proverbs with the concept of very practical wisdom. Because of its thirty-one chapters, some have even read the book as a month-long, chapter-a-day guide to wise living.

To interpret Proverbs correctly, however, we need to grasp what Proverbs' purpose is not and what it is. It is not, as some have seen it, some secular "advice book" on how to live well in the world—indistinguishable from irreligious wisdom literature found in other ancient cultures, such as Egypt. For instance, some scholars have wrongly argued that Proverbs "emphasizes the common morality and ethics applicable to all peoples."[26]

Instead, the wisdom within Proverbs is not just any kind; it is truth revealed from a covenant Lord to mold and shape and mature his covenant people so they live in proper covenant relationship with him on a practical level.[27]

---

[26] Shaye J. D. Cohen, *From the Maccabees to the Mishnah* (Philadelphia: Westminster, 1987), 42. As quoted in C. John Collins, "Proverbs and the Levitical System," *Presbyterion* 35, no. 1 (Spring 2009): 9.

[27] If the author intended for Proverbs to communicate generic guidance and maxims suitable to all peoples, one might expect a preference for the more generic Hebrew name for God (Elohim) in the book. However, that

More specifically, Proverbs takes the Torah—the covenantal instructions to the entire community—and brings them down to a real-world,
familial level. Indeed, in Proverbs, the parents are the primary purveyors
of wisdom. In other words, in the book, what Moses was to Israel as a
whole in the Pentateuch, the mother and father are to their children.
Like Moses with Israel, parents exhort and reprove children based on
divine revelation so that they become faithful members of the covenant
community.

Note, for instance, Prov 3:1–4: "My son, don't forget my teaching
[lit., Torah], but let your heart keep my commands; for they will bring
you many days, a full life, and well-being. Never let loyalty and faithfulness leave you. Tie them around your neck; write them on the tablet
of your heart. Then you will find favor and high regard with God and
people" (cf. Deut 6:5–9). That could just as well be Moses talking to
Israel, but it is the parent to the child.

So when you read Proverbs, think of practical wisdom on a family
level to raise up children to become healthy members of the covenant
community. This is what it means to "start a youth out on his way"
(Prov 22:6).

Now while the purpose of Proverbs is clear, its literary structure
is not. Simply based on style, one could divide the book into two
parts: chapters 1–9 (the longer discourses) and 10–31 (shorter, pithy
aphorisms). Based on the superscriptions in the text, one could divide
the book this way: 1–9; 10:1–22:16; 22:17–24:22; 24:23–34; 25–29; 30;
31:1–9; 31:10–31.

---

is not what we see. The authors/compilers of Proverbs refer to God almost
exclusively with his personal covenantal name Yahweh—some eighty-seven
times, in twenty of the thirty-one chapters. Strikingly, Elohim is used only five
times (Prov 2:5, 17; 3:4; 25:2; 30:9). And in three of those five occurrences, the
context is still covenantal.

A few important observations on the structure: The first concerns the personification of wisdom as a woman in chapters 1–9. The Hebrew word for wisdom is *hokmah*, and it is a feminine noun—thus the personification. This woman appears several times (1:20–33; 3:13–20; 8:1–9:18) in these opening discourses as a woman standing in the public square pleading for the naïve to learn from her. In other words, at the beginning of the book, wisdom is something commended and offered.

The end of the book is the famous acrostic poem (31:10–31) celebrating the virtuous wife as one who "speaks wisdom" (v. 26) and epitomizes a wise lifestyle. In other words, the book ends with wisdom realized.

In between, Prov 10:1–31:9 offers insight on how this offered wisdom may be gained and attained—by living a God-fearing life based on these general maxims that apply Torah to everyday existence. Interestingly, scholars have often noted the lack of arrangement in these chapters. The subject matter seems random, skipping from topic to topic. One verse might deal with family life, while the next deals with industry in employment, while the next deals with the dangers of the speech or sloth or self-indulgence.

Possibly the very disorder can serve a didactic purpose. We tend to encounter issues in life in such a random fashion. Perhaps too the author is saying that all of life is subject to wisdom—no matter the situation. And by the time we get to the end of the book, we hopefully have gained "prudent instruction in righteousness, justice, and integrity" (Prov 1:3).

Literary Structure/Message/Purpose—Ecclesiastes. You would be hard pressed to find a book in the Bible that speaks to the challenges of our postmodern culture more than Ecclesiastes. While all Scripture (including Leviticus and Chronicles) is profitable for every age and culture, some messages resonate more with the times. And Ecclesiastes is the book for our time.

The book famously deals with the issue of meaning in life. Postmodern society today has struggled with this issue of "ultimate

In Ecclesiastes, Qoheleth (sometimes identified with Solomon)
famously searches for ultimate purpose in life.

purpose"—often rejecting the possibility. Yet there is an unquenchable thirst for meaning among individuals today—whether a tomato farmer in small-town South Carolina or a tech guru from Silicon Valley.

But this book's own "meaning" is not easily accessible. Ecclesiastes has a notoriously Eeyore-ish tone.[28] It is also seemingly paradoxical in some of its statements. Different speakers are found in the text—a narrator, a teacher, and Qoheleth himself in the first person. And at times, the book seems to revolt against the standard, orderly, purposeful wisdom found in Proverbs, where everything seems so cut and dry.

---

[28] "Eeyore," *Wikipedia*, last modified January 23, 2019, https://en.wikipedia.org/wiki/Eeyore.

So how do you find the overall meaning of a book on the supposed meaninglessness of life? One method of finding the main theme is by looking to the orthodox assessment of the narrator (1:1–11 and 12:8–14). But if you do this, you ignore the struggle of the intervening chapters.

I think the best way to determine the "theme" of Ecclesiastes is by looking for *leitworts*—repeated words and phrases in the text. There are three of these: *profit*, *under the sun*, and *vanity/futility*.

First, *profit*. This word describes what Qoheleth wants out of life. Occurring some eighteen times in the text, the Hebrew root *ytr* does not describe profit in the monetary sense, but "advantage" or "something more" from life. As Eccl 1:3 states, "What does a person *gain* [from the root ytr] for all his efforts that he labors at under the sun?"

Qoheleth attempts to find this profit in many things—learning, levity, laughter, lasciviousness. As mentioned above, this quest unquestionably fits the experiences of Solomon in 1 Kings 10–11. But this materialistic search for profit is also a singular trait of modern secular culture.

Where did Qoheleth search for his profit? The second key phrase— *under the sun*—tells us. This phrase occurs some thirty times in the text and refers to our world of space and time. But it is that second characteristic of our world—time—that creates the problem for Qoheleth.

Time passes quickly until one "returns to dust" (3:20; 12:7) and to Sheol, the place of the dead (9:10). Qoheleth knew this; and every human in his or her navel-gazing moments also realizes this. As Qoheleth states: God "has made everything appropriate in its time. He has also put eternity in their hearts, but no one can discover the work God has done from beginning to end" (Eccl 3:11). Or, to quote the 1970s rock band Kansas, "All we are is dust in the wind."[29]

---

[29] "Kansas—Dust in the Wind (Official Video)," YouTube video, 3:19, posted by kansas, November 7, 2009, https://www.youtube.com/watch?v =tH2w6Oxx0kQ.

Death not only kills time, but it also kills any opportunity for profit and advantage. And we have no idea how much time we have left. As Eccl 9:12 states, "For certainly no one knows his time: like fish caught in a cruel net or like birds caught in a trap, so people are trapped in an evil time as it suddenly falls on them."

But this is the power of Ecclesiastes. Reading it is like going to a funeral. Like a wake, the book unnervingly wakes up the reader to the ephemeral nature of his or her own fragile existence.

The final *leitwort* tells us what Qoheleth finds after his search for profit under the sun: "vanity" or "futility," a word that occurs some thirty-three times in the text. A former professor of mine defined this term in a very technical manner: soap bubbles. In other words, "under the sun" profits aren't meaningless in and of themselves. They are meaningless because, like suds in a tub, they are here and gone. Qoheleth describes vanity as "pursuit of the wind" (1:14, 17; 2:11, 17, 26, etc.).

The question is, can we find meaning with such an existence, when all our toil, pleasures, knowledge, wisdom, relationships, words—everything that brings meaning to most people—perishes and passes away? In our zeal, we chase them like zephyrs that ultimately and unexpectedly dissipate.

What I love about Ecclesiastes is that Qoheleth does not deny the darkness. Yet Qoheleth, as the narrator, brings a light to the darkness. He offers a way out, by affirming three OT ideas that bring meaning to life. Ecclesiastes 12:13–14 reads: "When all has been heard, the conclusion of the matter is this: fear God and keep his commands, because this is for all humanity. For God will bring every act to judgment, including every hidden thing, whether good or evil."

As will be defined below, "fearing God" and "keeping his commandments" involve understanding and relating to God in covenant relationship. It is that covenant relationship with God and with others in the covenant community that brings meaning to this life. As early church father Augustine of Hippo famously wrote in his *Confessions*, "Thou hast made us for thyself, and our hearts are restless until they find their rest in thee."[30]

One last thing according to Qoheleth brings meaning to life: we must recognize the reality of God's judgment on every action under the sun. In other words, we need to have an eternal perspective on all that we do in life. As Jesus states in the Sermon on the Mount, "Don't store up for yourselves treasures on earth, where moth and rust destroy and where thieves break in and steal. But store up for yourselves treasures in heaven, where neither moth nor rust destroys, and where thieves don't break in and steal. For where your treasure is, there your heart will be also" (Matt 6:19–21).

To quote martyred missionary Jim Elliot,

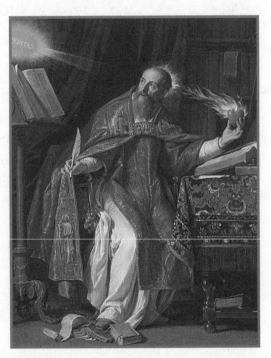

Early church father Augustine of Hippo famously wrote in his Confessions, "Thou hast made us for thyself, and our hearts are restless until they find their rest in thee."

---

[30] Project Gutenberg, "The Confessions of St. Augustine by Bishop of Hippo Saint Augustine," http://www.gutenberg.org/ebooks/3296?msg =welcome_stranger (accessed March 4, 2019).

"He is no fool who gives what he cannot keep to gain that which he cannot lose."[31]

Literary Structure/Message/Purpose—Song of Songs. One of the most purposely ignored books in the OT is the Song of Songs. Yet, as mentioned above, what I love about Song of Songs is that it presents a properly oriented sexually charged message for a promiscuously oriented sexually charged culture.

In the discussion of genre, we discussed how in church history, some have allegorized or avoided Song of Songs because of its "adult" subject matter. But I believe Danny Akin, who has an excellent commentary on the book, is correct when he labels it as "the Creator's ideas about love, intimacy, and marriage."[32] In other words, the book gives a proper biblical theology of sexuality.

What does it teach? Properly taught, Song of Songs guards against the Scylla of asceticism[33] and legalism and the Charybdis of hedonism.[34] Instead of pitting a legalistic, unappealing "no" against the unbridled, self-indulgent "yes" of modern Western culture (as many churches have done in the past), Song of Songs shows that God offers a better "yes."

Song of Songs presents a delicate, Edenic picture of God's "yes" within the confines of marriage. It also clearly teaches marriage as

---

[31] "Jim Elliot," *Wikipedia*, last modified March 6, 2019, https://en.wikipedia.org/wiki/Jim_Elliot.

[32] Danny Akin, *God on Sex: The Creator's ideas about Love, Intimacy, and Marriage* (Nashville: Broadman & Holman, 2003). This book is available on Amazon.com at https://www.amazon.com/God-Sex-Creators-Intimacy-Marriage/dp/0805425969/ref=sr_1_28?s=books&ie=UTF8&qid=1525185209&sr=1-28&refinements=p_27%3ADr.+Daniel+L.+Akin.

[33] "Asceticism," *Wikipedia*, last modified February 10, 2019, https://en.wikipedia.org/wiki/Asceticism.

[34] "Hedonism," *Wikipedia*, last modified February 11, 2019, https://en.wikipedia.org/wiki/Hedonism.

God's design and returns sexuality to an Edenic innocence (reversing the effects of the fall).

As Richard Hess writes, "In a fallen world in which the first couple was expelled from the garden of Eden, this song offers the hope that couples today may find something of that garden again and may see in their love that which is beautiful and good, from the good God."[35]

A triple version of the Song of Songs in Hebrew, Aramaic, and Arabic. The scribe copied each verse three times. Courtesy of the British Library

So the sexuality here is deeper, and more beautiful, than simple pleasure. The commitment expressed here between the lovers is covenantal. The repeated phrase—"I am my love's and my love is mine" (2:16; 6:3; 7:10)—demonstrates this connection. That is the view of

---

[35] Richard S. Hess, *Song of Songs*, Baker Commentary on the Old Testament Wisdom and Psalms (Grand Rapids: Baker Academic, 2005), 11.

sexuality that the world, and the church, needs to recover. See the Applying the Results section below for more details.

Theological Tools

Salvation History

Scholars have often labeled the Poetry and Wisdom Books as sort of the "red-headed stepchild" of biblical theology. In other words, some of the books seem to lack many of the redemptive historical themes found in the rest of the Hebrew Scriptures—particularly that of covenant or Torah. And none of the books contain narratives essential to the progression of the story line of Scripture.

So do they fit into the Bible theologically? If so, how? The answer is a clear yes.

The Wisdom Books are less obvious than the Psalms. But the themes are still there. Our discussion of Proverbs above demonstrates the role that that book played in the covenant community. Ecclesiastes also ties into these larger themes—demonstrating the meaning and purpose to be found in one's relationship with the covenant God (Eccl 12:13–14). Job shows that faith is based in a sovereign Creator. And Song of Songs recovers the polluted sexual relationship and restores it to its pre-fall covenantal quality.

Psalms more clearly fits into salvation history. In fact, due to the book's thousand-year composition history—covering virtually all the history found in the OT—the psalms do speak of most of the essential salvation historical themes and events. For instance, Psalm 136 celebrates God's creation and also his redemption in the exodus as an expression of his steadfast love that endures forever. Psalm 89 reflects on the failures of the Davidic kings. So it has been often and accurately stated that the psalms are in the Bible, but the Bible is also in the psalms.

Most famously, the Psalter contains psalms that anticipate and describe the central figure in salvation history—Jesus Christ.

Let's play a word association game. What is the first thing that comes to mind when I say, Jesus Christ? How about this question: what would a first-century Christian think of when that person first heard, Jesus Christ?

I believe the NT gives us evidence of what they would have thought of. When first-century believers described the Christ, the Messiah, and even when Jesus described himself, they used Scripture—particularly the psalms.

Look at Psalm 22 and see how it describes Jesus's crucifixion. Look at Psalm 2 and see how it describes Jesus's exaltation and victory over raging nations.

One of the primary Christological texts for the NT writers was Psalm 110.[36] Why? What does it tell us about Jesus? Take a look at it. Twice, God speaks in the psalm, and he does so with a prophetic-formula declaration—the same kind of words you find in the prophets: "the declaration of the LORD" in verse 1 and "the LORD has sworn" in verse 4. Thus, what God says in this psalm is sure and certain. And he *certainly* describes the Messiah in two ways.

First, God declares that the Messiah (Jesus) is the God-installed, reigning victorious King. In the psalm, the psalmist describes the Messiah as seated at the right hand of God. The right hand symbolized power. And whoever sat at the right hand of the king was next to him

---

[36] In fact, this text is cited in the NT in Matt 22:44; 26:64; Mark 12:36; 14:62; 16:19; Luke 20:42–44; 22:69; Acts 2:34–35; Rom 8:34; 1 Cor 15:25; Eph 1:20; Col 3:1; and Heb 1:3, 13; 5:6; 8:1; 10:12–13; and 12:2. In Matthew 22, the Pharisees ask Jesus, who is the Messiah? Jesus then quotes Psalm 110 and, as he often does, responds with a question to them: in Psalm 110, who is David's Lord? Look at Ps 110:1. If the first Lord is God, and David is the one talking as the author of the psalm (David is the "my"), who is the second Lord? Jesus says by implication, David's Lord is Jesus himself.

in rank and identified as the official empowered to represent the king and carry out his policy. But, as Mark 14:62 indicates, Jesus did not have just any power; it was the power to effect the will of God.

Second, the psalm identifies Jesus as the great, high priest in the order of Melchizedek. Your first reaction after I say that is probably, "Say what?" Who is this Melchizedek?

Though obscure, Melchizedek may be one of the most important characters in the Bible. He helps us to see clearly who Jesus is and how to put our Bibles together.

Though obscure, Melchizedek may be one of the most important characters in the Bible. He helps us to see clearly who Jesus is and how to put our Bibles together. Melchizedek originally appears in a mere three overlooked verses, Gen 14:18–20. Abraham has been in a battle to rescue his nephew Lot, who had been captured. Abraham comes back from his victory, and he meets a grateful ally named Melchizedek.

The key to understanding Melchizedek is how the text identifies him. In Genesis 14, Melchizedek is called the king of Salem (or Peace). His name means "king of righteousness." And he is identified as "a priest to God Most High" (God himself). By being a priest and king characterized by righteousness, Melchizedek provides a "type" or precursor of Jesus in Scripture. Why is it important for Melchizedek to hold both positions—priest and king—as it regards Christ?

What tribe is Jesus from? Judah, the tribe of the kings. What tribe are the priests from in Israel's history? Levi, the tribe of the priests. So how can Jesus serve us as a priest if he is not from Levi? Because he is of a priestly order predating Levi—the order of Melchizedek. And this priesthood is even greater than the Levitical one, because it precedes it (see Hebrews 7).

Why do we need a priest? A priest mediates between God and man, and we have rebelled against God. The only way to quell God's rage against the rebellion is for a proper propitiatory sacrifice to be made—not sacrifices that are here and gone, but a once-and-for-all sacrifice of the great High Priest himself.[37] That is our Priest-King Jesus.

So we see that Psalms, and the rest of the Poetry and Wisdom Books, really do add to our understanding of biblical theology.

Wisdom and Fear of the Lord

We have saved perhaps our most important theological tool in understanding the Wisdom Books of Job, Proverbs, Ecclesiastes, and Song of Songs until last. And that is the theological tool of Hebrew wisdom itself.

---

[37] Bible Study Tools, s.v., "Propitiation," accessed March 4, 2019, https://www.biblestudytools.com/dictionary/propitiation/.

What is wisdom? As I ask students this question, most answers include words such as *knowledge, intelligence*, or *experience*. But do these definitions comport with the biblical notion?

The Hebrew word for wisdom, *hokmah*, has a variety of connotations in the Bible. One basic and minor but instructive meaning is "skill in a craft" (see Exod 35:10). In other words, if you are a good carpenter, you could be called a carpenter with *hokmah*.

This connection of *hokmah* and "skill" is helpful to understanding the larger concept. I think the biblical conception of wisdom is something like "skill at life"—a way of deftly navigating life and life issues.

How is this done? For the biblical authors, this skill is found in one place. As Solomon writes, "The fear of the LORD is the beginning of wisdom" (Prov 9:10; cf. Prov 1:7; 15:33; Job 28:28).

But what is the fear of Yahweh? Most would answer something like "reverential awe." Sure, this is part of it, but it does not encapsulate the

The biblical conception of wisdom is something like "skill at life"—a way of deftly navigating life and life issues amid life's storms, based in the fear of the LORD.

entirety of the meaning. In Proverbs, fear of Yahweh is essentially theological, and it is often in parallel with "knowledge of Yahweh" (Prov 1:7, 29; 2:5; 9:10). The phrase depicts then that which is produced in people when they truly understand who God is and who they are in relation to him.

But how would Israelites understand Yahweh and their relationship with him rightly? This fear and knowledge was not of just any God. The author specifically attributes this fear as the fear of Yahweh, the covenant Lord of Israel. For the Israelite, wisdom and right living were impossible without knowing intimately their covenant Lord. As Grant writes:

> The fact that the authors and editors of Proverbs focus on the necessity to fear Yahweh if one is to be wise indicates that this is Israel's own brand of wisdom. They did not simply adopt other ancient wisdom ideas but rather adapted them to conform to Israel's own worldview. Therefore, they make it clear that true wisdom apart from relationship with Israel's covenant God is a *non-sequitur*—there can be no wisdom apart from covenant relationship.[38]

In other words, wisdom is essentially theological. For one to be truly wise, God must be the source of the wisdom, and our knowledge of and covenant relationship with him is the breeding ground for wisdom.

Do you see how this can be the beginning of wisdom? If wisdom is a proper way of navigating life and life issues, then this navigation begins with understanding who our covenant Lord is and who we are in relation to him in covenant.

Do you need to comprehend the nature of suffering and faith, as in Job? Understand our covenant Lord's sovereignty over all things.

---

[38] J. A. Grant, "Wisdom and Covenant," in *Dictionary of the Old Testament Wisdom, Poetry, and Writings*, ed. Tremper Longman and Peter Enns (Downers Grove, IL: InterVarsity, 2008), 860.

Do you need to avoid foolish behavior and adopt wise behavior as we find described in the book of Proverbs? Understand our covenant Lord's nature as holy and just and our own tendency to be foolish.

Do you need to find true meaning in a seemingly fleeting existence? Understand the eternal God that we serve. And understand that faith in the eternal covenant Lord is the only way to find personal meaning—not through temporary pleasures (Eccl 12:13–14).

Do you seek to understand the mysteries, meaning, pleasures, and pitfalls of the gift of sexuality? Understand the covenant nature of love and marriage as given by our covenant Lord.

So read the Wisdom Books to know and "fear" Yahweh, and you will find wisdom.

Putting the Tools to Use

The following will offer two examples showing how the use of tools can be helpful in interpreting biblical texts from the Poetry and Wisdom Books. Before reading the following, try it for yourself. Work through the following questions, and then see if you can discern the original meaning.

Example 1: Stargazing with King David and Psalm 8

Historical Tools

What is the level-1/level-2 historical context and how does that affect my reading of the text?

Literary Tools

What is the genre of the text? What type of psalm is it? How does the author use poetic tools?

Theological Tools

Are there any key theological terms or concepts in the text? How do I understand the text in light of Christ and the full testimony of the Bible?

Application

What does this text tell me about God? About myself? About the world? About how I relate to God?

Interpretation

I don't believe any little boy could emerge from the 1970s and 1980s without being a certified stargazer. *Star Wars*, *Battlestar Gallactica*, *Star Trek*, and *Buck Rogers* filled our collective childhood imaginations with speeding spaceships and epic interstellar battles, tapping into our innate desire for galactic gallantry and space swashbucklery. Even today, on clear nights outside, I find myself wondering and wandering about the heavens, posing on my porch like that iconic *Star Wars* image of Luke Skywalker gazing wistfully at the twin setting suns of Tatooine.

So when I came across a recent Hubble image published by NASA and reported by QZ.com, I couldn't help but be drawn to it as if caught in some Death Star tractor beam—being transported back in time to galaxies far away and childhood adventures rapidly fading into memory.[39]

The remarkable picture of the Andromeda galaxy—at some 1.5 billion pixels—is hailed as the most detailed space image ever and provides a partial glimpse into the vastness of one of the Milky Way's nearest neighbors. Incredibly, as you zoom in on the picture, the 100

---

[39] Zach Wener-Fligner, "This is the most crystal-clear image of space ever taken," *QZ*, January 22, 2015, https://qz.com/331406/this-is-the-most-crystal-clear-image-of-space-ever-taken/?utm_source=parFC.

*For Christians, our perception of the vastness of the universe
is, well, different. And, the best text in the Bible through
which to filter such feelings and experiences is Psalm 8.*

million visible stars become clustered and dense as sand, perhaps giving new meaning to God's promises to Abraham in Genesis 15. And this is just one of billions of galaxies!

Admittedly, the immediate and human reaction to such immensity is an overwhelming feeling of "smallness." As the QZ article states, "The vastness of space is so expansive, so inconceivable, that frankly, it makes humanity's lot in the universe seem pretty tiny and pointless." Similarly, secularist author and scientist Carl Sagan once wrote, "For as long as there have been humans we have searched for our place in the cosmos. Where are we? Who are we? We find that we live on an insignificant planet of a hum-drum star lost in a galaxy tucked away in some forgotten corner of a universe in which there are far more galaxies than people."[40]

However, for Christians, our perception and vision of the vastness is, well, different. For me, the best text in the Bible through which to

---

[40] "Galaxy," *Wikipedia*, last modified July 22, 2016, https://en.wikiquote.org/wiki/Galaxy.

filter such feelings is Psalm 8. And this is a great text to illustrate some of the tools we've learned in this chapter.

What I love about this psalm of David is its perspective. David, if he is the author, doesn't just leave the created world to one's imagination; he interprets it and gives it meaning and purpose. We are also able to trace out some of David's own thought patterns—some 3,000 years after the fact.

Reading the psalm, we note first that David too was struck by the "big" of creation and the "small" of humanity. No doubt, when David looked up at the thousands of visible stars from the Palestinian countryside, he had to wonder at the wonder of the universe. Indeed, how could David not note the stark contrast between the vast star-filled heavens and himself—a ruddy, shepherd boy turned king?

In Psalm 8, he asks the rhetorical question, "When I observe your heavens, the work of your fingers, the moon and the stars, which you set in place, what is a human being that you remember him, a son of man that you look after him" (vv. 3–4). The two terms used for man/human here denote weakness and frailty and mortality. David knew his relative significance.

Then an amazing thing happens. As David goes to his knees, in prostrate humility before God, he begins meditating on the Word of God.

And here is the key to the entire text and the entire dilemma of our "smallness" in light of creation: David interprets general revelation (creation) through the lens of special revelation (Scripture).

First, in verse 4, David notes that the God who creates is also the God who has "remembered" his people. God "remembered" the Israelites while they were in bondage in Egypt. God "remembered" the promises to the Patriarchs. God "remembered" his commitment to his covenant. And God had remembered David.

Then David begins to meditate on how God "visited" (or "looked after" in the CSB) his people. This term comes straight out of the exodus account. Any Hebrew reader would immediately think of how God had delivered his people out of slavery.

So David is thinking, "Here is a God so much more sovereign than us, so much more transcendent and holy, so much more 'other,' yet he is a God who has condescended to know us and love us and involve himself in our lives in a salvific manner."

At this point in the psalm, David's mind then drifts back to the beginning of the biblical story—to creation itself. He writes, "You made him little less than God and crowned him with glory and honor. You made him ruler over the works of your hands; you put everything under his feet; all the sheep and oxen, as well as the animals in the wild, the birds of the sky, and the fish of the sea that pass through the currents of the seas" (vv. 5–8).

The reference here in Psalm 8 is clearly to Gen 1:26–31. David thinks, "Not only has God saved us; he has given us a role to play. He has created us with a special dignity and crucial role to play in his creation." In both Genesis 1 and Psalm 8, the Bible describes humans as being made by God himself with special nobility and having a special status (as image-bearers).

As discussed in chapter 4, the imageness talked about in both passages has to do with rule and rank. God gave us to be his vice-regents in creation. His princes and princesses, if you will. God gave humanity the needed qualities to govern creation on his behalf as if he were physically present. In this regard, the Israelites' view of status was starkly different from that of their ancient Near Eastern neighbors, who reserved the status of "image of divinity" for kings and priests. The Bible on the contrary democratizes imageness.

Finally, all of these thoughts lead David back to his initial expression of praise—"LORD, our Lord, how magnificent is your name throughout the earth!" One thing even a casual reader will notice about this psalm is its clear structure. It begins and ends with the same idea—a Hebrew poetic technique called *inclusio*, but what I like to call "bookends." And if you begin and end with the same theme, it should tell you all you need to know about the theme of the middle.

What then is the theme of this psalm? What is David wanting us to see in all of this psalm and in all of his musing? What reaction should God's people have in the face of the vastness of creation and its Creator? Praising the magnificent name of God in creation.

In other words, God does not do these things (visitation, remembrance, bestowal of imageness) for us so that *we* might be praised. We do not experience the unexpected grace of God for our own glory. He does it so that he might be glorified.

As you gaze up at the heavens tonight, or as you look at Hubble images, think of his creation of trillions of stars. Also think of God's visitation of you in Christ, his remembrance of you in the new covenant, his giving you the status of image-bearer. Ultimately, may your passions be engaged to praise him who displayed his splendor in the heavens.

Example 2: Psalms 1 and 2 and the Secret to the "Blessed" Christian Life

Historical Tools

What is the level-1/level-2 historical context and how does that affect my reading of the text?

Literary Tools

What is the genre of the text? What type of psalms are they? How does the author use poetic tools?

Theological Tools

Are there any key theological terms or concepts in the text? How do I understand the text in light of Christ and the full testimony of the Bible?

Application

What does this text tell me about God? About myself? About the world? About how I relate to God?

Interpretation

How does the old adage go? If you want a barometer for the spiritual health of a Christian, check his or her checkbook. Perhaps this is true. But let me propose another barometer, this time for the spiritual health of Western Christianity—the Amazon.com top-selling Christian books list. And its measurements are not encouraging.

This list's array of Amish romance novels, mend-your-life manuals, and tales of heavenly experiences present a picture of popular Christianity that is—well—shallow, superficial, and self-centered. One has to look far down the list to find any thoughtful, theological treatises. For better or worse, we, as believers, are what we read.

The books on the best-seller lists that are most indicative of this dangerous narcissistic drift are the how-to volumes, dealing with the keys to the "blessed" Christian life—infamously telling you how to have "your best life now."[41] Even those words betray the evident egoism and self-absorption so common in our culture.

Yet when one looks at the Scriptures, one finds a much more simplistic and selfless understanding of the key to "blessedness"—an understanding that is less focused on materialism and "under the sun" profit and one that perhaps doesn't need book after book to address it.

The best-known of these descriptions is found in Jesus's Sermon on the Mount in Matthew 5—the Beatitudes. But another clear, though

---

[41] Amazon.com, "Your Best Life Now: 7 Steps to Living at Your Full Potential," https://www.amazon.com/Your-Best-Life-Now-Potential/dp/14 55532282 (accessed March 4, 2019).

lesser-known, set of "Beatitudes" is found in Psalms 1 and 2. Once again, our tools can help us to understand them.

The best-known description of blessedness is found in Jesus's Sermon on the Mount in Matthew 5—the Beatitudes. But another clear, though lesser-known set of "Beatitudes" is found in Psalms 1 and 2.

When you read these two psalms together (as they should be, since they provide a dual-introduction to the entire Psalter), you find that the two compositions are framed by a repetition of the word *blessing* (1:1 and 2:12)—another *inclusio*. In other words, these psalms focus on blessing as the foremost theme.

Two questions emerge upon noticing this. First, what does it mean to be "blessed"? And second, what is the means of receiving the "blessing"?

The word *blessed* in these psalms is often translated "happy," which frankly is a poor translation. In English, "happiness" is a feeling. For the Hebrews, blessedness is more a state. It is a state of being in a right relationship with God in covenant—that deep, committed, loving, redemptive relationship between God and his people. Just as wisdom is something grounded in the fear of the Lord, blessedness is something grounded in right relationship with the Lord.

But how does one achieve/receive this right relationship?

Psalm 1 asserts that blessing comes not by living life (walking, standing, sitting) as those who consciously and constantly rebel against God and his precepts, but instead by consciously and constantly delighting in and meditating on Torah, the covenant document. For the Hebrew people, the path to right covenant relationship and covenant blessing must necessarily follow the way lighted by the Word of God (Josh 1:8). Just as marital joy happens when spouses faithfully keep their vows to each other in covenantal love, so also the believer finds peace with God when, in response to his love, we love him by keeping his commandments (John 14:15).

Psalm 2 adds a second element to the equation. This messianic psalm begins with a statement about the kings of the earth raging futilely against God's Anointed (vv. 1–2), his Messiah. And it closes by promising blessing to those who give homage to and take refuge in this messianic King (vv. 11–12). In other words, to have the blessing found in right covenant relationship, one must submit to the Lord and King of the covenant relationship.

But one must remember that these psalms are not meant for merely individual consumption. Neither is God's relationship with us in covenant meant to "happen" individually, as "Lone Ranger" Christians. Psalms 1 and 2 are corporate songs and communal confessions; biblical blessing is achieved only when a believer is in right fellowship with fellow believers. Such a community—where members of the body sacrifice for one another, love one another, encourage one another—presents a ready remedy against the secular self-love saturating our society.

So believers should not ultimately look to popular books for the blueprint for blessing. Instead, they should meditate and delight in one Book in particular. They should submit desires, hopes, and happiness to their benevolent new covenant Lord, Jesus Christ. And they should do each of these while in fellowship with other Christians in a local church community.

If they do this, they will be "like a tree planted beside flowing streams that bears its fruit in its season and whose leaf does not wither. Whatever he does prospers" (Ps 1:3).

Applying the Results

Of all the OT books studied so far, the Poetry and Wisdom Books seem most readily applicable to the Christian life and the church. The following will offer two possible trajectories for application using what we have learned from the books.

Combating a Sexualized Generation with a Biblical Theology of Sex

While perusing the blogosphere one day, a disturbing headline caught my eye. A religion commentary on cnn.com asserted, "True love doesn't wait after all."[42]

Now we all know blogs can tend toward sensational "Chicken Little" claims and arguments and statistics. But the data given in this article, which was itself a commentary on an earlier article, "(Almost) Everyone's Doing It," in *Relevant* magazine, were truly staggering.

Both articles cited a 2009 study by the National Campaign to Prevent Teen and Unplanned Pregnancy.[43] In this study of the sexual activity of the broader populace of young adults, one statistic stood

---

[42] John Blake, "Why Young Christians Aren't Waiting Anymore," CNN Belief Blog, September 27, 2011, http://religion.blogs.cnn.com/2011/09/27 /why-young-christians-arent-waiting-anymore/?iref=allsearch.

[43] Power to Decide, https://powertodecide.org/ (accessed March 4, 2019).

out. Of the eighteen- to twenty-nine-year-olds who self-identified as "evangelical," some 80 percent had engaged at least once in unmarried sexual activity, even though 76 percent of them deemed it morally wrong. By comparison, 88 percent of all eighteen- to twenty-nine-year-olds surveyed had had premarital sex.

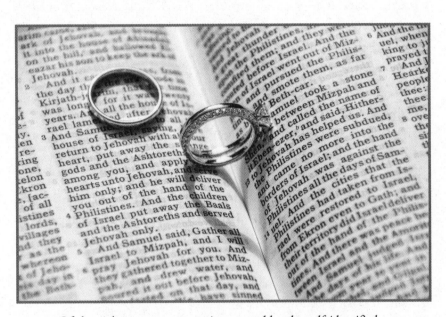

Of the eighteen- to twenty-nine-year-olds who self-identified as "evangelical," some 80 percent had engaged at least once in unmarried sexual activity, even though 76 percent of them deemed it morally wrong.

These statistics raise all kinds of questions, some of which are raised in both articles. Has the abstinence movement failed? What explains the disparity between the beliefs and practices of these evangelical Christians? What is the church not doing that perhaps it should? What about promise rings, vows of chastity until marriage, kissing dating good-bye? Are all of these "defenses" powerless in the face of the "in your face" sexuality of modern America?

All of these questions take on an even more pressing character as I interact with students every day at a Christian institution of higher learning, most of whom fall within the younger range of the cited age category. What can I do to head off this issue at the pass?

Obviously, no easy answers exist. But the longer we ignore or even wrongly attack the issue, the more casualties we will have from it—abortion, STDs, guilt, and subsequent marriages that suffer from pre-marital sexual union(s).

My sense is that a good start to attacking the problem is biblical in nature. The pattern of the Scriptures—both Old and New Testaments—has always been to ground right practice in right theological belief. If then evangelicals are to recover right sexual practice, perhaps it would behoove churches and families not to avoid the issue of sexuality, but to confront it head-on with biblical teaching.

In particular, I think we need to rediscover the rather ignored OT book, Song of Songs. As outlined above, the book gives a proper biblical theology of sexuality.

If we can recover the theology of sexuality—as a theological act, a meaningful act, and a covenantal act—perhaps our young people will see why it is such an important issue.

Although a good start, "good theology" by itself is not enough, as evidenced in Solomon's own life. One of the conundrums of the Bible is how the author of so many proverbs advising against sexual immorality could fall prey himself to the same vice.

Individual communities of faith must be more openly involved in the issue—teaching, modeling, and celebrating proper sexuality and God's "yes." This is exactly what Song of Songs commends. At the same time, we need to return to a sense of trust and accountability for male-female relationships within the church as well.

Again, there are no easy answers to this issue. One thing is for certain, we cannot ignore it anymore.

Embrace Robust Theology, so That in Tragedy, You Don't Have To

A few years ago, a friend of mine experienced an incomprehensible tragedy. His two-year-old developed medical complications. A day or two later, she died. A little girl—so full of life, so innocent—now dead and taken from her loving parents.

As a father of three boys, I can't imagine the questions, the grief. Words aren't enough.

Of course, as citizens of a fallen world, we face such tragedies all too often. The world has no answers for these events; frankly, many Christians do not either. People struggle to know to whom to turn in a world that seems deterministic, fatalistic, and cruel.

Where do we turn for answers, comfort, relief in a world dominated by a naturalistic worldview devoid of meaning and God? To friends? Family? Escapism? The nostalgic, postmodern spirituality as witnessed in response to the 9/11 tragedy?

As good Christians, we know the right answers. We know that our God invites our expressions of grief, and we know that he is good, and we know that he is sovereign and faithful. We know this intuitively. But it is when we face the darkness that we see our true theology coming to the forefront. This is our "rubber-meets-the-road" theology.

You may say that you believe that God is sovereign, but do you believe it when an earthquake takes everything you own? You may say that you believe that God is good, but do you believe it when God calls your two-year-old home? You may say that you believe God is faithful, but do you believe it when you lose your job and you have no prospects?

When the darkness of life comes, what is your theology? I heard John Piper preach once that he preaches the character of God in the present, so when darkness comes in the future, he doesn't have to and can focus on just "being there." As Christians, then, we must consistently embrace robust, biblical theology.

So if you read any biblical book, don't forget to examine the character of God that emerges from the text.

A great book to use for this purpose is the oft-neglected Ecclesiastes. As mentioned above, perhaps no other book speaks to our postmodern mind-set and its struggle for a sense of purpose than Ecclesiastes, a text known for dwelling on the darkness, the futility, the crisis that is life.

One thing I appreciate about the book is that no matter how much the author (Qoheleth in the Hebrew) struggles with questions, no matter how much he bemoans how everything under the sun is "chasing after the wind," he still maintains an orthodox view of God.

Qoheleth does not deny the darkness, but he (especially at the end, in the last few verses) brings light to the darkness. He invites us to maintain a proper perspective, grounded in a proper theology. Qoheleth sees God as sovereign. He is sovereign over time (3:1–14). He is sovereign over all events (1:15; 2:26; 7:13; 9:1). Like other biblical books, Qoheleth grounds God's sovereignty in God's creation. He is over all things because he made all things (11:5).

Inseparable from sovereignty are God's omniscience and omnipotence. God has decreed all that has happened and will happen (3:11). He is the source of knowledge (2:26). God knows all things, whereas man does not (11:5). God *made* everything appropriate for its time (3:11), even death.

Qoheleth sees God as just and righteous. God rewards humans on an ethical basis for both good and evil (8:12–13). And God will judge deeds (11:9; 12:14; 3:16–18). Regardless of what happens to us, God's justice is immutable. God's works are forever unchangeable (3:14).

The theology presented focuses on a God who brings light to darkness, which is why Qoheleth in the end states that only a fear of

*No matter how much the author of Ecclesiastes (Qoheleth in
the Hebrew) struggles with questions, no matter how much he
bemoans how everything under the sun is "chasing after the
wind," he still maintains an orthodox view of God.*

God brings ultimate meaning (12:13). This is robust theology. This is a
biblical theology.

So when you face the darkness of seemingly random circumstances
and tragedies, direct your attention to the light of an unchanging God
and the fullness of his nature and character.

During darkness, we must be grounded in the true character of
our God—the holy, awesome, sovereign, righteous, omnipotent, omniscience, omnibenevolent, all loving, all consuming God of the universe.

Application Questions

1. Why do you think people are so drawn to the Poetic Books of the OT? How have the poetic books (particularly the Psalms) impacted your life?

2. Turn to the famous Psalm 23 and see if you can identify some of the poetic features talked about in the chapter.

3. Read Psalm 22 in light of Jesus on the cross. Can you identify the prophecies fulfilled in the crucifixion?

4. How would you define wisdom? How does your definition differ from the one given in the Scriptures?

5. Can someone who does not know God be wise? Why or why not?

6. Can you relate to Job, or do you know people who have had Job-like experiences? What does this story teach about suffering and faith? Why do you think God does not answer Job's questions about why he has suffered?

7. Do you know people who live their lives like Qoheleth in the book of Ecclesiastes? Do you agree with Qoheleth that everything "under the sun" is vanity?

8. What is the culture's teaching on sexuality? How does Song of Songs respond to this view of sexuality?

7

Tools for Interpreting the Prophetic Books

Have you ever been locked out of your house, dorm, or apartment? Perhaps you misplace or forget your key and then find yourself faced with an impassable entrance—barring your access to the contents and comforts within. Frustrating, isn't it?

Well, the Prophetic Books of the Old Testament (OT) represent a vexing locked door for many Christians, rendering the contents and comforts of this section of Scripture inaccessible. The exegetical dead bolts encountered in the prophetic writings are myriad—archaic expressions and genres, fiery rhetoric, repetitive revelations of judgment, esoteric eschatological visions, and sometimes shocking sign-acts.

To make matters worse, the historical events behind these texts—dating from the preexile to the postexile (750 BC–late 400s BC)—represent some of the least known OT events. How do you understand someone's message if you don't know the situation that inspired it?

The Prophetic Books of the Old Testament represent a vexing locked door for many Christians, rendering the contents and comforts of this section of Scripture inaccessible.

The result is that many Christians selectively use these texts at best, reading them on a surface level; and at worst they avoid them completely.

I will not sugarcoat the real struggles presented by these texts. But I will say that I believe that with a few select tools, we may gain access, as O. Palmer Robertson writes, to "a body of literature unparalleled in human history."[1]

Indeed, the Prophetic Books present an opportunity to mine spiritual treasures relatively untouched by many Christians.

There one may gain insight on how God relates to us as individuals and as corporate covenantal bodies (today, the church). There

---

[1] O. Palmer Robertson, *Christ of the Prophets* (Phillipsburg, NJ: P & R Publishing, 2004), 1.

one sees displayed God's providential concern and plans for the nations—including Israel but not excluding the Gentiles. There one finds language and arguments and imagery that provide the backdrop for much of the language and arguments and imagery of the New Testament (NT). *See Wordsearch for an example of the NT appropriation of the prophetic texts.*

There one may behold the magnificent and multifaceted character of God—his holiness, sovereignty, faithfulness, righteousness, grace, and, yes, justice and wrath. And there one may experience hope and exhortation that may guide us as individuals and corporate bodies into a closer walk with our covenant Lord.

So let's examine the tools that allow us to access these spiritual treasures.

Understanding the Tools

I often tell my students that many keys may be used to unlock the Prophetic Books, but three are indispensable. The first two we find in the Historical Tools section below; the last we will unpack in the Theological Tools section. We will look at other tools as well, but these three are the "key" keys.

Historical Tools

The first of these keys is historical—understanding the ancient Israelite office of prophet.

The Prophetic Office

What's the first thing that comes to your mind when I mention "prophet"? Many might imagine a disheveled, placard-wearing subway preacher. Or Momma Leona, the palm reader in the strip mall on Main

Street. Or perhaps the late *Tonight Show* host Johnny Carson as Carnac the Magnificent.[2]

In other words, we probably think of those whose main occupation is to predict potentialities. In fact, we most often use the term *prophesy* with that connotation: "I prophesy that the Atlanta Braves will win the World Series."

But we should not think of biblical prophets in this way. In fact, while they did forecast the future at times, their main role was something different and more pressing. They were ambassadors between God and his covenant people, forthtelling rather than foretelling an often-urgent message to their contemporaries.

This representative role is perhaps best seen in an unexpected Scripture—Exod 7:1. Do you remember the dreaded analogies on the SAT—W is to X as Y is to Z? In this Exodus text, we have an analogy that tells us what a Hebrew prophet does. Go ahead and look it up.

Consider Moses. God has called him to go to Egypt to proclaim a message. But Moses protests that he possesses a speech impediment. So Exod 7:1 tells us that God gives Moses's brother, Aaron, to Moses to be his "prophet." The analogy goes: Moses—Aaron—Pharaoh is analogous to God—Prophet—People.

Whatever Aaron does for Moses, that's what a prophet does for God. And what is that duty? Delivering a message. Speaking for someone else. Aaron could say, "Thus says Moses," such that an equivalence existed between his words and Moses's words. In the same way, the prophets proclaim, "Thus says the LORD," so that God communicates his words "through" them (Jer 37:2).

This does not mean that the personalities, immediate concerns, and backgrounds of the prophets do not affect their messages. But it does

---

[2] "Carnac the Magnificent with Predictions about Snoopy and Taxi Driver on Johnny Carson's Tonight Show," YouTube video, 3:03, posted by Johnny Carson, July 31, 2011, https://www.youtube.com/watch?v=xuFSWcNe8hY.

mean that their words are 100 percent their own words, but also 100 percent the words of God (2 Pet 1:19–21).

The content of the prophetic message will be explored further in the Theological Tools below (the third key). For now, we can observe that these messengers fearlessly and faithfully served as spiritual consciences for the nation at critical times in the Israel's history—for example, the establishment of the monarchy (1 Samuel); the giving of the Davidic covenant (2 Samuel 7); the division of the kingdom (1 Kings 11–12); the threat of Assyria to Judah (2 Kings 19); the Babylonian exile (2 Kings 24–25); the postexilic malaise (Ezra and Nehemiah); among many others.

Although the prophets spoke divine messages, they did not always receive openhearted and enthusiastic responses. In fact, reactions were quite the opposite, especially from the maligned and wayward kings of Israel. Unlike prophets in other cultures, Hebrew prophets did not simply tell kings what they wanted to hear. They defied. They reproached. They threatened—not worrying about popularity or prosperity or even personal survival. See Amos 7:10–17, for example. *See Wordsearch for an example of how Jeremiah contrasted himself with the false prophet Hananiah in Jeremiah 28.*

This countercultural commissioning often put Israel's true prophets in the minority. In fact, many times the false prophets far outnumbered and outshouted the authentic ones (see 1 Kings 18 and 22). But the true prophets had a defining call from God, which many times is recorded in Scripture. See, for example, Isaiah 6, Jeremiah 1, Ezekiel 1–3, Amos 7, Exodus 3–4, 1 Samuel 3. They spoke out of a sense of compulsion (Jer 5:14), not acceptance. And their words never "fall to the earth" (2 Kgs 10:10 ESV), but always came true (Jeremiah 28; Deut 18:15–22), because their words were from God himself.

The first person to be labeled a prophet in Scripture is Abraham (Gen 20:7). But it is Moses who is presented in the Bible as the prophetic paradigm for all others (Hos 12:13; Deut 18:15–22). Then, for several

Prophets like Amos fearlessly and faithfully served as spiritual consciences for the nation at critical times in Israel's history.

hundred years after the conquest of the Promised Land, the prophetic voice steps into the background. In the dark period of the judges, God remained rather silent—save for a few such as the prophetess Deborah.[3]

With the advent of the monarchy, God begins to speak through his prophets once again. During the early part of the monarchy, numerous named (Samuel, Nathan, Micaiah, Elijah, and Elisha) and unnamed prophets appear. But their messages and ministries are accessed only through the biblical narrative. Though they may have written other texts, they did not transmit any scriptural compositions to us today.

Only in the later part of the monarchy, 170 years after the division of the kingdom in 931 BC, do we begin to encounter the "writing" prophets. These sixteen prophets left us a reservoir of revelation in the

---

[3] This is similar to God's several-hundred-year silence between the Testaments.

Hebrew Scriptures. In our English Bibles, we characterize them as major and minor prophets—not based on the quality of their writings, but the quantity. The major prophets comprise Isaiah, Jeremiah, Ezekiel, and Daniel. The minor prophetic writings are included in what the Hebrew Scriptures call the Book of the Twelve—Hosea through Malachi.

Major Prophets	
Isaiah	Ezekiel
Jeremiah	Daniel
Lamentations	
Minor Prophets—The Twelve	
Hosea	Nahum
Joel	Habakkuk
Amos	Zephaniah
Obadiah	Haggai
Jonah	Zechariah
Micah	Malachi

And to understand these books, we must understand their historical context—which brings us to our second major key in accessing these books.

Level-1 and Level-2 Historical Contexts

More than any other set of OT books, historical context is absolutely crucial in interpreting the Prophets. Imagine trying to understand the significance of Martin Luther King Jr.'s visionary "I Have a Dream"[4] speech outside of the context of the mid-1900s civil rights movement.[5]

---

[4] "Martin Luther King—I Have A Dream Speech—August 28, 1963," YouTube video, 17:28, posted by SullenToys.com, January 20, 2011, https://www.youtube.com/watch?v=smEqnnklfYs.

[5] "Civil rights movement," *Wikipedia*, March 6, 2019, https://en.wikipedia.org/wiki/Civil_rights_movement.

For the most part, for the Prophets, the level-1 and level-2 historical contexts are indistinguishable. That is, the context of the events described by the prophets and the context of the prophet and his audience are the same or at least close. That fact makes things a bit easier. The peculiarities of each book will be given in the literary section below. But the following will provide a general overview of the historical context of the writing prophets.

One can divide this context into three broad time periods: preexilic (760–late 600s BC), exilic (586 BC, the year of Jerusalem's fall to Babylon, and the years immediately prior and following), and postexilic (520–late 400s BC). Each epoch possesses its own unique challenges and crises.

The preexilic prophets include Isaiah among the major prophets and many of the minor prophets—Hosea, Amos, Jonah, Micah, Nahum, Habakkuk, Zephaniah, and possibly Joel and Obadiah.

The three great exilic prophets are all major prophets: Jeremiah, Ezekiel, and Daniel. One can also place the book of Lamentations in this group, because Jeremiah probably wrote this melancholy book in response to the exile.

Preexilic	Exilic	Postexilic
Hosea	Jeremiah	Haggai
Amos	Ezekiel	Zechariah
Jonah	Daniel	Malachi
Micah	Lamentations	Joel
Nahum		Obadiah
Habakkuk		
Zephaniah		
Joel		
Obadiah		

Finally, the postexilic prophets include Haggai, Zechariah, and Malachi, and, again, possibly Joel and Obadiah. Joel and Obadiah are listed as "possibly" because scholars dispute their context, and the books possess few internal clues that definitively place them in a particular period.

These historical periods were all developed in chapter 5. So here we will explore a few of the major issues concerning the prophets in each of the time periods.

During the preexilic period, God's people struggled with both internal and external issues. Remember that at this time, Israel has been divided between the northern kingdom (called Israel by the biblical authors) and the southern kingdom (called Judah) for some 150 to 200 years.

The northern kingdom experienced little spiritual success, with every king following in the lead of the first, the idolatrous Jeroboam I. Only two writing prophets direct their messages to Israel in the north—Amos and Hosea, with the latter being the only one from that area.

Amos and Hosea prophesied to the north near the end of Jeroboam II's reign (793–753 BC). This king had a long and capable rule according to worldly standards, and he successfully augmented the north's territory and economic prosperity. Politically, the regionally dominant Assyrian nation had occupied themselves with other concerns, which had given the Israelite king and nation room to maneuver. Socially and spiritually, however, the Israelite people, leadership, and culture had degraded.

A two-class economic system had created significant inequities and oppression. While the wealthy lived in ostentatious ivory palaces (Amos 3:15; 6:4), the beleaguered and tyrannized poor floundered. Spiritually, the people and religious leadership had compromised and perverted the Mosaic faith (Hos 4:4–9). They had merged Yahwism with Canaanite Baal worship (Hos 2:7, 17; 11:2) and had even engaged in sacred prostitution (Amos 2:7–8). The prophets vociferously confronted each of these evils, seeing them all as indicators of how far Israel had drifted from their covenant Lord.

*A decorative chain of ivory lotus buds from Samaria. The wealthy of
the northern kingdom of Israel possessed ivory furniture and inlays,
and the prophets believed these symbolized destructive excess.*

After the death of Jeroboam II, turmoil ensued in the monarchy of
the northern kingdom, which only worsened as Assyria grew more
powerful. Coups, countercoups, and assassinations produced an uncertain monarchy and an uncertain future. As discussed in the previous
chapter, the last Israelite king in the north was finally defeated by
the Assyrians in 722 BC, as the northern kingdom's capital,
Samaria, fell after a brutal three-year siege. The pitiless and impe-
rial Assyrians exiled and scattered much of the indigenous population such that Israel, as it had been known, ceased to exist (see
2 Kings 17). What the prophets had warned had occurred (Amos
7:17). The northern kingdom had met their God in judgment
(Amos 4:12).

> Her leaders issue rulings for
> a bribe, her priests teach for
> payment, and her prophets
> practice divination for silver.
> Yet they lean on the Lord,
> saying, "Isn't the Lord among
> us? No disaster will overtake
> us." Therefore, because of
> you, Zion will be plowed
> like a field, Jerusalem will
> become ruins, and the
> temple's mountain will be a
> high thicket. (Mic 3:11–12)

In the early preexilic period,
the southern kingdom of Judah experienced similar issues to those in
the north. The nation had its ups and downs spiritually, as did their

kings. Few of these lived up to the example of their forefather, King David. In addition, the other foundational institutions—the priesthood and even the prophets—also experienced corruption at unprecedented levels.

The prophets, priests, and kings all seemed motivated by prosperity and privilege, rather than covenantal obedience. Thus, the eighth-century Jewish prophets, such as Micah and Isaiah, proclaim prophecies comparable to their colleagues in the north.

The pressure on this tiny nation only increased with the exile of the north in 722 BC. The threat of an Assyrian onslaught and how to handle their menacing political presence became the dominant and immediate concern of both Micah and especially Isaiah. The stress from such a situation is hard for modern Western Christians to imagine.

The Assyrians were known to impale their victims on stakes, skin prisoners alive, count their slain enemies by the number of heads stacked at their king's feet, besiege cities until the occupants were reduced to cannibalism, and force mass deportations, separating families and nations. And the people of Judah in the southern kingdom only needed to look to their relatives in the north for evidence of this brutality.

Within this tumultuous world, small nations like Judah must have felt like a beach ball in F-5 tornado, tossed about at the mercy of the warring world. Picture yourself as a common person in that day, not knowing if within the next day or hour or minute marauding bands of Assyrians might consume you, your family, and your land as a locust plague (see Joel 1).

Such a context makes the prophetic messages of hope—for example, Isa 9:1–7 or Mic 5:1–5, which focus on a messianic deliverer—all the more powerful and palpable and pressing. This context changes how you "hear" the messages.

As discussed in the previous chapter, in approximately 700 BC, the Assyrian tornado had arrived on the rocky ridges of Jerusalem, after having conquered and destroyed every other walled city in Judah. The

An Assyrian soldier beheads an citizen of the Jewish city of Lachish. This relief was found in the palace of the Assyrian king Sennacherib. It celebrated the brutal victory over this second-largest Jewish city, and it demonstrates the cruelty of the Assyrians.

story of this event is found in Isaiah 36–39 (as well as 2 Kings 18–19 and 2 Chronicles 32). Amazingly, through the intervention of God and the leadership of the godly King Hezekiah and the ministry of the prophet Isaiah, Jerusalem survived. *See link to read about a recent archaeological discovery linking Isaiah and Hezekiah.*[6]

Also mentioned previously, after Hezekiah's death and this remarkable deliverance, Jerusalem lapses back into its old adulterous ways. Hezekiah is succeeded by his son Manasseh, who is considered

---

[6] Megan Sauter, "Isaiah's Signature Uncovered in Jerusalem: Evidence of the prophet Isaiah?" *Bible History*, February 22, 2018, https://www.biblical archaeology.org/daily/people-cultures-in-the-bible/people-in-the-bible /prophet-isaiah-signature-jerusalem/ (accessed March 4, 2019).

by the authors of Scripture to be the worst yet. Manasseh reigns for some fifty-five tragic years, and, as described in chapter 5, he becomes for God and his prophets the proverbial "last straw." Manasseh engages in both apostasy and atrocities—sacrificing his sons through fire in pagan religious rituals and filling Jerusalem with innocent blood (2 Kings 21).

Such is the level of Manasseh's evil that even the godly King Josiah (640–609 BC) cannot stave off the coming judgment on God's people. After Josiah dies prematurely in battle (2 Kgs 23:28–30), the four subsequent Jewish kings all fail politically and spiritually, leading to the exile.

During this period of covenant rebellion, seventh-century prophets such as Nahum, Habakkuk, and Zephaniah bring fiery messages of warning and woe. Knowing the level of spiritual adultery and the threat of God's just exile, we may understand why. Like Habakkuk, we might cry out,

> How long, LORD, must I call for help, and you do not listen or cry out to you about violence and you do not save? Why do you force me to look at injustice? Why do you tolerate wrongdoing? Oppression and violence are right in front of me. Strife is ongoing, and conflict escalates. This is why the law [Torah] is ineffective and justice never emerges. For the wicked restrict the righteous; therefore, justice comes out perverted. (Hab 1:2–4)

The Lord answers this prophetic cry for justice clearly. Habakkuk relates the Lord's words: "Look at the nations and observe—be utterly astounded! For I am doing something in your days that you will not believe when you hear about it. Look! I am raising up the Chaldeans, that bitter, impetuous nation that marches across the earth's open spaces to seize territories not its own. They are fierce and terrifying; their views of justice and sovereignty stem from themselves" (1:5–7).

The traditional grave of Habakkuk.

Three prophets span this exilic period—telling of the impending Babylonian exile and then seeing the exile realized. These are the great exilic prophets Jeremiah, Ezekiel, and Daniel. I will not retell the story of the exile related in chapter 5. Clearly each was deeply affected by this event, as were all God's people.

The Jews considered Jeremiah a traitor for his blunt predictions of Babylonian conquest. The Jewish kings hated him; the people persecuted him. Ezekiel was taken into exile by the Babylonians before the final destruction of Jerusalem (in an initial deportation in 597 BC), but his messages both predict and react to the annihilation. Daniel too was taken into exile before the final destruction (probably in 605 BC), and his life spans the entirety of the Babylonian domination of the Jews until the Persian/postexilic period (post-539 BC).

The exile for the Jews presented a crisis of faith. Everything upon which they had based their relationship with God—the Promised Land, the Davidic King, the covenant, the temple—had been lost or destroyed or compromised. And for the people, the event raised questions of divine impotence. How would you react to being dragged by bronze hooks in your nose across the desert to a foreign land, after seeing your entire life and nation and king obliterated?

As John Bright writes, "With evidences of undreamed-of wealth and power around them [in Babylon], with the magnificent temples of pagan gods on every hand, it must have occurred to many of [the exiles] to wonder whether Yahweh, patron God of a petty state which he seemed powerless to protect, was really the supreme and only God after all."[7]

It was left to these exilic prophets to explain the exile and also to encourage and exhort the exiles. So as you read Ezekiel or Jeremiah or even Lamentations (Jeremiah's poetic response to the exile), "feel" the message based on this context.

The last of the writing prophets are those of the postexile. As mentioned in chapter 5, the Persians conquered the Babylonians in 539 BC, and their ruler Cyrus the Great allowed conquered peoples to return to their native lands.

Though restored to Jerusalem, the people themselves were far from full restoration. The city and temple and the people's faith remained in ruins. Enter Zechariah and Haggai. The immediate concern of both was the rebuilding of the temple, which had begun in 536 BC, but had been put on hold due to indigenous opposition until 520 BC. These two prophets urged the people, as I explain in my classes, to "get off their hindquarters" and get to work. But these prophets also target deeper issues of attitude and doubt and continued covenant infidelity.

---

[7] John Bright, *A History of Israel*, 2nd ed. (Philadelphia: Westminster, 1972), 348.

The tomb of Cyrus the Great, approximately 1 km southwest of the palaces of Pasargadae. Cyrus's decree in 539 BC allowed the Jewish people to return from exile.

Yet the people continue in their old ways. So the OT ends with exhortations by the prophet Malachi in the late 400s BC for the people to return once again to God to stave off future devastating "days of the LORD." As mentioned in chapter 5, the OT period concludes with a cliff-hanger of sorts. Will the people return? Will God send another judgment? Will the Messiah ever come?

Literary Tools

Remember that the literary tools include things like literary structure/ message/purpose and genre. And once again, I will start our discussion with genre.

Genre

Generally speaking, the prophets use many different styles of writing—often with alarming and fiery language. All are used in service of the same goal. The prophets' purpose is to change the mind-sets and behaviors of a rebellious people and leadership strategically, systematically, and rhetorically.

Sometimes the prophets use poetry—especially in the early writing of the preexilic prophets. For instance, Obadiah, Nahum, Micah, and Habakkuk are almost completely poetic. A good majority of Isaiah's sixty-six chapters are also poetic. The repetition of Hebrew poetic verse particularly lends support to the prophets' rhetorical cause and helps make their messages memorable. See chapter 6 for a more detailed look at Hebrew poetic techniques.

Sometimes the prophets used common colloquial genres, such as parables (Isa 5:1–7; Ezekiel 23) or legal cases (Isaiah 1) or laments (Amos 5:1–3). These genres could be employed as a sports organist might play a funeral dirge at a key moment in a baseball game. The familiar form of a text heightens and highlights the prophetic function.

Native Hebrew speakers would understand the "rules" of these genres intuitively and could easily recognize any rhetorical modifications to them. The key with genre interpretation is first to note the typical structure and purpose, and then to analyze how the prophet manipulates or alters the typical to make a point.

To use a modern example, how should a typical fairy tale progress? From "once upon a time" to "happily ever after," correct? But what happens if the tale ends sadly or tragically? Does the surprise of this alteration of the norm not communicate a powerful, if not shocking, message?

Sometimes it is not just the prophets' language and genre that is alarming. Throughout the Prophetic Books, we find "sign acts"— where the prophet's actions themselves communicate the message. Perhaps most famous is Hosea's marriage to a scandalous adulteress to illustrate the spiritual infidelity of the nation against its loving covenant husband—God himself. One of the more humorous, and yet also serious, sign acts is when Isaiah walks naked and barefoot for not three days or three weeks but three years (!) as part of his message (Isaiah 20). Ezekiel's book is full of these disturbing acts as well. For instance, famously and tragically, Ezekiel's wife dies, and he is instructed not to mourn, as a sign of what would happen in the exile (Ezek 24:15–26).

With genre established, let's examine our next literary tool—that of the literary structure, message, and purpose of the books.

Literary Structure/Message/Purpose

The following will examine the message, purpose, and structure of the Prophetic Books in a chronological rather than canonical fashion. Though there is purpose and history behind the canonical structure, a chronological discussion allows us to keep the historical context central and primary. A detailed discussion of each book is not possible. The goal is to give hints and, well, tools that can help you to begin to unpack and access these wonderful texts.

Amos. The first prophet to be considered is Amos. Amos's name means "burden-bearer," which vividly illustrates the "heavy" calling and message of this prophet. He did not possess a typical prophetic pedigree, being a simple Judean sheepherder and raiser of fig trees (Amos 7:14). But as we have seen, God often chooses to use the unexpected for his purposes. God calls Amos to prophesy judgment against the northern kingdom at their political and economic apex. And he does so fearlessly. In particular, Amos emphasizes social justice and practical ethics and sees these as "spiritual barometers" for the nation—demonstrating the health or lack thereof of the people's covenant relationship with God (see the Theological Tools below). One of the distinctive traits of the Torah covenant is the call for God's people to care for the "least of these"; the people's current neglect of the widow, orphan, alien, and outcast demonstrates how far the people had fallen in covenant relationship. When the people lack proper fruit—justice and righteousness that roll down like waters—God "despises" any outward and traditional displays of their religion (5:21–24). While hope remains for the "fortunes of my people Israel" to be restored, it has to wait for the "fallen shelter of David" to be raised up again (9:11–15).

Hosea. Prophesying around the same time period (750 BC) in the same region is Hosea (from the same root as the name Jesus, meaning "salvation"). Again, Hosea is the only writing prophet actually from the northern kingdom. He is best known for embodying the message of Yahweh in a shocking sign act. Hosea is commanded to marry an unfaithful bride, Gomer, who bears him three children—one of whom is his, but the others possess uncertain paternal origins. Even the names of these children contain ominous messages of judgment (e.g., "Not My People" and "No Compassion/Mercy"). As expected, Hosea's adulterous spouse leaves him. Such infidelity illustrates, to use the words of Hank Williams Sr., the "cheatin' heart" of Israel, who has committed flagrant, unrepentant spiritual adultery against God.[8] Yet, with one of the most powerful demonstrations of grace in the Bible, God instructs Hosea to redeem his wife, to show how God would redeem his people (chap. 3). God's tender love is woven throughout the book. He loves and restores his wayward "bride" despite the Israelites' blatant breaking of his covenant.

Jonah. The unique book of Jonah represents one of the most controversial among the Prophetic Books. Oddly, the book contains mostly narrative and only one prophecy— "In forty days Nineveh will be demolished" (3:4). Yet the book as a whole presents a powerful prophetic message. Famously, God calls Jonah to preach against Nineveh, the capital of the brutal Assyrians (see the above discussion on historical context). Instead, Jonah (meaning "dove") flies, going down

Hosea is the only writing prophet actually from the northern kingdom. He is best known for embodying the message of Yahweh in a shocking sign act.

---

[8] "Hank William Sr—Your Cheatin Heart lyrics," YouTube video, 2:45, posted by theresa duplessis, June 7, 2009, https://www.youtube.com/watch?v=cS4LCoh0VGQ.

to Tarshish (1:3) and then going down into the Mediterranean Sea during a storm (1:15) and then going down into the belly of the fish (1:17). Inside the fish in the depths, Jonah understandably comes to his senses; he assents to go to Nineveh. He proclaims God's message and amazingly the people of Nineveh repent. Knowing Nineveh's reputation, one can perhaps forgive Jonah's initial reluctance to go. But his hesitation stems not from fear of personal harm, but from his desire to see the Assyrians reap their just rewards. He knows that God is a God of mercy (4:2, quoting Exod 34:6–7), and Jonah does not want God to give it to the Assyrians. Jonah is angry that all Nineveh needs to do to receive mercy is simple repentance (chap. 4). So the book's primary focus is a God who may freely bestow his compassion on whomever he wills. *See Wordsearch link to read a great article on this message, especially as revealed in the object lesson God gives Jonah in chapter 4.*[9] In this way, the book speaks clearly and hopefully to any today who might claim to be beyond the reach of God's mercy. In addition, the book represents a back-handed slap at the Israelites. Indeed, God's people received prophetic message after prophetic message and yet hardened their hearts. But the hardened and hated Assyrians receive just one—admittedly fishy and stomach-acid-stained—prophecy, and they and even their cattle (3:7; 4:11) repent.

Micah. Later in the eighth century BC is the prophet Micah (abbreviation for Micayahu, "who is like Yahweh?"). Micah shares many similarities in message with Amos. Like his northern counterpart, Micah focuses on social injustices, this time in the southern kingdom of Judah—iniquities that indicate spiritual deterioration. The primary offenders in the covenant abandonment are the leadership of Judah—the prophets, priests, and kings. Micah accuses them of being haters of good and lovers of evil (3:2), who eat the flesh of God's people (3:2–3), who "abhor justice" (3:9), and who build kingdoms through bloodshed

---

[9] John H. Walton, "The Object Lesson of Jonah 4:5-7 and the Purpose of the Book of Jonah," *Bulletin for Biblical Research* 2 (1992): 47-57.

(3:10). Structurally, the book is organized by the threefold call to "listen . . ." (1:2; 3:1; 6:1). In these sections, Micah alternates between messages of judgment and messages of hope. Like his contemporary Isaiah, Micah finds this hope in one place, a Davidic King born in humble Bethlehem (5:2), who would be for the embattled people "peace" (5:5). See the Applying the Results section in chapter 5.

Micah shares many similarities in his message with Amos. Like his northern counterpart, Micah focuses on social injustices, this time in the southern kingdom of Judah—iniquities that indicate spiritual deterioration.

Isaiah. The book of the prophet Isaiah (meaning "Yahweh is salvation") represents one of the most complex and majestic in the entire Bible. His ministry spanned a half a century (from the year of King Uzziah's death to the reign of King Hezekiah, mid-700s–early 600s

BC), and he served his nation and the Davidic kings of Judah during the turbulent time of the Assyrian threat. Such is the complexity of the book that many critical scholars have wrongly attributed the book to multiple authors. But for many reasons, Isaiah should be viewed as a unified whole written by the eighth-century Isaiah son of Amoz. Isaiah's call narrative sets the tone for the book. In chapter 6, Isaiah has a vision of Yahweh seated on his throne, lofty and exalted. Angelic seraphim ("burning ones") call out "Holy, holy, holy," and Isaiah finds himself on his knees, proclaiming himself to be a "man of unclean lips" who dwells among a people of unclean lips. After commanding the cleansing of Isaiah's chops with a coal from the altar, God calls this prophet to go proclaim a message of judgment to a people of hardened ears and hearts.[10] Thus, much of the first part of the book (chaps. 1–39) highlights this warning. Following a narrative of the Assyrian siege of Jerusalem in chapters 36–39, the remainder of the book focuses on comfort for God's people (see 40:1). The main source of hope is the Messiah.[11] In fact, as the apostle John writes, Isaiah "saw his [Jesus's] glory and spoke about him" (John 12:41). For a fuller discussion of Isaiah's multiple messianic prophecies, including the mind-blowing Song of the Suffering Servant in chapter 53, see the Putting the Tools to Use section below.

Nahum. The book penned by the prophet Nahum is the first of several books in the prophetic corpus focused solely on a foreign nation. Prophesying at the height of Assyrian power (mid–late 600s BC), Nahum foretells a fiery doom for this nation's malicious and imperialistic capital, Nineveh. With striking detail, Nahum describes the

---

[10] See https://www.youtube.com/watch?time_continue=1&v=vAXPV qFRw_k for a sermon by the author on Isaiah 6.

[11] See passages such as Isa 9:6–7; 11:1–2, 4; 42:1; 49:1–3; 50:4; 53; 59:1; 61:1–3; and 63:1–4.

"overwhelming flood" that would destroy Nineveh (1:8; cf. 2:3–4; 3:2–3)—a prophecy that became a reality in 612 BC, when the Medes and Babylonians overthrew Nineveh[12] after the flooding Tigris River breached the seemingly impenetrable city walls.[13] Nahum's name means "comfort," and for a threatened and imperiled Judah, his message certainly must have consoled. Regardless of how things might seem, God does not forget or forsake his people, even in judgment. Indeed, he is the Stronghold for his people and their Avenger, who will call the guilty to account (1:2–3, 7). This hopeful message of God's sovereign and coming justice is similar to what is found in the book of Revelation. There, a reigning and avenging Christ brings hope to a persecuted church.

Habakkuk. Distinctive among the Prophetic Books is the work of Habakkuk (meaning "embraced" [by Yahweh]). The first part of the book is uniquely styled as a dialogue between the distressed prophet and Yahweh himself. Prophesying during the difficult years immediately preceding the exile, Habakkuk questions why God has yet to check the unchecked spiritual infidelity of Judah (1:2–4). God responds by stating his discipline will soon arrive in the form of Babylon (1:5–11). A flabbergasted Habakkuk challenges God, asking how he could use and seemingly reward such an evil and brutal nation as Babylon (1:12–17). The prophet determines to take his stand on the watchtower to wait for God's response (2:1). Yahweh answers with clarity in 2:4–20. He promises punishment for Babylon. Indeed, being used as a divine agent does not excuse their conduct. Habakkuk then responds with a submissive

---

[12] "Battle of Nineveh (612 BC)," *Wikipedia*, last modified February 11, 2019, https://en.wikipedia.org/wiki/Battle_of_Nineveh_(612_BC).

[13] "3D Digital Art Ancient Nineveh—Ashurbanipal, Assyria," YouTube video, 2:39, posted by TheObserversTV, March 18, 2016, https://www.youtube.com/watch?v=XzFySIllqk8.

and humble psalm in chapter 3. The most striking verse in the book in Habakkuk is 2:4, where God affirms that the righteous one in Israel will live and survive the crisis by "his faith." The original intent of this verse is to prescribe the correct human response to God in the face of a moral and military crisis. Paul rightly expands this statement into a universal principle regarding the nature of salvation (Gal 3:11; Rom 1:17)—that is, that the salvation promised in the gospel is by faith alone.

Zephaniah. The last of the preexilic prophets is Zephaniah. His name appropriately means "Yahweh has stored up," and, indeed, in this book

Beginning of the Habakkuk Commentary or Pesher Habakkuk, 1QpHab, one of the first Dead Sea Scrolls discovered in 1947. Courtesy of the Israel Museum.

one finds the full fury of the Lord's stored-up discipline against his covenant people. Prophesying of the impending Babylonian exile (late 600s BC), the prophet speaks bluntly of an approaching "day of the LORD"—a day in which God would invade space and time for the purpose of enforcing his covenant. Undoubtedly this day refers to the destruction of Jerusalem by Babylon in 586 BC. And this day is fearful, being pictured as a reversal of creation (1:2–6). The justice meted out would ultimately extend to other nations (2:4–15). Yet even as the first part of the book is black and bleak, the last part is bright and blessed. As a diamond against black felt, like a beautiful sunset after the storm, Zephaniah's message of hope and restoration in 3:9–20 shines all the more against the darkness of judgment. Indeed, when God restores his people to right covenant relationship, this "warrior who saves" will exult over his people with loud singing (3:17). Such is the arresting beauty of God's grace that may be found at times in the prophets.

Jeremiah. With the prophet Jeremiah (meaning "Yahweh loosens" or "Yahweh exalts"), one finds the first of the great exilic prophets. As noted in the Historical Tools above, one cannot overstate the significance of the exilic crisis of faith for the Israelites. Known as the "weeping prophet," Jeremiah suffers incalculably for his blunt confrontation of the people, of the kings, and of the numerous false prophets, who tell the kings what they want to hear (see chap. 28). Jeremiah prophesies just before and during the Babylonian exile. Because he tells of the inevitable judgment, his people brand him a traitor. But this prophet remains faithful to God's call (chap. 1), even after the fall of Jerusalem and even after he is taken to Egypt against his will after the exile. Jeremiah is the longest OT book in terms of word count. And in his calling and message, he is very much a "prophet like Moses" (Deut 18:18). More than any other prophet, Jeremiah grounds his accusations based on the Torah of Moses (see the Theological Tools below). Indeed, for Jeremiah, outward displays of religion were no substitute for true covenant commitment (chap. 7) as prescribed in the Torah. Although Israel had failed in fulfilling its covenant responsibilities, Yahweh would not fail to fulfill his—for discipline and for restoration. At the heart of Jeremiah's message is hope—the hope of a new restored covenant people of God. Indeed, only in Jeremiah do we find the phrase "new covenant" (31:27–34)—although many other prophets anticipated it (see below). *See Wordsearch content for a brief discussion of the significance of the new covenant for the modern church.*

Lamentations. The book of Lamentations is not technically a prophetic book but a poetic lament over the Babylonian exile. Its placement in the canon is due to Jewish tradition (rightly, I believe) ascribing the book to the prophet Jeremiah. For a more detailed look at Lamentations, consider the discussion of it in chapter 3, where it is used as an illustration of the importance of historical context. As noted there, the book consists of a series of five laments composed as alphabetic acrostics (where each verse begins with a word that begins with a subsequent letter of the Hebrew alphabet—twenty-two in all). Acrostics communicate totality and perfection. Jeremiah, who experienced what he prophesied, uses this tool to express his complete and profound grief over the destruction of his people, his temple, and his land. Yet at the heart of the book is a profound assertion of profound hope, grounded in the author's continued belief in what everyone around him was doubting—God's faithfulness (3:19–38).

Ezekiel. My favorite prophet is another exilic envoy, the enigmatic Ezekiel (meaning "God strengthens"). Ezekiel wins the award for being the most creative and even bizarre among the writing prophets. In fact, in Jewish tradition, some of his messages were even restricted to adults. Taken into exile as a young priest in 597 BC, he is called by God to be a prophet (chaps. 1–3) while in Babylon in 593 BC, some seven years before the destruction of Jerusalem. His visionary call—complete with fearsome four-headed beings, glowing gems, and a floating divine throne—unnerves the prophet but communicates a clear message. This glorious God is free to move, and he is about to leave the corrupt and unfaithful city and allow its destruction (see the Applying the Results section below). God's glory departs Jerusalem (chap. 8) and does not return until some 600 years later. The bulk of Ezekiel's book describes the doom facing Judah, specifically for abandoning the covenant (chaps. 1–24) and becoming a fruitless vine (chap. 15) and unfaithful bride (chap. 16). The covenant curses (see the Theological Tools below) are coming, and thus, this section of the book is filled with bloodshed, climaxing in the disturbing Song of the Sword in chapter 21. Even the nations surrounding Judah do not escape God's wrath (chaps. 25–32). But something amazing happens in chapter 34. Starting with this chapter, death is not mentioned again in the book. Chapters 34–48 present some of the most striking messages of restoration found in the Bible. God will raise up the dry bones of his people (37:1–14) and shepherd them through his servant David (37:24–28; 34:23–24; cf. John 10). Yahweh will grant the people a new heart (36:26) and a covenant of peace (34:25), for his name's sake (36:22). The book closes with a splendid vision of a renewed temple (chaps. 40–48)—not one to be built, but one to symbolize how God will one day dwell with his covenant people forever (John 1:14; Rev 21:9–27).

Daniel. The book of Daniel (meaning "God is my judge") is perhaps the most popular Prophetic Book among many Christians. This esteem is primarily due to the well-known narratives concerning Daniel and his three friends (chaps. 1–6). These stories, such as Daniel in the lions' den and Daniel's friends in the fiery furnace, capture the imagination and make great Sunday school lessons and even fun Veggie

Tales videos.[14] But the book is much more than cool stories and object lessons. Taken into exile in 605 BC, almost twenty years before the destruction of Jerusalem, Daniel served the longest of any prophet, from the early Babylonian period to the early Persian period (which began in 539 BC). But he served more as a statesman and court official than a typical prophet per se. Like Joseph and Esther, Daniel is raised to power by God in a foreign land to serve and preserve his people. God uses Daniel to propel salvation history forward. The book includes a historical section (chaps. 1–6) and an apocalyptic section (chaps. 7–12), highlighted by a messianic vision of the "son of man" (see the part 2 introduction). The primary theological theme of the book is God's sovereignty, which is appropriate given the historical context. No matter how things seem, the Ancient of Days will bring the nations to justice through his chosen Messianic Son of Man; indeed, he controls the rising and falling of kings and kingdoms, including Babylon, Persia, and any other kingdom. And one day, he will raise his people to newness of life in the resurrection (12:1–3).

Joel. The book of Joel is hard to place historically, with scholars placing him anywhere between the ninth and fourth centuries BC. Hints at the exile and a vast destruction seem to place the book in the immediate exilic or postexilic period, but Jewish tradition and canonical position (between the preexilic Hosea and Amos) would push the date earlier. Regardless, the message (as embodied by Joel's name, "Yahweh is God") is timeless. As with earlier prophets, such as Zephaniah and Amos, Joel proclaims a coming day of Yahweh, but he perhaps presents the most developed portrayal of the theme. Joel initially shows the day as one of judgment—using the image of a locust plague. For

---

[14] "VeggieTales Daniel & The Lions Den," YouTube video, 27:24, posted by Larry the Cucumber, January 24, 2018, https://www.youtube.com/watch?v=LsqtKx2NRSw.

*Daniel served the longest of any prophet, from the early
Babylonian period to the early Persian period (which began in
539 BC). Like Joseph and Esther, Daniel is raised to power
by God in a foreign land to serve and preserve his people.*

the Jew, this judgment (as a covenant curse) can be due to only one thing—covenant infidelity (Deut 28:38; see the discussion on covenant curses in the Theological Tools below). Indeed, in ancient and modern history, these insects can prove devastating. But as Joel progresses in his description, the locusts seem to take on characteristics of human armies—perhaps even the Babylonians. In response to this divine discipline, God's people should rend their hearts and not their garments and return to him (2:12–13). But Joel also looks forward to another day of Yahweh—one of salvation (2:28–32). On this day, God will pour out his Spirit and renew and even expand his covenant people, and those who call upon his name will be saved. The apostle Peter rightly believes this prophecy to be fulfilled on the day of Pentecost (see Acts 2:14–21)—the birthday of the church.

Obadiah. Like Joel, Obadiah (meaning "servant of Yahweh") is difficult to date. Canonically, it is placed with the preexilic books, but in its message, the book seems to respond to the exile. Indeed, this shortest OT book, comprising a single chapter, is singular in its focus. Like Nahum, Obadiah proclaims God's judgment against a long-standing enemy of God's people, this time the Edomites. This people group possessed a lasting antagonism against Israel, which goes all the way back to their famous ancestor, Jacob's brother, Esau. In fact, from the very beginning and throughout the history of Israel, Esau and his children fought with his twin brother, Jacob/Israel, and his children. This antipathy culminates when Edom opposes and even cheers as the Babylonians level Judah in 586 BC. Other biblical writers also impugn Edom for this malicious participation in the exile (see Jer 49:7–22; Ezek 25:12–14; 35:5–6; Lam 4:21–22; and Ps 137:7). Because of its pride and sibling hatred, Edom will experience a "day of the LORD" (vv. 15–16)—a prophecy fulfilled in 312 BC, when the Nabataeans destroyed the Edomite capital of Petra. Also like Nahum, the book intends to give comfort to the persecuted people of God. This God is determined to establish his kingdom on earth (v. 21), and the godly may take consolation that their enemies will ultimately fall.

Haggai. The first of the postexilic writing prophets is the prophet Haggai (derived from a word meaning "pilgrimage festival"). This prophet possessed a short ministry (a little more than three months) and a very direct message. A contemporary of Zechariah, his main role was as encourager in chief in the rebuilding of the temple, which had been destroyed in 586 BC by the Babylonians. Construction of the second temple in Jerusalem had begun in 536 BC with Persian permission, but opposition from internal groups had delayed the building until 520 BC, some two decades after the original return from exile. Complacency had taken root. The people lived in comfort and "paneled houses," while God's house lay in ruins (1:4). Haggai reprimands the people for their apathy and misplaced priorities (1:1–11), and the effect of his exhortation is immediate. The people—led by Davidic descendant Zerubbabel and Joshua the high priest—respond with obedience and action (1:12–15). The remainder of this brief book describes a coming glory of the temple and calls the people to recognize and anticipate God's restoration, which would focus primarily on a future Davidic king (2:23).

A contemporary of Zechariah, Haggai's main role was as encourager in chief in the rebuilding of the temple, which had been destroyed in 586 BC by the Babylonians.

Zechariah. For me personally, Zechariah (meaning "Yahweh has remembered") represents the most complex and cryptic of the Prophetic Books. This prophet experiences a series of night visions (chaps. 1–6) of horsemen (chap. 1), measuring lines (chap. 2), golden lampstands (chap. 4), flying scrolls (chap. 5; students often mishear me, as if I'm saying "squirrels"!), and chariots (chap. 6)—all of which provide much fodder for the complex imagery of Revelation. Zechariah also includes several apocalyptic burdens (chaps. 9–14). All these texts are rather daunting exegetically. The key to understanding Zechariah is his historical context. Born in Babylon, he returns to Jerusalem with many other Jews in 538 BC. Like Haggai, Zechariah rebukes the people for their delay in rebuilding the temple. This seems to be the focus of chapters 1–8. The climax of this section is the stirring vision of chapter 3. In this revelation, God replaces the sullied clothing and tarnished turban of Joshua the high priest, as a way of demonstrating how he will cleanse the entire people of their sin. This cleansing will be accomplished in "a single day," when God brings forth his messianic King, "the Branch"

In his more apocalyptic visions (chaps. 9–14), Zechariah envisages a humble Messiah, who will ride into Jerusalem on a donkey bringing salvation (9:9). Of course, Christians know who this Messiah is—Jesus the Christ (Matt 21:5; John 12:15).

(3:8–9). Later, in his more apocalyptic visions (chaps. 9–14), Zechariah also envisages a humble Messiah, who will ride into Jerusalem on a donkey bringing salvation (9:9). Of course, Christians know who this Messiah is—Jesus the Christ (Matt 21:5; John 12:15). Zechariah further clarifies the identity of this Messiah. As a rejected "shepherd" (11:4–17), he will ultimately be smitten by the sword (13:7), but the result will be the ultimate restoration of God's people (13:9).

Malachi. The last of the Prophetic Books (and the last OT book) is Malachi (meaning "my messenger"). Little is known of this prophet personally, as the book itself provides our only access to him. Most scholars believe he wrote in the late fifth century BC, at the end of the OT period. Like Nehemiah, Malachi calls out and condemns the postexilic populace for their sin. In particular, he targets their covenant infidelity, irreverence in worship (1:6–14), lack of esteem for God's Word (2:1–9), intermarriage with foreign women (2:10–16), and greed (3:7–15). Because their core sin was covenantal in nature, Malachi warns of further covenant curses and even a coming "day of the LORD"—a day of covenant enforcement. Just as the NT ends with a distressing picture of the church (in Revelation 3, the church at Laodicea), so the OT ends on a similar dour note. But Malachi holds out hope for God's intervention. The "Messenger of the covenant you delight in" is coming into God's temple (3:1). And God will send forth another messenger, Elijah (John the Baptist) to prepare the Messiah's way (4:5). And so, as mentioned above, the OT ends with a sense of expectancy. See the Putting the Tools to Use section for more on Malachi.

Theological Tools

As important as historical keys are in interpreting the prophets, the third and final key to accessing the prophetic message is perhaps the most important—understanding the theological foundation for the

Malachi predicted that God would send forth another messenger,
Elijah (John the Baptist) to prepare the Messiah's way (4:5).

prophetic message. This basic message unites all of the prophets without exception.

Think of a modern-day preacher. When a preacher preaches, what is the basis of that exhortation? Of course, a good sermon derives from and is based on the Scriptures. Preachers take God's already received special revelation and "rebuke, correct, and encourage" a new generation of God's people based on that message (2 Tim 4:2).

Sometimes Bible scholars view the prophets as creative originators of the OT faith. But the prophets were not delivering some new message but preaching an old message in new ways. What was that old message? The message of God's covenant and his covenant history with his people—particularly as found in the Torah.

The Talmud, a record of Jewish rabbinic teachings dating back to the time of Christ, puts it this way: "Neither have [the prophets] diminished anything nor have they added anything to what is written in

Preachers like the late Billy Graham (above) take God's already received special revelation and "rebuke, correct, and encourage" a new generation of God's people based on that message (2 Tim 4:2).

the Torah." And again, "Moses had already spoken all the words of the prophets."[15]

As pointed out in chapter 4, you could argue that covenant is the central theme in all the Bible, so we should not be surprised to see how central it is in the Prophetic Books. Let's remember how we defined covenant in the chapter on the Pentateuch. A covenant is a solemn union of two individuals or groups, grounded in loyalty, love, promise, and commitment—kind of like a marriage today.

In chapter 4, we saw how God has been working in the world since creation to bring about redemption, and his chosen method of achieving this goal is through the covenant relationships he forms with his

---

[15] Quoted in Robertson, *Christ of the Prophets*, 122. Robertson's book is one of the best introductions to the prophetic message, for those interested in reading further.

people. He could have achieved salvation without us, but he chose to allow us to participate in his redemptive purposes.

His plan starts with Adam at creation (and the renewed covenant with Noah). Then God establishes a covenant relationship with one man, Abraham, through whom God will bring blessing to the nations (Gen 12:3). After several centuries, God calls an entire people (Israel) to himself to be a kingdom of priests to the nations (Exod 19:4–6). Finally, God chooses one man (the king David and the kings in his line) to represent his people, so that Israel is judged by and relates to God through the king (2 Sam 7:8–17; Psalm 89).

After the repeated failures of nation and king—Abraham's offspring—the OT also points forward to a new covenant—a new people of God with the Torah on their hearts and the Messiah at their heads (Jer 31:27–34; Ezek 34:23–24; among many others).

So where do the prophets stand in this redemptive history? After all the old covenants—particularly those with Abraham, Israel, and David—but before the new; their message draws on the old covenants and looks forward to the fulfillment of all of these in the new covenant.

Adam   Noah   Abraham   Israel   David   New

How does this work? *Looking back* to the Abrahamic covenant, the prophets urge the people to be mindful of the missionary purpose of their covenant with God (Gen 12:3). The prophets remind Israel of its special status as a nation and the accompanying promises. But the prophets also point out to the people that these promises are unconditional to the nation but not to individual generations, who could be cut off from the blessings of the covenant.

Looking forward based on the Abrahamic covenant, the prophets point to the eventual fulfillment of the Abrahamic promises in the restoration, led by the Davidic Messiah. When God's people are redeemed in this new covenant, the Abrahamic promises will be fulfilled, particularly the missional promise of being a blessing to the nations. "'Then the nations will call you blessed, for you will be a land of delight,' says YHWH of Hosts" (Mal 3:12; Cribb translation). "If you return, Israel . . . then the nations will be blessed by him and will pride themselves in him (Jer 4:1–2). "I will make them and the area around my hill a blessing" (Ezek 34:26).

Looking back, based on the Israelite covenant, the prophets explained more fully the commands of the Torah, and they call on people to fear and serve their covenant Lord and to be faithful to the covenant principles (Ten Commandments). As covenant enforcers, the prophets plead for repentance before the nation experiences the consequences of disobedience—the covenant curses. Indeed, the covenant curses from the Torah are hugely significant in explaining the overall prophetic message.

The curses can be found principally in three passages in the Pentateuch: Leviticus 26 and Deuteronomy 28 (the so-called curse sections of the covenant documents) and Deuteronomy 32 (the Song of Moses). These curses include calamities such as sword, famine, wild beasts, and pestilence (see Ezek 14:21). The prophets would often speak of these and use them rhetorically.[16]

In other words, when the prophets spoke of oppressing and overwhelming occupations, failed crops and famine, plagues and pestilence, bloodshed and blight, they were literally saying: "Look and see! You should not be surprised. You have breached the covenant. Now you see

---

[16] Douglas K. Stuart, *Hosea-Jonah*, Word Biblical Commentary, vol. 31 (Waco, TX: Word Books, 1987), xxxii–xxxiii. Indeed, as Stuart asserts, these prophetic covenant lawyers spoke about little besides the fulfillment of these blessings and cursings—i.e., "how and why God's people may expect to be punished by a variety of disasters soon, and how and why they may expect to be rescued and restored eventually."

the promised consequences. Remember the covenant that you have forsaken."

I liken the rhetorical function of the curses to parental discipline. When I tell my boys that they will not get dessert if they disobey my direction, I don't need to tell them what they have done when they do disobey. I just need to say, "No dessert for you."

Of course, as with parental punishments, the overarching goal was for the reprimands to result in repentance and a return to right covenant relationship. But so often, God's people simply ignored his curses (see Amos 4:6–13). And thus, the people needed someone to fulfill God's righteous requirements for them (see below).

Looking forward, the prophets used the covenant curses for another purpose. When they announce the withdrawal of the curses from the people, it becomes a powerful picture of covenant restoration. "I will make a covenant of peace with them and eliminate dangerous creatures from the land, so that they may live securely in the wilderness and sleep in the forest" (Ezek 34:25). In the place of the curses, God grants "showers of blessing" (v. 26) for his people who have returned to him. "'Test me in this way,' says the LORD of Armies. 'See if I will not open the floodgates of heaven and pour out a blessing for you without measure" (Mal 3:10).[17]

When will this happen? *Also looking forward,* the prophets anticipate a new covenant. In this new covenant, God will seek out his people and rescue them from the chief covenant curse—spiritual and physical exile (Ezek 34:11). God will then make a new covenant, and he will write the Torah on their hearts (Jer 31:33), so that they will be in right relationship with him. He will give them a heart of flesh to replace their heart of stone and put his Spirit within them (Ezek 36:26–27). And covenant relationship will be renewed: "I will be their God, and they will be my people" (Jer 31:33).

---

[17] See also the Ruth 1:6 discussion in chap. 5.

Finally, *looking back,* based on the Davidic covenant, the prophets call on the kings to lead the people in covenant relationship with God through Torah obedience. The prophets point out that the Davidic kings bear the primary responsibility for the spiritual well-being of the nation and thus bear the stricter judgment. As we've mentioned, as the kings go, so goes the nation. If the kings walk in covenant with God, then God will consider the nation to be righteous. And if the kings do not, the nation will experience the covenant curses.

Does that seem fair—that the people as a whole would experience harsh discipline because of the actions of the one?

But this also works in the opposite direction. *Looking forward,* the prophets anticipate a new covenant restoration centered on the figure of a Davidic Messiah, who would set all things aright. God's "servant" David would shepherd God's people rightly in covenant (Ezek 34:23–24), and because of his leadership, God's people "will follow my ordinances, and keep my statutes and obey them" (Ezek 37:24). The Messiah shall establish the righteousness of God "from now on and forever" (Isa 9:7). In fact, he will be our righteousness before God (Jer 23:6). When God looks at this eternal Davidic King, he will not see his people's sin, but the righteousness of the King himself.

Because of this King, the prophets can say that when God brings forward his "servant, the Branch," he "will take away the iniquity of this land in a single day" (Zech 3:8–9). Ironically and providentially, this removal of the people's sin will be accomplished by the suffering of God's kingly messianic Servant. As Isaiah so powerfully prophesies: "But he was pierced because of our rebellion, crushed because of our iniquities; punishment for our peace was on him, and we are healed by his wounds. We all went astray like sheep; we all have turned to our own way; and the LORD has punished him for the iniquity of us all" (Isa 53:5–6). See the Putting the Tools to Use section below for more on this song.

Of course, Christians know the identity of this King, Branch, Suffering Servant, and Messiah. In the NT book of Acts, Luke reports: "The eunuch said to Philip, 'I ask you, who is the prophet saying this about—himself or someone else?' Philip proceeded to tell him the good news about Jesus, beginning with that Scripture" (8:34–35).

Putting the Tools to Use

The following will offer two examples showing how the use of tools can be helpful in interpreting biblical texts from the Prophetic Books. Before reading my interpretation, try it for yourself. Work through the following questions, and then see if you can discern the original meaning.

Example 1: Who or What Is the Sun of Righteousness in Malachi 4:2?

Historical Tools

What is the level-1/level-2 historical context and how does that affect my reading of the text?

Literary Tools

What is the genre of the text? How does the author manipulate the genre for his purposes? What is the purpose and structure of the book? Where does this text fit into that purpose and structure?

Theological Tools

Are there any key theological terms or concepts in the text? How do I understand the text in light of Christ and the full testimony of the Bible?

Application

What does this text tell me about God? About Jesus? About myself?
About the world? About how I relate to God?

Interpretation

As an OT professor, I sometimes feel as if I have a neon sign on my
back flashing, "Ask me your most difficult Bible question." Rarely does
a week go by without some query about some "hard text"—whether
from emails from random visitors to our website, from students after
class, or from a layperson at church.

One I received recently concerned Mal 4:2. The text reads: "But
for you who fear my name, the sun of righteousness shall rise with
healing in its wings, and you will go out and playfully jump like calves
from the stall."

The person who asked the question was teaching the book of
Malachi to a women's group. In her preparation, she wondered if the
"sun of righteousness" and "its wings" are specific messianic references
to Jesus.

No doubt, the language of this text confuses. But as with any passage, the key to understanding its meaning is in using the tools.

As described above, Malachi is prophesying in the postexile, at the
end of the OT period. Though restored from captivity in Babylon,
Israel has not been reconciled to God. In fact, Malachi claims that
God's people have largely continued in their covenant infidelity that
led to the exile in the first place. Indeed, the threat of disciplinary covenant curses (famine, plague, pestilence, sword, etc.; see Leviticus 26) is
still very real for God's people.

Is there any hope for those who maintain covenant fidelity, in the
midst of this disobedient generation? That hope is found in a coming

"day of the LORD"—a primary theme in Malachi. This day is one in which Israel's covenant God will intervene providentially in space and time for his purposes—a day of covenant enforcement. Such intervention could involve judgment or salvation. In this case, the text seems to be referring to the "day of the LORD" as one of salvation for his people—for those who "fear" his name—that is, the people who have been faithful to God's covenant in the crooked and perverse generation of the postexile.

And when the "day of the LORD" comes, God will bring "healing" (from the covenant curses) and restored blessing (covenant blessings as pictured through the vigor of young calves). As stated above, the prophets considered the removal of these curses and the pouring out of covenant blessings (see Ezek 34:25–31) as a sign of full restoration to right covenant relationship.

Note that, as this passage states, this restoration comes only from the righteousness provided by God—pictured by Malachi as being as bright as the sun itself. The "wings" are an ancient Near Eastern way of describing the rays of the sun.

The question is, when will this "day of the LORD" and healing/blessing/covenant restoration take place? It will take place when the One who brings in the new covenant comes (Mal 3:1). Then, those who are in darkness will see a great light (Isa 9:2), and God will place over them "my servant David" as prince (Ezek 34:23).

I could be wrong, but I would argue that "sun of righteousness" focuses on the restoration that God would bring through his Messiah (who is God Our Righteousness; see Jer 23:4–6) and through his new covenant, rather than the "sun" being a one-to-one correspondence with the Messiah.

But the lines are blurred here, aren't they? After all, it is a "hard text." That's why we need the tools!

Example 2: Recognizing the Savior in Isaiah 52:13–53:12

Historical Tools

What is the level-1/level-2 historical context and how does that affect my reading of the text?

Literary Tools

What is the genre of the text? How does the author manipulate the genre for his purposes? What is the purpose and structure of the book? Where does this text fit into that purpose and structure?

Theological Tools

Are there any key theological terms or concepts in the text? How do I understand the text in light of Christ and the full testimony of the Bible? Check the cross-references to the New Testament.

Application

What does this text tell me about God? About Jesus? About myself? About the world? About how I relate to God?

Interpretation

It's difficult for Christians to maintain perspective around Christmastime. The endless barrage of strip-mall Santas and social events, novelty songs and nativity scenes can kick up enough mind-numbing nostalgia dust to cloud anyone's spiritual vision. Yet in the midst of the swollen schedules, we must come to grips with the significance of the Child in the manger whom the church celebrates.

The Bible attests of one individual who comprehended clearly the proverbial "true meaning" of Christmas. This man was Isaiah. Ironically, some seven hundred years before the birth of Jesus, this prophet perceived and proclaimed Christ, his person and his work, in a more lucid manner than most today who have the benefit of God's complete revelation. As mentioned above, the apostle John noted that Isaiah "saw his glory and spoke about him" (John 12:41).

What exactly did Isaiah "see" and "speak about" Christ? Among other things, he saw that the Messiah would be born of a virgin (7:14), would be both God and man (9:6), would perform miracles (35:5–6), and would preach good news (61:1).

However, in Isa 52:13–53:12, the Song of the Suffering Servant, we have the most precise of all Isaiah's prophecies regarding the work of Christ. This passage presents a straightforward and shocking depiction of our Savior's suffering and substitutionary work. So clear is its fulfillment that one could almost read the text and forget it is an OT passage. The use of tools can help us unpack its message and significance.

In the song, Isaiah presents several truths about the Savior, the Suffering Servant. Let us consider the significance of the Savior through Isaiah's eyes.

Because of the precision of the prophecy, many doubters throughout the centuries have identified the Servant of Isaiah 53 as someone other than Jesus. Suggestions include Israel, Isaiah, and Moses, among others.

True, the word *servant* does occasionally refer to Israel and Isaiah in chapters 40–55. However, in the four Servant Songs (others are in chaps. 42, 49, and 50), the clear referent is the Davidic Messiah. In fact, in the OT, the expression "my servant David" often functions as a messianic title (Ps 89:3, 20; Jer 33:26; Ezek 34:23; 37:25; Zech 3:8; see Luke 1:69).

The NT writers undoubtedly understood the Servant to refer to Jesus Christ. In fact, they cite or allude to Isaiah 53 some forty-eight times—a number eclipsed only by Daniel 7 (fifty-nine times).

In the initial words of the passage, we find partial evidence for why the Servant is said to be "suffering." Despite his sacrificial love described in the later verses and his exaltation before God (52:13–15), the world and the people he came to would despise him (53:3).

Humans are attracted to money, flash, majesty, fame—not sorrows, shame, and suffering. The Servant possessed no worldly attractiveness. Therefore, the world hated him. People still snub Christ because his humility and sacrifice do not fit their worldview, lifestyle, and values. Yet, in the wisdom of God, Christ was rejected that we might be accepted.

Isaiah makes evident the need for the Servant's sacrifice and suffering—"our sicknesses" (v. 4), "our pains" (v. 4), "our rebellion" (v. 5), "our iniquities" (v. 5), our straying (v. 6), "the iniquity of us all" (v. 6), "my people's rebellion" (v. 8), "the sin of many" (v. 12).

The essence of the biblical worldview is that humanity has a sin problem. And sin must either be covered or the sinner punished.

Isaiah wrote chapters 40–55 to comfort a people who would one day experience exile—God's forcible removal of his people from the Promised Land as precipitated by their covenant disobedience. Earlier passages in Isaiah give the people hope of a physical restoration to the land. Chapter 53 gives them hope that the very thing that sent them into exile in the first place—their sin—would be covered and forgiven (v. 4). This would be accomplished through the Servant.

Though innocent (v. 7), the Servant would vicariously suffer, even unto death, experiencing the punishment that God's people justly deserved (vv. 5–6) to bring them peace and healing (v. 5)—a doctrine we know today as penal substitutionary atonement.[18]

---

[18] "Penal substitutionary atonement," *Theopedia*, https://www.theopedia.com/penal-substitutionary-atonement (accessed March 4, 2019).

The image employed plainly recalls the death of the lamb in an OT sacrifice. Yet no animal would or could bear and atone for the sins of God's people; shockingly, it would be a human, a Servant, who would shed his blood sacrificially.

Perhaps most shocking to the modern mind are the final statements of Isaiah's song. Note who imposes the suffering on the Servant. God does. And more scandalous still, he was "pleased" to do it (v. 10).

But didn't the religious leaders frame Jesus? Didn't Judas betray Jesus? Didn't the Roman soldiers nail him to the cross? Yes, but it was the will of God that these things happen. It was God's "pleasure" for Christ to die.

Does this mean that those involved are absolved of guilt? No, but they did only what was permitted by God. Does this mean that God did not grieve to see his Son on the cross? No, the idea expressed with "pleasure" is "desire" or "will." God was willing to do it, because he sees all ends.

What were those ends? Simply, the Servant died for the justification of many and his own ultimate exaltation (vv. 10–12). Jesus "did not come to be served, but to serve, and to give his life as a ransom for many" (Mark 10:45).

This is the Christ that Christians celebrate at Christmas—a "man of sorrows" (Isa 53:3 KJV), slaughtered for our sin, but ultimately exalted at the right hand of the Father. To use the angels' words, "Glory to God in the highest heaven" (Luke 2:14).

Applying the Results

The OT Prophetic Books aim at changing the mindsets and behaviors of the readers. In other words, the goal of the prophets is application. The following will offer two possible trajectories for application using what we have learned from the books.

A Devotion on Isaiah 40: The Preciousness of Permanent Promises in a Life That Is Passing

Count me among the millions of readers who have been blessed over the decades by the writing—300-plus essays, articles, and books, such as *Knowing God*—and ministry of J. I. Packer.

So when it was revealed that the eighty-nine-year-old (ninety-two at that time of this writing) Packer had lost his vision and would not continue his writing ministry, I felt a twinge of sadness mixed with nostalgia.[19] Yet according to Packer, as he approaches life's finish line, he harbors no sorrow—only anticipation and assurance of God's providential care.

What is the source of Packer's perseverance and peace? Having read Packer, the answer is clear. For him, that which is most precious is that which is most permanent. Eyesight fades. Flesh fails. Possessions pass away. Divine promises endure.

I was recently reminded of this truth as I discussed a biblical text in one of my classes. Isaiah 40 is a chapter known for providing comfort to a suffering people—in this case, God's people who constantly faced the threat of exile and elimination. From where does this heavenly solace in the midst of suffering spring? God's enduring promises.

God promised that he would pardon them (v. 2). He would deliver them (v. 3). He would reveal his glory among them (v. 5).

But how could they trust in those promises when all—including their own flesh—seemed to fail and flounder in the face of the fury of raging nations (v. 6)? Isaiah reminds God's people that divine promises possess permanence.

He does this by drawing the minds of the hearer back to creation itself. In verses 6–8, four entities from Genesis 1–2 make an appearance.

---

[19] Ivan Mesa, "J. I. Packer, 89, on Losing Sight but Seeing Christ," The Gospel Coalition, January 14, 2016, https://www.thegospelcoalition.org /article/j-i-packer-89-on-losing-sight-but-seeing-christ/.

Two of these are created things: grass and flowers, as well as humanity itself. These wither and fade. They "dry up" as the waters of the flood (same word used in Genesis 8).

Grass, as well as humanity itself, withers and fades.
But the Word of God stands forever.

In contrast, two entities from the creation account stand forever: the breath (can also be translated as "Spirit") of God and the Word of God. Those things are uncreated and there at the beginning (Genesis 1), and thus they cannot be destroyed.

Of course, these promises find culmination and certitude in one Person—Jesus Christ. This side of the cross, we can see that the Word of God that never fails and cannot decay is the same glory of God that was revealed to his people some 700 years after Isaiah—Christ himself (see John 1). Because of Christ, God would pardon his people and deliver them from the enemies that have beset humanity since Genesis 3.

When you reach Packer's age, if God grants you such longevity, in what will you place your hope? Flesh that fades? Created things that crumble?

Or will that which is most precious to you be that which is most permanent?

A Sunrise Service and Ezekiel's Vision

I love sunrise services at Easter. Recently I had the opportunity of preaching one. On that morning, I encouraged the congregation to go back in time some 2,500 years to the ancient empire of Babylon.

There a strange, idiosyncratic prophet named Ezekiel is having a vision. An angelic being transports him in this vision from the flat, dry, alluvial plains of Babylon to the beautiful walls of Solomon's Temple in Jerusalem. The angel literally picks Ezekiel up by the lock of his hair.

Once there, God has his prophet dig through the wall to see all kinds of abominations in the temple. Idol worship of the worst kind. Innocent blood being shed.

In response, God tells Ezekiel a shocking thing: I'm leaving. Some 400 years earlier, when Solomon had built Jerusalem's magnificent temple, God's glory had descended in a visible cloud, and there it had remained as a tangible reminder of God's gracious presence among his people. But now God's glory was moving, turning his back on his adulterous people.

Ezekiel 11:22–23 reads: "Then the cherubim, with the wheels beside them, lifted their wings, and the glory of the God of Israel was above them. The glory of the LORD rose up from within the city and stopped on the mountain east of the city."

That mountain is the Mount of Olives. From there, God watched the destruction of the city long prophesied. The Babylonians broke in and leveled Solomon's magnificent temple to Yahweh.

Some seventy years later, the Persians allowed the Jews to return from exile, and the temple was rebuilt, but strangely the glory of God never returned. For centuries, the Jewish people waited, but it never happened. Centuries passed until . . .

A few years ago, I had the opportunity to go to Israel with some students. If you ever have the chance to go, you might find Jerusalem itself somewhat disappointing—lots of buying and selling, commercialism, and tourism.

The holy sites in Jerusalem and beyond, such as the Church of Annunciation,[20] the Church of the Holy Sepulchre,[21] and the Church of the Nativity,[22] all sit on places supposedly connected to Jesus's life and death. But none of these identifications are certain. Each church is ornately decorated, filled with candles, incense, and priests of various denominations. But none of these sites were tremendously meaningful to me.

But one place did cause me to break down in tears. Outside the Temple Mount, archaeologists have exposed some first-century steps leading into the city.

We stood on those steps and gazed at the scene. As I turned around, I looked to the east and saw the beautiful Mount of Olives, now crowned with thousands of tombstones—filled with dead Jews and Christians who believed this to be the location of the first or second coming, depending on your faith. The Mount of Olives is where Jesus prayed at Gethsemane. Where he pronounced judgment over Jerusalem. Where he assented to God's will for him to die for his people.

Then, it struck me. I was standing in the very place where Jesus himself had walked, as he entered the Holy City to go to his death.

---

[20] "Basilica of the Annunciation," *Wikipedia*, last modified February 15, 2019, https://en.wikipedia.org/wiki/Basilica_of_the_Annunciation.

[21] "Church of the Holy Sepulchre," *Wikipedia*, last modified March 4, 2019, https://en.wikipedia.org/wiki/Church_of_the_Holy_Sepulchre.

[22] "Church of the Nativity," *Wikipedia*, last modified March 2, 2019, https://en.wikipedia.org/wiki/Church_of_the_Nativity.

Standing on the first-century steps leading into Jerusalem—
steps that Jesus walked 2000 years ago to his death.

And as I looked at the Mount of Olives, I suddenly remembered that that location was also the place where God's glory had descended and remained never to return . . . until years later, Jesus of Nazareth— the Christ, the Suffering Servant, the King of the Jews, the Messiah to the nations, the Lord, the Alpha and Omega, the Word became Flesh— entered to die for us, humble and mounted on a colt, even the foal of a donkey (Zech 9:9).

God's glory had returned. As John states, "The Word became flesh and dwelt among us. We observed his glory, the glory as the one and only Son from the Father, full of grace and truth" (John 1:14).

And no cross, no beating, no crown of thorns could snuff that glory out.

Three days later, that glory was raised again. And that is what we celebrated that Easter Sunday morning at sunrise, some 2,000 years later.

The Bible tells us that Jesus was taken back into heaven from . . . guess where? The Mount of Olives. And one day, as Zechariah states, "His feet will stand on the Mount of Olives, which faces Jerusalem on the east. The Mount of Olives will be split in half from east to west, forming a huge valley, so that half the mountain will move to the north and half to the south" (14:4).

The very location where Jesus was betrayed and rejected will be the place where Jesus returns in triumph. So today, even as we look back to the victory of the glory of Christ over the grave, we await the return of that glory to us.

This is how it has always been for Christians—looking back with faith, looking forward with hope.

Application Questions

1. What is your notion of a prophet? How does that differ from the prophets of the OT? Have you ever met anyone who claims to be a prophet? What do you think they mean by that? Do you think there is a "gift of prophecy" today?

2. What does Isaiah 6 say about God's nature and character? How would you define holiness as ascribed to God? Is this how you conceive of God? What would you do if you were in Isaiah's shoes?

3. In considering the Suffering Servant passage in Isaiah 53, do you see how God has used that passage through the ages to convince many of the work of Christ on their behalf?

4. Does knowing the historical context of prophets like Ezekiel and Jeremiah help you to understand their messages better? Why or why not?

5. What does it mean to be a new covenant Christian? How do you see the promises in Jeremiah 31 (esp. vv. 31–34) fulfilled in the new covenant?

6. How does Ezekiel 37 speak to the regenerating power of God's Word?

7. Do you think it was cruel of God to ask Hosea to marry a prostitute? How does Hosea's sign-act help you better understand the grace of God and the seriousness of sin?

8. Do you think Jonah was really swallowed by a fish? Is it important for us to affirm this story as historical? Why or why not?

9. Picture yourself in Daniel's situation in Daniel 1. Do you think you would have reacted similarly? Why or why not?

10. Christ saw himself as fulfilling the "son of man" prophecy in Daniel 7. Can you describe the connection?

Part 3

Tools for Interpreting the New Testament

As a child, I loved to visit Midland, Texas. I'm not sure if you have ever been to this area of the country often referred to as the Permian Basin. There's not really a lot to see there except oil wells, tumbleweeds, and high school football stadiums. But that really didn't matter to me growing up. That's because two of my favorite people in the whole world lived there—Royce and Cherry Crisler. Or, as I affectionately called them, Mamaw and Papaw. I visited my grandparents every summer, at Thanksgiving, Christmas, and other special occasions. We spent most of our time just talking. I loved to hear my mamaw laugh and my papaw tells stories about my dad, or my uncle Lanny. We always seemed to congregate in the living room. Between our conversations, we usually watched some kind of ball game. I vividly remember watching, or yelling at, Dallas Cowboys games. It was all very familiar and very comforting. I miss those moments. But as I reflect on all that familiarity and comfort, I realize I missed something hanging just above the TV—a painting.

That painting was a permanent fixture in my grandparents' living room. It had always been there. I even looked at it a few times. I knew it depicted Jesus. It had some red, orange, and pink hues to it. I even knew that my dad had painted it as a young artist. Beyond that, I never gave it much thought. Like the rest of the room, that painting was familiar, comforting, and nice.

Not until I inherited the painting following the death of my papaw did I begin to "see" it. I hung it above my desk at home. Gradually I came to realize that the painting depicted Jesus carrying his cross to Golgotha. I also recognized that my dad had chosen the Lukan version of this event. All four Gospels describe Jesus carrying his cross. Only Luke's account includes weeping women to whom Jesus turns at one point and says, "Daughters of Jerusalem, do not weep for me, but weep for yourselves and your children" (Luke 23:28). I also came to see the Roman soldiers, Simon of Cyrene who carried the cross part of the way, the swelling crowd, and the ominous but hopeful skyline.

Before long, I wasn't just looking at the painting. I was interpreting it. The scales of familiarity and comfort had fallen from my eyes. By relocating the painting, looking at it from a different angle, looking at it with different lighting, "hearing" it without the familiar voices of friends and family, and thinking really hard about, I understood new things about something I had seen my own life.

I share this story because I think it is an apt analogy for many of you who are reading this book, especially as we come to this section on the New Testament (NT). Many readers probably feel a sense of comfort and familiarity here. You may have read the NT. You've probably heard it preached. Perhaps you've talked about. Perhaps you've sung about it. But have you really interpreted it?

That's what I want you to consider as you comb through the next several chapters. My hope is that you might recognize what you've been missing. It's a hope that you'll move from looking at the text to analyzing it.

That analysis requires the right tools, and that's precisely what this book supplies. The tools for interpreting the NT are similar to what you've seen in previous chapters. I will refer to them in what follows as historical, literary, theological, and responsive tools. I'll have much to say about them in what lies ahead. Before we begin making our way through the NT, let me use one more artistic analogy to help you see the bigger picture.

As you come to the NT, bring with you what you learned about the Old Testament (OT). You're going to need it. That's because there really is no separation between the Old and New Testaments. I know there are divisions in your Bible. I know different authors in different time periods penned the books contained in them. I know there are different genres and historical events. I know there are fields of OT and NT scholarship with OT and NT professors. But the reality is that all these pieces belong together like a beautiful painting. *See Wordsearch for a discussion about the inner unity of the OT and NT.*

In his teaching ministry, Jesus made this abundantly clear. In fact, just before his ascension, Jesus gave his disciples a "Bible Toolbox" of their own. He filled it up with the three tools from the Hebrew Bible—the Law, the Prophets, and the Writings (Luke 24:44)—a Hebrew Bible that was familiar to them, even comfortable. Yet Jesus managed to show them things about the sacred text that they had never seen before, himself. You see, Jesus took the pieces of the OT to help craft what would eventually come to be known as the NT. He started piecing Scripture together there on that mountainside. He was crafting. He was painting.

Luke tells us that the whole key to seeing this mosaic is Jesus himself, "Then he [Jesus] opened their minds to understand the Scriptures" (Luke 24:45). As you collect tools in the pages ahead, please remember two things. First, Jesus may be familiar and comfortable to you, or maybe he's not, but I assure you that there's more to see. Second, the

*This is the painting by my father, Larry L. Crisler, which now
hangs above my desk at home. (Photo courtesy of Erin Drago)*

most valuable exegetical tool in your toolbox will always be a cross and
an empty tomb. All of Scripture, whether Old or New Testament, finds
its ultimate meaning in God's crucified and risen Son. After all, when
Jesus "opened" the minds of the disciples to understand the Scriptures,
he said, "This is what is written: The Messiah would suffer and rise
from the dead the third day" (v. 46).

8

Tools for Interpreting the Gospels

I like to run. Let me correct that. I enjoy the benefits of running. I often cover the same terrain. The sights, sounds, and smells are all quite familiar. I know which dog and incline to avoid. I can tell you which house needs a fresh coat of paint and which one should be in a magazine. However, when I switch the direction that I run, I notice things I didn't before. It's the same terrain, same dog, same incline, and same house. What's different is the approach or angle that I take. It causes me to see something quite familiar from a totally different perspective. This is what happens when we read the four Gospels in the New Testament (NT). Matthew, Mark, Luke, and John provide both a unified and diverse portrait of Jesus. They do not offer competing presentations of him but complementary ones. It's the same Jesus from four different angles that makes our view of him slightly less foggy.

*The four Gospels are like mountain peaks which
collectively help us see Jesus more clearly.*

These four Evangelists craft the most important biography in history, the biography of Jesus the Nazarene. Despite their importance to the church and the world, the Gospels are some of the most misinterpreted books of the Christian Bible. The problem stems from our inability to properly understand narrative. We often want straightforward propositional statements that tell us exactly what the point is and what we should do with that information. That's not how the Gospels communicate to us. To be sure, they have incredible and life-changing points to make, but they play by a unique set of rules. Interpreters need to play by those rules using the proper exegetical tools.

That's what I offer here—tools for interpreting the most important biography ever written. I trust I don't have to say much more than that to pique your interest. Let me assure you that there are incredible treasures in the Gospels for those who have ears to hear and eyes to see.

Understanding the Tools

Historical Tools

There are three historical perspectives from which it is necessary to interpret the Gospels: (1) history *behind* the Gospels, (2) history *in* the Gospels, and (3) history *in front of* the Gospels. First, history *behind* the Gospels refers to historical features such as the original author, audiences, dates, and purposes of the Gospels. Here the questions are elementary but exegetically significant. Who wrote the Gospels? To whom did they write? Why did they write? What sources did they use to write? Next, history *in* the Gospels denotes the historical era, culture, focus, sequence, and nature of the events that the Gospel writers assume or explicitly describe in their respective writings. Finally, history *in front of* the Gospels has in view the expansive history of interpretation related to the four Gospels. Interpreters have endeavored to interpret the Gospels for 2,000 years now. To some degree, their interpretive findings can and should impact our own interpretation of the Gospels.

History behind the Gospels

Who wrote the Gospels? Technically, all four Gospels are anonymous writings. None of the authors explicitly identifies himself in his writings. Nevertheless, we have traditionally identified Matthew, Mark, Luke, and John as the four writers, known as Evangelists. There are good reasons to maintain this view. To begin, many ancient manuscripts of the Gospels contain titles that identify the authors as Matthew, Mark, Luke, and John. Additionally, some early church fathers (AD second century) explicitly connect the four canonical Gospels to these four authors. For example, Papias of Hierapolis recounts a statement made by a certain "John the Elder" regarding the Gospel of Mark, "Mark, having become Peter's interpreter, wrote down accurately everything he remembered, though not in order, of the things either said or done by Christ" (*Frag.*

of Papias 3:15). In any case, the identification of the authors has minimal impact on understanding what they wrote in the Gospels.

To whom did these Evangelists originally write? The most likely answer is that the four Evangelists did not direct their writings to a single group of people at one location in the first-century Mediterranean world.[1] Unlike Paul's Letters, which were originally directed toward specific churches or individuals, the four Evangelists directed their works toward two broad groups:

1. *Early Christians in need of exhortation.* The majority of early Christians never heard Jesus teach, witnessed his miracles, or ate a meal with him. Yet those followers of Jesus obviously needed to know more about him in order to rightly follow him. The Evangelists meet this need through their four Gospels.
2. *Early nonbelievers in need of evangelization.* There are also indications in their writings that the Evangelists wrote to people who had not yet believed in Jesus (see, e.g., John 20:30–31).

When reading and interpreting the Gospels, we should keep these two intended audiences in mind. We need to ask, How does this passage exhort believers to follow Jesus? How does this passage address the nonbeliever? After all, those are the kinds of people the writers had in mind when they penned their Gospels.

Why did the evangelists write? This is the most important question we can ask when it comes to thinking about the history behind the Gospels. Two of the four Evangelists explicitly stated why they wrote. In the prologue to his work, Luke tells Theophilus that he wrote his Gospel

---

[1] There are many scholars who would disagree at this point and attempt to identify a narrower historical audience for the Gospels. For example, some interpreters identify Mark's original audience as Christians in Rome due to certain features in Mark's Gospel such as latinisms (i.e., the retention of Latin words in the Greek text such as "centurion" in Mark 15:39). However, from my perspective, it is not possible to establish a narrower audience with any sense of certainty. What is more certain is that the Gospel writers anticipated a wide and diverse readership.

"so that you may know the certainty of the things about which you have been instructed" (1:4). The key word here is *certainty*. Luke aims for each of the episodes in his Gospel to provide certainty, or security, regarding what Jesus did and taught. This means that at every step of the way in reading Luke, the interpreter should ask, what certainty about Jesus does this episode provide? Similarly, the Gospel of John contains an explicit purpose statement, "But these things have been written in order that you might believe that Jesus is the Christ the Son of God and that by believing you might have life in his name" (John 20:31).

History in the Gospels

When thinking about history at the textual level of the Gospels, keep three items in mind. First, consider the culture of first-century Galilee. Jesus not only grew up in Galilee (Nazareth), but much of his earthly ministry took place there as well. His encounters with people did not take place in a vacuum. In the Gospels, Jesus shows an awareness of Galilean politics, past and current events, local customs, nagging concerns, everyday life, tragedies, and the like. His teaching and actions are wrapped up in Galilean culture. Therefore, interpreters must familiarize themselves with that culture and consider its impact on the meaning of the Gospels.

Second, we need a working knowledge of first-century Judea. Because Jesus's birth story, parts of his ministry, and passion are set in Judea, we must also consider this region's historical culture. Jerusalem and the temple are especially pertinent. After all, one of the main charges leveled against Jesus is that he threatened to destroy the temple (Mark 14:58; John 2:18–22).

Third, besides a working knowledge of Galilean and Judean culture, we also need a flexible outline of Jesus's life. It is helpful to know the basic sequence of events in Jesus's life, because individual episodes in the Gospels need to be set against the larger sequence. In this way, we avoid interpreting various episodes in isolation from the larger framework of

Jesus's life. The earliest such framework is embedded in the Gospel of Mark. Most scholars now agree that Mark is the earliest Gospel; therefore, it functions as the earliest written source for sketching an outline of Jesus's life. A very broad outline in Mark consists of the following:

The Gospel of Mark

Galilee

1. Jesus's baptism by John the Baptist (1:1–11)
2. Jesus's temptation (1:12–13)
3. Preaching ministry begins in Galilee (1:14–15)
4. Initial call of disciples (1:16–20)
5. Jesus heals, delivers, teaches, and reveals his identity in Galilee (1:21–8:22)
6. Peter confesses that Jesus is the "Christ" (8:23–30)
7. Jesus begins to warn his disciples about his impending death and resurrection (8:31–33)
8. Transfiguration of Jesus (9:2–13)
9. Jesus continues teaching and healing in Galilee (9:14–10:52)

Judea / Jerusalem

1. Triumphant entry at Jerusalem (11:1–10)
2. Jesus's enacted parable against the temple ("temple cleansing") (11:11–26)
3. Jesus's teaching challenged (11:27–12:44)
4. Apocalyptic teaching (chap. 13)
5. Plot to kill Jesus; Judas's betrayal; Passover/Last Supper/ Gethsemane (4:1–42)
6. Jesus's arrest and trial (14:43–72)
7. Crucifixion (chap. 15)
8. Resurrection (16:1–8)

When Matthew and Luke take up this outline of Jesus's life, they "supplement" it with items absent from Mark. For example, they both provide genealogies of Jesus (Matt 1:1–17; Luke 3:23–38). They explain various aspects of Jesus's birth, infancy, and even adolescence (Matt 1:18–2:23; Luke 1:5–2:52). Matthew and Luke also include parables, miracles, and events that Mark does not contain. These supplements are critical to the interpretive process, because they highlight the special emphases of Matthew and Luke. Even in material shared by the Synoptic Gospels, variations in certain details also underscore the special emphasis of each writer. "Synoptic" refers to the way that Matthew, Mark, and Luke "see Jesus together" in a similar way based upon the literary similarities that the three of them share.

For example, consider the difference between the Markan and Lukan versions of the centurion's confession at the moment of Jesus's death:

> When the centurion, who was standing opposite him, saw the way he breathed his last, he said, "Truly this man was the Son of God!" (Mark 15:39)

> When the centurion saw what happened, he began to glorify God, saying, "This man really was righteous!" (Luke 23:47)

Notice the different titles ascribed to Jesus here—"Son of God" and "righteous." The latter does not contradict the former. Luke uses Mark as a source for his Passion Narrative, but he interprets the centurion's "Son of God" statement as "righteous." That is because throughout his Gospel, Luke strives to depict Jesus the Son of God as *the* righteous One promised by God in the Old Testament (OT) and unmatched by all others. These kinds of variations occur frequently among the Synoptic Gospels. When two or more of these writers share the same literary episode, the interpreter must compare them side by side. The exegetical payoff will often be the recognition of a writer's particular point of emphasis.

Much of the discussion in this section has focused on the Synoptic Gospels. However, we also need to consider the history presented in the Gospel of John. While the story line of Jesus in John corresponds at certain points with the Synoptic Gospels, there are some unique features. For example, although John does not provide a birth narrative in the vein of Matthew and Luke, his explanation of Jesus's origin reaches further back than Bethlehem. John's prologue (1:1–18) portrays Jesus as the preexistent and incarnate Logos (Word) whose origin is ultimately eternal and divine. He is the eternal Word whose entrance into the world signals the definitive revelation and interpretation of God (1:18). Additionally, John highlights Jesus's frequent trips to Jerusalem (2:13; 5:1; 10:22–23), whereas the Synoptic Gospels choose to focus primarily on his initial Galilean ministry and subsequent entrance into Judea and Jerusalem which culminates in his death and resurrection. John also includes some key events in Jesus's life that are entirely absent from the Synoptic Gospels. Most notably, John alone reports how Jesus raised Lazarus from the dead four days after the time of his death (chap. 11). All of these events and others inform the history in the Gospel of John, and interpreters must pay attention to these features if they are to understand John's unique portrait of Jesus.

History in Front of the Gospels

An often unrecognized part of the exegetical process is assessing how the conclusions of previous interpreters impact our own understanding of the text. It is important to remember that we are neither the first nor the last interpreters to engage the Gospels. From the second century until today, readers with all kinds of backgrounds have interpreted the Gospels with different methods, aims, and outcomes. Their work impacts our own to varying degrees. Biblical scholars produce commentaries, monographs, articles, and other publications that collectively provide a rich reservoir of resources for interpreters. Pastors, missionaries, singers, political pundits, and a host of others also influence how we view the Gospels.

The history in front of the Gospels can be both a help and a hindrance to biblical interpretation. It is helpful when we use this reservoir of resources as a tool that enhances our understanding of the text. Everyone can and should use the vast supply of interpretive resources that have been produced in front of the Gospels. However, those same resources can become a hindrance when they function as a substitute for the difficult but rewarding task of biblical interpretation. As interpreters, we join rather than merely observe the history in front of the Gospels. We are participants in the interpretive process and not mere spectators.

With all of this in tow, let's consider one example of how history in front of the Gospels can impact our interpretation of them. In surveying the history of what interpreters have said about the Gospels, one significant development is often referred to as the "quest for the historical Jesus." This quest is an attempt by historians of various stripes to reconstruct the actual picture of Jesus the Nazarene. In its inception, and in many ways until today, many interpreters have argued that one cannot take the portrait of Jesus at face value. Their starting point is that the picture of Jesus in the NT Gospels reflects what the early church believed about Jesus rather than who Jesus was in first-century Palestine. For others, especially evangelical scholars, the Gospels reflect both the Jesus of history and what the early church (rightly) believed about him. These divergent starting points lead to divergent interpretations of the Gospels. If an interpreter does not believe that the Gospels offer a straightforward historical recollection of Jesus, then they will mine the Gospels for remnants of the historical Jesus. They will try to read between the proverbial lines. Contrastively, for those who believe that the Gospels present a historically reliable and accurate portrait of Jesus, they will read the Gospels as the Gospels stand without trying to get behind the text to reconstruct a picture of Jesus. The temptation that every interpreter of the Gospels must avoid is to see a picture of Jesus that reflects the interpreter rather than Jesus as the Evangelists actually portrayed him. For further discussion on the "Quest for the Historical Jesus," see Wordsearch content.

Many participants in the so-called "Quest for the Historical Jesus" only see a reflection of themselves in their interpretations of Jesus like those who stare into a pool of water and see nothing but a reflection of themselves.

Literary Tools

Genre

We often gravitate toward biographies of past and present figures. Biography is a genre that resonates with readers, because in it we find a way to relate to, admire, and emulate people whom we would otherwise not encounter. The ancient Mediterranean world had its fair share of biographers including Xenophon (430–354 BC), Plutarch (AD 46–120), Suetonius (AD 69–130), among others. We can add to these ancient biographers Matthew, Mark, Luke, and John.

From a first-century perspective, the four Gospel writers crafted biographies of Jesus the Nazarene. In an ancient library, they would have been shelved in the biography section, because the Gospels share some of the same aims and literary features as ancient biographies. For example, ancient biographers aimed to present a biographical subject that readers would remember, admire, and emulate. In some instances, they also aimed to defend the reputation of their biographical subjects against what they perceived as false or unfair criticism. To accomplish these aims, writers used literary devices such as biographical anecdotes. An anecdote usually highlighted a private or lesser-known deed of the biographical subject. For example, in sketching his biography of Alexander the Great, Plutarch did not focus solely on Alexander's very public and well-known military accomplishments. He moved the reader from the glory of the battlefield to more mundane settings such as Alexander rescuing a lone soldier on a mountainside. This kind of anecdote helped to humanize the biographical subject and underscore the subject's private character.

Matthew, Mark, Luke, and John also contain similar aims and devices. They, like other ancient biographers, want their readers to remember, admire, and emulate Jesus. There are even indications that they set out to defend Jesus against false accusations. For example, in Matthew's resurrection account, he specifically mentions that the religious leaders paid the soldiers at the tomb to falsely report that the disciples stole the body of Jesus. Matthew notes that such a report "has been spread among Jewish people to this day" (28:15). Matthew combats that false report circulating in his day through his resurrection account. To accomplish biographical aims, the Gospel writers use certain biographical devices such as biographical anecdotes. For example, in Mark 1:29–31, we find an extremely brief account of Jesus's healing Peter's mother-in-law. The episode is only a few lines long and contains no dialogue. Mark simply notes that the disciples come to Jesus and tell him that Peter's mother-in-law is ill with a fever. Jesus then goes to her, grasps her hand, and raises her up. The fever leaves her, and she begins to serve those in the house. On the surface, especially in comparison to what Mark reports before and after this episode, these verses are insignificant. All we have is one more miracle of Jesus, right? It is in fact much more than that. Based on the use of anecdotes in ancient biographies, this episode demonstrates that Jesus cares for the ill publicly and privately. It illustrates that his work is never really done and that his power to heal does not depend on circumstances or crowd size such as the very public healing of the man with a withered hand at the synagogue in Capernaum (Mark 1:23–28) or the throng that come to the house later that evening (vv. 32–34).

Of course, the Gospels are far more than ancient accounts of an individual who left his mark on an ancient culture and whose life is memorable, even worthy of emulation. Each of the four "biographers" of Jesus writes about a figure who died and rose again, one who came to the earth, departed, and promised to come again. Unlike other ancient biographers, the Gospel writers did not merely aim for their readers to admire, emulate, or remember Jesus. They wanted their readers to believe and trust in their biographical subject (Jesus) by encountering him in their Gospels. In this way, the best label for the genre of the NT Gospels is biographical-living testimony. Jesus is a first-century figure (biographical), but he is the risen Son of God (living) whom readers hear about and hear directly from (testimony) in the pages of the Gospels.

Parables

Parables make up approximately one-third of the Synoptic Gospels. Jesus did not invent the genre of parables but rather borrowed this form of communication from the OT and adapted it to his own culture.[2] Consequently, Jesus's parables are not timeless stories of morality but rather instructions about the kingdom of God from an OT and first-century perspective. Jesus ushers in that kingdom through his person, presence, and work (especially his death and resurrection).

Clearly, understanding parables is fundamental to understanding Jesus's teaching about the kingdom of God. Interpreters should hone their parable exegesis skills. Here are some tools that will be useful for the task.[3]

This is Rembrandt's depiction of Jesus's parable that likens the Kingdom of Heaven to a treasure hidden in a field (Matt 13:44).

---

[2] See, e.g., the parable in 2 Sam 12:1–16.

[3] I am helped here by Robert L. Plummer, "Parables in the Gospels: History of Interpretation and Hermeneutical Guidelines," *The Southern Baptist Journal of Theology* 13 (2009): 4–12.

Tools for Interpreting Parables

1. *Determine the "kingdom" point of the parable.* Remember that each of Jesus's parables teaches a specific point about the kingdom of God. The goal of your interpretation is articulating that point. Try to express the main point in one sentence.

2. *Recognize stock imagery in the parables.* The characters and actions in the parables symbolize things that Jesus's listeners would have been familiar with. That's what "stock imagery" means. For example, in Luke 18:1–8, the judge symbolizes God.

3. *Take note of the striking or unexpected details in the parable.* For example, in Matt 22:1–14, what is unexpected in this parable?

4. *Do not try to squeeze meaning out of every last detail.* Not every detail in a parable is significant. Some are simply meant to make the parable memorable and more interesting. For example, Matt 25:9 does not mean that we should not share.

5. *Notice the literary and historical context of the parable.* For example, in Luke 18:9–14, Jesus offers interpretive guidance. See also Luke 15. And the parable of the good Samaritan can be properly understood only in light of the historical relationship between Jews and Samaritans in the first century (Luke 10:33, 36).

6. *Determine how the parable is related to Jesus's death and resurrection.* None of the Gospels, along with the parables they contain, would have ever been written if Jesus had not been crucified and raised from the dead. With this in mind, how is the forgiveness and justification discussed in the Luke 18:9–14 parable related to Jesus's death and resurrection?

In addition to these steps, the interpreter should also look for OT echoes. Jesus often evokes events or figures from Israel's history in his parables.

Structure

Meaning is communicated by *what* is said and *where*. Literary structure deals with the literary *where* of the Gospels. The biographers of Jesus do not organize their thoughts about Jesus in a haphazard way. They are strategic in where they begin their accounts of Jesus, where they place certain events, where they embed transitional moments, and where they locate the highpoint of their biographies. Where these things occur contributes to the Gospel writer's overarching message. Let's briefly consider the basic structure of a Gospel.

Each structure consists of individual stories, acts, and cycles.[4] An individual story is the smallest unit of a literary structure. A string of related individual stories forms an act. A string of related acts forms a cycle. Here I will note the main cycles and the acts as they occur in Luke. However, it should be kept in mind that each act contains several individual stories that are linked by a similar theme or motif.

Outline of Luke

Prologue (Luke 1:1–4)

Cycle 1: *Responses* to the miraculous births of John the Baptist and Jesus; Jesus the adolescent in Jerusalem (1:5–2:52)
    Act 1—Angelic announcement of a son to Zechariah (1:5–23)
    Act 2—Angelic announcement of a Son to Mary (1:24–38)
    Act 3—Mary's visit with Elizabeth; Mary's Hymn (1:39–56)
    Act 4—Birth of John the Baptist; Zechariah's Hymn (1:57–80)

---

[4] Interpreters often differ on some of the finer points of literary structure. On stories, acts, and cycles, see Jonathan T. Pennington, *Reading the Gospels Wisely: A Narrative and Theological Introduction* (Grand Rapids: Baker, 2012), 183–210.

Act 5—Birth of Jesus in Bethlehem (2:1–7)

Act 6—Angelic announcement of Jesus's birth to shepherds (2:8–20)

Act 7—Jesus's circumcision; encounter with Simeon and Anna (2:21–40)

Act 8—Twelve-year-old Jesus at the temple in Jerusalem (2:41–52)

Cycle 2: *Responses* to the ministry of John the Baptist and the baptism of Jesus (3:1–22)

Act 1—John's baptism of repentance in preparation for One greater (3:1–20)

Act 2—Jesus's baptism and the voice from heaven (3:21–22)

Cycle 3: Genealogy and temptation of Jesus the Son of Adam, the Son of God (3:23–4:13)

Act 1—Genealogy of Jesus (3:23–38)

Act 2—Jesus defeats the tempter (4:1–13)

Cycle 4: Jesus brings the kingdom of God to Galilee (4:14–9:50)

Act 1—Jesus's inaugural sermon at Nazareth (4:14–30)

Act 2—Jesus teaches and miraculously discloses the kingdom in Galilee (4:31–9:17)

Act 3—Jesus's identity revealed to Peter and the other disciples (9:18–50)

Cycle 5: Jesus's journey to take the kingdom to Jerusalem (9:51–19:27)

Act 1—Growing resistance toward Jesus (9:51–62)

Act 2—Jesus sends seventy on mission (10:1–12)

Act 3—Jesus continues teaching and performing miracles on his way to Jerusalem (10:13–19:27)

Cycle 6: Jesus's arrival and week in Jerusalem (19:28–23:56)

    Act 1—Jesus's entry into Jerusalem (19:28–44)

    Act 2—Jesus's judgment/cleansing of the temple and consequences (19:45–20:19)

    Act 3—Religious authorities challenge Jesus's wisdom of the kingdom (20:20–47)

    Act 4—Jesus's "little apocalypse" (21:1–36)

    Act 5—Jesus's last days of teaching and Last Supper as enemies close in (21:37–22:53)

    Act 6—Jesus's arrest, trial, crucifixion, and burial (22:54–23:56)

Cycle 7: Jesus's resurrection, exegetical lessons, and ascension (24:1–53)

    Act 1—Angelic announcement of Jesus's resurrection to women at the tomb (24:1–12)

    Act 2—Jesus appears to two disciples on road to Emmaus and instructs them from the Scriptures (24:13–35)

    Act 3—Jesus appears to rest of disciples and instructs them from the Scriptures (24:36–49)

    Act 4—Jesus's ascension (24:50–53)

When analyzing an individual passage (story) in Luke, we should ask ourselves how that passage fits with the overarching emphasis of its cycle and act. *See Wordsearch for a discussion of the structures in Matthew, Mark, and John.*

Idiom

Think for a moment about your favorite singer, writer, entertainer, or speaker. If you know them well enough, you know their well-worn catch phrases, one-liners, facial expressions, even the inflection of their voice. These kinds of well-known traits exemplify what I mean by the "idiom" of the Gospel writers.

Each of the Gospel writers has his own style and manner of writing. We need to familiarize ourselves with the individualized idioms for a few reasons. First, how a writer communicates informs the message he is relaying to us. Second, when a writer deviates from his normal idiom, it is probably exegetically significant. However, if we are unfamiliar with that normal idiom, we will not be aware when he deviates from it.

Matthew's Idiom

Three key features of Matthew's idiom are (1) the verb *pleroo* (πληρόω), "to fulfill"; (2) "Immanuel" images; and (3) kingdom of heaven.

Matthew uses the verb *pleroo* ("to fulfill") sixteen times in his Gospel.[5] In fourteen places, the usage indicates Matthew's aim to demonstrate that Jesus completes, or fulfills, the promises that Yahweh made to Israel in the OT. These are promises that Jesus ultimately completes in his identity, his death, and his resurrection. For example, in recounting how Mary and Joseph hide their infant son in Egypt and return from there once God instructs them to leave, Matthew notes: "He stayed there until Herod's death, so that what was spoken by the Lord through the prophet might be fulfilled: Out of Egypt I called my Son" (2:15). The statement "Out of Egypt I called my Son" is a citation from Hos 11:1. In the original context of Hosea 11, the prophet recounts God's faithfulness to Israel during its enslavement in Egypt. He acted as a father toward his son. Yet Israel the son did not reciprocate his Father's faithfulness; therefore, the Father handed them over to judgment at the hands of their enemies (vv. 2–11). Matthew takes up Hosea's Father-son relationship (Yahweh-Israel) to identify Jesus. Jesus is the faithful and obedient Son who stands in stark contrast to the faithless and disobedient son Israel. Jesus the Son, like Israel the son, is handed over to

---

[5] See Matt 1:22; 2:15, 17, 23; 3:15; 4:14; 5:17; 8:17; 12:17; 13:35; 21:4; 26:54, 56; 27:9.

*Just as God called his son Israel out of Egypt, he also
called his Son Jesus out of Egypt (Matt 2:13-15).*

judgment and death. Yet his death is not the result of his own sin but
for the sins of Israel the son and others.

Matthew also uses phraseology and imagery that emphasizes
God's presence in the person of Jesus. He explicitly identifies Jesus as
"Immanuel" (God with Us). As the angel tells Joseph, "See, the virgin
will become pregnant and give birth to a son, and they will name him
Immanuel" (Matt 1:23; Isa 7:14). Additionally, when Jesus teaches his
disciples how to correct a sinful individual in the church, he promises,
"For where two or three are gathered together in my name, I am there
among them" (Matt 18:20).[6]

---

[6] See also Matt 25:31–46; 28:20.

While Mark and Luke prefer the phrase *kingdom of God*, the Matthean Jesus uses the phrase *kingdom of heaven*. Both expressions refer to the same kingdom announced by Jesus in his preaching ministry. However, by using "kingdom of heaven," Matthew underscores the truth that God's rule and reign in heaven has arrived on earth through the person, Spirit, and church of Jesus. Matthew explains that Jesus commenced his earthly ministry with an announcement of this kingdom's arrival, "From then on Jesus began to preach, 'Repent, because the kingdom of heaven has come near'" (4:17). Jesus then goes on to teach, heal, exorcise demons, supernaturally multiply food, walk on water, raise the dead, and the like. These actions manifest the kingdom of heaven that Jesus announces.

As you interpret Matthew, be mindful of his idiom. When working through a passage, check to see how Matthew may once again be explaining "fulfillment," "Immanuel," or "kingdom of heaven" as it relates to Jesus. He does not always do it in the same way.

MARK'S IDIOM

Two key features of Mark's idiom are (1) the expression *immediately* and (2) the motif of mystery.

Mark's Gospel is the "hurry-up" Gospel. He uses the adverb *immediately* (εὐθύς) repeatedly to move along his narrative in rapid fashion.[7] One explanation for the frequency of this expression is that Mark wants to rush the reader to the crucifixion scene, because it is at Golgotha (15:22) that Jesus's identity as the Christ (1:1) and Son of God (1:1) is fully disclosed.

---

[7] See, e.g., Mark 1:3, 10, 12, 18, 20, 21, 23, 28, 29, 30, 42, 43; 2:8, 12; 3:6; 4:5, 15, 16, 17, 29; 5:2, 29, 30, 42; 6:25, 27, 45, 50; 7:25; 8:10; 9:15, 20, 24; 10:52; 11:2, 3; 14:43, 45, 72; 15:1.

The motif of mystery is also a primary feature of Mark's idiom. Mystery is Mark's preferred way of describing the kingdom of God, which Jesus announces and reveals. The kingdom is mysterious in various ways for Mark. For example, Jesus teaches his disciples that he reveals the kingdom to some and conceals it from others. He explains to them, "The secret (μυστήριον) of the kingdom of God has been given to you, but to those outside, everything comes in parables so that they may indeed look and yet not perceive; they may indeed listen, and yet not understand; otherwise they might turn back and be forgiven" (4:11–12). Similar descriptions of the kingdom as a mystery are scattered throughout Mark, but he does not use the explicit term *mystery*. Instead, he makes this point by depicting the disciples and others as figures who struggle to discern the mysterious identity of Jesus.[8]

When reading Mark, take note of Mark's idiom. Observe how often Mark hurries readers along and where he slows them down. Trace how he develops his motif of mystery. There are of course other features in Mark's idiom. In general, interpreters should pay attention to repeated or rare expressions. These are often exegetically significant.

Luke's Idiom

Two noteworthy features of Luke's idiom are (1) the use of "righteousness" language and (2) the use of "it is necessary" (δεῖ) statements.

Luke often describes figures in his Gospel as "righteous" (δίκαιος), including Jesus. When he introduces the very first figures in his biography of Jesus, he describes them as righteous. "And they were both *righteous* before God, walking blameless in all the commandments and *righteous requirements* of the Lord" (1:6, Crisler translation). Luke describes Simeon, the elderly man who embraced the eight-day-old Jesus in the temple, as *righteous* (2:25). Jesus tells parables that underscore

---

[8] See, e.g., Mark 4:35–41.

who is truly "righteous" before God, such as the tax collector who begs for mercy rather than the Pharisee who trusts in his own piety (18:9–14). Luke climactically identifies Jesus as righteous in the crucifixion where the Roman centurion witnesses Jesus's last breath and announces, "Surely this man was *righteous*" (23:47, Crisler translation). Overall, Luke reworks the meaning of righteous around Jesus, both those who seek Jesus and Jesus himself.

Both in Luke and Acts, we find many "it is necessary" statements.[9] It is one of Luke's favorite theological expressions. For example, directly after Peter's confession that Jesus is "God's Messiah," Luke explains, "It is necessary that the Son of Man suffer many things and be rejected by the elders, chief priests, and scribes, be killed, and be raised the third day" (Luke 9:22). In many uses of the phrase, it signals God's obligation to carry out what he promised beforehand. It underscores the accomplishment of divine will even in the redemption history's darkest moment, namely the crucifixion of Jesus. Yet even here, especially here, God carries out his purposes. As Peter puts in one of his speeches, "There is salvation in no one else, for there is no other name under heaven given to people by which we must be [it is necessary for us to be] saved" (Acts 4:12).

Luke's idiom includes far more than these two examples. But they do represent some of his expressions that carry a great deal of meaning. Interpreters would do well to see how the uses of these expressions pile up in Luke's Gospel. We should ask exegetical questions, such as, How is Luke's use of "righteous" here related to previous and later occurrences? How do those other uses impact my understanding of the description in this instance?

---

[9] See, e.g., Luke 2:49; 4:43; 9:22; 11:42; 12:12; 13:14, 16, 33; 15:32; 17:25; 18:1; 19:5; 21:9; 22:7, 37; 24:7, 26, 44; Acts 1:16, 21; 3:21; 4:12; 5:29; 9:6; 14:22; 15:5; 16:30; 17:3; 19:21, 36; 20:35; 23:11; 24:19; 25:10, 24; 26:8; 27:21, 24, 26.

John's Idiom

John employs various phrases and expressions that are unique in comparison to the idiom of the Synoptic writers. Two examples are (1) "sign" (σημεῖον) and (2) "I am" (ἐγώ εἰμί) statements.

While the Synoptic writers often label Jesus's healings, exorcisms, and the like as miracles (δυνάμεις), John calls these kinds of actions signs.[10] A sign (σημεῖον), in John's usage of the term, refers to the wonders that Jesus carries out to produce faith in him. He even includes "signs" in the purpose statement of his Gospel (20:30–31). That is because the signs gradually reveal Jesus's identity within the flow of John's narrative. The first sign occurs at a wedding in Cana of Galilee where Jesus changes water to wine (2:1–11). The details of the event indicate that this sign implies Jesus is doing something "new" within Israel and the world. Although John notes that Jesus did many signs (20:30), he describes in detail six signs: (1) water to wine (2:1–11), (2) the healing of a royal official's son (4:46–54), (3) feeding 5,000 (6:1–14), (4) Jesus walking on water (6:16–21), (5) the healing of a man born blind (chap. 9), and (6) the raising of Lazarus from the dead (11:38–57). The seventh and climactic sign in John's Gospel is the resurrection of Jesus (20:1–29). This seventh and final sign completes the revelation of Jesus's identity.

John also makes frequent use of "I am" statements to unveil Jesus's identity.[11] As I will explain below, each of these "I am" statements has an OT background. The first such statement occurs in Jesus's conversation with the Samaritan woman who says to Jesus, "I know that the Messiah is coming (who is called Christ). When he comes, he will explain everything to us." Jesus responds, "I, the one speaking to you,

---

[10] See, e.g., John 2:11, 18, 23; 3:2; 4:48, 54; 6:2, 14, 26, 30; 7:31; 9:16; 10:41; 11:47; 12:18, 37; 20:30.

[11] See, e.g., John 4:26; 6:20, 35, 41, 48, 51; 8:12, 24, 58; 9:9; 10:7, 9, 11, 14; 11:25; 13:19; 14:6; 15:1, 5; 18:5, 6, 8.

Jesus's feeding of the 5,000 is a miracle that all four Gospel writers include in their biographical portraits of Jesus. However, John refers to this event, like others in his Gospel, as a "sign" (John 6:26).

am he" (4:25–26). Other uses of the phrase take up figures and events from Israel's history, including "I am the bread of life"; "I am the light of the world"; "I am the gate of the sheep"; "I am the good shepherd"; "I am the resurrection and the life"; "I am the way, the truth, and the life"; and "I am the true vine." Jesus's statement to a group of argumentative Pharisees might be the culminating use of "I am" statements in John, "Truly I tell you, before Abraham was, I am" (8:58). This statement echoes Yahweh's revelation of himself to Moses, "'I AM WHO I AM. This is what you are to say to the Israelites: I AM has sent me to you" (Exod 3:14). In this way, Jesus is including himself within the divine identity of Israel's God.

I have just scratched the surface here, because the Gospel of John is rich in its idiom. Interpreters will do well to interpret these "signs" and "I am" statements in relation to one another. They are, after all, mutually interpretive. If we wish to see how John answers the question, who is Jesus?, we must pay attention to these kinds of expressions. They carry a great deal of explanatory power.

Old Testament

I often tell students that the best commentary on the NT is always the OT. That is not to say that we should forgo historical-grammatical exegesis of the OT and simply observe how NT writers interpret the OT. However, if the biblical text is truly Christian Scripture, it follows that all Scripture finds its ultimate meaning in Jesus Christ. Jesus himself makes this point. For example, in a dispute with the religious elite, he asserts, "You pore over the Scriptures because you think you have eternal life in them, and yet they testify about me" (John 5:39).[12] Therefore, it is exegetically helpful to summarize some of the basic ways that each Gospel writer interprets and incorporates the OT into his biographical portrait of Jesus.

MATTHEW'S USE OF THE OT

The best description of how Matthew interprets and incorporates the OT into his Gospel is as typological fulfillment. In general, typology is a method of interpretation that sees events, figures, and other OT features as a "type" of event and or figure in the NT. The OT type foreshadows a greater reality in the NT. For example, Matthew notes that Jesus grew up in Nazareth "to fulfill what was spoken through the prophets, that he will be called a Nazarene" (2:23). Matthew speaks as

---

[12] See also Luke 24:27, 44; 2 Cor 1:20.

if an OT passage predicted that the Messiah would live in Nazareth and thereby be called a "Nazarene." However, no such passage exists in Israel's Scriptures. Therefore, what OT text does Matthew have in view?

This is where typological fulfillment is helpful. Matthew does not have a single text in mind but rather a particular group of figures from Israel's past, namely those who took a Nazirite vow. We first hear about Nazirites in the Mosaic law, "Speak to the Israelites and tell them: When a man or woman makes a special vow, a Nazirite (נזיר) vow, to separate himself to the LORD . . ." (Num 6:2).[13] It appears that Matthew is playing on the word *Nazirite* (Nazarene) from Numbers, but he is also evoking the idea that Jesus is "separated" for God's purposes in a way that far exceeds the Nazirites in Israel who came before him.[14] After all, he will not merely save his people from a political opponent in the way that Samson the Nazirite did before him. Instead, God sets Jesus the Nazirite/Nazarene apart to save the people from their sins (Matt 1:21).

Interpreters should stay alert for other instances in which Matthew links the OT to Jesus and his disciples through typological fulfillment. It is something he does from the introduction to the close of his Gospel. In Matt 1:1, he genealogically connects Jesus to both Abraham and David. For Matthew, Jesus fulfills both the promise to Abraham (Gen 12:1–3) and the promise to David (2 Sam 7:10–13). Jesus brings to earth the blessing of redemption to the nations promised to Abraham and the eternal kingship promised to David. Similarly, Matthew closes his Gospel by evoking one last time Isaiah's Immanuel motif through Jesus's promise to his disciples, "I am with you always, to the end of the age" (28:20).[15]

---

[13] In this example, Matthew seems to be using the Hebrew version of Num 6:2 rather than the Septuagint (LXX).

[14] Samson is an example of a Nazirite set apart to save Israel (Judg 13:5). See Judges 13–16.

[15] Cf. Matt 1:23 (Isa 7:14).

*Samson is described as a "Nazirite" who accomplished great feats such
as killing a lion with his bare hands (Judg 14:5-6). Likewise, Jesus the
"Nazarene" defeated sin, death, and Satan with his nail-scarred hands.*

MARK'S USE OF THE OT

One way Mark uses the OT in his portrayal of Jesus is by taking up
figures from Israel's Scriptures who suffer unjustly and yet serve sacrificially. The most prominent example is found in Jesus's self-description
to his disciples, "For even the Son of Man did not come to be served,
but to serve, and to give his life as a ransom for many" (10:45). This
description echoes the figure of the Suffering Servant in Isaiah 53:
"But he was pierced because of our rebellion, crushed because of our
iniquities; punishment for our peace was on him, and we are healed by
his wounds" (v. 5). As the fuller context of Isaiah 53 demonstrates, the
prophet provides a silhouette of a Suffering Servant whom Mark then

identifies as Jesus. He indeed suffers unjustly, but he does so to serve and redeem others from sin.

In this way, Markan interpreters should expect to find a picture of Jesus that is largely shaped by the suffering and or redemptive figures that preceded him. These include Moses/Joshua (Mark 6:34); David (10:48); and the prophets (8:28). Therefore, the Markan Jesus should be understood against the backdrop of these kinds of OT figures.

LUKE'S USE OF THE OT

Among the various ways that Luke employs the OT in his biography of Jesus, two features stand out. First, Luke sees the arrival of Jesus as the answer to God's long-awaited promise of redemption that is laid out in the OT. This is most evident in the hymns sung by Mary (1:46–55) and Zechariah (1:67–79). Both hymns underscore that through Jesus God has "remembered" the redemption he promised to Abraham and his descendants. As Mary exclaims, "He has helped his servant Israel, remembering his mercy to Abraham and to his descendants forever, just as he spoke to our ancestors" (1:54–55).[16] For Luke, the birth, life, death, and resurrection of Jesus complete God's prior promise to forgive his people, deliver them from their enemies, and serve him without fear.

Second, Luke portrays Jesus as a righteous sufferer such as the figures often found in the Psalms of Lament. In these psalms, the righteous sufferer trusts God in the face of betrayal and even divine silence before his enemies. It is against this backdrop that Luke often portrays Jesus. This is most clearly seen in the crucifixion scene. With his last breath, Jesus cries out, "Father, into your hands I entrust my spirit" (23:46). The phrase "into your hands I commit my spirit" is a cry of trust uttered by the psalmist, "Into your hand I entrust my spirit; you have redeemed me, LORD, God of truth" (Ps 31:5). In the wider context of the psalm,

---

[16] See also Luke 1:72–73.

the speaker cries out against unjust enemies who have overtaken him and seeks vindication from God. Jesus's circumstances and needs are similar. Yet one difference between Jesus and the lamenter in Psalm 31 is that Jesus asks God to forgive his enemies (Luke 23:34). God will vindicate Jesus from his enemies by raising him from the dead, but he will also forgive those who crucified him per the request of his Son.

Interpreters will miss the richness of Luke's salvation history and Christology if they fail to hear these kinds of OT echoes. They are not coincidental but intentionally woven into Luke's mosaic of Jesus whose work as the righteous One brings the promise of redemption to completion.

JOHN'S USE OF THE OT

The OT definitively shapes the literary and theological characteristics of John's Gospel. This OT influence is especially evident in John's well-known "I am" (ἐγώ εἰμί) statements. As noted above, Jesus routinely uses "I am" statements to reveal his identity and thereby the identity of his Father. For each "I am" statement in John, there is an OT counterpart.

For example, shortly after the miraculous feeding of the 5,000, Jesus exclaims "I am the bread of life." He likens his feeding of the 5,000 to the way Yahweh fed Israel in the wilderness with manna (Exodus 16). Jesus explains to those who question him on this matter, "Truly I say to you, Moses didn't give you the bread from heaven, but my Father gives you true bread from heaven" (John 6:32). Jesus then identifies himself as the true bread, "I am the bread of life. No one who comes to me will ever hunger, and no one who believes in me will ever be thirsty again" (John 6:35). Jesus builds upon this OT connection and teaches his disciples that the one who "eats my flesh and drinks my blood" will have true life (John 6:54–55). We see an escalation here between the manna Yahweh gave in the wilderness and the "bread of life" that he gives in the ministry of Jesus. Manna gave life for a limited span of time to one group of people. By contrast, Jesus, as the bread of life, gives eternal life to the entire world (John 6:33).

The other six "I am" statements have a similar OT link. Therefore, the interpreter must not only identify this link, but also seek to understand how that link illuminates the portrait of Jesus. If we fail to make this connection, we miss one of the primary ways that John answers the question, who is Jesus?

USE OF OT—SUMMARY

Overall, the Gospel writers use the OT in two main ways. First, to portray Jesus as both God and man. On the one hand, both the Synoptic Gospels and John attribute to Jesus characteristics that are normally reserved for Yahweh. The synoptic writers tend to communicate these attributes through what Jesus does. For example, although readers familiar with the Gospels may think of Jesus walking on water as somewhat routine for him, Yahweh is the only figure in Israel's Scriptures who is capable of such power over creation's most chaotic and foreboding location. In describing God's past acts for Israel, the psalmist notes:

> Others went to sea in ships, conducting trade on the vast water. They saw the LORD's works, his wondrous works in the deep. He spoke and raised a stormy wind that stirred up the waves of the sea. Rising up to the sky, sinking down to the depths, their courage melting away in anguish, they reeled and staggered like a drunkard, and all their skill was useless. Then they cried out to the LORD in their trouble, and he brought them out of their distress. He stilled the storm to a whisper, and the waves of the sea were hushed. They rejoiced when the waves grew quiet. Then he guided them to the harbor they longed for. (Ps 107:23–30)

When we set the psalmist's description of how God calms the storm alongside Luke's description of Jesus calming the storm, we see how he includes Jesus in the identity of Israel's God:

> And as they were sailing he fell asleep. Then a fierce windstorm came down on the lake; they were being swamped and were in danger. They came and woke him up, saying, "Master, Master, we're going to die!"
>
> Then he got up and rebuked the wind and the raging waves. So they ceased, and there was a calm. He said to them, "Where is your faith?"
>
> They were fearful and amazed, asking one another, "Who then is this? He commands even the winds and the waves, and they obey him!" (Luke 8:23–25)[17]

The psalmist can answer the disciple's "who?" and by evoking Psalm 107 in this episode Luke echoes that answer. In addition to these kinds of actions by Jesus, the synoptic writers also have Jesus participate in Yahweh's identity through his teachings.[18]

John also identifies Jesus as divine by using the OT. His approach is somewhat different from the synoptic writers. For example, in his prologue (1:1–18), John gives Jesus a unique title and situates him in the eternal presence and work of God. This is clear from the opening line alone, "In the beginning was the Word, and the Word was with God, and the Word was God." The phrase "in the beginning" evokes Gen 1:1, "In the beginning God created the heavens and the earth." John places Jesus, who is the Word, at creation, prior to creation, and intimately involved in the work of creation (1:3, 8:58; 17:24). Against this OT

---

[17] See also Matt 8:23–27; Mark 4:35–41.

[18] See, e.g., the Sermon on the Mount in Matthew 5–7, where Jesus speaks about the "fullness" of the Mosaic law based on his own authority, whereas Moses acted only as a prophetic messenger.

In the well-known story of Jesus walking on water, we often miss the divine implications of the scene. Jesus does something that only Yahweh is described as doing in the OT.

backdrop, John clearly identifies Jesus as the eternal Son of God who became a man (1:14).

In thinking about how the Gospel writers use the OT to portray Jesus as a man, we should consider three things. First, they discover many "types" of Jesus in the OT whose characteristics and roles in YHWH's purposes illuminate Jesus's identity. These "types" of Jesus include people, places, and even events. They can be categorized as figural people, places, and events.[19] The chart below identifies some of these figures. It is important to read these references in light of their wider contexts in the OT and the Gospels.

---

[19] By "figural," I do not mean ahistorical. It is simply a way of referring to the fact that one of the ways the Gospel writers interpret the OT is to see how it typifies, foreshadows, or prefigures Jesus.

Figural People, Places, and Events in the Gospels

Figural People

Adam (Gen 2:7; Luke 3:38)

Abel (Gen 4:1–16; Matt 23:35; Luke 11:51)

Noah (Genesis 6–8; Matt 24:37–38; Luke 17:26–27)

Moses (Num 21:4–9; John 3:14–15)

David (2 Sam 8:13–14; Ps 110:1; Matt 12:3; 22:45)

Solomon (1 Kgs 10:1–9; Matt 12:42)

Son of Man (Dan 7:13–14; Mark 14:62)

Prophets (Amos 7:10–17; Luke 13:31–34)

Figural Places

Tabernacle (Exod 40:34–38; John 1:14)

Temple (1 Kgs 8:10; 9:1–9; Matt 12:6)

Figural Events

Creation (Gen 1:1–2; John 1:1–5)

Flood (Gen 6:11–13; Matt 24:37–38)

Divinely orchestrated birth (Isa 7:14; Matt 1:23)

Deliverance from Egypt (Hos 11:1; Matt 2:15)

Passover (Exod 12:1–28; Luke 22:13–20)

Feast of Booths (Lev 23:39–44; John 7:37–39)

Giving of law (Exod 20:1–17; Matt 5:17–48)

Installation of king (Psalm 2; Mark 14:62)

Entrance into paradise (Gen 2:15–23; Luke 23:43)

Second, the Gospel writers also indicate that Jesus is a human being. He shares in the experiences and hurts of the human beings whom he encounters. Therefore, he is accessible, approachable, and empathetic just as Yahweh promised. Jesus makes this clear in invitations such as, "Come to me, all of you who are weary and burdened, and I will give you rest" (Matt 11:28).

Third, the Gospel writers do not pry apart Jesus's divine and human identity when they use the OT to describe him. Instead, they use the

OT to hold these identities together and define them. We find that Jesus is indeed the messianic Son of David and Son of Man promised in the OT. Yet Jesus reshapes those identities with the result that he is a man sent by God but not just a human agent of God. God is within him in a way that is both expected and unexpected.

Another primary way that the Gospel writers use the OT is in their presentation of those whom Jesus encounters, including disciples, the needy, and enemies. For example, Jesus likens those who follow him to OT prophets. He warns that his disciples will be persecuted like the prophets who came before them (Matt 5:12). Similarly Jesus teaches and heals those whose pain echoes the needy found in the pages of the OT. Luke makes this very point in Jesus's inaugural sermon at Nazareth where he stands in the synagogue and reads from the scroll of Isaiah, "The Spirit of the Lord is on me, because he has anointed me to preach the good news to the poor. He has sent me to proclaim release to the captives and recovery of sight to the blind, to set free the oppressed, to proclaim the year of the Lord's favor" (4:18–19). Finally, the Gospel writers also use the OT to portray Jesus's enemies. This is especially evident in the Passion Narrative where the description of Jesus's opponents echo the description of enemies in the Psalms of Lament. For example, the mockers at the crucifixion bear a striking resemblance to the psalmist's scoffers:

> Those who passed by were yelling insults at him, shaking their heads, and saying, "Ha! The one who would destroy the temple and rebuild it in three days, save yourself by coming down from the cross!" (Mark 15:29–30)

> Everyone who sees me mocks me; they sneer and shake their heads: "He relies on the Lord; let him save him; let the Lord rescue him, since he takes pleasure in him." (Ps 22:7–8)

The similarities between these two passages are not merely coincidental. Mark uses the psalmist's description of his enemies to depict those who afflicted Jesus at this darkest moment.

We have covered a lot of ground in this summary section on the use of the OT in the Gospels. If you are wondering what the exegetical lesson is in all of this, please note the following:

1. Interpreters should always consider how any episode in any Gospel echoes the OT.
2. Specifically, interpreters should identify what role the OT is playing in the depiction of Jesus, the disciples, the needy, and Jesus's enemies.
3. The OT is most often the source for the language, imagery, and theology present in the Gospels.

Theological Tools

Theology is a term that writers use in a variety of ways, including

1. *Descriptive theology.* This refers to what a NT writer believed in the first century about God, Jesus, the Spirit, people, salvation, the world, the end of all things, and so forth. These various areas often receive labels from systematic theology such as Christology (study of Jesus), pneumatology (study of the Holy Spirit), anthropology (study of people), soteriology (study of salvation), ecclesiology (study of the church), cosmology (study of the world), and eschatology (study of the end of all things). In the Gospels, Christology includes and ultimately defines these categories.
2. *Redemptive history theology.* We can also approach theology from the standpoint of how the various books of the Bible present an overarching story line in which God carries out his redemptive purposes.
3. *Systematic (dogmatic) theology.* This is the category that people most often associate with the term *theology*. Here an attempt is made to bring together teachings of Scripture into a consistent or "systematic" whole.

As interpreters of the Gospels, we must engage in theological analysis. That analysis will inevitably involve an overlap among these three categories of theology. However, since the Gospels are devoted to the figure of Jesus, our theological analysis will be guided by Christology. Quite simply, what did the four Gospel writers believe about Jesus?

Matthew's Theology

The most prominent feature of Matthew's Christology is his emphasis on "Immanuel" as the One who brings the "kingdom of heaven" near (1:23; 28:20). Matthew drives home the point that God is present to rule the world and his people in the person of Jesus. Matthew's Immanuel Christology defines his entire understanding of God, people, salvation, the end of all things. In other words, Immanuel Christology defines all of Matthew's theology. In this way, salvation from sin (1:21) comes through God's presence in Jesus. The church's mission unto the end of all things depends on Jesus's presence with his disciples (28:16–20). Likewise, the church's unity depends on God's presence in Jesus (18:15–22). Immanuel is the location of God's rule (kingdom of heaven) over sin, death, Satan, and his people. Interpreters should observe how individual passages in Matthew may reflect this Immanuel Christology.

Mark's Theology

Mark's Christology revolves around God's authority over sin, death, and Satan as it is unveiled in the mystery and suffering of his Son. Mark constantly highlights how the disciples and others struggle to understand who Jesus is (4:10–12, 35–41). Jesus and the kingdom he reveals is in fact a mystery. Although Jesus clearly demonstrates his kingdom authority, his identity remains enigmatic until the crucifixion. It is there that an unidentified Roman centurion rightly confesses, "Truly

*Notice in this depiction of the crucifixion scene that the Roman
centurion flings his arms wide open before the crucified Jesus. It
is a visual representation of the centurion's very telling confession
"Surely this man was the Son of God" (Mark 15:39).*

this man was the Son of God!" (15:39; 1:1). Yet even at the end of
Mark's Gospel, there is uncertainty. The women at the tomb receive an
angelic command to go and announce the resurrection of Jesus to the
disciples (16:5–7). And in Mark's last verse, there is a cliff-hanger, "They
[the women] went out and ran from the tomb, because trembling and
astonishment overwhelmed them. And they said nothing to anyone,
since they were afraid" (16:8). Mark ends his Gospel with the same
note of mystery with which it began. Interpreters should pay close

attention to the way Mark weaves this theme of mystery and suffering throughout his work.

Luke's Theology

What sets Luke's Christology apart from the other three Gospels is his emphasis on Jesus the righteous One. Just as in Mark, the crucifixion scene is pivotal for understanding all of Luke's Christology. After watching Jesus take his last breath, the Lukan centurion confesses, "This man really was righteous!" (23:47). This confession sheds light on all that Luke has written about Jesus up to this point. Jesus's miracles, teachings, response to his opponents, and relationship to his Father can be summed up as righteous. Jesus is the Son of God who stands righteous before God, because he entrusts himself to the Father's will. He teaches, heals, gathers disciples, and endures suffering in obedience to the Father. Jesus definitively reveals his righteous identity at the cross where he both answers the cry of a repentant criminal and himself cries out in trust, "Father, into your hands I entrust my spirit" (23:46). God then answers the cry of the righteous One by raising him from the dead. The lesson for interpreters in all of this is that they should read Luke's Gospel in relation to the centurion's climactic confession at the cross, "This man really was righteous!"

John's Theology

John's prologue (1:1–18) alerts the reader to Jesus's identity before the narrative even begins to unfold. Jesus is the "Word [who] became flesh" (1:14). John expects the reader to take this Christological identification into the succeeding chapters. Everything that John says about God, Jesus, salvation, and the like must be filtered through the opening lines of his Gospel.

Responsive Tools

We now come to one of the most critical elements of interpretation. We must ask, how do the Gospel writers want their readers to respond to their works? Obviously, since all four writers have Jesus as their biographical subject, there is some overlap among their intended responses. They all want the reader to believe in Jesus. But what does each writer specifically want the reader to believe? What is the exact nature of that belief?

Responding to Matthew

The intended response to Matthew most certainly has something to do with fulfillment and Immanuel. Specifically, God fulfills his promises to his people through his very presence in Jesus, in the crucified and risen Immanuel. Even more, Jesus is with his people as he sends them out to make disciples.

Responding to Mark

Given Mark's literary and theological features, his intended response revolves around the mystery of the kingdom as it is revealed in Jesus and the struggle involved in following him. The answer to this mystery and discipleship struggle is a continual return to Golgotha where Mark unveils the identity of the Son of God.

Responding to Luke

Luke tells us plainly from the outset how he wants us to respond. In a word, have certainty. Luke wanted Theophilus to have certainty, and the same is true for subsequent readers. The response is certainty about Jesus's teaching, miracles, mission, death, resurrection, and ascension.

It is not just certainty that these things happened. It is a certainty that Jesus is the righteous One who entrusted himself to the Father in life, death, and in resurrection on my behalf. The reader, like the lamenting thief at the cross, should cry out, "Jesus, remember me when you come into your kingdom" (23:42).

Responding to John

John also tells us plainly how he intends his readers to respond. He wants them to believe. Specifically, they are to believe in the identity of the Logos made flesh (1:14). The one who was in the beginning with God is also the Christ and the eternal Son of God. Faith in the Logos who was crucified and risen results in eternal life.

Putting the Tools to Use

We could spend several more chapters just working through individual passages in the Gospels. However, given the sizable use of parables in the Synoptic Gospels, I think it will be helpful to work step by step through Luke 18:9–14. You can also consult the "tools for interpreting a parable" section above. The steps you take here can be applied to any number of passages in the Gospels.

1. *Reading and preliminary exegetical statement*. Read the parable several times until you are quite familiar with it. Prior to completing any of the following exegetical steps, write a preliminary exegetical statement that reflects what you think the parable means.

   Preliminary statement:

2. *Literary context*. Discuss the micro-context (i.e., what occurs directly before and after the parable; how does it impact the

interpretation of the parable?) and the macro-context (i.e., how does the parable fit within the overall literary context of the book? how does it impact the interpretation of the parable?).

Micro-context:

Macro-context: (Act? Cycle?):

3. *Lexical considerations.* Identify and discuss key terms in the parable. (Consult a critical commentary for help.)
4. *Stock imagery.* Identify and discuss the stock imagery of the parable. (You may have to consult a commentary or two to adequately discuss the stock imagery.)
5. *Unexpected features.* Identify and discuss the unexpected features of the parable.
6. *Potential overinterpreted elements.* (See Tips discussion above.) What elements in the parable might an interpreter overinterpret in a way that Jesus did not intend?
7. *Jesus's exegesis.* Does Jesus exegete his own parable? If so, identify the verse in which he does and discuss it.
8. *Synoptic context.* Does this parable occur in the other Synoptic Gospels? Does the parallel use of the parable shed any interpretive light on the parable you are interpreting? Explain.
9. *Kingdom point.* What point is Jesus making about the kingdom of God?
10. *Death and resurrection.* The interpreter who skips this step has missed the point of Luke's entire Gospel. With that in mind, how might this parable be linked to Jesus's death and resurrection?
11. *Theological perspective.* Does this parable touch on any of Luke's wider theological motifs? Explain.
12. *Final exegetical statement.* Carefully construct a final exegetical statement that reflects your interpretive work up to this point. Make sure you include Luke's intended response for the reader.

13. *Response*. How did Jesus want the original listeners to respond
    to this parable (see Lk 18:9)? How might we respond today in
    light of both the parable and the good news of Jesus' death and
    resurrection that is not explicitly mentioned here?

9

Tools for Interpreting Acts and Paul's Biography

Understanding the Tools for Acts

The book of Acts opens with Jesus's last instructions to the apostles followed by his ascension (1:1–11). The apostles are instructed by Jesus to wait for the gift of the Spirit, which will empower them to bear witness to the crucified and risen Jesus in Jerusalem, Judea, Samaria, and to the ends of the earth (1:7–8). Their instructions come upon the heels of a question related to when God would restore the kingdom to Israel in accordance with his prior messianic promise (1:6). Of course, as we see in Acts, the people of God are being reworked around the person of Jesus who empowers them and promises to return. Therefore, Luke situates the early church's mission between two poles of "waiting"—wait for the Spirit and wait for Jesus's return. Between those two poles, they are to be active witnesses empowered by the Spirit.

These opening instructions and events set the program for the entire book. What we find is an early church on mission highlighted by two prominent figures, Peter and Paul. The former dominates Acts 1–12 while the latter dominates Acts 13–28. Paul's biography is especially prominent and provides an invaluable tool for the latter interpretation of his letters.

Speaking of tools, we will once again consider the historical, literary, theological, and responsive tools needed for the interpretation of Acts. The guiding question in Acts is simply this: how does Jesus continue his work from the right hand of the Father? (7:55) The answer unfolds in the pages of Acts. Let's make sure we have the right tools to discover that answer.

Jesus's work does not end after his ascension described in Acts 1.
Instead, Jesus continues his work from the right hand of the Father.

Historical Tools

History behind Acts

As a reminder, the questions here include the following: Who is the author of Acts? When was Acts written? To whom was Acts originally written? Why was Acts originally written? We should not underestimate the interpretive importance of these questions. The last two questions are especially pertinent as I will discuss below.

AUTHOR

The traditional view is that Luke authored the book of Acts. The external evidence for this view stems once again from the writings of the early church fathers. For example, Eusebius explains, "Now it would be clear from Paul's own words and from the narrative of Luke in the Acts that Paul, in his preaching to the Gentiles, laid the foundations of the churches from Jerusalem round about unto Illyricum."[1]

So what do we know about Luke? First, based on the prologues in Luke 1:1–4 and Acts 1:1–2, it is clear that Luke was fairly well educated. He opens both of these works using phrases and an approach to his task that is normally reserved for advanced pieces of historical writing. Second, the "we" passages in Acts indicate that Luke accompanied Paul on many of his missionary journeys. The narration in Acts shifts from third person to first person beginning in Acts 16:10, "After he had seen the vision, we immediately made efforts to set out for Macedonia, concluding that God had called us to preach the gospel to them." The author clearly includes himself in the travels of Paul. Third, Paul mentions Luke in two of his letters (Col 4:14; 2 Tim 4:11). We glean additional biographical information from these two references. In the Colossians reference, Paul refers to Luke as a "doctor" (ὁ ἰατρός). It

---

[1] Eusebius, *Ecclesiastical History* 3.4.

is possible that Luke served Paul as his medical physician, or perhaps the reference is metaphorical. From the 2 Timothy reference, we learn that Luke stayed with Paul up until the last moments of his life. Paul wrote 2 Timothy during his last Roman imprisonment, which would end in his death (2 Tim 4:6–8). In this context, Paul mentions to Timothy, "Demas has deserted me, since he loved this present world, and has gone to Thessalonica. Crescens has gone to Galatia, Titus to Dalmatia. Only Luke is with me. Bring Mark with you, for he is useful to me in the ministry" (4:10–11).

However, as with all other books of Christian Scripture, doubts about the traditional authorship of Acts arose in the wake of the Enlightenment.[2] Some scholars put forward the following reasons against traditional authorship:

1. The views of the early church and early church fathers are unreliable.
2. The use of "we" in the text of Acts is a rhetorical device rather than a reference to the author of the book.
3. The author distorts the "historical Paul." Quite simply, the depiction of Paul in Acts is incongruent with the historical and theological picture of him in his letters. Therefore, a true companion of Paul would have never depicted the apostle in the way that the writer of Acts does.

These kinds of arguments against traditional authorship ultimately falter at various points. First, to suggest that early church fathers identified Luke as the author of Acts based solely on their own readings of Luke and Acts is historically unlikely. Early church fathers did not base their identification of Luke as the author of Acts solely on inferences

---

[2] I am helped here by the summary in D. A. Carson and Douglas J. Moo, *An Introduction to the New Testament*, 2nd ed. (Grand Rapids: Zondervan, 2005), 291–96.

they drew from the text. It is more likely that their views reflect a wider and earlier Christian tradition that identified Luke as the author. Second, the suggestion that the use of "we" in Acts is a rhetorical device lacks explanatory power. Why would the author of Acts suddenly shift from the third person to the first person? What rhetorical impact is this supposed to make? It seems more likely that the shift reflects the author's participation in the events that he describes. Finally, the well-worn argument that the Paul of Acts and the Paul of his letters are incongruent is based on a number of faulty assumptions. For example, this view assumes that both Acts and Paul report every journey that the apostle ever took. Based on this assumption, some interpreters claim large inconsistencies between Paul's trips to Jerusalem as mentioned in Acts and those mentioned in the Letters.[3] We should remember that neither Acts nor Paul sets out to give an exhaustive biographical sketch of the apostle's movements.

DATE

Although different scholars identify different dates for the writing of Acts, I prefer a date in the early 60s AD for two primary reasons. First, Luke does not include any references to Neronian persecution of Christians that we know took place during the mid-60s. Second, Luke portrays first-century Judaism as a religion that abided by Roman law; this would not have been the perception of it from AD 66 and forward, when Jewish rebels launched a war against Rome.

---

[3] Paul's Letters report three trips to Jerusalem; Acts reports five such trips. Carson and Moo, *An Introduction to the New Testament*, 319.

AUDIENCE

While some scholars attempt to locate a specific and narrow original audience for the book of Acts, its original audience, much like the Gospel of Luke, is probably much broader. Given the emphasis that Luke places on Jesus working through the church by the Spirit to fulfill God's promised plan of salvation, the audience of Acts is early Christians who need to be encouraged that God is faithfully fulfilling his saving work in the Mediterranean and beyond.

PURPOSE

This being the second volume written by Luke, the purpose of his Gospel prologue applies also to the purpose of Acts. As I noted in the previous chapter, Luke dedicates his Gospel to Theophilus and writes to give him "certainty" about what Jesus said and did (Luke 1:1–4). That purpose of certainty continues in Acts. The difference in Acts is that now Jesus's work takes place *from* the right hand of the Father *through* the Spirit *in* the apostles and early church. Nevertheless, Luke still writes to give Theophilus, and those like him, certainty as it relates to Jesus's continued work in Jerusalem, Judea, Samaria, and to the end of the earth.

This geographical focus stems from Jesus's instructions to the apostles in Acts 1:8, "You will receive power when the Holy Spirit has come on you, and you will be my witnesses in Jerusalem, in all Judea and Samaria and to the end of the earth." This statement also indicates to us Luke's purpose in Acts. Quite simply, he is giving certainty about Jesus's missional work through the early church beginning in Jerusalem (2:1–4) and reaching all the way to Rome (28:16–31).

Interpreters should keep this overarching purpose in view when analyzing individual episodes in Acts. Although each episode contains unique features that need to be appreciated, each episode ultimately informs Luke's overarching purpose in Acts. Therefore, "certainty" will be a part of each episode's meaning. Each episode, in its own way, functions to give certainty about Jesus's continued work in the early church.

History in Acts

The story that Luke tells in Acts revolves around the enthroned Jesus who sends the Holy Spirit to empower his message and apostles in their mission to be his witnesses to the end of the earth all in accordance with what God promised beforehand in the Old Testament (OT) and what Jesus promised in Luke's Gospel.

Luke underscores Jesus's enthronement in Peter's Pentecost sermon where the apostle proclaims, "Therefore, let all the house of Israel know with certainty that God has made this Jesus, whom you crucified, both Lord and Messiah" (Acts 2:36). Similarly, at the close of another sermon, just before he is stoned to death, Stephen testifies, "Look, I see the heavens opened and the Son of Man standing at the right hand of God!" (7:56). Jesus's authoritative position is consistent with what he promised at his trial, "From now on, the Son of Man will be seated at the right hand of the power of God" (Luke 22:69). In Acts, everything that transpires is a result of the crucified, risen, and enthroned Jesus.

The pivotal moment in Acts occurs at Pentecost when the apostles receive the Holy Spirit, as Jesus had promised, who then empowers their mission (1:7–8; 2:1–13). The arrival of the Spirit is marked by the apostles' ability to speak in languages not native to them. They proclaimed the "magnificent things of God" in dialects ranging from Parthians to Cretans and Arabs who were all present in Jerusalem to celebrate Pentecost. Some have suggested that in this event God reverses his actions at Babel where he confused the languages of various peoples and scattered them across the earth. In the arrival of the Spirit at Pentecost, God has gathered representatives of various nations and spoken to all of them with the same language, namely the message of the gospel spoken through the Spirit in the apostles. As the narrative moves forward in Acts, Luke continually emphasizes how the Spirit empowers the testimony of the apostles to the end of the earth.[4] Additionally, Jesus confirms the testimony about him through various miracles carried out by the apostles. Each of these miracles mirrors what Jesus did in Luke's Gospel. Luke's point in drawing these parallels is to establish the continuity between what Jesus did on the earth and what he is still doing on earth from heaven.

The movement of the testimony to the end of the earth progresses geographically through the story in Acts. After the Pentecost episode in Jerusalem, the apostles carry the testimony throughout Judea, Samaria, and beyond.

One way to trace the unfolding action in Acts is to follow how Jesus's witnesses obey his command (Acts 1:8) by moving from Jerusalem, to Judea, to Samaria and toward the end of the earth.

---

[4] See, e.g., Acts 6:10.

The story that unfolds in Acts is in accordance with what God promises in the OT and what Jesus promised in Luke's Gospel. Acts contains numerous OT citations and allusions that collectively underscore the link between what the early church experiences and what God had promised beforehand. For example, at Pentecost, by appealing to prophetic promises Peter explains the arrival of the Holy Spirit and the apostles' ability to speak in various languages. He notes, "This is what was spoken through the prophet Joel: And it will be in the last days, says God, that I will pour out my Spirit on all people; then your sons and your daughters will prophesy, your young men will see visions, and your old men will dream dreams" (Acts 2:16–17). At the same time, what the early church experiences in Acts corresponds with what Jesus promised in Luke. For example, Jesus assures his disciples, "Therefore make up your minds not to prepare your defense ahead of time, for I will give you such words and wisdom that none of your adversaries will be able to resist or contradict it (Lk 21:14–15). Luke then alludes to this prior promise from Jesus when describing Stephen's Spirit-empowered wisdom before those who oppose him, "But they were unable to stand up against his wisdom and the Spirit by whom he was speaking" (Acts 6:10). Stephen's unmatched wisdom also exemplifies Jesus' promise that the Spirit would empower those who testified to his death and resurrection (Acts 1:7–8).

History in Front of Acts

Over the past 2,000 years of interpretation, various issues have occupied interpreters of Acts. Three issues are noted here.

First, interpreters have often highlighted the emphasis that Luke places on "salvation history" in his two-volume work. From Luke 1 to Acts 28, Luke shows how God's long-awaited promise of redemption finds its completion in Jesus and his church. Luke underscores this point in the Pentecost narrative where Peter explains that the arrival of the

Holy Spirit signals how the end of God's redemptive plan is drawing near. As Peter puts it, citing the prophet Joel, "And it will be in the last days, says God, that I will pour out my Spirit on all people" (Acts 2:17).

Second, modern-day Christians often struggle to determine if the church's experiences in Acts are prescriptive or descriptive. Does Luke intend for the reader to consider healings, speaking in tongues, and the like as normative or exceptional for Christians?

Third, from a historical perspective, interpreters are often divided in their views on the many speeches that are found in Acts. Specifically, questions arise about the historicity of these speeches. Does Luke present them as they originally occurred, or are the speeches his own literary creation? Some interpreters have pointed to the practice of the fourth-century BC historian Thucydides, who explains that he often placed speeches on the lips of the historical figures whom he wrote about.

Consequently, it is suggested that Luke adopted the same practice. However, it is more likely that the speeches in Acts are based on the following: (1) eyewitness testimony, (2) written sources, and (3) paraphrases.

Literary Tools

Genre

While the Gospel of Luke is an ancient biography, the overarching genre of Acts is historical monograph. This means that the author attempts to make one overarching point about something that occurred in the first-century context. That one ("monograph") point informs and holds together every episode in Acts. It becomes an exegetical compass for interpreters, because one of the main questions they can pose to each episode is, how does this episode inform the one overarching point of Acts? Based on common threads found in the various episodes of Acts, the overarching point of this historical monograph is that *God has installed Jesus his Son as Lord and Christ*

Some scholars have wrongly suggested that Luke's speeches are created in the same way that Thucydides and other ancient historians created speeches. "But I have used language in accordance with what I thought the speakers in each case would have used, adhering as closely as possible to the general sense of what was actually spoken." —*Thucydides,* History of the Peloponnesian War *1.22*

at his right hand in heaven (2:29–36; 7:55–56) so that Jesus continues his work of redemption to the end of the earth through the Spirit who empowers the apostles and early church to proclaim the saving message of the gospel. It is this point that Luke attempts to make through every episode he includes in Acts. The task of the interpreter is to determine how each episode sheds light on that singular purpose. *See Wordsearch video for an example of how the singular purpose of Acts impacts the interpretation of individual episodes.*

Structure

Some interpreters suggest complex structures for the books of the NT. However, sometimes simpler is better. There are two simple ways to interpret the structure in Acts.

First, Jesus's statement in 1:7–8 functions as the axis around which the rest of Acts rotates. In these verses, Jesus gives the apostles one last command: "It is not for you to know the times or periods that the Father has set by his own authority. But you will receive power when the Holy Spirit has come on you, and you will be my witnesses in Jerusalem, in all Judea and Samaria, and to the end of the earth." This statement provides a road map for the literary structure in Acts. Testimony about the risen Jesus begins in Jerusalem and progresses in the geographical locations that Jesus mentions in Acts 1:8:

Acts 1:12–8:4—Witness of the risen Jesus in Jerusalem and Judea

Acts 8:5–15:41—Witness of the risen Jesus in Jerusalem, Judea, Samaria, and beyond

Acts 16:1–28:31—Witness of the risen Jesus all the way to Rome

Second, the structure of Acts is also organized around two key figures: Peter and Paul. Peter is the dominant figure from Acts 1–10; Paul dominates Acts 13–28. One of the indicators of this structure is the way that Luke draws parallels between the experiences of Peter and Paul. For example, both figures perform miracles, face resistance as they bear witness to the risen Jesus, are mistaken as divine figures, and provide leadership to the early church.

When dealing with various passages in Acts, interpreters should situate each episode within the wider structure of the book. This prevents us from tearing a passage out of its literary context and interpreting it in a vacuum.

Idiom

Many expressions and literary devices that Luke uses in his Gospel also appear in the book of Acts. For example, Luke once again uses the language of "necessity" (*dei*). God continues to complete his prior promises in the life of the early church. For example, Peter insists that the apostles replace Judas the betrayer of Jesus based on God's prior promise in the OT. He explains, "Brothers and sisters, it was necessary that the Scripture be fulfilled that the Holy Spirit through the mouth of David foretold about Judas, who became a guide to those who arrested Jesus" (Acts 1:16). A few lines later Peter cites Ps 69:26 and 109:8, "For it is written in the Book of Psalms: Let his dwelling become desolate; let no one live in it; and Let someone else take his position" (1:20). Based on these scriptural statements, Peter concludes that Judas must be replaced (1:21–26). Similar divine "necessities" in Acts include:

1. Necessity for Jesus to die and be raised from the dead (17:3)
2. Necessity for Jesus to ascend to the right hand of the Father (3:21)
3. Necessity to call on the "name" of the Lord and be saved (4:12; 16:30–31)
4. Necessity to obey God by testifying to Jesus rather than obey people by not testifying (5:29)
5. Necessity for Jesus's witnesses (disciples) to suffer (9:6, 16; 14:22)

Additionally, as I mentioned above, speeches are the primary way that Luke presents how Jesus is at work in the apostles and the early church. Approximately one-third of the material in Acts comes in the form of speeches. Therefore, we need to familiarize ourselves with some basic features of ancient speeches to interpret them. Let's consider three important components of ancient speeches.

TYPES OF RHETORIC

First, in antiquity and the book of Acts, there are three types of speeches (rhetoric): (1) deliberative rhetoric, (2) forensic rhetoric, and (3) epideictic rhetoric. In deliberative rhetoric, the speaker's aim is to move the audience toward a decision. The speakers in Acts use this kind of rhetoric, and the decision they generally seek from their audience is repentance, faith, and baptism. For example, toward the conclusion of Peter's Pentecost sermon, many of his listeners ask, "Brothers, what should we do?" (2:37). Peter responds, "Repent and be baptized, each of you, in the name of Jesus Christ for the forgiveness of your sins, and you will receive the gift of the Holy Spirit" (2:38). Peter's speech and many others in Acts aim for this kind of decision.

Second, Acts also contains a fair amount of forensic rhetoric. In forensic rhetoric, the speaker defends himself or a cause. Both Peter and Paul make use of forensic rhetoric as they defend themselves and their testimony about Jesus. Paul defends himself before religious leaders, Roman authorities, and even raucous crowds. He is sometimes quite shrewd in his forensic strategies. For example, faced with opposition by both Pharisees and Sadducees, Paul stirs things up. Luke notes, "When Paul realized that one part of them were Sadducees and the other part were Pharisees, he cried out in the Sanhedrin, 'Brothers, I am a Pharisee, a son of Pharisees. I am being judged because of the hope of the resurrection of the dead!'" (Acts 23:6). Paul recognizes that he can best defend himself by pitting the Sadducees, who do not believe in the resurrection of the dead, against Pharisees, who do believe in the resurrection of the dead (23:7–9).

Third, epideictic rhetoric focuses on praise or blame with the ultimate aim of agreeing or rejecting some value.[5] We find an example

---

[5] Ben Witherington III, *Conflict and Community in Corinth: A Socio-Rhetorical Commentary on 1 and 2 Corinthians* (Grand Rapids: Eerdmans, 1995), 43.

of this rhetoric in Herod Antipas's speech (Acts 12:20–23). He speaks with the intention of the crowd heaping praise upon him, which they do. In fact, they attribute a divine quality to him proclaiming, "It's the voice of a god and not of a man" (12:22). When Herod accepts such praise, Luke tells us that an angel of the Lord took his life (12:23).

It should be noted that in ancient speeches all three types of rhetoric could be blended together. That is certainly the case with the speeches in Acts. Interpreters should note how speakers combine deliberative, forensic, and epideictic rhetoric to accomplish their aims.

ART OF RHETORIC

In addition to the general types of rhetoric, Aristotle provides some helpful observations about characteristics of ancient speeches in his well-known work *Art of Rhetoric.* He notes that a speaker must tap into three areas to communicate effectively: ethos, logos, and pathos. Ethos refers to the speaker's ability to connect with the audience in a way that ensures the audience deems the speaker worthy of being heard. Of course, once the speaker establishes ethos, the speaker must make a convincing argument. This is what Aristotle calls logos. Finally, an effective speaker must engender pathos, wherein the speaker encourages the audience to respond to the message.

I mention Aristotle's perspective on speeches, because it is relevant to the analysis of the many speeches in Acts. I am not suggesting that Luke read Aristotle's work. These ideas were "in the air" in the first-century world, a world quite familiar with rhetoricians of various types plying their speaking trade all over Mediterranean cities. The speakers recorded in Acts, namely Peter and Paul, would have been familiar on some level with the notion of ethos, logos, and pathos, even if they did not use those descriptive phrases or had no familiarity with Aristotle's work. Ethos, logos, and pathos are inherent to a speech, whether it is done well or poorly.

*Aristotle believed an effective speech needed to contain three
elements: ethos, logos, and pathos. Interpreters of Acts should
look for the same elements in the book's many speeches.*

When interpreters evaluate speeches in Acts, part of their analysis
should include pinpointing the presence and nature of a given speaker's
ethos, logos, and pathos. It provides a helpful exegetical lens for reading
and understanding a speech in Acts.

PARTS OF RHETORIC

In addition to the types and art of rhetoric, an ancient speech usually
consisted of six successive parts:

Introduction to argument—the beginning part of the speech,
   aimed at making the audience receptive to the speech
Explanation of problem—the explanation of the disputed matter
Thesis—the main proposition(s)
Support for thesis—specific arguments to support the proposition

Disputation of opposition—disputation of arguments of an opponent

Summary of main points—repetition of the main arguments (probation) and appeal to gain a positive response from the audience[6]

The speeches in Acts contain these parts of rhetoric to varying degrees. For example, consider Paul's speech before Agrippa in Acts 26:

Introduction to argument (26:1–3)—Paul attempts to make King Agrippa receptive to his speech by complimenting Agrippa's familiarity with Jewish controversies and customs.

Explanation of problem (26:4–7)—Paul explains that the "disputed matter" revolves around his claim that Jesus has been raised from the dead, which is in fact the hope of Israel.

Thesis (26:8)—The main proposition of Paul's speech is stated in the form of a question, "Why do any of you consider it incredible that God raises the dead?"

Support for thesis (26:9–20)—Paul supports his *propositio* my recounting his former persecution of the church and his subsequent encounter with the risen Jesus on the road to Damascus.

Disputation of opposition (26:21–23)—Paul weakens the accusations by the religious elite by noting that his testimony of the crucified and risen Jesus is in accordance with what Moses and the prophets promised.

Summary of main points (26:24–32)—The speech closes with Paul's admonition to Agrippa that he believe the testimony about the risen Jesus, "King Agrippa, do you believe the prophets? I know that you believe" (26:27).

---

[6] I am helped in the description of these rhetorical parts by Witherington, 44.

Interpreters can analyze the many speeches in Acts by identifying these various parts of a speech. It helps us to see what the main point of the speech is, how the speaker supports that main point, and what the speaker aims to accomplish.

Use of the OT

Just as the Gospel of Luke contains copious OT echoes, the Acts of the Apostles is likewise filled with references to Israel's Scriptures. It is undoubtedly the "substructure" for how Luke presents the work of Jesus by the Spirit in the early church. There are many ways to assess the function of the OT in Acts. Quite simply, we are asking, how, or for what purpose, does Luke use the OT in this work? In answering this question, we will briefly consider four interrelated uses.

CHRISTOLOGICAL USE OF THE OT

Just prior to his ascension in Luke 24, Jesus twice explains his identity to the apostles by using the OT. Luke explains, "Then beginning with Moses and all the Prophets, he interpreted for them the things concerning himself in all the Scriptures" (24:27). He also notes, "He told them, 'These are my words that I spoke to you while I was still with you—that everything written about me in the Law of Moses, the Prophets, and the Psalms must be fulfilled.' Then he opened their minds to understand the Scriptures" (24:44–45). This instruction provided the apostles the interpretive guidance they needed to preach and teach about Jesus just as we see in Acts.

Figures in Acts frequently incorporate the OT into their speeches to explain the following: (1) Jesus's death and resurrection, (2) Jesus's relationship to the Father, (3) Jesus's position, and (4) Jesus's ongoing work in the church and world. For example, when Paul preaches at the synagogue in Antioch of Pisidia, he proclaims, "And we ourselves proclaim to you the good news of the promise that was made to the ancestors. God has fulfilled this for us, their children, by raising up Jesus as it is written in the second Psalm: You are my Son; today I have become your Father" (13:32–33). Paul cites Ps 2:7 and in doing so he explains something about Jesus's resurrection, his relationship to the Father, and its significance for the audience to whom Paul preaches. In short, God raises Jesus to fulfill his prior promise of redemption to Israel. Jesus is now the firstborn from the dead, which implies that there are more to follow. That is part of the ongoing work carried out by Jesus in the church.

SOTERIOLOGICAL USE OF THE OT

Luke also uses the OT to explain the nature and means of salvation in the early church. The nature of salvation in Acts involves deliverance from sin, death, Satan, and divine judgment. However, the experience of that salvation takes place through the preaching of a saving message. After all, Jesus commissions the apostles to be his "witnesses." This presentation of salvation is grounded in the OT. For example, when Paul defends himself before Agrippa by recounting his conversion experience on the road to Damascus, he alludes to a passage from Isaiah that helps shape how the apostle understands the saving message he preaches. He recounts what Jesus said to him on the road, and it echoes the words of Isaiah:

> But get up and stand on your feet. For I have appeared to you for this purpose, to appoint you as a servant and a witness of what you have seen and will see of me. I will rescue you from your people and from the Gentiles. I am sending you to them to open their eyes so that they may turn from darkness to light and from the power of Satan to God, that they may receive forgiveness of sins and a share among those who are sanctified by faith in me. (Acts 26:16–18)

I am the LORD. I have called you for a righteous purpose, and
I will hold you by your hand. I will watch over you, and I will
appoint you to be a covenant for the people and a light to
the nations, in order to open blind eyes, to bring out prisoners from the dungeon, and those sitting in darkness from the
prison house. (Isa 42:6–7)

There is clear overlap between these two passages. Paul sees himself
as the one addressed in Isaiah. Jesus takes him by the hand and directs
him to be a light to those mired in the darkness of sin and Satan which,
if left unresolved, has eternal judgment as its outcome. Similar examples
of this interplay between the OT and Acts are scattered throughout the
book where Luke's soteriology can be clearly seen. Once again, Luke's
soteriology requires a divinely appointed witness preaching a saving
message, and this comes straight from the pages of the OT, which Jesus
reworked around himself (Luke 24:27, 44–45).

ECCLESIASTICAL USE OF THE OT

As I will discuss further below, the identity of God's people is a key
theological motif in Acts. Who are the people of God? This question
underlies the entire book. However, the answer to this question is complex. The complexity stems from the relationship between Jews and
Gentiles in the early church. We find that in Acts the people of God
are not composed of ethnic Jews with a genealogical connection to
Abraham (Gen 12:1–3). Instead, the people of God are defined by their
faith in the Son whom Israel's God raised from the dead. Therefore,
"membership" in this group rests entirely on God's grace. Luke does
not present this definition of the people of God as something entirely
new. It stems from the OT.

A primary example of this can be found in the so-called Jerusalem
Council recorded in Acts 15. Here we find the early church at a

*Peter, James, and other church leaders at Jerusalem determined
that Gentile Christians, like Jewish Christians, should only rely
upon God's grace for entrance into the people of God.*

crossroads. Will the Jewish Christian leadership force Gentile Christians
to live like Jews to be saved and to be part of the people of God? Peter
answers this question by observing that salvation and inclusion in God's
people rest solely on grace for Jew and Gentile alike:

> And God, who knows the heart, bore witness to them by giv-
> ing them the Holy Spirit, just as he also did to us. He made no
> distinction between us and them, cleansing their hearts by faith.
> Now then, why are you testing God by putting a yoke on the
> disciples' necks that neither our ancestors nor we have been
> able to bear? On the contrary, we believe that we are saved
> through the grace of the Lord Jesus in the same way they are.
> (Acts 15:8–11)

Although Peter's response does not include an explicit OT citation, his reference to "our ancestors/fathers" certainly evokes Israel from the patriarchal period to the first century. Peter takes a wide look at the whole history of Israel and concludes that they could not bear the yoke. In other words, they were not able to stand before God as his people through obedience to the law. Instead, they, like the Gentiles, found salvation before God and membership in his people only through grace ultimately revealed in the crucified and risen Jesus. James follows Peter and makes a similar point though he appeals to a specific OT text:

> After they stopped speaking, James responded: "Brothers and sisters, listen to me. Simeon has reported how God first intervened to take from the Gentiles a people for his name. And the words of the prophets agree with this, as it is written: After these things I will return and rebuild David's fallen tent. I will rebuild its ruins and set it up again, so the rest of humanity may seek the Lord—even all the Gentiles who are called by my name—declares the Lord who makes these things known from long ago." (Acts 15:13–18)

James here cites Amos 9:11. He interprets the prophet's reference to a rebuilt and risen tent of David as a reference to the crucified and risen Jesus. Through this risen "tent," God forms a people that includes Gentiles. The people of God are reworked around the person of Jesus, and all of this is in accordance with Scripture.

It is also worth noting that Luke uses the OT for other ecclesiastical concerns including: the church's message (Acts 8:32–35), the church's mission (Acts 13:47), and opposition to the church (Acts 7).

ESCHATOLOGICAL USE OF THE OT

Luke's understanding of the "last things" (eschatology) in Acts is sometimes underappreciated. Although he does devote the most space to how things unfold in the formative years of the church, it is all within an eschatological framework informed by the OT. For example, the backdrop of many speeches in Acts is the return of Jesus and the judgment that follows. Peter's speech at Pentecost is framed within a focus on the end times, which evokes the OT. The opening lines of his speech are a citation from the prophet Joel:

> And it will be in the last days, God says, that I will pour out my Spirit on all people; then your sons and your daughters will prophesy, and your young men will see visions, and your old men will dream dreams. I will even pour out my Spirit on my servants in those days, both men and women and they will prophesy. I will display wonders in the heaven above and signs on the earth below: blood and fire and a cloud of smoke. The sun will be turned to darkness and the moon to blood before the great and glorious day of the Lord comes. Then everyone who calls on the name of the Lord will be saved. (Acts 2:17–21)

The phrase *in the last days* is not present in either the Hebrew or Greek version of Joel. It represents Peter's interpretation of Joel and the events of Pentecost. In short, the end has come; therefore, judgment is just upon the horizon. The pouring out of the Spirit on the apostles indicates that the end has come just as Joel prophesied. Consequently, Peter's listeners must respond as Joel exhorted, "Call on the name of the Lord." In Acts, just as in Joel, only those who cry out to the Lord before the judgment arrives will live beyond it.

Peter's use of Joel is programmatic for the rest of Acts. Luke carries forward both the prospect of coming judgment and Joel's charge to call on the Lord's name before that time arrives (Acts 9:14, 21; 22:16). Calling on Jesus's name is not only a response to the apostolic message in Acts. It is also an eschatological response in which one finds deliverance from the judgment to come.

As you work through Acts, it is critical that you pay attention to the OT's function in the book. The interaction between OT texts and episodes in Acts highlights points that Luke makes about Jesus, salvation, the church, and the future.

Theological Tools

I have already talked around several theological motifs of Acts. It is helpful to discuss a few of them in greater details. Specifically, we will consider Luke's emphasis on the Spirit and salvation history in Acts.

Witness and Work through the Spirit

There is no denying that Luke places great emphasis on the Holy Spirit in the book of Acts. His pneumatology (doctrine of the Holy Spirit) is extensive. This is not entirely surprising given the way he describes the Spirit in his Gospel.[7] In the Gospel of Luke, we find that the Spirit's presence marks the beginning and duration of Jesus's ministry (3:22). Jesus's inaugural sermon at Nazareth highlights the role of the Spirit in his own work, "The Spirit of the Lord is on me" (4:18; Isa 61:1). The Spirit is present and at work as Jesus preaches to the poor, releases captives from sin and Satan, and opens "eyes" (both physically and spiritually). Additionally, Jesus prays in the Spirit (10:21), promises that the Father will give the Spirit to the disciples (11:13), and indicates that the Spirit will teach the disciples what to say in moments of tribulation (12:12).

The presence of the Spirit among the apostles in Acts mirrors the Spirit's presence with Jesus in Luke. The beginning of the apostles' mission, like Jesus's, is marked by the dramatic arrival of the Spirit. At

---

[7] See, e.g., Luke 1:15, 35, 41, 67; 2:25–27; 3:16, 22; 4:1, 14, 18; 10:21; 11:13; 12:10, 12.

Jesus's baptism, the Spirit descends on Jesus like a dove and the Father speaks from heaven (Luke 3:22). At Pentecost, the Spirit descends on the apostles like "flames of fire that separated" (Acts 2:3) and they speak in languages that are not native to them. Just as the Spirit was present in Jesus's ministry, as indicated by various miracles, the Spirit is present in the apostles' ministry also indicated by various miracles.[8] Jesus promises the disciples that the Spirit would teach them what to say in moments of tribulation. We see this unfold at various moments in Acts. For example, when Peter is arrested, brought before religious authorities, and commanded to give an account of how he healed a crippled

" There appeared unto them cloven tongues like as of fire."—*Acts* ii. 3.

The Spirit's arrival at Pentecost in Acts 2 parallels the Spirit's arrival at Jesus's baptism in Luke 3:21-22.

---

[8] See, e.g., Acts 3:1–10; 14:8–10.

man, Luke prefaces Peter's response by noting "Then Peter was filled with the Holy Spirit and said to them . . ." (4:8; cf. 13:9).

So what is the theological significance of this clear overlap between Jesus and the Spirit in Luke and the apostles and the Spirit in Acts? The overlap indicates that Jesus is present through the Spirit in the witness and work of the apostles just as he promised (Acts 1:8). The power needed for the church to complete its God-given mission does not reside in human ability but in the Son of God and the Spirit he pledged. The Spirit empowers those who proclaim his death and resurrection and confirms the truth of that proclamation through miracles that echo those performed by Jesus in the Gospel.

One way to assess Luke's description of the Spirit in Acts is by comparing it to his description of the Spirit in Luke. We should take note of the overlap between the Spirit's presence with Jesus and the apostles.

Salvation History as Salvation to the Ends of the Earth

The songs by Mary and Zechariah in Luke 1 are an early indicator to the reader that the author views the figure of Jesus through the lens of a long and winding history of redemption. Acts expands upon this motif by placing the work that Jesus does in the early church within a salvation-historical framework. Within this framework, Luke does not try to provide an exhaustive explanation of God's ways from Genesis 1 up to the time of the early church. While some interpreters speak about a straight line of salvation history that exists between the "beginning" and "end" of God's ways, Luke does not.[9] What he offers is an explanation of how God completes prior promises in Christ and his church.

---

[9] E.g., Oscar Cullmann, *Christ and Time: The Primitive Christian Conception of Time and History* (London: SCM, 1945), 51.

The prime example is embedded in the book's key verse, "But you will receive power when the Holy Spirit comes on you, and you will be my witnesses in Jerusalem, in all Judea and Samaria, and to the end of the earth" (Acts 1:8). It is the last phrase that echoes God's prior promises in the OT: "to the end of the earth." A similar phrase and usage occurs in various OT passages, particularly Isaiah:

> Turn to me and be saved, all the ends of the earth. For I am God, and there is no other. (Isa 45:22)

> It is not enough for you to be my servant raising up the tribes of Jacob and restoring the protected ones of Israel. I will also make you a light for the nations, to be my salvation to the ends of the earth. (Isa 49:6)[10]

These passages illustrate that Israel's God had always planned and promised to save people from all parts of the world. Isaiah's prophecy is in fact built upon other OT texts that promise this very thing. We see this in God's promise to Abraham that through his descendants "all the peoples on earth" would be blessed (Gen 12:1–3). From Luke's salvation historical perspective, this promise given to Abraham and echoed in Isaiah is being realized through Jesus's work in the early church. The conclusion of Peter's speech in Acts 3:11–26 captures this perspective perfectly:

> All the prophets who have spoken, from Samuel and those after him, have also foretold these days. You are the sons of the prophets and of the covenant that God made with your ancestors, saying to Abraham, And all the families of the earth will be blessed through your offspring. God raised up his servant and sent him first to you to bless you by turning each of you from your evil ways. (vv. 24–26)

---

[10] See also Isa 48:20; 52:10.

Peter makes it clear that God fulfills his promise to Abraham through the resurrected Jesus. Consequently, all of salvation history finds its ultimate aim and purpose in the person of Jesus.

Interpreters should stay alert for the way Luke explains and develops his view of salvation history. The interpretive question here is, in Acts, how does Luke relate the work of Jesus in the early church to God's prior promise that he would go to the end of the earth to save people?

Responding to Acts

We saw in the previous chapter that Luke wants readers of his Gospel to have certainty concerning the things they heard about Jesus (Lk 1:4). The intended response of certainty carries over into Acts as well. Luke wants the reader to respond in faith at least three different ways.

First, Luke wants the reader to believe that Jesus continues his work through the Spirit in the church despite any and all obstacles. In fact, Luke wants the reader to understand that God actually uses the obstacles to the church's mission to propel that very mission.

Second, based on this faith, Luke urges the reader to "join the mission." He recounts episode after episode wherein Peter, Stephen, Paul, and others are on mission bear witness to the crucified and risen Jesus with all of its implications. Some of the figures, such as Paul, are dramatically drawn into this mission (Acts 9:1–22). Through these accounts, Luke wishes to draw the reader into the mission as well.

Third, Luke confronts the reader with the certainty of Jesus' return and the final judgment that will ensue. Throughout the numerous and diverse speeches of Acts, one common trait is the certainty of Jesus' return that will usher in final judgment. In fact, the church's mission begins with angelic figures assuring the stunned apostles that Jesus would return in the same way that they witnessed him departing (Acts

1:9–11). Luke then tethers this certainty of Jesus' return to the certainty of the judgment that he would enact.[11]

Putting the Tools to Use in Acts

It is now time to put this information to use. While using the preceding overview, consider the following questions to analyze Acts 22:1–30.

Historical Tools

1. How does this passage inform Luke's original and overarching purpose in Acts?
2. How is this passage related to the overarching history in Acts?

Literary Tools

1. How does Acts 22:1–30 fit within the larger structure of the book?
2. What are the type(s), art, and parts of rhetoric in Paul's speech?
3. What kind of OT uses are present in the passage? Read the wider contexts of those OT passages and consider how those wider contexts influence your reading of the Acts passage. (Hint: see Acts 22:6; read Psalm 16, Isaiah 26.)

Theological Tools

1. How is the Spirit involved in this episode? How does that involvement compare to the Spirit's involvement elsewhere in Acts?

---

[11] See e.g., Acts 10:42; 17:31.

2. How are Paul's actions related to salvation history as Luke understands it in Acts?

Response

In what specific way does this episode fit with the responses that Luke aimed to evoke from his readers?

Paul's Biography in Acts and His Letters

We now shift our attention to one of the key figures in Acts and the early church in general. Paul, or Saul, of Tarsus became one of the most important figures in the history of early Christianity. As a preacher,

Paul's impact on Christian history is incalculable. His writings have led to the conversions of well-known figures such as Augustine, Martin Luther, and John Wesley.

teacher, missionary, and letter writer in the first century, it is almost impossible to overstate Paul's importance. His missionary efforts resulted in the spread of the gospel and establishment of churches throughout the ancient Mediterranean world. Even more, his letters have served as one of the main pillars of theological reflection in Christianity over the past 2,000 years. Leading lights such as Augustine, Martin Luther, John Wesley, and countless others attribute their conversions and much of their theological formation to the study of Paul.

What follows is a brief biographical sketch of Paul the apostle. In the next chapter, we will discuss the interpretation of Paul's Letters. In preparation for that discussion, we need to give special attention to Paul's life, because his background and experiences directly impacted what he wrote in his letters. The interpreter needs a basic sense of Paul the man to rightly understand Paul the letter writer. This biographical sketch includes a brief look at Paul's life and theology.

Paul's Life

The flash point of Paul's life occurs on the road to Damascus. Luke provides three accounts of this event in Acts (9:1–18; 22:3–21; 26:9–20). Armed with authorization from the Sanhedrin in Jerusalem to arrest Christians, Paul charges toward Damascus "breathing threats and murder against the disciples of the Lord" (9:1). His journey is interrupted by a sudden appearance of Jesus on the road. Luke notes:

> As he traveled and was nearing Damascus, a light from heaven suddenly flashed around him. Falling to the ground, he heard a voice saying to him, "Saul, Saul, why are you persecuting me?"
>
> "Who are you, Lord?" Saul said.
>
> "I am Jesus, the one you are persecuting," he replied. "But get up and go into the city, and you will be told what you must do." (9:3–6)

Luke further explains that Paul subsequently suffered three days of blindness (9:9). That blindness is an ironic commentary on Paul's life before and after Jesus revealed himself to him on the road to Damascus. It is ironic in the sense that prior to the Damascus road encounter Paul was zealously confident that he knew, or "saw," the God of Israel, confident to the point of carrying out violence against those who followed Christ. Yet it is only when he is blinded by the appearance of Christ that he sees who God really is. A radical shift takes place in this moment. To understand the significance of this shift, we need to sketch a picture of Paul "before" and "after" the revelation of Jesus on the way to Damascus.

Paul before the Damascus Road Revelation

Only a handful of references scattered throughout Acts and his letters provide a window into Paul's pre-Damascus encounter with Jesus. We have only a few specific details about his upbringing and adult life, including

1. Born in Tarsus
2. Circumcised on the eighth day in accordance with Mosaic law
3. Genealogical roots in the tribe of Benjamin
4. Educated in the law and Jewish ancestral tradition in Jerusalem by Gamaliel
5. An up-and-coming leader in the Pharisaic sect
6. An ardent opponent of the early Christian movement

These details are not entirely insignificant for understanding some of the basic contours of Paul's pre-Damascus life. However, the best insight on this period comes from the apostle's own description of it.

In both Acts and his letters, Paul makes some brief comments about his pre-Damascus life from which we can draw a few inferences. First, Paul wanted to excel in his life as a Pharisaic Jew far beyond those around him. He tells the Galatians, "I advanced in Judaism beyond many contemporaries among my people, because I was extremely zealous for the traditions of my ancestors" (Gal 1:14). Paul may have measured his advancement in Judaism by how much he outshined other Pharisaic Jews. Pharisees were known for living out their lives before God through strict adherence to the Mosaic and Oral law (Acts 23:6; 26:5; Phil 3:5), and Paul, at least from his own perspective, did it better than any of his peers.

Second, pre-Damascus Paul unashamedly and zealously persecuted Christians. However, there is no indication in Acts or the Pauline Letters that he felt badly about his actions during the time in which he carried them out. It seems that pre-Damascus Paul saw his actions against Christians as something in keeping with a person zealously dedicated to God. As he recounts to the Philippians, "Regarding zeal, persecuting the church; regarding the righteousness that is in the law, blameless" (Phil 3:6). This does not sound like someone having second thoughts about spearheading the arrest and oppression of Christians. It is possible that the "zealous" pre-Damascus Paul saw himself through the lens of famous zealots from Israel's past, such as Phinehas, who slew a man who defiled the Israelite camp with a Midianite woman (Num 25:6–8), or Judas Maccabeus, who led an army of Jewish rebels against the tyranny of Antiochus Epiphanes during the intertestamental period. Paul also resorted to violence in his effort to defend Israel's God and people from the danger of Christ's disciples.

This brings us to a third inference regarding Paul's campaign, seeing Christians as a danger to Jews. Why did Paul violently and zealously persecute Christians? Although Paul never provides a list of reasons, his pre-Damascus hatred probably stemmed from the following:

1. To pre-Damascus Paul, the notion of a crucified Jesus probably sounded more like a man cursed by God than the Jewish Messiah (see Deut 21:23; Gal 3:13).

2. Pre-Damascus Paul probably found the Christian veneration and worship of Jesus as a blasphemous violation of the Mosaic law (see Deut 6:4; 1 Cor 8:4).

3. He was probably troubled by the way that Christians reworked salvation so that faith in Jesus became the basis of eternal life rather than one's covenant status and possession of the Mosaic law.

4. Pre-Damascus Paul may have been concerned that Christians posed a threat to the tolerance that the Roman Empire showed toward Jews. If Rome interpreted the early Christian confession "Jesus is Lord" as a slight toward "Lord Caesar," it could potentially result in a loss of privileges and freedoms granted to those who followed the God of Israel.

Of course, when Jesus revealed himself to Paul, these reasons became invalid for Paul. The experience radically transformed his thoughts about God, salvation, the people of God, and other matters. This transformation is summarized in the way Paul initially responds to Jesus's voice on the road to Damascus, "Who are you, Lord?" (Acts 9:5).

Paul after the Damascus Road Revelation

After Paul encounters Jesus, the identity of the Lord ("Who are you, Lord?") and everything related to him is reconfigured. Paul's perspective on his past life and the trajectory of the life ahead of him takes a drastic turn. In retrospect, Paul comes to see his persecution of the church as a shameful and foolish act rather than zealous obedience to God. It is a past act that forever shapes how he sees his role as an apostle:

> For I am the least of the apostles, not worthy to be called an apostle, because I persecuted the church of God. But by the grace of God I am what I am, and his grace toward me was not in vain. On the contrary, I worked harder than any of them, yet not I, but the grace of God that was with me. (1 Cor 15:9–10)

> I give thanks to Christ Jesus our Lord who has strengthened me, because he considered me faithful, appointing me to the ministry—even though I was formerly a blasphemer, a persecutor, and an arrogant man. But I received mercy because I acted out of ignorance in unbelief, and the grace of our Lord overflowed, along with the faith and love that are in Christ Jesus. (1 Tim 1:12–14)

These statements indicate that Paul never forgot how he persecuted Jesus's church. Although he did not move about the Mediterranean in sackcloth and ashes chanting "woe is me," Paul never forgot what he did to other believers. That is because his persecution of the church clearly indicated to Paul that God called him to be an apostle entirely out of grace and mercy. God called Paul to salvation and apostleship based on divine grace, given the pre-Damascus Paul's persecution of the church, which qualified as persecution of Christ himself (Acts 9:3). Moreover, Paul saw his conversion and calling as an example for others. As he tells Timothy, "But I received mercy for this reason, so that in me, the worst of them, Jesus Christ might demonstrate his extraordinary patience as an example to those who would believe in him for eternal life" (1 Tim 1:16). In this way, Paul's biography is an embodiment of the gospel he preached.

After Damascus, the preaching of the gospel became the impetus for all of Paul's actions and the defining characteristic of his identity. As he tells the Corinthians, "I do all this because of the gospel, so that I may share in the blessings" (1 Cor 9:23). Paul summarizes the crux of his gospel message as "Christ died for our sins according to the Scriptures, that he was buried, that he was raised on the third day according to the Scriptures" (1 Cor 15:3–4). His sermons in Acts and thirteen letters elaborate on this gospel and spell out the implications of it for the church and for the world. Nevertheless, at its heart, Paul's gospel consistently remained a message of salvation from sin, death,

Satan, and condemnation, salvation through Jesus's death and resurrection. This is the message that defined his identity as an apostle, preacher, teacher, and missionary. For more reflection on apostleship and the uniqueness of Paul's apostleship, see link in Wordsearch.

Paul never considered his apostolic ministry as something that elevated him above the rest of the church, nor did he see himself or his message as something that other people controlled. He simply referred to himself as the Lord's "servant": "Paul, a servant of Christ Jesus, called as an apostle and set apart for the gospel of God" (Rom 1:1).[12] Paul sees himself as someone whom God called to serve through preaching the gospel to Gentiles in the same way that prophets from Israel's past saw themselves as heralds of a God-given message. For example, he compares himself to Jeremiah:

> I chose you before I formed you in the womb; I set you apart before you were born. I appointed you a prophet to the nations. (Jer 1:5)

> But when God, who set me apart from my mother's womb and called me through his grace, was pleased to reveal his Son in me, in order that I might preach him among the nations, I did not immediately consult with flesh and blood. (Gal 1:15–16, Crisler translation)

From Paul's perspective, only God long ago (even before birth) had decided to make him an apostle of the gospel. Neither his gospel nor apostleship came from human beings (Gal 1:1, 11–12). Consequently, no human being could undercut his apostleship or change the truth of the message that God had entrusted to him. Paul's confidence in the divine origin of his apostleship and gospel are on full display in his public confrontation with the apostle Peter which he recounts to the Galatians:

---

[12] See Gal 1:10; Titus 1:1.

But when Cephas [Peter] came to Antioch, I opposed him to his face, because he stood condemned. For he regularly ate with the Gentiles before certain men came from James. However, when they came, he withdrew and separated himself, because he feared those from the circumcision party. Then the rest of the Jews joined his hypocrisy, so that even Barnabas was led astray by their hypocrisy. But when I saw that they were deviating from the truth of the gospel, I told Cephas in front of everyone, "If you, who are a Jew, live like a Gentile and not like a Jew, how can you compel the Gentiles to live like Jews?" (Gal 2:11–14)

This public spat did not lead to permanent discord between the two apostles, but it clearly demonstrates that Paul located the authority of his position and message in Christ alone. He did not even need the approval of someone as prominent as Peter. In reading accounts such as these, one gets the sense that Paul had a boldness as a servant of Christ. Yet that boldness could often be hidden in weakness.

In fact, this is precisely how Paul describes his life as an apostle. He suffers, but it is in his weakness that he is strong: "I take pleasure in weaknesses, insults, hardships, persecutions, and in difficulties, for the sake of Christ. For when I am weak, then I am strong" (2 Cor 12:10). Paul's sufferings included the following:

1. Physical illness (Gal 4:13–14)
2. Opposition by Jewish religious leaders (Acts 17:4–10; 21:27–28; 2 Cor 11:24)
3. Opposition by various Mediterranean community leaders (Acts 16:16–40)
4. Opposition by false teachers (2 Cor 11:5–6; Gal 5:7–12; 6:11–12; Phil 3:2–3)
5. Opposition by Satan (2 Cor 12:7; 1 Thess 2:18)

6. Dangers and depravation in his missional travels (2 Cor 11:25–28)

7. A constant concern for the well-being of various churches (2 Cor 11:28)

8. Ongoing struggles with sin (Rom 7:7–25)

9. Concern for his Jewish kinsmen who rejected Jesus (Rom 9:1–5; 10:1–2)

10. Financial needs for his mission and for others (Rom 15:24; 1 Cor 16:1–3)

These kinds of sufferings defined Paul's life as an apostle. In many ways, Paul's physical wounds are indicative of his entire experience serving Christ, "From now on, let no one cause me trouble, for I bear on my body the marks of Jesus" (Gal 6:17).

These "marks," whether they be physical, mental, or spiritual, are indicators of the hurt and hope that God mingled together in Paul and in those who heard his message. Hoping in and proclaiming the gospel hurt Paul. It was a kind of death, and it exemplified what Paul meant when he told the Romans, "and if [we are] children, also heirs—heirs of God and coheirs with Christ—if indeed we suffer with him so that we may also be glorified with him"

God hid the power that he gave to the Apostle Paul in his various sufferings like a treasure hidden in an earthen vessel (2 Cor 4:7).

(Rom 8:17). Paul embodied what it meant to die with Christ and still hope that one might be raised with Christ (1 Cor 9:23; Phil 3:7–11).

Of course, not everyone understood Paul's suffering or gospel. Some saw Paul's pain as an indication that God might be displeased with him (2 Cor 10:10–12). Some would disfigure Paul's gospel (Gal 1:6–10) or misrepresent it (Rom 3:8). Others would draw false conclusions about it (Gal 2:17). A persistent misunderstanding involved the relationship between the grace of the gospel and how believers should deal with sin. Paul recognized that some drew the conclusion (wrongly) that grace in Christ meant believers could go on living in sin. In response to such erroneous conclusions, he asks the Romans, "What should we say then? Should we continue in sin so that grace may multiply? Absolutely not! How can we who died to sin still live in it?" (Rom 6:1–2). Clearly, misrepresentation and misunderstanding also marked Paul's life as an apostle.

The Ultimate Goal and End of Paul's Life

We have barely scratched the surface here in terms of Paul's biography. There is more that could be said about Paul's life, especially if we had space to consider the cultural milieu in which he lived and breathed.[13] Paul he did not live in a vacuum. Just as we are influenced by the cultures we live in, so was Paul. Nevertheless, I think it is appropriate to end this biographical sketch by highlighting what Paul saw as the goal of his work and how that work ended. This apostolic goal and the end of his life dovetail with each other.

Resurrection from the dead and new creation are what Paul saw as the goal of his apostolic ministry. It is in fact what creation, the children of God, and even the Holy Spirit "groaned" for (Rom 8:19–27).

Although Paul recognized that only God could ultimately accomplish such a goal, he sensed he had a key part to play in all of this. For his part, Paul aimed to reach as many Gentiles as he could with the

---

[13] See, e.g., Wayne Meeks, *The First Urban Christian: The Social World of the Apostle Paul*, 2nd ed. (New Haven, CT: Yale University Press, 2003).

gospel because of the impact it would have on unbelieving Jews. He explains to the Romans, "Now I am speaking to you Gentiles. Insofar as I am an apostle to the Gentiles, I magnify my ministry, if I might somehow make my own people jealous and save some of them. For if their rejection brings reconciliation to the world, what will their acceptance mean but life from the dead?" (Rom 11:13–15). Paul had other motivations in reaching Gentiles with the gospel, namely making Jews jealous by bringing Gentiles into the family of God so that Jews would begin to believe in Jesus, which would ultimately involve the return of Jesus who would raise the dead.

Although Paul suffered until the end of his life, his faith in the gospel did not waiver.

Although Paul did not witness the realization of this goal in his lifetime, his life does not end in bitterness and disappointment. Instead, although facing execution during his second Roman imprisonment, he tells Timothy, "I have fought the good fight, I have finished the race, I have kept the faith. There is reserved for me the crown of righteousness, which the Lord, the righteous Judge, will give me on that day, and not only to me, but to all those who have loved his appearing" (2 Tim 4:7–8). Notice the lasting phrase "to all who have loved his appearing." Even in his last days, Paul did not give up on the hope that Christ will return, raise the dead, and make all things new. He remained confident that God would remember the work he did as an apostle and remember that he promised the second "appearance" of Jesus on the earth. Paul died as he lived after the Damascus revelation, by faith. Paul did not change "religions" after he encountered the risen Jesus. Instead, he came to believe that in the crucified and risen Jesus all the promises to Israel and the world were yes (2 Cor 1:20). In other words, he found the true meaning and completion of what it meant to be a Jew (Rom 2:25–29). Would God remember what Paul had done as an apostle? Yes. Would God finish what he started in all the churches Paul planted (Phil 1:6)? Yes. Would God make good on the ultimate hope of the gospel, namely resurrection from the dead (Rom 8:24)? Yes. Paul died believing that God's answer to everything he had ever promised, whether Paul saw it or not, was yes in Christ.

Response to Paul's Biography

As we have seen, Paul's biography is scattered across Acts and his letters. We cannot connect all the dots of his life, and there are some things we simply do not know about him. What we do know is that Paul saw his life as an example for others. As he told the Corinthians, "Imitate me, as I also imitate Christ" (1 Cor 11:1). In other words, Paul's biography demands a response from those who hear it. Here are a few questions to consider:

1. How does the grace that God showed Paul apply to me and you today?
2. What motivated Paul in his mission as an apostle, and what might that same motivation look like in my life?
3. What was hidden in Paul's suffering, and what might be hidden in my own suffering as a believer?
4. As we look to the next chapter and Paul's Letters, we need to take his biography with us. Paul's experiences influenced many of the things he wrote in his letters. He did not separate what he lived from what he wrote.

10

Tools for Interpreting Paul's Letters

I once taught a course on Paul's life and Letters in which a student admitted to me on the first day that he did not really like the Pauline Epistles. He respected them as part of the biblical canon, but they did not exactly get his spiritual and theological blood pumping. I was intent on changing his mind over the course of the semester. As the weeks went by, I could see why the student had a distaste for these books of the Bible. He simply did not know how to approach them. He did not know how to follow Paul's argument or what he should be looking for when he did manage to follow along. He certainly did not know how to respond to the Letters beyond finding a few key verses that could be proof texted for various purposes.

Some of you may feel the same way. You might not dislike Paul's Letters, but you keep them at arm's length because they can be hard to understand. Remember that even the apostle Peter admitted Paul's

*Just as Paul asked for a fair hearing before philosophers in Athens,
he asks for a fair hearing from those today who read his letters.*

Letters have "some things in them that are hard to understand" (2 Pet 3:16). Of course, I am not suggesting that as interpreters we are doomed to exegetical frustration, never knowing if we are getting Paul right or not. What will help is having the right tools and using them the right way.

There is obviously a lot of ground to cover here. Paul pens thirteen letters; each of them has unique historical, literary, theological, and responsive features that help shape our interpretive tools.

Understanding the Historical Tools
for Paul's Letters

There are several historical features to consider in Paul's Letters, but none of them is as important as the "situational" nature of each document. The historical situation of Paul and his recipients stands behind each letter. The events unfolding in the life of Paul and those to whom he writes have the largest impact on the contents of the Letters themselves. A lot of the attention here is devoted to identifying these situations and how they inform the purpose of each letter.

History behind the Letters

The historical questions here are simple, but they greatly influence our understanding of the Letters. Who wrote the Letters? When were they written? To whom were they written? Why were they written?

Author

All thirteen letters explicitly identify Paul as the author.[1] That has not prevented many scholars from questioning the Pauline authorship of at least some letters, particularly Ephesians, Colossians, 2 Thessalonians, and the Pastoral Epistles (1 & 2 Timothy, Titus). Denials of Pauline authorship most often stem from the same set of issues: (1) absence of key theological motifs, (2) change in vocabulary and syntax, and (3) advanced ecclesiology in the Pastoral Epistles.[2] In short, some interpreters feel that the language and theology of some letters attributed to Paul are so different from others that both groups of letters could not have possibly been written by the same person. So how do these interpreters explain that all thirteen letters explicitly identify Paul as the author? One of the main responses involves so-called pseudonymous authorship. Those who deny Pauline authorship of letters such as the Pastoral Epistles argue that in the first century pseudonymous

---

[1] See, e.g., Rom 1:1; 1 Cor 1:1; 2 Cor 1:1; Gal 1:1; Eph 1:1.

[2] See, e.g., 1 Tim 3:1–13.

authorship was quite acceptable in literary works.[3] Therefore, even early Christian communities would accept a letter bearing Paul's name even though they were aware that someone other than Paul wrote it. The problem with this argument is twofold. First, acceptance of pseudonymous authorship in early Christian communities has not been established with the amount of historical certainty that some scholars assert. Second, it seems unlikely that early Christians would accept someone creating the kinds of autobiographical counts of Paul's life that we find in the Pastoral Epistles (2 Tim 4:6–20).

Overall, the differences between so-called authentic letters of Paul and pseudonymous ones are overstated. While Paul's Letters use a variety of words, constructions, and theological motifs, those variations are *not* best explained by appealing to non-Pauline authorship. A better explanation for the differences includes (1) the use of different amanuenses (secretaries who performed the physical act of writing) for different letters, (2) different needs in different churches called for different written responses, and (3) Paul's ability to write in different styles with differing points of emphases. Finally, it should also be noted that for several centuries no one questioned the Pauline authorship of these thirteen letters. Only with the dawn of the Enlightenment and the general skepticism toward the Bible that ensued do we find many interpreters questioning Pauline authorship. It seems unlikely to me that interpreters from the eighteenth–twenty-first centuries could better establish the authorship of Paul's Letters than those in the early patristic era (second–third centuries AD) who attributed the authorship of all these documents to the apostle.

---

[3] For a helpful discussion on the traditional authorship vs. pseudonymous authorship of the Pastoral Epistles, see Terry L. Wilder, "Pseudonymity, the New Testament, and the Pastoral Epistles," in *Entrusted with the Gospel: Paul's Theology of the Pastoral Epistles*, ed. Andreas J. Köstenberger and Terry L. Wilder (Nashville: B&H Academic, 2010), 28–51.

So in what ways does identifying Paul as the author of these thirteen letters impact our interpretation of them? First, it should prompt the interpreter to keep Paul's biography close at hand when reading his letters. The previous chapter provided a biographical sketch of Paul both before and after Jesus revealed himself on the road to Damascus. Paul often alludes to or explicitly discusses those experiences in his letters. Second, the connection between the biography and the Letters is analogous to a song writer and a song. Although a song may not say anything directly about the songwriter, the songwriter's own life experiences influence his or her depiction of life in the song. Songwriters do not compose songs in a vacuum. Rather, they write from what they know. Paul does something similar in his letters. He responds to crises

A songwriter's lyrics are often influenced by his or her own experience. Similarly, Paul's experiences influence much of what he writes in his letters.

in the lives of the recipients whom he addresses from what he knows and has experienced in Christ.

Date

It is important to connect the dots between the dates that Paul penned his letters and the dates of key events in his life. After all, what is happening in his life at the time that he writes to a church or person impacts what he says in the letter itself. For example, Philippians is one of the so-called Prison Epistles. Paul writes to the Philippians during his first Roman imprisonment (Phil 1:12–18). Paul's imprisonment shapes both the content and tone of the letter.

Here I offer a basic chronology that helps situate the dates of Paul's Letters within the arc of his life. I am largely following the chronology suggested by Michael Bird.[4] These dates are largely based on material from the book of Acts and Paul's Letters.

Life of Paul

Event	Production of Letter	Date
Paul's birth		5 BC to AD 10
Death of Jesus		AD 29–30
Paul persecutes Christians		AD 30–33
Damascus Road revelation		AD 33
Ministry in Arabia/Damascus		AD 34–37
First Jerusalem visit		AD 37

---

[4] Michael Bird, *Introducing Paul: The Man, His Mission and His Message* (Downers Grove, IL: InterVarsity, 2008), 31–32. It should be noted that Pauline interpreters continue to debate the precise chronology of the apostle's life.

Ministry in Syria & Cilicia		AD 37–46
Ministry in Antioch		AD 47
Second Jerusalem visit		AD 48
First missionary journey		AD 48
Confronts Peter at Antioch		AD 48
	Writes Galatians	AD 48–49
Meets with Apostolic Council		AD 49–50
Second missionary journey		AD 50–52
Travels in Macedonia/Greece		AD 51–52
	Writes 1 & 2 Thessalonians	AD 52–53
Travels to Antioch		AD 52
Third missionary journey		AD 53–57
Ministry at Ephesus		AD 53–55
	Writes 1 & 2 Corinthians	AD 55
Ministry at Philippi		AD 55
Ministry at Corinth		AD 55–56
	Writes Romans	AD 55–56
Final trip to Jerusalem		AD 57
Imprisoned at Caesarea Maritima		AD 57–59
Travels to Rome to appear before Caesar		AD 59–60
House arrest in Rome		AD 60–62
	Writes Ephesians, Colossians, Philippians, Philemon	AD 60–62
More missionary travels in Asia Minor		AD 62–64
Nero's pogrom against Christians		AD 65–68
	Writes Pastoral Epistles	AD 67–68
Beheaded		AD 67–68

Recipients (First Auditors) of Paul's Letters

Paul's Letters are addressed to both churches and individuals. However, even the letters addressed to Timothy, Titus, and Philemon are intended for a wider readership. Interpreters need to step into the first-century situations of the various recipients to understand both what Paul writes to them and how they would receive what he writes. Therefore, you should dig into primary and secondary resources that help you understand ancient life in the locations to which Paul writes, including Rome, Corinth, Ephesus, Philippi, Crete, Thessalonica, and Galatia.

Purpose (Situation)

The purpose of a Pauline letter is like the axis around which every individual piece of it rotates. When one gets into the details of Paul's argumentation, it is easy to get confused or lose sight of what he is trying to accomplish. Knowing the purpose of the letter mitigates that confusion. If we know the overarching purpose for which Paul writes, we know that each paragraph he pens is somehow linked to that purpose.

Of course, Paul does not always explicitly state why he is writing. Sometimes we must cobble together clues to reconstruct the original historical purpose of the letter. These clues include (1) What does Paul keep emphasizing? (2) Does Paul mention any opponents or false teachers; if so, how does he describe them? (3) What is the focus of the letter's introduction? (4) What is the focus of the letter's conclusion?

Although the historical situations behind each letter are different, there is one commonality in all of them. The recipients, and their author, are in a situation that involves suffering of some kind. Therefore, one question an interpreter should ask when reading these letters is, how are Paul and/or his recipients suffering at this moment?

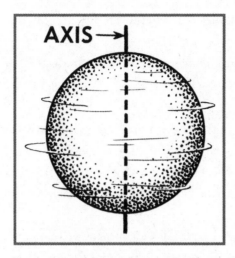

Imagine that the vertical line is the purpose of a Pauline letter.
Everything else in the letter revolves around that line.

Romans (ca. AD 55–59). Interpreters have often struggled to identify the exact situation that prompted Paul to write to the Christians in
Rome. On the surface, it appears to be the least situational of his letters.
That is why many have often treated it more like a theological treatise
than a situational letter. However, it does in fact contain a historical
situation that Paul addresses and a unifying purpose. Paul's overarching purpose is to address concerns about the relationship between the
way God has revealed his righteousness in the gospel and the way he
is revealing his wrath in the world (Rom 1:16–18). The Romans have
ongoing struggles with sin and the law (7:7–25), affliction by inimical
forces (8:18–39), worries about Israel's unbelief in the Messiah (chaps.
9–11), conflict between the "strong" and "weak" in faith (14:1–15:6),
and false teachers (16:17–20). The Romans might interpret these struggles as an indication that they are "under God's wrath" like the rest of
the world. Paul writes to them and wants to make his way to Rome to
give them a "spiritual gift" (1:11), namely to strengthen one another in
the belief that in Christ they are no longer under divine condemnation

(8:1). When reading the lengthy argumentation of Romans, interpreters should keep asking one question: how is the particular unit of
thought addressing concerns about the wrath of God? *See Wordsearch
video for further discussion about the overarching purpose of Romans.*

1 Corinthians (ca. AD 53–54). Luke tells us that Paul first preached
the gospel in Corinth during his second missionary journey (AD
50–52; see Acts 18). He spent a year and a half there. After his departure, it appears that both Peter and Apollos later ministered in Corinth
(1 Cor 1:10–17).

The purposes behind 1 Corinthians are not difficult to identify.
First Corinthians 1:10–6:20 addresses multiple problems involving the
Christians at Corinth that associates of Chloe (1:11; 16:17) reported to
Paul. These include

1. Factions/divisions among the Corinthians (1:10–17; 3:1–23)
2. Criticism of Paul's ministry by some of the Corinthians (chap. 4)
3. Unchecked sexual immorality (chap. 5)
4. Lawsuits by Corinthian Christians against one another (chap.
    6)

Paul also responds to questions asked him by the Corinthians ("in
response to the matters you wrote about," 7:1).[5] These problems include

1. Uncertainty and questions about marriage (chap. 7)
2. Eating in idols' temples and eating idol foods (chap. 8)

---

[5] There are indications in 1 & 2 Corinthians that both Paul and the
Corinthians penned letters that are no longer extant. In 1 Cor 5:9, Paul mentions a previous letter that he wrote to the Corinthians. In 1 Cor 7:1, Paul
refers to a letter that the Corinthians wrote to him. Additionally, in 2 Cor 2:4,
Paul mentions another letter that he wrote to the Corinthians often referred
to as the "tearful letter" in which he expresses his love for them but also
makes clear how they must live as the body of Christ. See Carson and Moo,
Introduction to the New Testament, 420–24. (see chap. 9, n. 2).

3. Criticism of Paul's apostleship (chap. 9)
4. Temptation, idolatry, and eating idol foods (chap. 10)
5. Head coverings and conduct of women in worship service (11:1–17)
6. Inappropriate conduct at the Lord's Supper (11:18–34)
7. Questions about spiritual gifts and conduct in worship service (chaps. 12–14)
8. Denials of resurrection from the dead (chap. 15)

Obviously, Paul addresses several issues that had been reported to him by associates of Chloe and issues directed toward Paul by the Corinthians themselves. Nevertheless, the one purpose that ties these subsidiary purposes together is that many of the Corinthians are not conducting themselves as those who are "being saved" through faith in the word of the cross (1:18). They are proudly and boastfully (1:31; 5:2) engaged in factions, sexual immorality, infatuation with "showy" spiritual gifts, and an overall lack of love for one another. Paul writes to remind and further explain to the Corinthians how through the crucified and risen Christ God has set them apart as the body of Christ. That "body" must be wise and sanctified in the way that they live and love one another. Therefore, Paul must show them once again how Christ provides all such needs, "It is from him that you are in Christ Jesus, who became wisdom from God for us—our righteousness, sanctification, and redemption" (1:30).

2 Corinthians (ca. AD 54–55). Obviously the historical situation in 2 Corinthians is closely tied to the events of 1 Corinthians.[6] The specific events that transpired between the writing of the first and second letters include the following:

---

[6] I am helped here by Carson and Moo, 420–24.

1. After Paul wrote 1 Corinthians, Timothy visits Corinth and reports to Paul that the situation there has not improved entirely. Some in Corinth still resist Paul fiercely.

2. Then so-called "super-apostles" (11:5) enter the congregation at Corinth who push a "Jewish/Judaizing" form of Christian faith and relished power.

3. Paul makes a "painful visit" (2:1) to Corinth in which the opponents insult Paul and threaten the gospel that he preaches (2:5–8, 10; 7:2).

4. Paul leaves Corinth after this "painful visit," and he sends (through Titus) the so-called "tearful letter" (2:4) urging the Corinthians to live in the truth of the gospel and oppose the leader of the opponents (2:3–9; 7:8–12).

5. Some kind of danger forces Paul to leave Ephesus (1:8–10). In Macedonia, Titus reports to Paul that the Corinthians have responded well to his "tearful letter" (chaps. 6–7).

6. Paul then writes 2 Corinthians, thankful that the Corinthians have responded positively (chaps. 1–9). During the course of writing 2 Corinthians, Paul most likely receives news that trouble is once again brewing in Corinth. Therefore, 2 Corinthians also contains stern warnings (see chaps. 10–13).

Given all of these events and the contents of the letter itself, Paul's overarching purpose for writing 2 Corinthians is to defend his apostleship, defend and further explain his understanding of the gospel against opponents ("super-apostles"), encourage the Corinthians in the midst of their own suffering (1:3–7), and exhort them to participate in the collection for poor Christians in Jerusalem.

Galatians (ca. AD 48–49). The historical purpose behind Paul's letter to the churches in Galatia stems from their lives, as experienced in the "present evil age" from which Christ died to free them (Gal 1:4) and the enslaving activity of false teachers who preach a "different" or counterfeit gospel (1:6–7).[7] It is difficult to pinpoint the precise contents of this false gospel, but clues in the letter indicate that it involved the following claims:

1. A right standing before God (justification) requires faith in the gospel and a law-observant lifestyle.

2. Inclusion in the Abrahamic people of God, and all of the blessings that come with that inclusion, requires faith in Jesus Christ *plus* a Jewish way of life marked by circumcision, dietary regulations, and the like (3:26–29; 5:2–6; 6:11–13).

3. Faith in Christ alone is not sufficient for the ongoing struggle with sin. Gentile believers also need to live like Jews through observance of the Mosaic law and various regulations.

Paul responds to these kinds of claims by reiterating the truth of the gospel. Justification is on the basis of faith in the promise of Jesus's death and resurrection rather than works of the law (Gal 2:15–21). Just as Abraham was justified by faith in the gospel apart from works (3:6–9), Gentile believers are as well. Therefore, they share in the blessings promised to Abraham by faith not a law-observant lifestyle. The "freedom" from divine wrath against the present evil age (1:4) and from sin that the opponents promise through their false gospel is actually a

---

[7] Among often-discussed historical issues related to Galatians, the debate about "North or South Galatia" stands toward the top of the list. North Galatia refers to geographical Galatia founded by the Gauls and visited by Paul during his second and third missionary journeys. South Galatia refers to the Roman province of Galatia and the church that Paul help start during his first missionary journey. Over the years of interpreting Galatians, I have not found this issue pivotal to understanding the letter's contents. See helpful summary of evidence for both theories in H. Wayne House, *Chronological and Background Charts of the New Testament*, 2nd ed. (Grand Rapids: Zondervan, 2009), 136–39.

forfeiture of the Galatians' freedom in Christ and entry into a divine curse (3:10–14) from which Christ died to liberate them.

Ephesians (ca. AD 60). The historical situation that stands behind this letter is not as obvious as many of the others in the Pauline corpus. Paul is offering some broader admonitions here for the church in Ephesus and the worldwide church. Specifically, he wants the Christians in Ephesus and elsewhere to gain a better grasp on what God has really given them in Christ. His prayer for the Ephesians is—

> I never stop giving thanks for you as I remember you in my prayers. I pray that the God of our Lord Jesus Christ, the glorious Father, would give you the Spirit of wisdom and revelation in the knowledge of him. I pray that the eyes of your heart may be enlightened so that you may know what is the hope of his calling, what is the wealth of his glorious inheritance in the saints, and what is the immeasurable greatness of his power toward us who believe, according to the mighty working of his strength. (1:16–19)

This hope and "wealth" finds its basis, as always with Paul, in what God predestined (1:3–14) through the crucified and risen Jesus and what he accomplishes for the believer. Armed with this better understanding, the Ephesians are urged to live wisely (5:15), in a way that reflects the worth of the gospel they believe (4:1), and be alert to the invisible and wicked forces that they face (6:10–20).

In addition to these broader concerns for the church in general, there are some indications of a more specific need in Ephesus involving the relationship between Jewish and Gentile Christians. We see this especially in chapter 2, where Paul explains that Jesus's crucifixion resulted in the destruction of the "dividing wall" that separates Jew from Gentile.

This is the theater in ancient Ephesus, a city that presented many challenges for Paul and the believers who called it home.

Philippians (ca. AD 59). Paul writes this letter from prison (Phil 1:12–18).[8] The Philippians' situation is not as dire as imprisonment, but Paul does express concerns about their unity (2:1–3, 14–16) and the presence of false teachers whom he refers to as "dogs" (3:2). Paul sees his imprisonment as the divine means for advancing the gospel rather than its hindrance (1:12–18), and he is confident that, though he prefers to die and be with Christ, he will survive his imprisonment to help the Philippians (1:19–26). Part of that help is offered in the letter itself wherein Paul admonishes the Philippians to outdo one another

---

[8] Paul's imprisonment during this time could have been at Rome, Caesarea Maritima, or Ephesus.

*Paul's first experience in ancient Philippi involved imprisonment,
an earthquake, the conversion of the Philippian jailer, and a Roman
apology for an unlawful incarceration (Acts 16:11-40).*

in their love for one another, lowering themselves for the others' sake
in the same way that Christ lowered himself from heaven to the cross
with the result that God raised him and exalted him to the highest
position (2:5–11). In Christ, a similar experience awaits Paul and the
Philippians despite what they currently experience (3:7–20). With
respect to the "canine" opponents, Paul admonishes the Philippians to
ignore their religious pedigree, noting that he himself has a far superior
Jewish résumé, which he now regards as "rubbish" in comparison to
the knowledge of the crucified and risen Christ.

Colossians (ca. AD 60). This letter is also penned from prison (Col
4:10). Once again, the work of false teachers prompts Paul to write.
The nature of the false teaching, or "philosophy" (2:8) in Colossians
is a combination of worries over certain "powers" and spirits (astral/
magical) that can negatively impact the Christians in Colossae and the

need to placate those powers through adopting Jewish customs/rituals (circumcision, dietary restrictions, observance of certain days/times).[9] Paul responds with robust teaching about the person and work of Jesus Christ. God was pleased for all the fullness of Deity to dwell in the preexistent Christ (1:19), who stripped away the authority of any supposed cosmic powers through his death and resurrection (2:11–15). All that the Colossians need is found in him, not in the ritual and customs that the opponents trumpet.

1 & 2 Thessalonians (ca. AD 50). The historical purpose behind the Thessalonian correspondence can be summarized in one phrase, *eschatological confusion*. Eschatology is a theological term that refers to the study of the things and the time pertaining to the end. As I will discuss below, Paul's thought is thoroughly eschatological. Paul saw everything through the dawn of the end brought about by Jesus's resurrection and the consummation of that end at his return. However, this eschatological emphasis could be easily bumbled and disfigured. That is precisely what happens in Thessalonica. In 1 Thessalonians, Paul writes for two interrelated eschatological purposes: (1) admonish the Thessalonians to be ready for Jesus's return and (2) reassure the Thessalonians about the condition of those who die before Jesus's return. Readiness for the return includes receiving the word of the gospel (1:5), enduring

---

[9] Clinton Arnold notes that in this part of Asia Minor, "Deities and intermediaries were seen primarily in terms of their power. The tremendous fear of spirits prompted people to call on helpful spirits or angels and engage in rituals of power. Various forms of ritual initiation could help to charm one against the powers and provide the much-sought-after protection. Fasting and other forms of ascetic practices often accompanied the ritual and incantations. It is in this area where we see the highest degree of syncretism among the Jews of western Asia Minor." Clinton E. Arnold, *The Colossian Syncretism: The Interface between Christianity and Folk Belief at Colossae* (Grand Rapids: Baker, 1996), 310.

affliction and suffering (2:14; 3:1–13), abstaining from sexual immorality (4:3–8), showing brotherly love (4:9), giving mutual encouragement (5:11), respecting church leaders (5:12–13), and praying constantly (5:17). To reassure the Thessalonians about their brothers and sisters in Christ who died before his return, Paul explains that the deceased live in Christ and will return with him on the last day (4:13–17).

In 2 Thessalonians, the eschatological confusion continues, only this time there are Christians in Thessalonica who are worried that they have missed the "day of the Lord" or return of Jesus (2 Thess 2:1–2). Paul reminds them of his prior teaching, namely that the return of Jesus is preceded by certain events that have not yet occurred. Therefore, the Thessalonians must continue to believe in the gospel and trust that God will vindicate them when his Son returns (1:3–10). Meanwhile, all those in the believing community are admonished to continue working to provide for their families (3:11–12) and to not grow weary (3:13).

1 & 2 Timothy and Titus (ca. AD early to mid 60s). These three letters are often referred to as the Pastoral Epistles, because they contain pastoral admonitions to Timothy, Titus, and the congregations at Ephesus (1 Tim 1:3) and Crete (Titus 1:5). However, these letters are still very much "situational" in nature.

In 1 Timothy, Paul writes to instruct Timothy on how he should deal with the following issues at the church in Ephesus: (1) false teachers (1 Tim 1:3–11; 4; 6:1–5), (2) prayer for all kinds of people (2:1–8), (3) conduct of women at the church, (4) qualifications for elders and deacons (chap. 3), (5) care for widows (5:1–16), (6) treatment of elders (5:17–22), (7) warnings about wealth (6:1–19), and (8) a charge for Timothy to keep watch over the gospel ministry entrusted to him (6:20–21).

In 2 Timothy, Paul writes during his second Roman imprisonment, which will end with his execution, as he indicates in the letter:

"For I am already being poured out as a drink offering, and the time for my departure is close" (2 Tim 4:6). While Paul once again addresses the issue of false teaching (3:1–9), he mainly writes to exhort Timothy who most likely was distressed by Paul's imminent death. After all, Paul likened this relationship to a father and son, "But you know [Timothy's] proven character, because he has served with me in the gospel ministry like a son with a father" (Phil 2:22). Given their closeness, Paul tells Timothy to guard the gospel and renew his gifts as a preacher of the gospel until the end (2 Tim 1:6–7; 2:14–4:5), to not be distraught by his (Paul's) suffering but join along with him in suffering for the gospel (1:8–18) like a soldier, farmer, and athlete (2:1–7). Many have deserted Paul in his imprisonment (4:10–12), but he asks for Timothy to travel to see him (4:13–22).

In Titus, Paul writes to instruct Titus on the following matters: (1) appointment of elders (Titus 1:5–9), (2) how to deal with false teachers in Crete (1:10–2:15), and (3) how to admonish believers in Crete (chap. 3).

Philemon (ca. AD 60). The situation that prompted Paul to write this small letter is unique. During his first Roman imprisonment (see chronology above), Paul befriended a runaway slave named Onesimus (Phlm 10). Onesimus apparently served Paul in some capacity during his imprisonment (v. 13). However, Paul sends Onesimus back to his master, Philemon, "I am sending him back to you—I am sending my very own heart. I wanted to keep him with me, so that in my imprisonment for the gospel he might serve me in your place. But I didn't want to do anything without your consent, so that your good deed might not be out of obligation, but of your own free will" (vv. 12–14). Paul writes to facilitate the reunion between Onesimus and Philemon by pointing out that this relationship is no longer defined by master and slave. Instead, they are brothers in Christ (vv. 15–16).

Summary of Purposes (Situations). The situations that prompted Paul to pen these thirteen letters vary. Nevertheless, the common thread that runs throughout them is that Paul writes to address the suffering of early Christians. From Paul's perspective, these recipients had to endure in their belief in the gospel and live in a way that reflected the power and worth of the gospel regardless of the obstacles they faced. Yet he ultimately knew and wrote that their endurance depended on God's work in Christ through the Spirit. Adherence to his explanations and exhortations depends not on the power of his rhetoric or apostolic gravitas. Instead, it depended on God's power, hope, love, and faithfulness revealed in his Son's death and resurrection. What Paul said to the Philippians applied to all of his recipients, "I am sure of this, that he who started a good work in you will carry it on to completion until the day of Christ Jesus" (Phil 1:6). In all of these distressing situations, Paul's confidence rests in God rather than himself. That is why he begins and ends each letter with a prayer. It is the acknowledgment that the salve to heal the ailments of his recipients is given only by God in Christ.

History (Story) in the Text

Although the genre of a Pauline letter is "ancient epistle," Paul writes with a story in view. There is a "narrative substructure" to these letters that interpreters should have in view as they read them. Simply put, Paul is operating with a story about Jesus. His letters are like "theological reflection" on this story.[10] It is not possible to trace that entire story

---

[10] Richard Hays uses the description "narrative substructure" in his study on Galatians. Hays notes, "A story about Jesus Christ is presupposed by Paul's argument in Galatians, and his theological reflection attempts to articulate meaning of that story." Richard B. Hays, *The Faith of Jesus Christ: The Narrative Substructure of Galatians 3:1–4:11*, 2nd ed. (Grand Rapids: Eerdmans, 2002), xxiv.

Beneath the surface and structure of Paul's Letters is a story
about the crucified and risen Jesus that Paul narrates in a
way that addresses the situation of his recipients.

here. However, it will be helpful to summarize three main strands of it.
All three of the strands are intertwined with and inform one another.

Jesus Reveals God's Righteousness

One strand of Paul's "Jesus story" is that God reveals his righteousness
in the crucified and risen Jesus. The phrase *righteousness of God* summarizes a number of divine actions in Paul's thought, and those actions
are largely informed by his reading of the Old Testament (OT).[11] These
actions include

1. God condemns his enemies.
2. God saves his people.
3. God answers the cry of those who cry out to him for deliverance.

---

[11] See "righteousness of God" in Rom 1:17; 3:5, 21, 22; 10:3; 2 Cor 5:21.

4. God answers that cry by condemning and saving.
5. Those who believe in God's promised answer are declared and regarded as "righteous" before him.

In Paul's story of Jesus, God condemns Jesus to death like an enemy at the cross and raises him from the dead since Jesus is actually righteous. He does this to save those who cry out to him. God declares as righteous ("justifies," Gal 2:16) those who believe this promise. Of course, Paul does not have to use the phrase *righteousness of God* to have this idea in mind. This is part of the story that Paul then interprets in his letters. Specifically, he teaches his recipients the meaning of this story, its implications for their lives, and how they should respond to God in light of it.

In the Eternal Son We Find the Yes to All of God's Prior Promises

Paul explains to the Corinthians, "For every one of God's promises is "Yes" in him. Therefore, through him we also say "Amen" to the glory of God" (2 Cor 1:20). Similarly, he begins his epistle to the Romans by describing the gospel as that which God "promised beforehand through his prophets in the Holy Scriptures" (Rom 1:2). What these statements and many others like them indicate is that Paul links one large strand of his "Jesus Story" to the promises of the OT. For Paul, the crucified and risen Jesus is not merely the fulfillment or completion of God's promises, as if Jesus stood as act 3 in a five-act play. Paul identifies Jesus as the eternal Son of God who existed prior to the moments when Yahweh promised Abraham and his descendants anything. God made his promises to Israel with Jesus in mind and with Jesus present. He then fulfilled those promises when his Son became a man, suffered crucifixion, and was raised from the dead. The miniaturized version of this story is captured in the Philippians hymn:

Adopt the same attitude as that of Christ Jesus, who, existing in the form of God, did not consider equality with God as something to be exploited. Instead he emptied himself by assuming the form of a servant, taking on the likeness of humanity. And when he had come as a man, he humbled himself by becoming obedient to the point of death—even to death on a cross. For this reason God highly exalted him and gave him the name that is above every name, so that at the name of Jesus every knee will bow—in heaven and on earth and under the earth—and every tongue will confess that Jesus Christ is Lord, to the glory of God the Father. (Phil 2:5–11)[12]

Paul undoubtedly sees God's faithfulness to his prior promises as a main feature in his Jesus story. However, he also sees Jesus as someone who preceded the promises themselves.

The Risen Jesus Brings the End of the Ages

Paul believes that the "end" of the story has already begun with the arrival, life, death, and especially resurrection of Jesus. For Paul, Israel's Scriptures promised an end that would be marked by resurrection from the dead, worldwide judgment, and new creation. Paul locates the beginning of that "end" in Jesus. We see this when Paul refers to Jesus as the "firstfruits of those who have fallen asleep" (1 Cor 15:20), or when he describes believers as a "new creation" (Gal 6:15). These are not mere metaphors. Instead, they are expressions that abbreviate an entire story, a story in which the risen Jesus has ushered in the end of the ages. Resurrection from the dead meant imminent judgment and newness. For Paul, that has already begun in the risen Jesus.

Paul brings this "Jesus story" with its varying strands to his letters. The story is a reference point from which he understands and responds

---

[12] See also Col 1:15–20. This hymn is also a "miniaturized" story that is worked around the eternal Son of God.

to the various situations in his own life and in the life of the church. Therefore, interpreters need to probe constantly for the strands of this story in Paul's Letters and assess how that story impacts what Paul says to his recipients.

History in Front of the Text

The history of Pauline interpretation is vast. We could explore any number of issues, but here I will limit the focus to one "recent" development in the field of Pauline interpretation known as the New Perspective on Paul.[13] This so-called "new perspective" on Paul stems in large part from a reevaluation of how we should understand Jewish faith in the first-century world. Working to correct what he perceived as a caricature of Judaism in Paul's day, E. P. Sanders famously coined the phrase "covenantal nomism" as an abbreviation for his reevaluation.[14] He explains, "Briefly put, covenantal nomism is the view that one's place in God's plan is established on the basis of the covenant and that the covenant requires as the proper response of mam his obedience to its commands, while providing means of atonement for transgression."[15] This means that rather than scrambling to find a right standing/salvation through their obedience to the law Jews in Paul's day viewed themselves as already being in God's grace through the covenant that he established with them. They simply needed to remain in that gracious covenant through their obedience to the law.

---

[13] The phrase "New Perspective on Paul" is a misnomer. This interpretation of Paul and the Judaism of his day in now well over thirty-five years old if one takes as a starting point J.D.G. Dunn's 1983 essay entitled "The New Perspective on Paul."

[14] See, E.P. Sanders, *Paul and Palestinian Judaism: A Comparison of Patterns of Religion* (Minneapolis: Fortress, 1977).

[15] Sanders, *Paul and Palestinian Judaism*, 75.

In light of Sanders' covenantal nomism, some Pauline scholars have argued that when Paul spoke against the law, or "works of the law," he did not mean to suggest that Jews were using the law to make themselves right with God.[16] Instead, Paul is addressing whether or not Gentile Christians needed to live like Jews by taking up "Jewish badges of identity" such as circumcision, Sabbath observance, and dietary restrictions.[17] This would mean that Paul's discussions about grace and the law were not a matter of salvation but how to handle disputes about the ethnic/national differences between Jews and Gentiles in the church.

The New Perspective interpretation obviously challenges some traditional readings of Paul, particularly Paul's view of grace and the law. However, while the New Perspective provides some healthy correctives about Judaism in Paul's day, it is not without its problems. Other Pauline scholars have noted that Paul's problem with the law in relation to grace cannot be reduced to ethnic/national concerns. Sanders and those who followed in his train have "overstated" their conclusions about how Jews in Paul's day understood their covenant of grace in relation to the law.[18] As Hagner rightly notes, there is literary evidence that many Jews thought of their salvation as somehow dependent upon their obedience to the law.[19] Therefore, Paul is in fact reacting to both Jews and potentially Gentiles who somehow based their right standing with God, their salvation, on obedience to the Mosaic Law. Paul's response to such an attempt is summarized in statements such as, "I do not reject the grace of God; for if righteousness ("a right standing/not

---

[16] See e.g., Gal 2:15–21.

[17] See the helpful discussion and critique of the "New Perspective" in Donald Hagner, *How is the New Testament? First-Century Judaism and the Emergence of Christianity* (Grand Rapids: Baker, 2018), 2–5.

[18] Hagner, 5.

[19] Hagner.

guilty verdict") comes through the law, then Christ died for nothing"
(Gal 2:21, translation mine).

Understanding the Literary Tools
for Paul's Letters

Paul's Letters present some of the most complex argumentation in the
biblical text. It is easy to miss, or misunderstand, how Paul links together
each part of his argument. What an interpreter needs is a proper understanding of a letter's genre, structure, and OT usage. Identifying these
elements enables the interpreter to see how the large pieces of the
argument fit together. They can function like a color-coded map that
helps you see "where" things are in a Pauline letter.

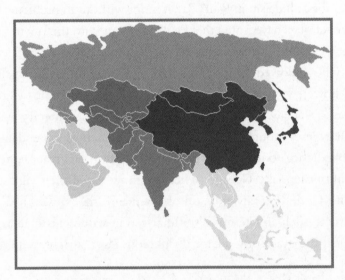

When we understand the layout of Pauline letters with
all their parts, they become easier to follow.

Genre

It is necessary to evaluate Paul's Letters in relation to the forms of communication that existed in his day. Many interpreters believe that Paul "chose to cast his letter in rhetorical forms."[20] That means Paul shaped his letters like a formal oral speech and used certain elements that his recipients would recognize. We need to familiarize ourselves with these elements if we are to read Paul's Letters effectively.

Types of Rhetoric

Ancient rhetoric consists of three types, as follows:

1. Deliberative rhetoric—a speech aimed to persuade or dissuade the audience
2. Forensic rhetoric—a speech aimed to accuse or defend
3. Epideictic rhetoric—a speech aimed to praise or blame

Paul mixes these types of rhetoric together to make points that address the various historical situations of his recipients. For example, in persuading the Galatians (deliberative) to continue in the truth of the gospel, he defends his apostleship (forensic) and blames (epideictic) the Judaizing opponents for attempting to change the gospel.

---

[20] Witherington, *Conflict and Community in Corinth*, 39. (see chap. 9, n. 6). I am helped here by Witherington's discussion of ancient rhetoric and its use in Paul's Letters.

Parts of Rhetoric

Any type of ancient rhetoric (deliberative, forensic, epideictic) has an arrangement of parts that collectively helps make the speaker/writer's point.[21] These parts are as follows:

Introduction to argument—the beginning part of the speech where the speaker aims to make the audience open to what is about to be said

Explanation of problem—some of the specifics of the disputed matter

Thesis—essential proposition

Support for thesis—arguments to support the thesis

Disputation of opposition—arguments to disprove or weaken opponent's arguments

Summary of main points—summary of main points that support thesis and seek to gain favorable response

Paul uses these elements in his own way and for his own purposes. Galatians once again provides a good example:

Introduction to argument—Due to Paul's anger with the Galatians, he skips this part as indicated by the anger he expresses in Gal 1:6–10.

Explanation of problem (1:6–2:14)—Paul explains that the opponents in Galatia are both challenging his apostolic authority and attempting to change the gospel he preached.

Thesis (2:15–21)—Paul lays out his essential point in these verses. He argues that justification is by faith in Christ and

---

[21] We discussed these parts of rhetoric in the previous chapter with respect to the speeches in Acts.

not by works of the law, because if justification was through works of the law, it would mean Christ died for nothing.

Support thesis and disprove opposition (3:1–6:10)—Paul supports his *propositio* (2:15–21) by explaining the relationship between God's saving work in Christ, faith, and the law. This *probatio* simultaneously functions as a *refutatio* in which Paul disproves the arguments of the false teachers.

Summary of main points (6:11–18)—Paul summarizes his main point and supporting points by giving a final warning about the false teachers and exclaiming that he boasts only in the cross of Jesus which makes works of the law, such as circumcision, meaningless. What matters is that believers are a "new creation" through faith in the crucified and risen Christ.

The Form of a Letter

Besides its rhetorical types and parts, interpreters can also analyze a letter based on its form. The broadest and simplest form of the letter contains four parts: (1) letter opening, (2) body, (3) *paraenesis* (ethical exhortation), and (4) closing. Each part contains various features. Galatians will once again provide a good example.

Letter Opening (Gal 1:1–5)

Name of Writer (1:1)—Paul

Name of Addressees (1:2)—Churches of Galatia

Greeting (1:3–5)—"Grace to you and peace from God the Father and our Lord Jesus Christ, who gave himself for our sins to rescue us from this present evil age" (v. 3).

Body of Letter (Gal 1:6–4:31)

Prayer/Prayer Report—Due to Paul's anger over the situation in Galatia, this letter does not contain a prayer or prayer report.[22]

Main Argument (1:6–4:31)

Paranesis (Ethical Exhortation) (5:1–6:10)

Ethical exhortation can occur anywhere in a Pauline letter. However, much of his exhortation is concentrated in the latter parts of the letter.

Closing (6:11–18)

The letter's closing summarizes the contents of the whole letter. Additionally, it can contain a closing prayer, a summary of travel plans, or closing greetings (see 6:18).

There is of course more to interpreting a Pauline letter than identifying its four major parts. You must dig into all four parts and then follow the progression of Paul's argument. Nevertheless, it is helpful to see the broad contours of the whole argument before analyzing its smaller parts. For a few more tips on interpreting the parts of a Pauline letter, click here.

Use of the OT

Paul's Letters are chock-full of OT echoes. He cites and alludes to various texts from the Law, the Prophets, and the Writings. Paul uses the

---

[22] A "prayer report" is not an actual prayer but a summary of what the writer prays about.

OT for a variety of reasons; a key interpretive question in analyzing any passage in a Pauline letter is, how is Paul using the OT in this particular passage? To answer that question, we need to consider the various ways that Paul uses the OT in his thirteen letters.

Christological Use

I find it fascinating that early Christians routinely used the OT to better understand and explain the identity of Jesus. They did not depend solely on their personal encounters with Jesus. They looked to the sacred text of the OT. Paul certainly uses the OT in this way. He interprets Jesus in relation to at least three OT figures: (1) Yahweh, (2) the Davidic Messiah, and (3) priest/sacrifice.

Jesus and Yahweh. Paul portrays Jesus as the eternal Son who has always participated and will always participate in the identity of Israel's God. For example, Paul warns the Corinthians about the dangers of idolatry and sexual immorality by recounting what God did to the Israelites who wandered in the wilderness. In using this analogy, he notes that the Israelites "All drank the same spiritual drink. For they drank from the spiritual rock that followed them, and that rock was Christ" (1 Cor 10:4). Paul here alludes to Exodus 17 in which Moses recounts how God provided the Israelites with water from a rock. Yahweh commanded him, "'I am going to stand there in front of you on the rock at Horeb; when you hit the rock, water will come out of it and the people will drink.' Moses did this in the sight of the elders of Israel" (Exod 17:6).[23] In evoking this passage, Paul does not mean to say that Jesus was literally a rock. He is indicating that in the wilderness wanderings Yahweh and Jesus provided the Israelites with water.

---

[23] See also Num 20:7–11.

After the Damascus revelation, Paul takes a retrospective look at Israel's Scriptures and sees Jesus in the actions of Israel's God.

Paul retrospectively looks back at ancient Israel's wilderness wanderings. He places Jesus in the wilderness with them, providing them with water.

Jesus and David. Paul also views Jesus as the Davidic Messiah. For instance, in the opening to the letter to the Romans, Paul describes Jesus as being "a descendant of David according to the flesh" (1:3). Similarly, in 2 Tim 2:8, his admonishment includes a Davidic reference: "Remember Jesus Christ, risen from the dead and descended from David, according to my gospel." Although he does not explicitly speak at length about the connection between Jesus and David in his letters, these examples indicate that Paul views Jesus through the lens of Davidic kingship. That kingship is reworked around the person of Jesus with the result that God's work in his Son is at the same time *expected* based on the OT's description of a Davidic Messiah but also *unexpected* (mysterious) based on what Jesus actually did and does.

Jesus and Priest/Sacrifice. A third Christological use involves the priestly and sacrificial system present in both the OT and the Judaism of Paul's day. Paul subtly portrays Jesus as an eternal high priest who intercedes for God's people, "Who is the one who condemns? Christ Jesus is the one who died, but even more, has been raised; he also is at the right hand of God and intercedes for us" (Rom 8:34). This Christological description echoes Ps 110:1, "This is the declaration of the LORD to my Lord: 'Sit at my right hand until I make your enemies your footstool.'" Of course, Paul is not merely echoing one verse of the psalm. He evokes the entire psalm in which the psalmist goes on to describe this "Lord" who is at the Lord's right hand in a priestly fashion. That description includes an explicit reference to the mysterious priest from Genesis 14, "The LORD has sworn an oath and will not take it back: 'You are a priest forever according to the pattern of Melchizedek'" (Ps 110:4).[24] In this way, Paul identifies the crucified and risen Jesus as the priestly Lord who sits at God's right hand in Psalm 110. Besides viewing Jesus as a priest, Paul also sees him as the ultimate sacrifice. While admonishing the Corinthians to deal with the sexual immorality in their congregation, Paul refers to Jesus as a Passover lamb: "Cleanse out the old leaven that you may be a new unleavened batch, as indeed you are. For Christ our Passover lamb has been sacrificed" (1 Cor 5:7). This description echoes OT passages such as Exod 12:21, "Then Moses summoned all the elders of Israel and said to them, 'Go, select an animal from the flock according to your families, and slaughter the Passover animal.'" The Passover lamb commemorated Yahweh's hurried deliverance of Israel from Egypt

---

[24] See Gen 14:16–20. See also Heb 5:6, 10; 6:20; 7:1, 10, 11, 15, 17.

and the final plague in which all the firstborn were struck dead. For Paul, Jesus is that ultimate Passover Lamb whose sacrifice brings forgiveness and deliverance from the final judgment that awaits all the living and the dead.

Apostolic Use

Paul also uses the OT to understand and describe his mission as an apostle. As I noted in the previous chapter, Paul sees himself in the vein of an OT prophet. God set him apart to be an apostle even before his birth in the same way he set apart Jeremiah and Isaiah (Jer 1:5; Isa 49:1; Gal 1:15). But Paul also uses the OT to understand the following things about the apostolic message he preached.

The Content of His Message. The heart of Paul's message is the death and resurrection of Jesus (1 Cor 15:3–4). Yet he interpreted and shaped the content of that core message through the Scriptures. For example, he sees the promise to Abraham as the gospel in its seedling form as he tells the Galatians (3:8), "Now the Scripture saw in advance that God would justify the Gentiles by faith and proclaimed the gospel ahead of time to Abraham, saying, All the nations will be blessed through you." Paul cites Gen 12:3, which includes the promise of worldwide blessing through the descendants of Abraham. For Paul, that promised blessing is the promise of salvation and the key Abrahamic descendant is Jesus (Gal 3:15–18). There are other ways that the OT shapes the content of Paul's apostolic message, and interpreters should take note of them.

The "Location" of His Message. As an apostle, Paul even used the OT to determine "where" he would preach the message of the gospel. It is not that he used the OT as a lockstep map. Yet, at least in principle, the OT influences Paul to preach where no one has yet preached Christ. As he explains to the Romans (15:20–21), "My aim is to preach the gospel where Christ has not been named, so that I will not build on someone else's foundation, but as it is written, Those who were not told about him will see, and those who have not heard will understand." Paul cites Isa 52:15, which is part of Isaiah's famed Suffering Servant motif. For Paul, the description of God's servant (Isa 52:13–53:12) indicates the location where the saving work of the servant should be proclaimed, namely wherever his name/work have not yet been proclaimed.

The Target(s) of His Message. Paul refers to himself as the "apostle to the Gentiles" (Rom 11:13; Gal 2:8). This is, after all, the apostolic assignment he received from Christ on the road to Damascus (Acts 9:15). However, Paul also understands the "target" of his apostolic based on his reading of the OT. This is exemplified in a chain of OT citations that Paul weaves together in Rom 15:7–13. The common theme in the citations that come from Deuteronomy, 2 Samuel, the Psalms, and Isaiah is that God's saving work would be proclaimed among the Gentiles, and Gentiles would hope in the announcement of that saving work. Yet, in reaching Gentiles, Paul hoped to provoke his Jewish kinsmen to jealousy so that they would turn and believe in Christ (Rom 11:13–14). This "indirect target" of Paul's mission to the Gentiles is also rooted in his reading of the OT, "I will make you jealous of those who are not a nation; I will make you angry by a nation that lacks understanding" (Rom 10:19; Deut 32:21).

The Financing of His Message. Paul even appeals to the OT to explain that he and other apostles should be monetarily supported for their gospel ministry. For example, while discussing this matter with the Corinthians, Paul notes:

Who serves as a soldier at his own expense? Who plants a vine-yard and does not eat its fruit? Or who shepherds a flock and does not drink the milk from the flock?

Am I saying this from a human perspective? Doesn't the law also say the same thing? For it is written in the law of Moses, Do not muzzle an ox while it treads out grain. Is God really concerned about oxen? Isn't he really saying it for our sake? Yes, this is written for our sake, because he who plows ought to plow in hope, and he who threshes should thresh in hope of sharing the crop. (1 Cor 9:7–10)

In this explanation, Paul cites Deut 25:4 "Do not muzzle an ox when it treads out grain." The wider context of Deuteronomy 25 contains miscellaneous laws, but most of them involve care that Israelites were to show to one another in various relationships and scenarios. Paul applies those instructions to the care that churches were to show to apostles. He even appeals to the authority of Scripture in making this point ("Doesn't the law say the same?").

Anthropological Use

Paul has a great deal to say about believers and unbelievers alike. Much of that reflection stems from reading the OT through the lens of his encounter with the risen Jesus. This combination shapes Paul's anthropology in various ways.

Humans as Divine Enemies. Paul describes all human creatures as God's enemies by appealing to the OT. For example, Rom 3:10–18 contains citations from Ecclesiastes, Psalms, and Isaiah which collectively portray humans as those whose deeds and words demonstrate they have "no fear of God before their eyes" (Rom 3:18). This last line is a citation from Psalm 36 where the psalmist complains about wicked enemies who afflict him. His description of those enemies includes, "There is no dread of God in front of his eyes" (Ps 36:1 CSB note). For Paul, all those who are "under sin" (Rom 3:9) play the part of those enemies.

Adam and Christ. To explain the origin, implications, and solution for these rebellious creatures, Paul portrays Adam as a "type" of Jesus ("a type of the Coming One" Rom 5:14). For example, in Rom 5:12–21, Paul reflects on the origin and implications of human sin by comparing Adam and Jesus. Paul explains that sin and death entered the world through Adam's sin in the garden (Rom 5:12–14; Genesis 3). He then compares the disobedience of Adam and its results with the obedience of Jesus and its results. Adam's disobedience results in death and condemnation while Jesus's obedience results in life and justification.[25] The comparison between these two figures also includes a contrast between the "first" and "last" Adam, "So it is written, The first man Adam became a living being; the last Adam became a life-giving spirit" (1 Cor 15:45). Paul goes back to the beginning of humanity (Genesis 1–2) to explain the end that believers can expect. Specifically, Jesus, the "last Adam," surpasses the "first Adam," because he makes the believer live eternally. At this return, Jesus will transform the perishable, corruptible, and mortal material bodies of his people into imperishable and immortal ones (1 Cor 15:50–54).

Soteriological Use

Paul often appeals to the OT when discussing the salvation that God provides to those who believe in the crucified and risen Jesus.

---

[25] See also 1 Cor 15:22.

Abraham and Justification. For example, he links the promise of justification by faith and the pattern of justification by faith to Abraham. Both Romans 4 and Galatians 3 echo the Abrahamic narrative, especially Gen 15:6. "Abraham believed God, and it was credited to him for righteousness" (Rom 4:3, 9, 23; Gal 3:6). Contextually Yahweh repeats his covenant promise to Abraham: "Do not be afraid, Abram. I am your shield; your reward will be very great" (Gen 15:1). Abraham (Abram) responds that he has no descendant; therefore, he does not see this "reward" of descendants through whom the nations will be blessed (Gen 12:1–3). God then promises Abraham, "'Look at the sky and count the stars, if you are able to count them.' Then he said to him, 'Your offspring will be that numerous'" (Gen 15:5). The narrator then notes, "Abraham believed the LORD, and he credited it to him as righteousness" (15:6). For Paul, this Abrahamic episode is both an early form of the gospel and a pattern for believers. The promise of blessing to the nations through Abraham's descendant finds its completion in Jesus (Gal 3:15–18). Furthermore, when Abraham believes God's promise, it becomes an example for future believers. Abraham trusted in the promise of a redeemer who would come from his genealogy, and believers trust in the promise that Jesus is that redeemer. Therefore, just as God justified Abraham because he believed the promise, believers are justified in the same way. I will talk more about justification by faith below.

Forgiveness and Atonement. The OT also shapes Paul's thinking on forgiveness and atonement for sin that God provides through Jesus. For example, he describes Jesus as the One whom God "presented . . . as an atoning sacrifice [propitiation] in his blood, received through faith" (Rom 3:25). "Propitiation," sometimes translated as a "sacrifice of atonement," evokes the sacrificial system outlined in both Exodus and Leviticus. Specifically, the language Paul uses (ἱλαστήριον; hilastērion) alludes to the mercy seat that sat atop the ark of the covenant:

*For Paul, Jesus is the ultimate mercy seat foreshadowed
in Leviticus and the priestly system.*

Make a mercy seat [*ha-kappŏet/hilastērion*] of pure gold, forty-five inches long and twenty-seven inches wide. (Exod 25:17)[26]

The LORD said to Moses: "Tell your brother Aaron that he may not come whenever he wants into the holy place behind the curtain in front of the mercy seat on the ark or else he will die, because I appear in the cloud above the mercy seat." (Lev 16:2)

When he slaughters the male goat for the people's sin offering and brings its blood inside the curtain, he will do the same with its blood as he did with the bull's blood: He is to sprinkle it against the mercy seat and in front of it. (Lev 16:15)

---

[26] See also Exod 25:18–22; 31:17; 35:12; 38:5–8; Num 7:89.

As these passages indicate, on the Day of Atonement, the priest sprinkled the blood of the sacrificial offering on the mercy seat in order to cleanse the people of their sin (expiation) and thereby satisfy God's wrath for sin (propitiation). The mercy seat functions as the location, or sacred space, where forgiveness and atonement were secured. For Paul, God puts forward Jesus as the "mercy" seat where once and for all there is expiation and propitiation for sin.

Ecclesiastical and Ethical Use

The OT helps shape Paul's thinking about the people of God and how those people should live. He sees a direct correlation between ancient Israel and the church.

Sin in Israel and the Church. Paul warns the Corinthians about idolatry and sexual immorality by referring to God's judgment against Israel's wilderness generation. He explains, "Let us not test Christ as some of them did and were destroyed by snakes. And don't complain as some of them did, and were killed by the destroyer" (1 Cor 10:9–10). The wider context of Paul's explanation (10:1–13) appeals to specific events, such as Israel's grumbling about a lack of water (Exod 17:1–6), grumbling about a lack of food (Num 11:4), idolatry with the golden calf (Exodus 32; Numbers 14), and fornication with Moabite women (Numbers 25). Paul underscores that some of the people involved in these events perished (1 Cor 10:8, 10). He concludes his warning by noting, "These things happened to them as examples, and they were written for our instruction, on whom the ends of the ages have come. So, whoever thinks he stands must be careful not to fall" (10:11–12).

Paul is not reducing ancient Israelite history to nothing more than an example for the church. He is underscoring the fact that God demands holiness from the people he saves. However, in demanding such holiness, Paul does not direct the Corinthians to redouble their ethical efforts or to look inwardly for the spiritual fortitude to be holy. Instead, he points them again and again to Christ. From the very outset of the letter, even before he gives these warnings about living unethically in the church, Paul reminds the Corinthians, "It is from him that you are in Christ Jesus, who became wisdom from God for us—our righteousness, sanctification, and redemption, in order that, as it is written, Let the one who boasts, boast in the Lord" (1:30–31). In other words, the holiness that God demands is found by faith in who Christ is, what he has already done, and in the empowering presence of the Holy Spirit. As Paul tells the Romans, "Everything that is not from faith is sin" (14:23). And as he tells the Galatians, "I say then, walk by the Spirit and you will certainly not carry out the desire of the flesh" (5:16).

The Mosaic Law and the Church. Paul speaks at length about the Mosaic law for various purposes. His view of the law plays a key role in his view of Christian ethics but not in a way we might expect. Two points on this issue appear often in his letters.

First, Paul describes the law as a "guardian" or "tutor" that God placed Israel under with the aim of bringing them to faith in Christ (Gal 3:24). The law could not give life or empower their obedience to God. Instead, it condemned them in their sin and confined them under divine judgment (Gal 3:21–24). Consequently, the law has the same function for Gentile Christians in Galatia contemplating a turn to a Jewish way of life. Such a turn would result in the same judgment and indicate a misunderstanding of the purpose of the law, namely, to be a tutor that leads to faith in Christ. The inability to do the law is meant to turn people to the grace of God in Christ. In this way, the law always condemns and points to a need for Jesus. Paul does not think the law is sinful (Rom 7:7). He merely points out that the power of sin uses the

"The law, then, was our guardian until Christ, so that
we could be justified by faith" (Gal 3:24).

law against people and that people have a propensity for using the law
in a way that God did not intend (Rom 7:7–25).

Second, Paul also summarizes the entire Mosaic law as divine
instruction on "love." Much like Jesus, Paul sums up the whole law
by noting, "Do not commit adultery; do not murder; do not steal; do
not covet; and any other commandment, are *summed up* by this commandment: Love your neighbor as yourself. Love does no wrong to a
neighbor. Love, therefore, is the fulfillment of the law" (Rom 13:9–10,
emphasis added). Of course, for Paul, love for God and one another is a
result of the love that God pours into the heart of the believer through
the Holy Spirit (Rom 5:5).

"Connective Tissue" in a Pauline Letter

Much of what we've discussed in this literary section pertains to seeing how one unit of thought fits within the larger framework of Paul's argument. However, what should we do with smaller pieces—a paragraph, a sentence, even a single clause? It is critical that we see how Paul *connects* paragraphs, sentences, and even single clauses if we are to understand his main argument and the points that support it.

This is analogous to the connective tissue in the human body. Connective tissue refers to the small fibers that connect and support key organs. In Paul's Letters, conjunctions and other grammatical particles act like tissue that connects and supports the "heart" of Paul's argument. We here briefly discuss some of Paul's favorite conjunctions and particles.

Inferential Conjunction: Therefore. The use of *therefore* indicates that Paul is drawing a conclusion (or summarizing) based on what he has just said. Sometimes Paul is drawing a conclusion based only on the previous paragraph. At other times, Paul may use *therefore* to draw a conclusion based on several previous paragraphs. For example, in Rom 5:1, Paul writes, "Therefore, since we have been declared righteous by faith, we have peace with God through our Lord Jesus Christ." Paul is most likely reaching all the way back to Rom 3:27–4:25, where he meticulously explains how a person is justified by faith apart from works using both Abraham and David as examples. Based on that larger argument, what conclusion/inference does Paul draw for the reader? In a word, *peace*. Based on justification by faith that Paul describes in 3:27–4:25, Paul concludes that believers have "peace with God."

Causal Conjunctions: For/Because. Paul likes to provide the basis (cause) for the arguments that he makes. For example, notice how the three causal conjunctions (emphasis added) function in the thesis statement of Paul's letter to the Romans, "*For* I am not ashamed of the gospel, because [*for*] it is the power of God for salvation to everyone who believes, first to the Jew, and also to the Greek. *For* in it the righteousness of God is revealed from faith for faith, just as it is written: The righteous will live by faith" (1:16–17). To understand how this first *for* is functioning, we must look back to the immediately preceding verses where Paul tells the Romans "I am eager to preach the gospel to you also who are in Rome" (1:15). Paul wants to preach the gospel in Rome, because/for he is not ashamed of the gospel. This brings us to the second *for*. Paul is not ashamed of the gospel, because/for the gospel is the power of God that results in salvation to those who believe. And this brings us to the third *for*. The gospel is the power of God that results in salvation because/for the gospel reveals God's righteousness.[27]

Understanding the Theological Tools for Paul's Letters

We have already touched on several theological motifs in Paul's Letters. Nevertheless, it is helpful to summarize some of the main ones here. After all, a big part of interpreting a Pauline letter is understanding how various "theological pieces" fit into the apostle's entire theology. The problem we have here is that Paul writes only situational letters. He never pens a summary of his basic beliefs. That does not mean he lacked basic beliefs. It simply means we must recover those beliefs in piecemeal fashion. Each letter provides bits and pieces of his theology. When we stitch these together, we catch a glimpse of a Pauline theology.

---

[27] I've only included a few examples of conjunctions in Paul's letters. For an extensive discussion of Paul's grammar, see Tom Schreiner, *Interpreting the Pauline Epistles*, 2nd ed. (Grand Rapids: Baker, 2011), 69-96.

What is the "center" of Paul's theology? That is often a question that occupies the attention of Pauline interpreters. What is the theological axis around which everything else turns and makes sense? I will not solve that riddle here. What I do offer is a summary of six theological motifs that have the crucified and risen Christ as their centerpiece.

Is there one central idea in Paul's theology around which all his other thoughts revolve?

Justification by Faith

This is the teaching (doctrine) most often associated with Paul. It is legal (forensic) in nature. From Paul's perspective, God is the cosmic judge who puts the sinner in a right standing with himself or declares him "not guilty," based on the sinner's belief that, just as God promised, Jesus Christ died for sinners, was buried, was raised on the third day, and that he saves all those who call upon his name (Rom 10:8–13). This justification that believers receive now anticipates the verdict they will receive on the day of judgment (Gal 5:5). While this doctrine does not appear in many letters besides Romans and Galatians, it is clearly one of Paul's main theological motifs. Moreover, the crucified and risen Christ is the centerpiece of this doctrine.

Key Texts: Rom 3:27–31; 4:1–8, 23–25; 5:15–21; 8:28–39; 1 Cor 1:30; 2 Cor 5:20–21; Gal 2:15–21; Phil 3:7–11.

Death and Life "in Christ"

The phrase *in Christ* and related expressions occur some ninety times in Paul's Letters. Although scholars sometimes debate the precise meaning of the expression, it is fair to say that it is both "locative" and "relational" in nature. By "locative," I am referring to a spatial metaphor where Paul portrays the believer as someone who is "located" with Christ by faith and thereby sharing in all the benefits that he secured through his death and resurrection. In various ways, Paul expresses this "in Christ" relationship in many of his letters:

> Are you not aware that all of us who were baptized into Christ Jesus were baptized into his death? Therefore we were buried with him by baptism into death, in order that, just as Christ was raised from the dead by the glory of the Father, so we too may walk in newness of life. (Rom 6:3–4)

> I no longer live, but Christ lives in me. The life I now live in the body, I live by faith in the Son of God, who loved me and gave himself for me. (Gal 2:19–20)

> If you have been raised with Christ, seek the things above, where Christ is, seated at the right hand of God. (Col 3:1)

These examples demonstrate that being "in Christ" revolves around what he secures for the believer in his death and resurrection.

These benefits include death (freedom) from sin, new life and eventually a risen life, the gift/presence of the Spirit (Rom 5:5; Eph 1:11–15), deliverance from condemnation, and future glory.[28]

Key Texts: Rom 6:1–11; 8:17; Gal 2:15–21; 3:25–28; Eph 1:3–14; Phil 1:21–26; Col 2:11–15; 3:1–4; 2 Tim 2:9–10.

Predestined and Elected as God's Children in Christ

I sometimes encounter students who tell me they do not believe in predestination and election. What they really mean to say is, I do not believe in certain explanations of predestination and election. Paul clearly uses this language (Rom 8:28–30). There is a tension in Paul's teaching on predestination and election. It is a tension between human responsibility and divine sovereignty. What is the responsibility of a person with respect to salvation? Over what is God sovereign as it relates to salvation? Although these are important and legitimate questions, Paul never answers them to our satisfaction. What is clear is that Paul evokes the language of predestination and election out of pastoral concern for his recipients. In the face of their uncertainties and afflictions in the world, Paul can appeal to God's eternal ways and purposes to reassure them of God's love and deliverance of them.

Key Texts: Rom 8:28–30; 9:11; 11:5, 7, 28; Eph 1:5, 11; 1 Thess 1:4.

Jesus as Cosmic Lord

Some people have a really small Jesus. By this I mean that they do not realize the full scope of his power. They should read more Paul, because he did not have this misconception. For Paul, God exalted his preexistent and risen Son as Lord over everything. Jesus is "far above every

---

[28] This is not an exhaustive list of benefits. You should stay alert for others when you encounter the "in Christ" motif while reading Paul's Letters.

ruler and authority, power and dominion, and every title given, not only in this age but also in the one to come" (Eph 1:21). As Paul tells the Philippians, "For this reason God highly exalted him and gave him the name that is above every name, so that at the name of Jesus every knee will bow—in heaven and on earth and under the earth—and every tongue will confess that Jesus Christ is Lord, to the glory of God the Father" (Phil 2:9–11). Paul admonishes the believer "call on . . . the name of the Lord" (Rom 10:13). To confess that Jesus is Lord (1 Cor 8:6) is to confess that he rules over everything, including sin, death, Satan, and creation. As Paul poetically puts it in Rom 8:38–39, "For I am persuaded that neither death nor life, nor angels nor rulers, nor things present nor things to come, nor powers, nor height nor depth, nor any other created thing will be able to separate us from the love of God that is in Christ Jesus our Lord."

Key Texts: Rom 13:14; 1 Cor 1:8–9; 8:6; 12:3; 15:55–57; 2 Cor 4:5; Eph 1:15–23; 4:5; 1 Thess 4:13–17.

The Revelation of God's Righteousness in Christ

Scholars have exerted a great deal of energy trying to determine what Paul means by the phrase *righteousness of God* (e.g., Rom 1:17). The importance of this teaching in Paul's theology cannot be gauged by how many times the actual phrase appears in his letters. What the phrase abbreviates is the divine action in which God saves through judgment, and this is something that informs much of Paul's thinking. Like all of Paul's theological motifs, this one is grounded in OT theology and then reworked around the crucified and risen Jesus. In the OT, God delivers the Israelites from slavery in Egypt by judging the pharaoh, the Egyptians, and their gods through a series of plagues. Simply put, he saves Israel through judging Israel's enemies. To put it another way, God reveals his righteousness.

For Paul, God ultimately reveals his righteousness through the death and resurrection of Jesus. However, in this instance, God judges his righteous Son rather than a wicked enemy. He does this to deliver the sinner who believes in him. God pours judgment out on Jesus in place of the sinner to mercifully save the sinner. God then raises his son from the dead, because his son is righteous. God's judgment is both "against" Jesus (crucifixion) and "for" Jesus (resurrection). In all of this, God saves the sinner through the judgment of Jesus. To put it another way, God reveals his righteousness in Christ.

Key Texts: Rom 1:16–17; 3:21–26; 10:1–4; 2 Cor 5:20–21.

Redemption in Christ

Paul often uses the metaphor of redemption to describe what Christ has accomplished in his death and resurrection and the hope that his accomplishment produces. The literal sense of redemption in both ancient Hebrew and Greek has to do with buying something back or releasing a person from debt. Paul specifically draws the language of redemption from both the OT and his Greco-Roman environment. In the OT, God "redeems" his people from slavery in Egypt in accordance with his prior promise:

> Therefore tell the Israelites: I am the LORD, and I will bring you out from the forced labor of the Egyptians and rescue you from slavery to them. I will redeem you with an outstretched arm and great acts of judgment. I will take you as my people, and I will be your God. You will know that I am the LORD your God, who brought you out from the forced labor of the Egyptians. I will bring you to the land that I swore to give to Abraham, Isaac, and Jacob, and I will give it to you as a possession. I am the LORD. (Exod 6:6–8)

Yahweh redeems (recovers/frees) his people from Egyptian bondage through judging Israel's enemies. For Paul, God's quintessential
act of redemption (recovering/freeing) takes place in Jesus's death and
resurrection. Jesus's work secures "redemption" for the believer, and
Paul defines that redemption in two interrelated ways: (1) "In him we
have redemption through his blood, the forgiveness of our trespasses,
according to the riches of his grace" (Eph 1:7). And (2) "Not only
that [the creation], but we ourselves, who have the Spirit as the first
fruits—we also groan within ourselves, eagerly waiting for adoption,
the redemption of our bodies" (Rom 8:23).

Redemption in the crucified and risen Jesus is the forgiveness
of sins before God. The implication is that without Christ's work a
person is enslaved, even dead, in sin (see Eph 2:1–3). However, Paul
also sees a future component to redemption. That is why he speaks
about the "redemption of our bodies" (Rom 8:23). The implication
here is that the material body needs to be freed from death and corruption. This is not an escape from the body. Rather, it is the body
being freed from death and given new life just as Christ was raised
from the dead by God's Spirit (Rom 8:11). So we see that Paul's
understanding of redemption in Christ has both a present and a
future aspect.

Key Texts: Rom 8:23; 1 Cor 1:30; Eph 1:7, 14; 4:30; Col 1:14.

Responding to Paul's Letters

There is no question that Paul intended for his original recipients
to respond to his letters. He did not write them for nothing. These
responses varied from letter to letter, but they also overlap with one
another. They include repentance, renewal of the mind, endurance,
forgiveness toward others, and rejecting false teaching. In all of this,
Paul wanted his recipients to remain "in Christ" by faith, holding onto
what God had done in Christ, what he was doing in Christ, and what

Although Paul has much to say about Jesus and his church, he acknowledges that his understanding is partial at best. There is a dimness to what he knows which will only become clear with the arrival of Jesus.

he would do in Christ until his return and the judgment that would immediately follow.

Another way to summarize Paul's intended responses is that he wants his readers to "understand" and "imitate" him by faith. He repeatedly uses language that pertains to understanding. As he tells the Ephesians, "So don't be foolish, but understand what the Lord's will is" (5:17).[29] Of course, Paul is aware that some things (perhaps many things) remain a mystery that will not be fully understood until Christ returns. He acknowledges, "For we know in part, and we prophesy in part, but when the perfect comes, the partial will come to an end" (1 Cor 13:9–10). There is a "dimness" to Paul's knowledge, even the knowledge he passes on to his readers: "For now we see only a reflection as in a mirror, but then face to face. Now I *know* in part, but then I will *know* fully, as I am fully known" (1 Cor 13:12, emphasis added). Nevertheless, there is much that can be known through what God

---

[29] See also Rom 6:6; 1 Cor 2:16; 11:3; 2 Cor 1:13; Eph 3:4.

revealed in Christ. Therefore, Paul wants his readers to "understand" what has been revealed. Additionally, Paul wants his readers to imitate him. As he tells the Corinthians, "Imitate me, as I also imitate Christ" (1 Cor 11:1). Paul wants his readers to imitate his faith, endurance, and obedience in Jesus.

Putting the Tools to Use

It is now time to put all this reflection on Paul to good exegetical use. We will use Phil 3:17–21 as an example of how you can approach any Pauline passage.

Historical Tools

1. How does the letter to the Philippians fit into the chronology of Paul's life?
2. What is the historical purpose for which Paul wrote Philippians? How might Phil 3:17–21 fit that purpose?
3. Are there any indications that Phil 3:17–21 is related to the "Jesus story" in some way? Explain.

Literary Tools

1. What is the rhetorical type(s) contained in this passage? Explain your answer.
2. What "part" of rhetoric is Phil 3:17–21, and how is it related to the other parts of rhetoric in the letter?
3. How does the passage fit with the larger "form" of Philippians?
4. Read Hosea 4 (note especially v. 7). How does Paul's language in Phil 3:17–21 echo Hosea 4? Which of Paul's OT usages (discussed above) is this? How does Hosea 4 shed light on what Paul is saying in Phil 3:17–21?
5. How is each verse in Phil 3:17–21 related to the others?

Theological Tools

1. Does this passage evoke one or more of the theological motifs discussed above? How so?
2. Does this passage have parallels with theological motifs found in any of Paul's other letters? Explain.
3. How does Rom 8:23–25 and 1 Cor 15:35–55 shed light on Paul's statement in Phil 3:21?

Responsive Tools

1. Compare Phil 1:21–23 to 3:21. How did Paul want the Philippians to think about their ultimate hope in Christ?
2. Based on Phil 3:17–21 and the wider admonitions in the letter, what would it look like to imitate Paul (3:17) in your context today?

11

Tools for Interpreting the General Epistles & Revelation

We now come to some of the most neglected books in the Bible and then also one of the most confusing. The so-called General (Catholic) Epistles include Hebrews, James, 1 & 2 Peter, 1, 2, & 3 John, and Jude. Compared to the Gospels and Paul's Letters, the General Epistles receive far less attention. That is unfortunate, because these books provide some of the richest portraits of Jesus and instructions for Christians in all of the New Testament (NT). Additionally, for many interpreters, the book of Revelation (John's Apocalypse) is hands-down the most debated and confusing book in the biblical text. This is also unfortunate, because Revelation has an incredibly powerful and always timely word for the people of God. Given this neglect and confusion, we will need some tools for our exegetical toolbox.

The label General Epistles has been applied to these books since the time of Eusebius (AD 265–340). Often referred to as the church's

"I looked, and there was a white horse. Its rider held a bow; a crown was given to him, and he went out as a conqueror in order to conquer" (Rev 6:2).

first historian, Eusebius coined the phrase *Catholica/General Epistles* while discussing the books of James and Jude, noting, "Such is the story of James, whose is said to be the first of the epistles called *catholic*." He notes that the book of Jude was also called *catholic* by those who used it in the church.[1] Whatever Eusebius meant by the description "catholic" (not Roman Catholic) or general, it is apt. These eight documents lack some specific historical details such as the geographical location of the original audience and, at least in the case of Hebrews, the identity of the author. Despite these kinds of obstacles, the historical, literary, theological, and responsive tools discussed in the previous chapters are up to the exegetical task. However, they need to be "adjusted" to fit the unique qualities of each book.

---

[1] Eusebius, *Ecclesiastical History* 2.23.

Understanding the Tools for Hebrews

Historical Tools

Some of the same historical tools discussed in the previous chapter are applicable here. For example, Hebrews is still a situational document. The author writes in response to a certain crisis. Hebrews also contains a "story" within a story, and a very high volume of Old Testament (OT) citations and allusions.

History behind Hebrews

Hebrews contains some pressing historical questions. Who wrote it? When was it written? To whom was it written? Why was it written?

Author. Technically, Hebrews is an anonymous writing. The author never identifies himself although he was surely known to the original audience. Scholars have spilled a lot of ink over the years trying to identify the author. Suggestions include Paul, Luke, Apollos, Barnabas, Priscilla & Aquila, and Clement of Rome.[2] Of these candidates, Paul and Luke have consistently remained the most probable throughout the history of interpretation.

Arguments for Pauline authorship include (1) circumstances described in Hebrews 13 have similarities with those described in the Pauline Letters; (2) some theological motifs are similar, such as Christology and two covenants; (3) some Pauline terminology is used; and (4) Pauline authorship was accepted by some patristic writers (e.g., Clement of Alexandria).[3] Arguments against Pauline authorship include

---

[2] I am helped here by House, *Chronological and Background Charts,* 145–50. (see chap. 10, fn. 7).

[3] On the similarities between Heb 13:18–25 and Pauline situations, see Rom 15:30; 2 Cor 1:11–12; Phil 1:24–25; 1 Thess 5:28; 2 Thess 3:18; 1 Tim

(1) other people besides Paul could have the experiences described in Hebrews 13; (2) Paul does not discuss the high priesthood of Christ in the way the writer of Hebrews does; (3) there are 292 words that occur in Hebrews that never occur in Paul's Letters; and (4) many patristic writers did not identify Paul as the author (e.g., Irenaeus, Hippolytus, Gaius of Rome).

Arguments for Lukan authorship include (1) similar styles between Luke-Acts and Hebrews, (2) any Pauline thoughts in Hebrews could be a result of Luke's connection to Paul, and (3) similarities between Stephen's speech in Acts 7 and Hebrews. Arguments against Lukan authorship include (1) similar styles could be attributed to Luke and the writer of Hebrews using the same traditional material from the early church and (2) did Stephen or did Luke write the speech in Acts 7?

In the final analysis, the patristic writer Origen might have said it best: "But who wrote the epistle, in truth God knows." If we could definitively identity Luke, Paul, or anyone else as the author, what impact would it have on interpretation? One small impact it might have is that interpreters would more readily interpret Hebrews in relation to Paul's Letters or Luke-Acts. Yet that is something we can do regardless of whom we identify as the author. In fact, interpreting one part of the NT in relation to another should always be part of the interpretive process.

Date. The most likely range of dates for Hebrews is AD 55–62.[4] The evidence within Hebrews for this range of dates includes (1) the writer is addressing a second generation of Christians (Heb 2:3), which would mean they arose not earlier than the 50s AD; (2) there is a reference to

---

3:9; 2 Tim 1:2; and Phlm 22.

[4] I am helped here by Carson and Moo, *Introduction to the New Testament,* 605–08. (see chap. 9, n. 2).

*While we should think hard about the authorship of
Hebrews, Origen's conclusion may still be the best one:
"But who wrote the epistle, in truth God knows."*

Timothy (13:23), which means Hebrews was penned during his lifetime; and (3) the references to sacrifices (10:1–2) seem to indicate that
the temple in Jerusalem, destroyed in AD 70, was still standing at the
time Hebrews was written.

Audience. The author most likely wrote to a group of Christians
perhaps located in Jerusalem, given the emphasis on the priesthood,
temple, and use of OT, or the city of Rome. Many identify Rome as
the location of the original audience due to the writer's statement in
13:24, "Greet all your leaders and all the saints. Those who are from
Italy send you greetings." However, it simply is not possible to identify
the location of the original audience with certainty. This is one of the
features of the book that qualifies it as a "general" epistle.

Beyond concerns over location, the original audience was most likely composed of both Jewish and Gentile Christians who were in danger of turning away from faith in Christ altogether and toward a Jewish way of life or toward a form of Christianity that wrongly focused on a Jewish way of life.

Purpose. The most important historical issue for the interpretation of Hebrews is identifying its original purpose. Why did the author pen this document in the first place? That purpose can be summed up in one word—*apostasy*. All the historical clues in Hebrews point to the author's chief concern that his recipients are on the brink of turning away from their faith in Jesus (committing apostasy) and turning away from faith in Christ toward a Jewish way of life or toward a form of Christianity that wrongly focused on a Jewish way of life. That is why he issues warnings, such as, "Watch out, brothers and sisters, so that there won't be in any of you an evil, unbelieving heart that turns away from the living God" (3:12).

The author combats the threat of apostasy through a long and complex argument that aims to show that Jesus is "superior" to whatever alternative form of faith the recipients are considering. Therefore, as the writer makes clear from the outset, the recipients must hold onto the saving word that God has given through his superior Son (1:1–4). This is the purpose that interpreters must keep before them when analyzing every passage in Hebrews. We must ask ourselves, how does this unit of thought contribute to the author's aim of preventing apostasy among his original recipients?

History in Hebrews

Like Paul, the writer of Hebrews is working with a story/history of Jesus as he instructs the recipients. It is a story that accentuates two points: (1) God's prior promise of rest, new covenant, and Jerusalem from above and (2) the Son's superior role as the eternal High Priest. There is a close link between these two points.

God's Prior Promises. Hebrews evokes key pieces of Israel's story from the OT including (1) God's word spoken to the prophets (Heb 1:1–2), (2) Moses's ministry (3:1–6), (3) Israel's wilderness wanderings (3:7–19), (4) Joshua brings the people to "rest" in the Promised Land (4:1–10), (5) priesthood of Levi and Melchizedek (5:1–10; 6:19–7:28; 9:1–10:31), and (6) a new covenant (8; 12:18–24). The writer of Hebrews binds all these pieces together through "promise" and "faith." In short, God promised to establish a new covenant with his people and bring them into eternal rest. Moses's ministry, the Mosaic law, the priestly system (with its tabernacle/temple, priests, and sacrifices), the wilderness wanderings, Joshua's "rest," and the preaching of the prophets were all preparatory and promissory in nature. Through all of this, God promised and prepared his people for something better. That "better" is found in the crucified and risen Jesus who gives better rest, mediates a better covenant as a better mediator, and leads the people to a better Jerusalem.

Superiority of the Son. This better rest, covenant, mediation, and even Jerusalem are made possible through the superiority of the Son. Throughout Hebrews, the writer explains that Jesus is superior to the following: the angels, Moses, Joshua, priests, sacrifices, and tabernacle or temple. Jesus's superiority stems from his better status and work. From the very outset of the sermon, the writer summarizes the Son's superior status and work:

> Long ago God spoke to the fathers by the prophets at different times and in different ways. In these last days, he has spoken to us by his Son. God has appointed him heir of all things and made the universe through him. The Son is the radiance of

God's glory and the exact expression of his nature, sustaining all things by his powerful word. After making purification for sins, he sat down at the right hand of the Majesty on high. So he became superior to the angels, just as the name he inherited is more excellent than theirs. (Heb 1:1–4)

Clearly, the writer portrays Jesus as preexistent (God "made the universe through him") and as a divine participant in God's identity ("exact expression of his nature"). He also underscores Jesus's work, which includes creating, upholding all things, making purification for sin, and sitting at God's right hand. In all of this, Jesus inherited a better "name," which is most likely either Son, Lord, or both. *Name* signals a person's identity and work. For Jesus, that means he is the superior and eternal Son whose work is creative and redemptive. All of this makes him superior to the figures and work that preceded him in Israel's story. In fact, those figures and actions were a shadow of the real thing who is Jesus. Therefore, the recipients must hold fast to the word God has spoken through his "superior" Son if they are to participate in the new covenant and eventually reach eternal rest in the Jerusalem that will descend from above.

Literary Tools

There are several literary tools that we need for the interpretation of Hebrews. We need a grasp of the following items: (1) genre, (2) literary structure, (3) literary devices, and (4) OT usage.

Genre

The genre of Hebrews is genuinely unique in comparison to the other twenty-six documents of the NT. That is because Hebrews is an ancient homily or sermon. Although there is a letter closing (Heb 13:18–25), the bulk of the book is a sermon. Hebrews "sounds," or reads, as a sermon. The oscillation between exposition and exhortation bears the marks of a sermon.

Structure

Scholars rarely, if ever, agree on the precise structure of any book in the NT, including Hebrews. Nevertheless, the notion of a "sermonic" structure in Hebrews has strong support. The key to this structure is the

Charles Spurgeon is one of the most gifted preachers from the 19th century. His sermons consisted of explaining the biblical text followed by exhortation from the text. The structure of Hebrews follows a similar pattern.

back-and-forth movement between the writer's exposition of Jesus's superiority and his exhortation based on that exposition. These expositions and exhortations are tied to the sermon's main idea: the recipients must hold onto the saving word spoken by God through the superior Son.

Hebrews

(1:1–4) *Main idea of sermon*—Hold onto the saving word spoken by God through the superior Son.

(1:5–14) *Exposition 1*—Jesus is superior to the angels.

(2:1–4) *Exhortation 1*—Do not drift away from the saving word.

(2:5–3:11) *Exposition 2*—Jesus is superior to angels; nullified work of devil; superior to Moses.

(3:12–15) *Exhortation 2*—Beware of an unbelieving heart and encourage one another in the saving word.

(3:16–19) *Exposition 3*—Wilderness generation did not enter "rest" due to unbelief in saving word.

(4:1–3) *Exhortation 3*—Fear not entering the eternal rest.

(4:4–10) *Exposition 4*—An eternal Sabbath rest remains for God's people.

(4:11–16) *Exhortation 4*—Be eager to enter the eternal rest and, because you have a great high priest, hold to confession of the saving word.

(5:1–10) *Exposition 5*—Jesus is a better high priest who offers better help than other priests.

(5:11–6:17) *Exhortation 5*—The lazy and immature recipients need to move on to maturity in hearing the saving word to avoid falling away from grace.

(6:18–10:18) *Exposition 6*—Jesus is from a better priestly order (Melchizedek), mediating a better covenant, serving in a better sanctuary, and offering a better sacrifice.

(10:19–31) *Exhortation 6*—Draw near to Jesus by faith rather than falling away in the hands of judgment (10:31).

(10:32–11:40) *Exposition 7*—The righteous have always lived by faith in the word of promise.

(12:1–29) *Exhortation 7*—Look to Jesus, proclaimed in the word of promise.

(13:1–17) *Concluding exhortations*

(13:18–25) *Closing*

Although I have neatly divided exposition and exhortation here, there is overlap between all of them. They overlap with the author's concern that the recipients cling to the saving word that God spoke through Jesus rather than face the consequence of turning away from it.

Literary Devices

The writer of Hebrews uses several different literary devices throughout his sermon. These devices serve multiple purposes.[5] Overall, they hold the sermon together and move it forward. Interpreters should attempt to identify these devices and determine how they are being used in the sermon.

Anaphora. This is the repetition of a certain word within a unit of thought. The writer repeats a term for emphasis and/or because it is

---

[5] I am helped here by George Guthrie's discussion of literary devices in Hebrews. See G.H. Guthrie, *The Structure of Hebrews: A Text-Linguistic Analysis* (Grand Rapids: Baker, 1998).

critical to his argument. For example, in Heb 3:11–4:13 the term *rest* appears ten times.[6] The entire section revolves around the theme of rest.

Antithesis. The author juxtaposes two contrasting concepts. For example, the author contrasts the priesthood of Aaron and the priesthood of Melchizedek to show that Jesus's priesthood is superior (Heb 7:1–19).

Hook-Words. When the writer wishes to connect one section to the next, he "hooks" them together by using the same term at the end of one section and the beginning of the next. For example, the author refers to Melchizedek in Heb 6:20, which ends a section, and then uses Melchizedek in 7:1 to begin a new section.

Use of the OT

I sometimes tell students that if you took the OT "stuff" out of Hebrews there would be nothing left. The author cites and alludes to passages from every part of the OT. Overall, he uses the OT to explain and support the overarching point of his sermon—hold onto the saving word of God spoken through Jesus (1:1–4). I will highlight here two primary ways that the author makes use of the OT.

Christological Use. The author of Hebrews views Jesus through the lens of key figures, moments, and covenants from Israel's past. First, he links Jesus to the identities of OT figures, including (1) Yahweh, (2) Moses, (3) Joshua, and (4) high priests. Hebrews 1 makes it clear that Jesus participates in Yahweh's divine identity. He also explains that Jesus

---

[6] Heb 3:11, 18; 4:1, 3, 5, 8, 9, 10, 11.

surpasses the work done by Moses, Joshua, and Israel's high priests. The interpreter should pay close attention to how Jesus participates in Yahweh's identity and how he surpasses prominent figures from Israel's past. Second, the author of Hebrews evokes the Mosaic covenant, especially highlighting its priestly system and requirements, to show that Jesus surpasses it. The writer bases Jesus's superiority to the Mosaic covenant and its sacrificial requirements on the fact that it served only as a shadow or introduction to the better things brought about by Jesus. For example, he writes, "Since the law [Mosaic law] has only a shadow of the good things to come, and not the reality itself of those things, it can never perfect the worshipers by the same sacrifices they continually offer year after year" (10:1). Given the historical situation behind Hebrews (see above), this kind of description of the Mosaic law is fitting. One cannot turn away from the "true form" (i.e., Jesus) to the "shadow" of him (i.e., sacrificial system in Mosaic law).

Ecclesiastical Use. The author also uses the OT to explain how the recipients in this early Christian community should live by faith in the word God spoke through Jesus (Heb 1:1–2). One of the sermon's common exhortations is to "hold fast" to faith in the crucified and risen Jesus (3:6; 4:14; 6:18; 10:23). The nature of that faith is exemplified both negatively and positively by figures from Israel's past. Negatively, the author points to Israel's wilderness generation (3:7–19). He attributes their failure to enter the Promised Land to unbelief, "So we see that they were unable to enter because of unbelief" (3:19). The author warns the recipients not to fail in the same unbelieving way. Positively, the author appeals to a panoply of figures from the OT who persevered in their belief that they would eventually inherit what God had promised them. The one who is right before God (righteous; 10:36–39) must live by the kind of faith exemplified in a wide range of OT figures. (See chart.)

Old Testament Faith Noted Exemplarily in Hebrews

OT Figure	Hebrews	OT Reference
Abel	11:4	Genesis 4
Enoch	11:5	Genesis 5:21–24
Noah	11:7	Genesis 6–9
Abraham	11:8–10, 17–19	Genesis 12–25
Sarah	11:11–12	Genesis 17 & 21
Isaac	11:20	Genesis 27:27–29
Jacob	11:21	Genesis 48
Joseph	11:22	Genesis 50:24
Moses's Parents	11:23	Exodus 2
Moses	11:24–29	Exodus 1–15
Rahab	11:30–31	Joshua 2; 6:14–16:25
Gideon	11:32–38	Judges 6
Barak	11:32–38	Judges 4
Samson	11:32–38	Judges 13
Jephthah	11:32–38	Judges 11–12
David	11:32–38	1 Samuel 16–2 Samuel 24; 1 Kings 1–2 Kings 2:11
Samuel	11:32–38	1 Samuel 1:1–28:20
Prophets (esp. Elijah & Elisha)	11:32–38	1 Kings 17:1–2 Kings 2:14; 2 Kings 2:1–13:21

The faith in God's saving word that "pleases" him is the kind demonstrated by these various figures (Heb 11:6). Specifically, these figures died without seeing what God promised them (11:12–16, 39–40). The author focuses especially on figures from Genesis and Exodus. The interpreter should read the wider narratives that describe the various figures evoked by the author of Hebrews.

The common thread in these OT figures is a faith in God's promise that endured unto death even though they did not actually see the fulfillment. In this way, the readers of Hebrews must believe in what God promised through Jesus even unto death.

Theological Tools

The theological motifs in Hebrews revolve around the saving word spoken through Jesus and Jesus's superiority. Enduring faith in Jesus's word is well placed because of who he is, and faith in him has a blessed outcome.

The Superiority of Jesus

The picture of Jesus's superiority in Hebrews is marked by three main features. First, Jesus has a better "name" than the angels or any other figure whom God has sent. The writer notes that Jesus, having made purification for sins and having sat down at God's right hand, "inherited" a better name (Heb 1:1–4). "Name" is a shorthand way of referring to Jesus's person, work, and status. He is the eternal Son of God (1:2–3) whose eternal priestly work is based on his death and resurrection. Jesus is the eternal Son of God (1:5–9) who always intercedes as the eternal high priest for the believer (7:25) and never changes (13:8). He surpasses Moses in the way he "builds" an eternal people of God, because he builds as God's eternal Son not merely as a servant (3:1–6). He surpasses Joshua, because he brings the people into an eternal "rest" in the new Jerusalem (3:7–4:11). He surpasses earthly high priests for the following reasons: (1) his sanctuary is in heaven before God, not on the earth; (2) he is without sin, unlike earthly priests who must first offer a sacrifice for their own sin; (3) as a sacrifice he offered his own blood, not merely the blood of goats and bulls; (4) his sacrifice was "once and for all," rather than repeated day by day and year by year; and (5) earthly priests must be replaced because they die, while Jesus was raised from the dead. Clearly, the superiority of Jesus means the recipients must hold to the word God spoke through him.

The "Completion" of Jesus as the Source of the Believer's Completion

The writer of Hebrews uniquely crafts a high view of Jesus's superiority. For as high as the writer portrays Jesus, he also brings him quite low. We find that Jesus's superiority includes what he experienced and accomplished during his time on earth. He refers to Jesus's earthly ministry at various points in his sermon: "During his earthly life, he offered prayers and appeals with loud cries and tears to the one who was able to save him from death, and he was heard because of his reverence. Although he was the Son, he learned obedience from what he suffered. After he was perfected, he became the source of eternal salvation for all who obey him" (5:7–9).

The phrase *was perfected* does not imply that Jesus, either before his incarnation and after it, was somehow morally imperfect. In fact, it is the writer of Hebrews who assures us that "we do not have a high priest who is unable to sympathize with our weaknesses, but one who has been tempted in every way as we are, yet without sin" (4:15). Instead, "was perfected" refers to Jesus completing the will of God (10:7) through suffering (2:10), especially in his life and death.

This "completion" of Jesus has two results for the writer of Hebrews. First, Jesus's completion (i.e., doing the will of God) becomes the source and guarantee of the believer's completion. The law and its sacrifices could never complete people (10:1). In other words, those things never sufficed for doing God's will as he required it. Yet, in Jesus being "perfected" (completed; doing God's will), he becomes the "source of eternal salvation for all who obey him" (5:9). The ultimate goal of that completion is resurrection from the dead with all the people of God in the new Jerusalem (11:39–40; 12:18–29). Second, Jesus's "completion," which came through the earthly suffering that his Father subjected him to, provides a pattern for the recipients of the sermon. God the Father is completing and disciplining them as

The writer of Hebrews speaks of another Jerusalem, a heavenly
one that will come from above in a new heavens and earth.

sons, which means they must suffer. As the writer explains, "For the
Lord disciplines the one he loves and punishes every son he receives
(12:6; Prov 3:12).

The Goal of a Heavenly Jerusalem

There is only one reference to Jerusalem in the sermon of Hebrews. It
occurs toward the end: "Instead, you have come to Mount Zion, to the
city of the living God (the heavenly Jerusalem), to myriads of angels, a
festive gathering" (12:22). However, the number of occurrences is not
a good measure of its importance to the writer's theology. As noted in
the previous section, Hebrews emphasizes the completion of those who
are holding to God's saving word in Christ. Metaphorically, they are
moving toward a goal. They are approaching the "heavenly Jerusalem"
through the superior and priestly work of Christ (12:23–25). However,
this does not mean that the goal is ultimately escape through death

followed by entrance into heaven.[7] The writer exhorts his listeners to look for the city, which is to come to them, "For we do not have here a lasting city, but we seek the city that is to come" (13:14). Earlier in the sermon, he refers to the "world [that is] to come" (2:5). So when we consider the eschatology (teaching on the last things) of Hebrews, we find that the writer exhorts his hearers to seek what is coming to them, which is a new world (2:5), a new homeland (11:14), and a new Jerusalem (12:22), which is coming to them (13:14) as they hold fast to the saving word and find their completion in their eternal high priest.

Responsive Tools

If you read Hebrews and miss the response the author seeks from his listeners, you are not reading closely enough. There is a repeated emphasis on "holding fast" to, or enduring in, the saving word that God spoke through his Son (Heb 3:6, 14; 10:23). The author explains at length what stands behind this exhortation. In short, the reader must hold fast to the saving word in Christ, because he is superior to anyone or anything that one might turn to including the Mosaic law and its priestly prescriptions. After all, those things are meant only to introduce and foreshadow the superior person and work of the eternal Son.

Putting the Tools to Use for Hebrews

It is now time to put these various tools to interpretive use. Heb 2:14–18 provides a good test case.

---

[7] This is not the goal in any of the NT's eschatology. The NT writers repeatedly point to bodily resurrection from the dead as the goal. See, e.g., John 5:25; Rom 8:23–25; 1 Cor 15:35–57; 1 Thess 4:13–17.

Historical Tools

1. How is this passage linked to the sermon's original historical purpose?
2. How does the history/story in Hebrews (see above) inform our understanding of this passage?

Literary Tools

1. Is Heb 2:14–18 exposition or exhortation? How does Heb 2:14–18 fit into the overall structure of the sermon?
2. What is the "hook word" that connects Heb 2:14–18 to 2:10–13? Explain this connection.
3. Does the writer make any Christological or ecclesiastical use of the OT in this passage? Explain.

Theological and Responsive Tools

1. Which of the sermon's theological motifs is reflected in Heb 2:14–18? Explain.
2. How does the writer want the listener to respond to this passage? How does that response compare to the overarching response to the sermon?

Understanding the Tools for James

Historical Tools

History behind the Text

Author. In James 1:1, the author identifies himself as "James a servant of God and of the Lord Jesus Christ." He could have also introduced himself as "James the brother of Jesus." That is because the author of this book is most likely James, the half-brother of Jesus, Mark 6:3 provides the names of Jesus's brothers, and one of them is "James." Although the NT mentions several people by the name of James, James the brother of Jesus is most likely the author of this book.[8] The following points support this identification:

1. *Name recognition.* The writer in James 1:1 does not attempt to identify himself with any more specificity than "James." This implies that the author was a well-known James.

2. *The only remaining well-known James.* Most likely, the only well-known James alive during this time was James the brother of Jesus. James the son of Zebedee and brother of John is the other well-known James from the early church, but he suffered martyrdom at a date earlier than the production of this document (Acts 12:2).

3. *Authority of author.* James the brother of Jesus possessed a great deal of authority in early Christianity, especially at the church in Jerusalem (Acts 12:17; 15:13; 21:18; Gal 1:19).[9]

Date. The book of James has an early date. James most likely penned the work in the early to middle 40s AD.

Audience. The author does not identify the audience explicitly. Yet the instruction he gives indicates that the recipients are hurting due to many causes. Based on these comments in the book, the following picture of this early Christian community emerges:

---

[8] E.g., James the son of Zebedee—one of the twelve disciples (Mark 1:19; 5:37; 9:2; 10:35; Acts 12:2); James the son of Alphaeus—one of the twelve disciples (Matt 10:3; Mark 2:14; 3:18; Luke 6:15; Acts 1:13); and James the father of Judas (Luke 6:16; Acts 1:13).

[9] I am helped here by the conversation in Köstenberger, Kellum, and Quarles, *Cradle,* 703–11. (see chap. 2, n. 12).

"Isn't this the carpenter, the son of Mary, and the brother of James, Joses, Judas, and Simon? And aren't his sisters here with us?" (Mark 6:3).

1. *Externally afflicted community.* In James 1:1, the author addresses his recipients as "the twelve tribes dispersed abroad." This is obviously a metaphorical reference, but it does indicate that the recipients may have especially being experiencing the pain of feeling like outsiders in their community and of being away from the Lord (cf. 1 Pet 1:1). The precise nature of their external affliction is difficult to pinpoint. However, if these are Christian readers who had been "scattered" from Jerusalem due to persecution (Acts 11:19), then James is ministering to his "scattered flock by mail."[10]

2. *Internally afflicted community.* The congregation's affliction may not have come from external forces alone. Some of the document's instructions and warnings may indicate internal

---

[10] Carson and Moo, *Introduction to the New Testament*, 629.

problems such as tensions between wealthy and poor Christians (James 1:9–11; 2:1–13).

Purpose. The preceding description of the community hints at part of the book's original purpose. External and internal afflictions arose that required James's "wisdom," a wisdom that comes "from above" (James 3:15). However, the wisdom that James discusses transcends this historical moment in the community. James sets this wisdom against the backdrop of final judgment. He provides the wisdom that will help them through their current affliction, but, more important, it is wisdom that will prepare them for Christ's return and the day of judgment he brings. This backdrop of final judgment occurs in various places in the book:

> What good is it, my brothers and sisters, if someone claims to have faith but does not have works? Can such faith save him? (2:14)

> Not many should become teachers, my brothers, because you know that we will receive a stricter judgment (3:1).

> Brothers and sisters, do not complain about one another, so that you will not be judged. Look, the judge stands at the door! (5:9).

History in the Text

The history, or story, that James works with in his wisdom letter is built on at least two main pillars.

The Gospel Is Axiomatic. It is true that James does not contain explicit references to the death and resurrection of Jesus. This is surprising, given the central role that the crucified and risen Jesus plays in all the other documents of the NT. However, it does not follow that James neglects the gospel, challenges it, or changes it. Instead, he assumes it. It is taken for granted, or axiomatic, that the letter's recipients have received by faith the good news of Jesus's death and resurrection. In fact, he briefly hints at this experience in at least two passages:

> By his own choice, he gave us birth by the word of truth so that we would be a kind of firstfruits of his creatures. (1:18)

> Therefore, ridding yourselves of all moral filth and the evil that is so prevalent, humbly receive the implanted word, which is able to save your souls. (1:21)

James refers to the gospel as the "word of truth" and "implanted word." He acknowledges that it is this "word," or gospel, that makes his recipients a new "creation" and saves them. Interpreters must understand that for James the gospel is axiomatic. Although he does not discuss in detail Jesus's death and resurrection, he assumes that message and its power to save his recipients.

Wisely Prepare for the Lord's Arrival. James's story in his wisdom letter is also built on the Lord's arrival and the final judgment that will ensue. James writes to believers who must prepare for that arrival in two contrasting ways. On the one hand, they need to consider how they speak, if they act impartially toward others, the nature of saving faith, and related concerns. On the other hand, they should find comfort in the truth that Jesus will return and judge their oppressive enemies. James warns these oppressors, "Look! The pay that you withheld from the workers who mowed your fields cries out, and the outcry of the harvesters has reached the ears of the Lord of Hosts" (5:4). He follows this warning by addressing the oppressed, "Therefore, brothers and sisters, be patient until the Lord's coming. See how the farmer waits for the precious fruit of the earth and is patient with it until it receives the early and the late rains" (5:7). In this way, James operates with a story in which the believer must (1) prepare for the Lord's return by living wisely but also (2) patiently wait for the Lord to return and make things right.

Literary Tools

Genre

As I have noted in previous chapters, genre is like a "contract." The author agrees to write in a certain way and follow certain literary conventions. Some interpreters have identified James as an ancient sermon. Although it does have some sermonic features, the book is primarily an ancient Christian wisdom letter.[11] It shares similarities with other wisdom writings, such as Proverbs and the Sermon on the Mount (Matthew 5–7). James provides wisdom for Christian living, and he covers a wide range of topics in the process, including the following:

1. Seeking wisdom from God (1:1–8)
2. How to view wealth and poverty (1:9–11)
3. The source of temptation (1:13–15)
4. The divine source of good and wisdom (1:17–18)
5. Relationship between faith and works (1:19–20; 2:14–26)
6. Nature of "true religion" (1:27)
7. The believer's speech (1:19–20, 26; 3:1–12)
8. Avoiding friendship with the world (4:1–10)
9. Make future plans humbly (4:13–17)
10. Wait for vindication in Christ (5:1–12)
11. Sickness, suffering, and prayer (5:13–20)

---

[11] Some scholars refer to this as a "literary letter." Carson and Moo, *Introduction to the New Testament*, 629.

Literary Structure

James has the loosest structure of any NT document. At many points in the letter, it is very difficult to see how one unit of thought is related to preceding and subsequent units of thought. What clearly holds the whole letter together is James's emphasis on wisdom for everyday living until the day of the Lord. Therefore, each piece of wisdom that James gives is part of a larger structure that collectively tells the Christian how to live by faith and wisdom until the Lord's arrival.

Echoes of Jesus

James demonstrates a familiarity with the teachings of Jesus. At various points, James echoes the teachings of Jesus, particularly those found in the Sermon on the Mount (Matthew 5–7).[12]

The Sermon on the Mount as Echoed in James

James	Sermon on the Mount
Testing (1:2)	Matt 5:11–12
Call for perfection (1:4)	Matt 5:48
Asking/Receiving from God (1:5, 17; 4:2–3)	Matt 7:7–11
Anger and righteousness (1:20)	Matt 5:22
Doing the word (1:22–23)	Matt 7:24, 26
Inheritance of kingdom by poor (2:5)	Matt 5:3, 5
Judgment without mercy (2:13)	Matt 7:1–6
Fruit of good works (3:12)	Matt 7:16–18
Divided loyalties (4:4)	Matt 6:24

---

[12] This chart is an adaption of a chart in Köstenberger, Kellum, and Quarles, *Cradle,* 706.

Blessing of pure in heart (4:8)	Matt 5:8
Warning about wealth (5:1–3)	Matt 6:19–21
Persecuted like prophet (5:10)	Matt 5:11–12
Oaths forbidden (5:12)	Matt 5:33–37

James did not write with a copy of Matthew in front of him. Rather, he and Matthew use the same Jesus tradition preserved through oral teaching and eyewitnesses. The interpreter should consider the overlap between James's wisdom and the wisdom Jesus shares in the Sermon on the Mount. Considering this overlap may illuminate the wisdom James shares.

Use of the OT

James makes judicious use of the OT. He draws from a wide range of OT books, including Genesis, Exodus, Leviticus, Deuteronomy, Joshua, 1 Kings, Job, Psalms, Jeremiah, Proverbs, Ecclesiastes, and 2 Chronicles. Not surprisingly, given the book's genre, James's concern with wisdom dominates his use of the OT. Two examples are offered here.

Justification by a Faith That Really Works and Saves. In James 2:14–26, James combines two passages from the Abrahamic narrative as part of his effort to explain that only a faith that is accompanied by works can save (2:14). First, he alludes to Genesis 22 and the binding of Isaac. James asks, "Wasn't Abraham our Father justified by works in offering Isaac his son on the altar?" (2:21). Second, he cites Gen 15:6 and adds to it a description of Abraham from 2 Chr 20:7. He writes, "And the Scripture was fulfilled that says, Abraham believed God, and it was credited to him as righteousness, and he was called God's friend" (2:23). He also evokes the figure of Rahab from Joshua 2 as part of his argument, "In the same way, wasn't Rahab the prostitute also justified by works in receiving the messengers and sending them out by a different route?" (2:25).[13]

Abraham and Rahab provide James with two figures who exemplify the kind of faith he has in view. James contrasts a living faith and a dead faith, or a faith that saves and one that does not. It is works that distinguish the two kinds of faith. James does not suggest that one is made right with God (i.e., justified) through faith and works. Instead, he argues that only one kind of faith justifies, and it is one that is accompanied by works, such as those carried out by Abraham and Rahab. For example, God reckoned Abraham's faith as righteousness (i.e., a right standing with him). Abraham then, by faith, offered his son Isaac as a sacrifice as commanded even though God did not ultimately take his son. In this way, Abraham's justifying faith was accompanied by a work done out of faith. It is the kind of faith that James has in mind. In short, a faith that works is a faith that saves.

Exemplars of Eschatological Patience and Righteous Prayer. James 5 evokes two key figures from Israel's Scriptures. First, while exhorting his recipients to patiently wait on the Lord's return as they suffer, James evokes the figure of Job: "See, we count as blessed those who have endured. You have heard of Job's endurance and have seen the outcome that the Lord brought about—the Lord is compassionate and merciful" (5:11). Job's story touches on many elements related to suffering and God's ways. James focuses specifically on the patience Job demonstrated in his suffering. From James's perspective, Job exemplifies the patience and hope that early Christians needed to live with as they awaited God's compassion and mercy they would experience at the return of Jesus (5:7–9). Just as God showed Job compassion and mercy in the end (Job 42:10–17), the same awaits those who patiently wait on the Lord Jesus.

---

[13] Joshua 2; 6:17–25.

Similarly, James evokes Elijah as an example of how God answers the prayer of a righteous person who suffers (James 5:13–20). He explains, "Elijah was a human being as we are, and he prayed earnestly that it would not rain, and for three years and six months it did not rain on the land" (5:17). This reference to Elijah echoes the account in 1 Kings 17–18 that includes the prophet's prediction of a three-year drought that will not end except "by my word" (1 Kgs 17:1). After conquering the prophets of Baal and reviving a widow's son, he prays for the drought to end, and the rains come (1 Kgs 18:41–45). James sees Elijah as an assurance that God answers the cries of the righteous. Therefore, the recipients of his letter can pray with the same assurance.

James encourages his recipients to pray like the OT prophet Elijah, believing that God answers the cries of the righteous.

Theological Tools

James, Paul, and Justification by Faith

Interpreters are often baffled by the apparent contradiction between the ways that James and Paul discuss justification by faith. On the surface, when you juxtapose some of their statements, it can be theologically jarring:

> If Abraham was justified by works, he has something to brag about—but not before God. For what does the Scripture say? Abraham believed God and it was credited to him for righteousness. Now to the one who works, pay is not credited as a gift, but as something owed. But to the one who does not work, but believes on him who declares the ungodly to be righteous, his faith is credited for righteousness. (Rom 4:2–5)

> The Scripture was fulfilled that says, Abraham believed God, and it was credited to him as righteousness, and he was called God's friend. You see that a person is justified by works and not by faith alone. (James 2:23–24)

So Paul insists a person is justified apart from works, while James insists a person is not justified by faith alone. What should we conclude? Some have concluded that James is combating Paul's theology of justification by faith alone. Therefore, James and Paul contradict each other in their views of justification. However, such a conclusion does not adequately consider the wider contexts of James's argument and Pauline theology. James contrasts two kinds of faith. One of them can save from eternal judgment and one of them cannot. This is evident in his question, "What good is it, my brothers and sisters, if someone claims to have faith but does not have works? Can such faith save him?" (2:14). The answer is clearly no—because faith that saves is accompanied by works. In his argument, James *never* says, "A person is justified by works." He says, "A person is justified by works and not by faith alone." The "not by faith alone" is a reference to the useless faith (i.e., a faith that cannot save) that he has in view from the outset of his argument. His argument comes down to one issue: what kind of faith really saves? Answer? A faith that produces or is accompanied by works.

Paul says the same thing in a different way and context. Like James, Paul was accustomed to combating erroneous views of faith. For example, in discussing with the Romans God's grace, Paul anticipates the false conclusion one might draw. He asks, "What shall we say then? Should we continue in sin so that grace may multiply? Absolutely not! How can we who died to sin still live in it?" (Rom 6:1–2). This is Paul's version of James's question: is that kind of faith able to save? The answer is "absolutely not." Although neither Paul nor James teaches that salvation/justification is by works, they do teach that saving faith is accompanied by or produces works. As Paul tells the Galatians, "For in Christ Jesus neither circumcision nor uncircumcision accomplishes anything; what matters is faith working through love" (Gal 5:6).

Divine Vindication at the Lord's Return

One of the most underappreciated theological motifs in the NT is the believer's vindication. By "vindication," I am referring to that moment in which God judges the enemies of his people to show that he and his people were in the right all along despite all they suffered. James picks up this motif, especially in the last section of his letter. He does so in two ways. First, James condemns an unidentified group of rich people who oppress the poor, "Come now, you rich people, weep and wail over the miseries that are coming on you" (5:1). He notes that the cries of the oppressed have reached God, "Look! The pay that you withheld from the workers who mowed your fields cries out, and the outcry of the harvesters has reached the ears of the Lord of Hosts" (5:4). This is an ominous note. If one reads between the lines, the implication is that God has heard, and he will judge you (see Exod 22:22–24). James goes on to accuse the rich oppressors of self-indulgence and murder of the righteous (5:5–6). Second, James turns his attention to the oppressed believers and assures them of vindication (5:7–12). Specifically, Jesus will vindicate them upon his arrival. Therefore, he admonishes "You also must be patient. Strengthen your hearts, because the Lord's coming is near" (5:8).

We tend to think of Jesus's return as an ominous event. Yet, for the believer, the return of Jesus is portrayed as a joyful event for those who are prepared. James sets out to prepare believers for that moment. He wants it to be joyful for them. However, he knows the realities of life. He knows that they are being or will be oppressed by those outside the believing community. Such experiences could cause believers to lose heart, or become disgruntled (5:9). That is why James assures his recipients that God will vindicate them against their enemies when the Lord returns. Until then, they must be patient and supportive of one another.

Responsive Tools in James

In a nutshell, James wants his readers to be wise. He wants them to be wise in the way they pray, in the way they treat others with impartiality, in the way they speak, in the way they care for the marginalized, in the way they plan for the future, in the way they face temptation, in the way they respond to mistreatment, in the way they respond to sickness, and in the way they respond to sinners who wander from God (5:19–20). He gives wisdom with the assumption that his readers have already received the word of the gospel that has been implanted in them and is able to save them (1:21). Yet they must wisely receive that word and live it out until the return of the Lord.

Putting the Tools to Use for James

Very quickly, let's put these tools to work in James. We will use James 1:2–4 as a test case.

Historical Tools

1. How is James 1:2–4 related to the overall purpose of the letter?

Literary Tools

1. Does this passage echo any part of the Sermon on the Mount (see above)? How does that echo influence your interpretation of James 1:2–4?

Theological Tools

1. If the reader heeds the wisdom of James 1:2–4, how might that impact the reading of justification in James 2:14–26?

Responsive Tools

1. Is James asking us joyfully to deny the pain we experience as Christians? Explain in light of James's emphasis on vindication.

Understanding the Tools for 1 & 2 Peter

Historical Tools

History behind the Text

Author. According to 1 Pet 1:1 and 2 Pet 2:1, the apostle Peter is the author of both these letters. Peter's authorship of 1 Peter is not hotly contested. However, many scholars have questioned the Petrine authorship of 2 Peter. Reasons for their skepticism include the following:

1. Eusebius (fourth century) questioned the authenticity of 2 Peter.[14]
2. 1 Peter contains many OT allusions; 2 Peter does not.
3. 60 percent of vocabulary in 2 Peter is not found in 1 Peter.
4. The Greek style seems out of reach for a Galilean fisherman.
5. Different literary styles are evident in 1 Peter and 2 Peter.

These points are representative of the arguments often made against Petrine authorship of 2 Peter. Notice that many of them are linked to comparisons with 1 Peter. Arguments for Petrine authorship of 2 Peter include the following:

1. Patristic writings such as 1 Clement and *Epistle of Barnabas* attribute the letter to Peter.
2. 2 Peter 2 evokes multiple OT passages.
3. Vocabulary differences between 1 & 2 Peter could be explained by Peter's use of different scribes for the two letters or by the fact that we do not know the extent of Peter's vocabulary.

---

[14] I am helped here by House, *Chronological and Background Charts*, 150.

The same Peter who denied Christ and found restoration
in him is the same one who penned 1-2 Peter.

4. The Greek style in 2 Peter is not necessarily impossible for a Galilean fisherman. Additionally, we do not know everything about Peter's "intellectual" background.

While there are stylistic and theological differences in 1 & 2 Peter, the differences do not rise to the level of different authorship.

Date. Peter most likely penned 1 Peter around AD 63–64 and 2 Peter shortly thereafter (ca. AD 65).

Audience. First Peter begins by mentioning locations in northern Asia Minor (modern-day Turkey), "Peter, an apostle of Jesus Christ: To those chosen, living as exiles dispersed abroad in Pontus, Galatia, Cappadocia, Asia, and Bithynia" (1 Pet 1:1). These geographical references represent as a "crescent-shaped region of northern Asia Minor."[15] Second Peter presumably addresses the same recipients.

Beyond geographical locales, Peter refers to these recipients as the dispersion (1 Pet 1:1; cf. James 1:1). The metaphor evokes images of a people on the move but not really at home. Peter later refers to the audience as "strangers and exiles" (1 Pet 2:11). These descriptions coincide with Peter's emphasis on the suffering of believers in both letters.

Purpose. The historical purpose behind 1 Peter is the encouragement of believers in Asia Minor who are suffering some form of persecution and social ostracism. Their hurt is directly linked to their faith in Christ and the righteous lifestyle that results from it. This is evident in one of Peter's admonitions, "For there has already been enough time spent in doing what the Gentiles choose to do: carrying on in unrestrained behavior, evil desires, drunkenness, orgies, carousing, and lawless idolatry. They are surprised that you don't join them in the same flood of wild living—and they slander you" (1 Pet 4:3–4). In encouraging them to endure their sufferings until the return of Jesus (1 Pet 1:3–9), Peter wants to make sure they suffer for doing good rather than evil (1 Pet 2:20; 3:17). Additionally, as they suffer and wait, they must live holy lives in the church, in the home, and in the world.

The historical purpose behind 2 Peter also stems from a need for believers in Asia Minor to wait upon the Lord as they suffer. However, the source of their suffering in 2 Peter stems from false teachers/prophets who are especially immoral in their conduct. Peter devotes more space to their conduct than to the content of their false teaching and likens them to "irrational animals" (2 Pet 2:12), "springs without water"

---

[15] Köstenberger, Kellum, and Quarles, *Cradle,* 736.

Peter, like Paul (1 Cor 10:1-13), saw parallels between the early church and ancient Israel who, after the Exodus, wandered in the wilderness as "strangers" longing for the Promise Land.

(2:17), and "slaves of corruption" (2:19). He puts them in the same class as rebellious angels (2 Pet 2:4; Gen 6:1–4), flood generation (2 Pet 2:5), and citizens of Sodom and Gomorrah (2 Pet 2:6). Faced with such enemies, Peter reminds his recipients that God has given them divine power to live godly lives in a wicked generation (2 Pet 1:3–11). Their hope is grounded in the prophetic word of the gospel (2 Pet 1:12–21) and the return of Christ that will usher in the new heavens and earth in which righteousness, not wickedness, dwells (2 Pet 3:13).

History in the Text

If Peter has one "story" in view as he writes: it is a story about Christian "exiles/sojourners" waiting for the end, when Jesus returns (1 Pet 1:7; 5:4), judges both the righteous and unrighteous (1 Pet 4:17–19; 2 Pet 2:3–5), and ushers in the new heavens and earth (2 Pet 3:1–13). Their waiting is not marked by complacency or participation in the world's wickedness (1 Pet 4:1–11). Instead, they recognize that God's grace (1 Pet 1:3–9) and power (2 Pet 1:3–11) in Christ enables them to live holy lives in the church and in the world (1 Pet 1:16). They must keep themselves from deceit (2 Pet 3:17) and grow in God's grace (2 Pet

3:18) until the chief Shepherd appears (1 Pet 5:4). Interpreters should have this broader story in view as they read 1 & 2 Peter.

Literary Tools

Since these books are ancient letters, we are helped by what we learned previously in our reflection on Paul's Letters. Specifically, we need to consider the nature of Peter's rhetoric in his letters as well as his use of the OT.

Types of Rhetoric

As a reminder, there are three basic types of ancient rhetoric:

1.   Deliberative rhetoric—a speech aimed to persuade or dissuade the audience
2.   Forensic rhetoric—a speech aimed to accuse or defend
3.   Epideictic rhetoric—a speech aimed to praise or blame

First and Second Peter employ elements of all three types of rhetoric. Peter seeks to persuade his audience that they should endure what they suffer, continue in their faith, and prepare for the Lord's arrival (deliberative). In this persuasion, Peter also defends (forensic) the righteous conduct of his recipients (1 Pet 4:1–11) along with the promise of Jesus's return (2 Pet 3:1–13). On the other hand, he accuses the false prophets of wickedness by classifying them with some of the OT's worst offenders (2 Peter 2). Both letters shower praise on God (epideictic). Peter praises the mercy that God demonstrates through the new birth he gives to believers (1 Pet 1:3–10) and the power he supplies to believers so they might live godly lives and be certain about their election in Christ (2 Pet 1:3–11).

Parts of Rhetoric

As a reminder, the parts of rhetoric consist of the following:

> *Introduction to argument*—the beginning part of the speech where the speaker aims to make the audience open to what is about to be said
>
> *Explanation of problem*—some of the specifics of the disputed matter
>
> *Thesis*—essential proposition
>
> *Support for thesis*—arguments to support the thesis
>
> *Disputation of opposition*—arguments to disprove or weaken opponent's arguments
>
> *Summary of main points*—summary of main points that support thesis and seek to gain favorable response

It is helpful to identify these parts in both 1 & 2 Peter, because it is one way to see how the parts of each letter fit together.

Parts of Rhetoric in 1 Peter. Here is a summary of parts of rhetoric used in 1 Peter.

> *Introduction to argument* (1:3–12)—Peter makes the audience well disposed toward him by praising God for mercifully giving believers a new birth through Jesus Christ, preserving their eternal salvation, and refining their faith in preparation for Jesus's return so that they will receive the full salvation that OT prophets promised.
>
> *Explanation of problem and thesis* (1:13–17)—The recipients, or exiles (1:17), must set their hope on the return of Jesus and live in holiness, because at his return God will judge his people.

Support for thesis (1:18–3:22)—These exiles can live in hope and holiness, because of the following:

> (1:18–21)—God ransomed them through death and resurrection of Christ.
>
> (1:22–25)—God gave them new birth through a "word" that does not perish.
>
> (2:1–10)—God is making them into a spiritual house (2:5) in which Jesus is the cornerstone and each of them is a living stone.
>
> (2:11–17)—As God's exiles (2:11) in the earth, they must battle against fleshly desires and live righteously before governing authorities.
>
> (2:18–25)—Christ's atoning suffering exemplifies how the recipients must endure suffering.
>
> (3:1–7)—Wives and husbands must live exemplary lives before others.
>
> (3:8–17)—The recipients/exiles must not respond to evil with evil, and they must suffer for doing good rather than evil.
>
> (3:18–22)—Christ the righteous One (3:18) suffered for the unrighteous. His work (death/resurrection/descent into hell?) and position at the right hand of God is the source of recipients' salvation and hope.

Disputation of opposition (4:1–19)—Peter argues against the recipients continuing in the life of sin that they once lived (4:1–6). Instead, they should suffer, be wise, stay awake in prayer, and use their spiritual gifts as the return of the Lord draws near (4:7–11). They should not be surprised by their suffering nor should they lose sight of the coming judgment, which will begin with "God's household" (4:17).

Summary of main points (5:1–14)—Peter ends the letter as he began it—with a focus on the "chief Shepherd's" return (5:4). He exhorts elders/shepherds of the church to be humble examples to the flock since God resists the proud but gives grace to the humble (5:5). His closing exhortation focuses on casting burdens on Jesus due to his great care for his people (5:7).

Interpreters of 1 Peter should recognize that Peter gives comfort to a hurting group of believers by directing their attention to the hope of the "Chief Shepherd's" (Jesus's) return (1 Pet 5:4).

Parts of Rhetoric in 2 Peter. And here is a corresponding summary for 2 Peter.

Introduction to argument (1:3–11)—Peter makes the audience well-disposed toward him by explaining to his readers that

God has given them everything they need to live godly lives and enter the eternal kingdom of God (1:12).

Explanation of problem (1:12–15)—The problem that Peter addresses is that his life is nearing its end (1:14); therefore, he is eager to remind them of gospel truth so that they will recall it after he is gone.

Thesis (1:16–21)—The thesis of Peter's letter is that his message about Jesus is from God, and his readers should resist the false teachers among them.

Support for thesis (2:1–22)—Peter supports his *propositio* by explaining that God will judge the false prophets (2:1) among them, despite all appearances otherwise. He criticizes the immorality of the false teachers and likens them to some of the worst examples of evildoers from the OT.

Disputation of opposition (3:1–13)—Peter argues against the false claim that Jesus will not return.

Summary of main points (3:14–18)—Peter concludes his argument by admonishing the recipients to be ready for Jesus's return by keeping themselves unstained by sin (3:14) and resisting false teachers (3:15–16). They must grow in the grace that God grants them in their Savior Jesus Christ (3:18).

Use of the OT

Both letters make extensive use of the OT. Peter uses the OT to encourage the recipients as they suffer and to combat false teachers. He draws primarily from the books of Genesis, Exodus, Leviticus, Psalms, Proverbs, and Isaiah. We will look at one example from 1 Peter and one from 2 Peter. However, note that there are many other OT usages from both letters that we could discuss at length.

The Church as God's Holy People. Both letters use key passages from the Pentateuch to describe what the recipients must be and what they must suffer. These churches in Asia Minor must be "holy" as their God is holy (1 Pet 1:16). This is a brief reference to Lev 11:44, "For I am the LORD your God, so you must consecrate yourselves and be holy because I am holy." Of course, the wider Leviticus context defines holiness in ancient Israel as abstention from certain foods, purification regulations, observance of certain days, and the like. For Peter, holiness is defined by redemption through the blood of Christ in whom believers live holy in every walk of life (1 Pet 1:16–21).

Peter also combines passages from Exodus and Isaiah to describe God's holy people. He tells his recipients, "You yourselves, as living stones, a spiritual house, are being built to be a holy priesthood, to offer spiritual sacrifices acceptable to God through Jesus Christ" (1 Pet 2:5). Peter's description echoes Exod 19:5–6, "'Now if you will carefully listen to me and keep my covenant, you will be my own possession out of all the peoples, although the whole earth is mine, and you will be my kingdom of priests and my holy nation.' These are the words that you are to say to the Israelites." Peter then draws from Isaiah to describe the foundation of this "spiritual house" made up of a holy priesthood, "See, I lay in Zion, a chosen and honored cornerstone, and the one who believes in him will never be put to shame" (1 Pet 2:6; Isa 28:16).

When you put these two OT pieces together in Peter's argument, what is the result? In short, Peter's sojourners, like those in ancient Israel, are God's chosen and holy people. As a "spiritual house," they are called to be holy and act as priests who offer up spiritual sacrifices that are acceptable only through the crucified and risen Jesus who is the cornerstone of the house itself. Clearly, Peter is reading passages such as Exodus 19 typologically. For further reflection on biblical typology, click here.

God's Judgment of the Wicked Does Not Change. As noted above, the recipients of 2 Peter are troubled by false teachers/prophets (2 Pet 2:1). Peter explains that though their judgment may not be seen currently, it does not follow that God's judgment of the wicked is "idle" or "asleep" (2 Pet 2:3). By evoking the judgment of angels from Gen 6:1–4 and the judgment against Sodom and Gomorrah from Genesis 19, Peter makes the point that God's judgment of the wicked does not change. These false prophets, like the wicked from the "ancient world" (2 Pet 2:5), will likewise face divine condemnation.

Theological Tools

These letters contain rich theological motifs that the interpreter must seek to identify and articulate. We will briefly consider two of these motifs.

Holiness Is a Gift

It is significant that Peter begins both letters by explaining what God has given to these believers. In 1 Pet 1:3–11, Peter praises God for the new birth, hope, and inheritance given in Christ. This divine graciousness serves as the sole basis for Peter's admonition that his recipients must be holy as God is holy (1 Pet 1:16). It is their redemption in Christ that sets them apart for holiness and enables it. Peter makes a similar point in 2 Pet 1:3–11. He assures the recipients, "His divine power has given us everything required for life and godliness through the knowledge of him who called us by his own glory and goodness. By these he has given us very great and precious promises, so that through them you may share in the divine nature, escaping the corruption that is in the world because of evil desire" (2 Pet 1:3–4). It is only because of the power that God gives for holiness that Peter can exhort the recipients to be holy (2 Pet 1:5–11). Therefore, in Peter's theology, holiness is a gift.

The End Is Still Near

As previously noted, the widest backdrop for both letters is eschatological in nature. Peter specifically underscores the nearness of Christ's return and final judgment. For example, he declares, "For the time has come for judgment to begin with God's household, and if it begins with us, what will the outcome be for those who disobey the gospel of God?" (1 Pet 4:17). Peter realizes that some scoff at the notion of imminent judgment: scoffers will say, "Where is his 'coming' that he promised? Ever since our ancestors fell asleep, all things continue as they have been since the beginning of creation" (2 Pet 3:4). Peter explains the falsehood of this perspective:

> They deliberately overlook this: By the word of God the heavens came into being long ago and the earth was brought about from water and through water. Through these the world of that time perished when it was flooded. By the same word, the present heavens and earth are stored up for fire, being kept for the day of judgment and destruction of the ungodly.
>
> Dear friends, don't overlook this one fact: With the Lord one day is like a thousand years, and a thousand years like one day. The Lord does not delay his promise, as some understand delay, but is patient with you, not wanting any to perish but all to come to repentance.
>
> But the day of the Lord will come like a thief; on that day the heavens will pass away with a loud noise, the elements will burn and be dissolved, and the earth and the works on it will be disclosed. (2 Pet 3:5–10)

Here we find Peter reflecting extensively on the nearness of the end. Despite mockers who deny God's judgment in the day of Noah (Genesis 6–8) and the judgment to come, Peter insists the end is near. Scoffers deny the end deliberately. Moreover, the time of nearness is determined by God. Therefore, as believers hope for new creation, they should prepare by growing in grace and leaving the judgment of the wicked to God.

Responsive Tools

The argument of Peter's letters indicates that he wants his readers to respond in at least two ways. First, Peter wants the reader to keep hoping in the crucified, risen, and returning Jesus whom they cannot see (1 Pet 1:8). Their suffering is necessary, but it is not God's final word to them (1 Pet 1:6). Despite what others might say, Jesus will usher in a new creation (2 Pet 3:10–15). Second, Peter wants the reader to prepare for the return of Jesus by living in holiness (1 Pet 1:16), entrusting themselves to God (1 Pet 4:19), and trusting that God will judge false teachers (2 Peter 2); he wants them to consider the absence of Jesus as God's patience (2 Pet 3:14) for salvation.

Understanding the Tools for 1, 2, & 3 John

Historical Tools

History behind the Text

These three letters lack historical specificity. Nevertheless, there are some internal clues that allow us to get a sense of the history behind 1, 2, & 3 John.[16]

---

[16] I am helped here by Köstenberger, Kellum, and Quarles, 783–90; Carson and Moo, *Introduction to the New Testament*, 670–75.

Author. The traditional view of authorship is that John the son of Zebedee penned 1 John based on patristic writings (Irenaeus) and the many similarities between this letter and the Gospel of John. In the early centuries of the church, some questioned the Johannine authorship of 2 & 3 John. Nevertheless, they also have patristic support and congruence with the Gospel of John which points to John the son of Zebedee as the author.

Date. These letters are some of the latest documents in the NT. John likely penned these three letters somewhere between AD 90 and 95.

Audience. It is difficult to pinpoint where John's original audience resided. There are some indications that 1 John was a circular letter intended for the church in Ephesus and the surrounding area.[17] Second John is addressed to "the elect lady and her children" (v. 1). This is probably a metaphorical reference to various local congregations. Third John is addressed to "my dear friend Gaius" (v. 1).

Purpose. What historical occasion prompted John to write these three letters? The occasion behind 1 & 2 John involves false teachers who had recently departed from the congregation (most likely in Ephesus). We find in 1 John 2:19, "They went out from us, but they did not belong to us; for if they had belonged to us, they would have remained with us." These false teachers made some audacious and heretical claims, such as (1) the claim to be without sin (1 John 1:5–10), (2) the claim that Jesus was not the Christ (1 John 2:22–23), and (3) the claim that Jesus had not come in the flesh (1 John 4:2–3). Additionally, given the emphasis that John places on loving one another in 1 John, these false

---

[17] E.g., 1 John does not contain specific names of people or places. This could indicate a broader or moral general audience.

teachers did not love those in the congregation. The occasion behind 3 John involves an individual named Diotrephes. John notes, "I wrote something to the church, but Diotrephes, who loves to have first place among them, does not receive our authority" (v. 9).

John's overarching response to these crises can be summed up in two words: *truth* and *love*. The false teachers confused the recipients and raised questions about who and how someone had eternal life. John brings clarity to the confusion by underscoring two simple truths that are summed up in one robust commandment, "Now this is his command: that we believe in the name of his Son Jesus Christ, and love one another as he commanded us" (1 John 3:23).[18]

History in the Text

John works with a history, or "story," about Jesus that focuses on his incarnational work. From John's perspective, Jesus came in the flesh to undo the work of Satan, who continues to oppose Jesus's work through the Antichrist. This "story" is abbreviated in a single statement, "The one who commits [practices] sin is of the devil, for the devil has sinned from the beginning. The Son of God was revealed for this purpose: to destroy the devil's works" (1 John 3:8), which have been murderous and unloving from the time of Cain to the present (1 John 3:11–12). The interpreter should engage each individual passage in relation to this larger narrative framework.

---

[18] John states several times why he wrote the letter. Those statements repeatedly underscore truth and love. See 1 John 2:1, 7, 12, 13, 14, 21, 26; 5:13.

For John, Jesus came to undo the works of the devil that he traces as far back as Cain's murder of Abel (Gen 4:1-16).

Literary Tools

Literary Structure

Once again, it is helpful to see the parts in relation to the whole. Individual passages are not written in a vacuum but as part of a larger argument. I will limit the analysis here to the parts of the rhetoric in 1 John and brief outlines of 2 & 3 John.

Parts of Rhetoric in 1 John.

Introduction to argument (1:1–4)—John reaches out to his audience by reassuring them that he has seen, touched, and heard the risen Jesus. Knowing that the departure of false teachers from the congregation really stung and confused those who remained, John assures them that he is writing because he wants the recipients to have fellowship with Jesus and one another.

Explanation of problem (1:5–10)—The disputed matter in this letter revolves around the false claims of those who left the congregation (see above). They downplayed the reality of sin and denied the identity of Jesus as the incarnate Christ.

Thesis/Propositio (2:1–2)—Due to this disputed matter, John's thesis is that Jesus is indeed the Christ (and "righteous one") who is the recipients' "advocate" with God the Father and the propitiation or atoning sacrifice for their sins.

Support for thesis and disputation of opposition (2:3–4:21)—John supports his thesis by explaining to the recipients what Jesus requires of them and how they can know that they "have" him along with the life he promises. He also refutes the false claims of those who departed from this early Christian community, claims such as that Jesus did not come in the flesh.

Summary of main points (5:1–21)—John sums up how individuals can know if they are "born of God." He exhorts them to believe, pray for sinful believers, and to "keep themselves from idols" (v. 21).

Outline of 2 John.

Salutation (vv. 1–3)—"to the elect lady and her children"

Body of letter (vv. 4–11)—John praises the recipients for walking in truth and encourages them to continue loving one another in obedience to Jesus's love command. He warns them to watch out for deceivers who do not abide in the teaching of Christ.

Closing greetings (vv. 12–13)—John indicates he wishes to speak further with them face to face.

Outline of 3 John.

Salutation and prayer (vv. 1–2)—"to my dear friend Gaius, whom I love in the truth"

Body of letter (vv. 3–12)—John once again praises the recipients for walking in truth. They are showing hospitality to fellow believers who are traveling (vv. 5–8). He also warns them about Diotrephes, who is speaking against John.

Closing greetings (vv. 13–15)—John once again indicates that he wishes to speak further with them face to face.

Use of the OT

First John does not contain explicit OT citations, but it does contain some key allusions. To reiterate, one of the most important steps in interpretation is to understand how a NT writer's thought is shaped by his reading of the OT. Johns draws from Genesis and Deuteronomy.

Children of the Devil Kill like Cain. Genesis 4:1–16 records creation's first murder. John evokes Cain's murder of Abel to show that one's love, or lack of love, indicates whose child a person really is. John distinguishes two sets of children based on brotherly love or hatred, noting, "This is how God's children and the devil's children become obvious. Whoever does not do what is right is not from God, especially the one who does not love his brother or sister" (1 John 3:10). He then evokes Cain as an example of someone who hated his brother and, thereby, was a child of the Devil, "For this is the message you have heard from the beginning: We should love one another, unlike Cain, who was of the evil one and murdered his brother. And why did he murder him? Because his deeds were evil, and his brothers were righteous" (3:11–12).

Avoid Christological Idolatry. First John contains one of the most enigmatic endings in the entire NT. The last line of the letter is the command, "Little children, guard yourselves from idols" (5:21). The clouds of exegetical confusion begin to lift when the interpreter understands how John's statement echoes the OT and the wider motifs of the letter. John's statement echoes a warning from Deut 4:15–16, "Diligently watch yourselves—because you did not see any form on the day the Lord spoke to you out of the fire at Horeb—so you don't act corruptly and make an idol for yourselves in the shape of any figure: a male or female form." This statement is just one of many imperatives in which Moses warns the Israelites about the two fundamental transgressions against the Mosaic covenant, idolatry and a lack of love for another. If the Israelites fail to keep themselves from idols, a lack of brotherly will surely follow. These transgressions go hand in hand. John's use of this Deuteronomic warning is ironic. While Moses notes that the Israelites saw no image of God at Horeb (Deut 4:15–16), John begins his letter by underscoring how he himself had seen, touched, and heard Jesus. What is idolatrous for John is the denial that Jesus came in flesh. A Jesus who did not come in the flesh is an idolatrous Jesus fashioned after the image of the false teachers. Moreover, this Christological idolatry leads to a lack of love, which John presses repeatedly in the letter.

Theological Tools

Knowledge of God's Love in the Incarnate Son

John's first letter contains one of the most oft-cited verses in Christian and even non-Christian circles, "The one who does not love does not know God, because God is love" (1 John 4:8; see also 4:16). It is the last phrase that gets repeated. When ripped out of context, the statement "God is love" becomes abstract and untethered from John's understanding of God's love. Contextually John is driving home the difference between those who are "from God" and those who are "from the world." Those "from the world" do not love and thereby do not really know God. Contrastively those "from God" love others, because they have come to know God's love revealed in his Son. As John puts it: "God's love was revealed among us in this way: God sent his one and only Son into the world so that we might live through him. Love consists in this: not that we loved God, but that he loved us and sent his Son to be the atoning sacrifice for our sins. Dear friends, if God loved us in this way, we also must love one another" (1 John 4:9–11).

Cleary John grounds his well-known statement "God is love" in the death of Jesus which cleanses from sin and thereby satisfies God's wrath (i.e., propitiation, 1 John 2:1–2; 4:10). John, like the rest of the NT writers, never detaches divine love from the crucified and risen Son of God. In fact, one can know God's love and know that "God is love" only by knowing him in his Son.

The False Doctrine of the Antichrist

John is not shy about discussing the works of the Devil and the Antichrist. First and Second John contain the only explicit references to the Antichrist in the entire NT (1 John 2:18, 22; 4:3; 2 John 7).[19] For John, the Antichrist attempts to take the place of ("anti") the true Christ. His attempt is spearheaded by a false doctrine that consists of two pillars. First, types of an Antichrist have already entered the world

---

[19] The figure of the Antichrist overlaps with other figures in the NT, including the "man of lawlessness" (2 Thess 2:3) and "the beast" whose number is "666" (Rev 13:18).

(1 John 2:18). Second, the spirit and teaching of the Antichrist is that Jesus did not really come in the flesh. One of the ways that John combats this false doctrine is by reassuring his readers that he saw, heard, and touched Jesus in the flesh (1 John 1:1–4).

Responsive Tools

John wants his readers to "know" and "love." These two responses go hand in hand. True knowledge of God will result in love, and that love indicates such knowledge. So what does John want his readers to know? He wants them to know that they have come to know God in a way that results in eternal life. This objective is clear in several statements.[20] They know God and his Son by faith and through the gift of the Spirit (1 John 3:24; 4:6). Their faith in the crucified and risen Jesus overcomes the world (1 John 5:4–5) and is accompanied by love for one another. However, their knowledge is ultimately incomplete until Jesus returns. As John puts it, "Beloved, we are God's children now, and what we will be has not yet appeared; but we know that when he appears we will be like him, because we shall see him as he is" (1 John 3:2; cf. 1 Cor 13:9–10).

Understanding the Tools for Jude

Historical Tools

Jude is nestled between John's letters and the book of Revelation. It is small and neglected in the history of interpretation. Yet it contains a powerful message.

---

[20] See 1 John 2:3, 4, 14, 21, 29; 3:1, 14, 16, 19, 24; 4:2, 6, 8, 13, 16; 5:2, 13, 15, 18, 19, 20; 2 John 1; 3 John 12.

History behind the Text

Author and Date. Although some scholars label the book pseudony-mous, the author of Jude is most likely the brother of James (James 1:1) and the half-brother of Jesus (see Mark 6:3). Jude most likely penned this brief letter somewhere between AD 55 and 62.

Audience. There are no clues that reveal the geographical location of Jude's audience, though some have suggested somewhere in Asia Minor. It is clear that Jude's recipients are being afflicted by false teach-ers. Therefore, it is fitting that Jude refers to his audience as "those who are the called, loved by God the Father and kept for Jesus Christ" (v. 1). Despite what they face, Jude's recipients are called, loved, and kept by God in Christ.

Purpose. Jude writes to warn about false teachers who, much like the false prophets in 2 Peter 2, are morally bankrupt. Jude describes them as those designated for condemnation, ungodly, perverting God's grace, and denying Jesus (v. 4). Again as with 2 Peter, he places these teachers in the same category as rebellious angels (v. 6), Sodom and Gomorrah (v. 7), Cain (v. 11), Balaam (v. 11), and Korah (v. 11). In other words, they will surely face judgment for their actions. Jude admonishes his recipients to contend for their "once for all" faith (v. 3) against these teachers.

History in the Text

The story that Jude operates with is steeped in the narratives of the Pentateuch. God's people are once again being afflicted by enemies who are sexually immoral like the Sodomites, murderous like Cain, greedy like Balaam, and rebellious like Korah.

Literary Tools

Literary Structure: Parts of Rhetoric

Here is a summary of the parts of rhetoric as evident in Jude.

Introduction to argument and explanation of problem (vv. 3–4)—
Jude wastes no time getting to his point. He immediately
exhorts his recipients to contend for the faith (v. 3). The
matter at hand (*narratio*) is that false teachers have entered
the believing community. He warns, "For some people,
who were designated for this judgment long ago, have
come in by stealth; they are ungodly, turning the grace of
our God into sensuality and denying Jesus Christ, our only
Master and Lord" (v. 4).

Thesis (v. 5–7)—Jude's thesis is that just as Jesus delivered Israel
from Egypt and destroyed those who did not believe (v. 5),
Jesus will do the same thing to these false teachers.

Support for thesis (vv. 8–16)—The support for Jude's thesis cen-
ters on describing the nature of the false teachers and the
outcome of their work. In short, the recipients can leave
the judgment of these teachers to God who will deal with
them in accordance with his prior judgments (e.g., Sodom,
Cain, Balaam, Korah) and promises.

Disputation of opposition (vv. 17–19)—Jude does not directly
refute the false teachers, but he does appeal to the prior
predictions of the apostles, "But you, dear friends, remember what was predicted by the apostles of our Lord Jesus
Christ. They told you, 'In the end time there will be scoffers living according to their own ungodly desires'" (vv.
17–18).

Summary of main points (vv. 20–25)—Jude concludes his letter
by admonishing the recipients to avoid the division caused

by the false teachers; they should do so by building one another up in faith and prayer, waiting for the mercy of God to be revealed at the return of Christ.

Use of the OT

Jude does not cite the OT explicitly, but he does evoke several OT narratives. He especially draws from Genesis and Numbers. Jude also makes mention of two noncanonical texts, which I will discuss below.

JESUS DELIVERED ISRAEL FROM EGYPT

In Jude 5, we find a jarring statement: "Now I want to remind you, although you came to know all these things once and for all, that Jesus saved a people out of Egypt and later destroyed those who did not believe." What should give us pause is that Jude identifies Jesus as the one who delivered Israel from Egypt. He takes Yahweh's quintessential saving action in Israel's history and includes Jesus in it. Obviously, such a statement implies the preexistence of Jesus. How could he have saved Israel from Egypt thousands of years prior to his birth in Bethlehem unless he existed prior to both of those events? Jude's statement speaks to the exalted view of Jesus in the early church as well as the nature of Jesus's saving work. Specifically, Jesus has delivered believers through his death and resurrection just as he delivered Israel from Egypt. Yet just as he judged the Israelites who did not believe after the exodus, he will do the same to those who have not believed after his saving work at the cross.

The Ancient Way of False Teachers. Jude places the false teachers in the same category of notorious rebels from Israel's past, "Woe to them! For they have gone the way of Cain, have plunged into Balaam's error for profit, and have perished in Korah's rebellion" (v. 11). There is

Jude includes Jesus in Yahweh's deliverance of the ancient Israelites from Egypt.

a particular "way," or manner of life, that defines these false teachers. It is murderous (Cain), greedy (Balaam), and rebellious (Korah). It is the ancient way of false teachers, but God ultimately judges them all as the OT narratives about Cain, Balaam, and Korah demonstrate.[21]

Jude's Use of Noncanonical Texts. Jude incorporates two texts into his letter that are not found in the canonical OT. First, Jude refers to a story in which the archangel Michael argues with the Devil about the corpse of Moses, "When Michael the archangel was disputing with the devil in an argument about Moses's body, he did not dare utter a slanderous condemnation against him but said, 'The Lord rebuke you!'" (v. 9). The OT does not contain such a story. In fact, neither Deuteronomy 34 nor any other OT passage contains the account mentioned by Jude. He is most likely referring to a tradition from a Jewish pseudepigraphal work titled the *Assumption of Moses* (or *Testament of Moses*). This is a first-century AD document, but the one extant copy is incomplete and

---

[21] See Gen 4:1–16; Num 16:32–34; 31:8.

does not contain the story that Jude references.[22] Second, Jude cites a line from the book of *1 Enoch*. Jude writes: "It was about these that Enoch, in the seventh generation from Adam, prophesied: 'Look! The Lord comes with tens of thousands of his holy ones to execute judgment on all and to convict all the ungodly concerning all the ungodly acts that they have done in an ungodly way, and concerning all the harsh things ungodly sinners have said against him'" (vv. 14–15).

Jude links the false teachers of his day to Enoch's prophecy that the Lord would arrive on the earth to judge such individuals. The only description of Enoch in the OT is found in Gen 5:22–24. The Genesis account does not mention Enoch prophesying. Rather than using the OT, Jude refers to a prophecy located in the first-century AD pseudepigraphal work titled *1 Enoch*. The passage from 1 Enoch 1:9 fits Jude's emphasis on God's final judgment against the false prophets.

By using the tradition from the *Assumption of Moses* and a citation from *1 Enoch*, it does not follow that Jude saw these kinds of works as Scripture or having the same authority as Scripture. The preponderance of OT citations scattered throughout the NT indicates that the early church viewed the OT as authoritative. By comparison, Jude's usage of these two noncanonical works is unusual. Jude is most likely appealing to well-known traditions to drive home the point that God will ultimately judge false teachers.

Theological and Responsive Tools

An Ancient and Unchanging Faith

Jude exhorts readers to guard the "faith" that "was delivered to the saints once for all" (v. 3). Specifically, they must guard the faith from

---

[22] See Ben Witherington III, *Letters and Homilies for Jewish Christians: A Socio-Rhetorical Commentary on Hebrews, James and Jude* (Downers Grove: IVP, 2007), 617.

those who attempt to change its content and who live immoral lives. At its core, God's saving work through the crucified and risen Jesus, and everything related to it, is the message, or "faith," that Jude references.

This "faith" is obviously ancient, but, as Jude reminds us, it is unchanging. Despite centuries of history, political and intellectual revolutions, advancements in sciences, and a slew of other changes, the saving message of Jesus Christ has not, should not, and will not be changed.

Putting the Tools to Use for James, 1 & 2 Peter, 1, 2, & 3 John, Jude

Rather than focus on one single passage, let's do a little work in all these books we've been discussing.

Historical Tools

1. What does 1 John 4:1–3 tell us about the historical situation of the original recipients?
2. What does 2 Pet 3:1–13 tell us about the history in the text of 2 Peter?

Literary Tools

1. How does James 5:12 echo Jesus's teaching on the Sermon on the Mount?
2. List some of the ways that Peter supports his *propositio* in 1 Peter (hint: look at his *probatio*).
3. In 1 John 3:12 and Jude 11, how do these two authors make use of the episode in Genesis 4 to support their arguments?

Theological Tools

1. How are the theological motifs in 2 Peter and Jude similar?

2. What role does eschatology play in James's wisdom? Provide specific examples.

Responsive Tools

1. What do we do with an unchanging faith (Jude 3) in a world that seems to change all the time?

2. How does Peter (1 Peter & 2 Peter) want his recipients to respond to suffering? What would that look like today?

Understanding the Tools for Revelation

We now turn our attention to the most confusing book in all of Christian Scripture. I sometimes refer to the book of Revelation as the Bermuda Triangle of biblical exegesis: Some biblical readers avoid Revelation, because they are afraid they will get lost in its bizarre imagery and never come out of it with a clear understanding of John's message. By contrast, others sometimes enter Revelation and never come out at all. Instead, every book of the Bible and all of Christian theology gets filtered through Revelation. In what follows, I would like to suggest that we can avoid both extremes. *For a discussion about exegetical fears surrounding Revelation see Wordsearch video.*

Revelation does not have to be confusing or scary. It does not have to engulf us exegetically. We do not need a special formula or lens to view its contents. We simply need some of the same "tools" that we've discussed throughout this entire book. When you come to the last book of the Bible, you do not need to throw out your whole toolbox. You simply need to make sure that the toolbox contains what you need to read one of the most uplifting books in all of Scripture. Yes, I just called Revelation uplifting. Let's see how.

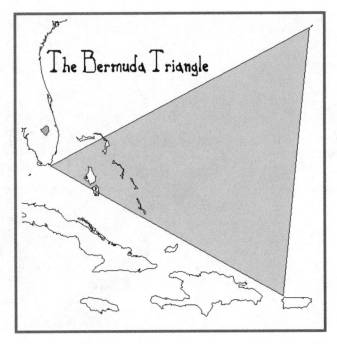

Bible readers sometimes fear the book of Revelation in an almost superstitious way like those who avoid or supposedly disappear into the Bermuda Triangle.

Historical Tools

Students are often surprised when I remind them that John lived in real space and real time. While he saw heavenly visions, his feet were still planted on Patmos (Rev 1:9). Moreover, his recipients also lived in first-century Asia Minor. I make this rather obvious point, because it is so often forgotten in the interpretation of Revelation. While there are future elements in the book, it meant something to people in the first-century world. Even more, John uses first-century language and imagery to communicate to them and to us. The bottom line is that Revelation is just as historically oriented as the other books of the NT. Therefore, we need to treat it as such.

Although Revelation contains fantastic imagery, John had these visions in real space and time on the Island of Patmos.

History behind the Text

Author and Date. The traditional view is that John the apostle penned this work. It is the same John who wrote the Gospel of John and 1, 2, & 3 John. Two different dates are often proposed for this work. Some argue that John wrote Revelation in AD 68–69 just after Nero's reign ended. Others argue that John wrote in AD 95–96 during the reign of Emperor Domitian. One factor that tips the scales in favor of 95–96 is the evidence that Domitian made a point to emphasize his deity.[23] This is reflected in Revelation.[24]

---

[23] Carson and Moo, *Introduction to the New Testament*, 709.

[24] See Rev 13:4, 15, 16; 14:9–11; 15:2; 16:2; 19:20; 20:4.

Audience. In Revelation 2–3, Jesus addresses the seven churches of Asia Minor: Ephesus, Smyrna, Pergamum, Thyatira, Sardis, Philadelphia, and Laodicia. These are the original recipients of the entire book. The "letters" addressed to them in Revelation 2–3 reveal some troubling circumstances with a few bright spots. Overall, the troubles brewing in these communities include waning affections for Jesus (2:4; 3:16), Satanic opposition in human/political form (2:9–10, 13), false teachers (2:6, 14-15; 3:9), tolerance of sexual immorality (2:20–22), a need for repentance (3:3). The author John finds himself in trouble of his own as he is exiled on the island of Patmos when he receives this apocalypse (Rev 1:9).

Purpose. Based on the various troubles plaguing the seven churches, John writes to warn and encourage them with his divine vision just as Jesus commanded (Rev 1:1–2). He even promises a blessing for those who read and listen to his vision, "Blessed is the one who reads aloud the words of this prophecy, and blessed are those who hear the words of this prophecy and keep what is written in it, because the time is near" (1:3). Although subsequent readers have been confused by what John wrote, he intended to instruct, encourage, even bless. In this way, his historical purpose is the same as the other NT writers. The interpreter of Revelation must not lose sight of this original purpose.

History in the Text

John works with a story in which God through the Lamb has already overcome the "dragon," the beasts, and the harlot. Yet the dragon continues to wage war against the people who bear witness to the Lamb. Therefore, God works to vindicate his people, showing that he indeed loves them and that in the Lamb they have overcome the dragon, despite all appearances. That victory will be on full display as an answer to the prayers of his people when Jesus returns to slay and condemn his wicked enemies forever. As we will see, unpacking this kind of symbolism is one of the exegetical keys to understanding the book.

History in Front of the Text

Revelation has a long history of interpretation. While many have avoided it, others have developed interpretive models for the whole book and the enigmatic passage in Rev 20:1–10. The model one chooses has a significant impact on how one interprets the whole book and individual passages. I will briefly summarize those models here.[25]

Interpretive Models for Revelation. There are five main models used to interpret the book of Revelation. As we will see, much of the discussion revolves around the timing of the events that John describes.[26]

1. *Preterist.* All of the events occurred prior to AD 70. John is telling the churches in the first century that God will deliver them from the Roman Empire and the evils associated with it.
2. *Idealist.* John presents a symbolic battle between good and evil rather than a prediction of future events. In this way, Revelation offers timeless truths about God overcoming the enemies of his people.
3. *Historicist.* Revelation is an outline of church history from the first century until Jesus's return. As a result of this model, interpreters tend to identify features in Revelation with events in

---

[25] See House, *Chronological and Background Charts*, 152.

[26] I am helped with these definitions by J. Daniel Hays, J. Scott Duvall, and C. Marvin Pate, *Dictionary of Prophecy and End Times* (Grand Rapids: Zondervan, 2007).

their own day. For example, many Reformers (sixteenth century) identified the pope and the Roman Catholic Church in that day with Revelation's description of the Antichrist and Babylon.

4. *Futurist.* In this model, Revelation 4–22 essentially portrays a time just before and at Jesus's return.

5. *Eclectic.* This approach takes the best pieces of models 1–4 while attempting to avoid the weaknesses of them.

It should be noted that there are variations to many of these models. Additionally, all five models see Revelation 2–3 as a historical address to first-century churches. After that, agreements among them are hard to find.

Millennial Views and Revelation 20:1–10. This passage is one of the first (or only!) that comes to mind in discussions on Revelation. The debate really turns on John's reference to a 1,000-year reign (thus "millennial debate") of Christ on the earth. There are six "thousand years" references in these ten verses. In short, John sees a vision in which Satan is bound in chains for 1,000 years (20:1–2). He is not allowed to deceive the nations during that 1,000-year period (20:3). There are some who reign with Christ on the earth during this 1,000-year period (20:4–6). Once the 1,000-year period is over, Satan is unbound and allowed to deceive the nations for a time until he is finally thrown into the lake of fire (20:7–10). The pressing questions for interpreters of this passage are (1) Is this a literal reign of Christ on the earth? (2) If it is literal, when does this 1,000-year reign occur? In trying to answer these kinds of questions, three schools of thought have emerged. I define them here in alphabetical order.

1. *Amillennialism.* John is speaking symbolically about Christ's reign in the lives of believers—not a literal 1,000-year reign.

2. *Premillennialism.* A literal reading of the passage in which Christ returns before ("pre") the 1,000-year reign and then inaugurates that 1,000-year reign followed by final judgment.

3. *Postmillennialism.* A literal reading of the passage in which Christ returns after ("post") 1,000 years of improving conditions in the world due to gospel success.

Literary Tools

Genre

Revelation blends three genres together: apocalypse (1:1), prophecy (1:3), and epistle (1:4).

From a literary standpoint, apocalypse is a type of literature in which an author receives a vision from God. Broadly speaking, the vision portrays the world as rebelling against God and persecuting his people. Therefore, God intervenes to save his people in the end and establish his kingdom forever. The presentation of these saving events is always highly symbolic. John's work employs all of these features, but he uses them in his own unique way. Above all, he reworks everything around the "Lamb." One of the unique features of John's Apocalypse is that God's victory against Satan and the world is already secured in the Lamb's death and resurrection. In John's vision, whatever happens at the end of all things is grounded in what God already did through the Lamb.

With respect to prophecy, John takes his cues from OT prophets. On the one hand, he sees visions of things that will happen in the future. However, the impetus of his message is to warn and encourage the saints. They must respond to John's "prophecy" in repentance and faith just as we saw with OT prophets. Additionally, John gives a prophetic warning at the close of his work: "I testify to everyone who hears the words of the prophecy of this book: If anyone adds to them,

God will add to him the plagues described in this book. And if anyone takes away from the words of the book of this prophecy, God will take away his share of the tree of life and the holy city, which are written about in this book" (Rev 22:18–19).

The epistolary elements of Revelation are seen in a few different places. For example, at the outset of the work, John writes, "John: To the seven churches in Asia. Grace and peace to you from the one who is, who was, and who is to come, and from the seven spirits before his throne" (Rev 1:4). There are also epistolary features in Revelation 2–3 and at the end of the work (Rev 22:21).

As Richard Bauckham notes, John combines all three of these genres. He explains, "Thus Revelation seems to be an apocalyptic prophecy in the form of a circular letter to seven churches in the Roman province of Asia."[27]

Structure

Interpreters have not reached a consensus on the structure of Revelation. Much of the disagreement swirls around the middle section in chapters 6–16. This section is highlighted by three series of seven: seven seals, seven trumpets, and seven bowls. There are pauses, or interludes, between the first six series (seals, trumpets, bowls) and the seventh (seal, trumpet, and bowl). Clearly, John is symbolically portraying divine judgments. The question becomes, what is the interrelationship between the seals, trumpets, and bowls? Suggestions include

1. *Simultaneous view.* The three series of seven judgments are occurring at the same time. John portrays the same events three times with an increased intensification each time.

---

[27] Richard Bauckham, *The Theology of the Book of Revelation* (Cambridge: Cambridge University Press, 1993), 2.

2. *Consecutive view.* The three series of seven judgments represent twenty-one judgments.

3. *Telescopic view.* The seventh seal introduces the six trumpets, and the seventh trumpet introduces the seven bowls.

Here is one proposed structure based on the simultaneous view:

1:1–8—Prologue

1:9–3:22—Jesus addresses seven churches

4:1–5:14—Heavenly worship of One on the throne and Lamb who is worthy to break the seals of the scroll

    6:1–17—Jesus opens six seals of the scroll

        7:1–17—Interlude: Sealing of 144,000

    8:1–5—Jesus opens seventh seal of scroll

    8:6–9:21—Six trumpets blown

        10:1–11:14—Interlude: Eating little scroll and the two witnesses

    11:15–19—Seventh trumpet blown

        12:1–13:18—Interlude: Woman and dragon; emergence of first and second beasts

        14:1–20—Interlude: Lamb and the 144,000; messages of angels; harvest of earth

        15:1–16:21—Angels with seven last plagues bowls

17:1–18:24—The fall of the whore/Babylon

19:1–10—Heaven rejoices for Babylon's fall

19:11–21—The rider on the white horse and the defeat of the beast

20:1–10—The thousand-year reign

20:11–15—Judgment of the dead

21:1–8—Vision of new heaven and new earth

21:9–27—Vision of new Jerusalem

22:1–7—Vision of river of life

22:8–21—Epilogue, warning, and closing prayer

Notice that it is possible to organize all of this imagery into a discernible structure. Once again, while we need to respect the genre and unique complexities of Revelation, we also need to keep using the kinds of tools we've been discussing throughout this book.

Imagery

When dealing with individual units of thought in Revelation, nothing is more important than rightly interpreting the imagery. G. K. Beale offers a simple and helpful four-step method.[28] Ask the following questions:

1. *Linguistic level.* What does the text actually say? What are the actual images?
2. *Visionary level.* What is John's experience?
3. *Referential level.* What is the historical reference in the vision?
4. *Symbolic level.* What does the symbolism tell us about the historical reference in the vision?

The approach sounds simplistic, but it works. For example, in Rev 12:1–6, we find a symbolic story about a pregnant woman, her child, and a dragon.

> A great sign appeared in heaven: a woman clothed with the sun, with the moon under her feet and a crown of twelve stars on her head. She was pregnant and cried out in labor and agony as she was about to give birth. Then another sign appeared in heaven: There was a great fiery red dragon having seven heads and ten horns, and on its heads were seven crowns. Its tail swept away a third of the stars in heaven and hurled them to the earth. And the dragon stood in front of the woman who was about

---

[28] G. K. Beale, *The Book of Revelation*, New International Greek Testament Commentary (Grand Rapids: Eerdmans, 1999), 52–53.

The imagery of a red dragon, a pregnant woman, and a child in Revelation 12 are highly symbolic. However, they communicate very real events.

to give birth, so that when she did give birth it might devour her child. She gave birth to a Son, a male who is going to rule all nations with an iron rod. Her child was caught up to God and to his throne. The woman fled into the wilderness, where she had a place prepared by God, to be nourished there for 1,260 days.

When we filter the symbols through Beale's four levels of interpretation, here's what we discover.

1. Linguistic level
   a. Woman—clothed with the sun and moon under feet; crown of twelve stars; in agony of child birth; flees to wilderness after giving birth; nourished for 1,260 days
   b. Dragon—red; seven heads; ten horns; seven crowns; tail sweeps a third of stars of heaven to earth; poised to eat the child

    c.   Child—male; he is to rule all of the nations with a rod of iron; caught by God to his throne

2. Visionary level—John simply says in 12:1 a sign appeared in heaven, and he recounts what he saw

3. Referential level

    a.   Woman—based on OT background and Jesus's story, the woman refers to Israel, Mary, and the church. Jesus comes into the world as a child through all of them in some way.

    b.   Dragon—based on OT background, early Christian belief, and broader context of Revelation, the dragon refers to Satan.

    c.   Child—based on early Christian belief and the broader context of Revelation, the child refers to Jesus.

4. Symbolic level

    a.   Woman—The woman is the people of God (Israel/Mary/church) from whom the incarnate Christ came. Her painful pregnancy symbolizes the difficulties of God's people leading up to his arrival/birth. Her time in the wilderness symbolizes the people of God's experience on the earth until Christ returns. It is a wilderness wandering, but God cares for his people. He has even set a time limit on their suffering—1,260 days.

    b.   Dragon—The dragon's red hue symbolizes Satan's violent and murderous ways. He failed in his murder of Jesus, because the child was raised from the dead. The horns and crowns symbolize the political/royal forces of the world that he uses to carry out his violence and rule. Yet God "snatched" the child up to the throne to rule from heaven.

    c.   Child—The child's dramatic rescue symbolizes Jesus's resurrection, ascension, and installment as king. He rules with the iron rod from above, and from that location cares for the "woman" (people of God) from whom he came.

Use of the OT

John makes more use of the OT than any other NT writer. He evokes various figures and events to communicate his apocalyptic visions. Not surprisingly, he draws widely from apocalyptic works such as Daniel, Ezekiel, and Zechariah. Yet he also draws from Genesis, Exodus, the Psalms, Isaiah, and other OT texts. I will highlight two main uses here.

God's Vindication of His People. John draws clear lines of demarcation between the righteous and the wicked throughout his Apocalypse. In doing so, he divides the righteous from the wicked. As is common in the Psalms, the righteous suffer and the wicked prosper. Therefore, the righteous pray for God to deliver them and vindicate the trust they have in him before their enemies. John takes up this motif from the Psalms. In Rev 6:9–11, Christians who have already died cry out for vindication from underneath the heavenly altar. Their cry echoes the Psalms of Lament, "They cried out with a loud voice: 'Lord, the one who is holy and true, how long until you judge those who live on the earth and avenge our blood?'" (Rev 6:10). This is the way the righteous cry out in the book of Psalms, begging for vindication before their enemies. For example, "There are no signs for us to see. There is no longer a prophet. And none of us knows how long this will last. God, how long will the enemy mock? Will the foe insult your name forever?" (Ps 74:9–10). The psalmist's prayer sheds light on what the Christians under the heavenly altar want. They are asking that God show their scoffing and reviling enemies that, despite what they suffered on the earth, the Lamb was victorious, God loves them, and they are his people.

New Creation and Temple. John's Apocalypse frequently evokes creation, Jerusalem, and temple imagery from the OT:

> Then the temple of God in heaven was opened, and the ark of his covenant appeared in his temple. There were flashes of

lightning, rumblings and peals of thunder, an earthquake, and severe hail. (Rev 11:19)

I also saw the holy city, the new Jerusalem, coming down out of heaven from God, prepared like a bride adorned for her husband. (Rev 21:2)

I did not see a temple in [the city], because the Lord God the Almighty and the Lamb are its temple. (Rev 21:22)

John's descriptions echo Genesis 1–2, Isaiah 65–66, and numerous OT passages involving Jerusalem and the temple. However, John reworks in the Lamb all of this imagery around what God has done and will do. Atoning sacrifices and Davidic rule are found in the Lamb. God reigning and ruling from Zion is found in the Lamb. The promise of a return to Eden with the waters of life is found in the Lamb.

Yet John also describes that Lamb as Lion whose return will definitively show what the Lamb has already secured in his death and resurrection—salvation for his people and judgment for his enemies. These are all OT motifs that John evokes to describe the vision given to him by Jesus.

Theological and Responsive Tools

Several theological motifs emanate from Revelation. What stands above all of them is God's sovereignty over evil for this people through the Lion and the Lamb. The one who sits on the throne and the Lamb are the "Alpha and Omega" (Rev 1:8; 21:6; 22:13). That means they plan, act, and fulfill the prior promise to God's people. Although there are ghastly images of evil in Revelation (dragon, beast, harlot, etc.), John gives his readers the assurance that despite what they see and what they suffer God is carrying out his redemptive purposes. The response of the reader should not be one of confusion or terror. It should be one of repentance, faith, and confidence. The Lion was hidden in the Lamb all along, securing all that the people of God needed for this life and the new creation to come. They are not foolish to believe despite what the scoffers might claim. No, God's people must wait patiently, confidently, and hopefully knowing that they have overcome and will overcome by the blood of the Lamb, the word of their testimony, and the arrival of the King of kings and Lord of Lords (Rev 12:11; 19:16).

Putting the Tools to Use in Revelation

Let's put what we've discussed to work by looking at Rev 8:1–5.

Historical

1. How is Rev 8:1–5 related to the book's original historical purpose?
2. How might a preterist interpreter deal with this passage? How is that different from a futurist interpretation?

Literary

1. What is the relationship between Rev 8:1–5 and the overall structure of Revelation?
2. Work through the imagery using the four levels of interpretation discussed above.
3. What OT echoes are present in Rev 8:1–5? How does that illuminate the meaning of the text?

Theological and Responsive

1. How does Rev 8:1–5 fit with the main theological motif of Revelation?

SCRIPTURE INDEX

Genesis

1 *98, 100, 101, 146, 267, 327*
1:1 *69, 367*
1:1–2 *369*
1:1–2:3 *69, 98, 101*
1:2 *100*
1:26 *103*
1:26–31 *102, 135, 267*
1:27 *103*
1–2 *326, 457, 547*
1–3 *135*
1–6 *106*
1–11 *69*
2:4 *98*
2:4–4:26 *103*
2:7 *369*
2:15–23 *369*
2:24 *186*
3 *103, 104, 457*
3:15 *85, 104, 107, 131*
4 *105, 488, 533*
4:1-16 *369, 524*
5 *105*
5:1 *98*
5:21–24 *488*
5:22–24 *532*
6 *105*
6:1–4 *510, 517*
6:1–5 *106*
6:5 *105*
6:9 *98*
6:11–13 *369*

6:18 *135*
6–8 *369, 519*
6–9 *135, 488*
6–11 *106*
8 *327*
9:1 *105, 106*
9:1–2 *135*
10 *106*
10:1 *98*
11 *87, 105, 136*
11:4 *105*
11:10 *98*
11:27 *98*
12 *93, 107, 134, 135, 136*
12:1–3 *362, 398, 405, 458*
12:3 *64, 107, 131, 133, 135, 315, 454*
12–25 *488*
12–50 *234*
14 *260, 453*
14:18–20 *259*
15 *107, 134, 135, 136, 265*
15:1 *458*
15:5 *458*
15:6 *107, 134, 136, 458, 500*
15:13–15 *108*
15:13–16 *114*
17 *134, 135, 136, 488*
19 *93, 182, 517*
20 *93*
20:7 *283*
21 *488*

549

22 *87, 108, 500*
22:12–14 *108*
24 *194*
24:1 *194*
25 *108*
25:12 *98*
25:19 *98*
25:27–34 *109*
26 *93*
27 *109*
27:27–29 *488*
32:22–32 *109*
35 *108*
36:1 *98*
36:9 *98*
37:2 *98*
37–50 *58, 109*
48 *488*
50:20 *110*
50:24 *185, 488*

Exodus
1 *94*
1:7 *109, 112, 128, 131*
1–15 *488*
1–18 *112, 115*
2 *488*
2:23–25 *113*
3 *113*
3:14 *360*
3:14–15 *114*
3–4 *283*
4:31 *185*
5–11 *113*
6:1–8 *114*
6:2 *114*
6:6–8 *469*
6:8 *114*
7:1 *282*
7:17 *114*
10:2 *114*
12:1–28 *369*
12:21 *453*
13:19 *185*
15 *115*
15:11 *114*
16 *365*
17 *451*
17:1–6 *460*

17:6 *451*
17:14 *89*
19 *18, 66, 115, 516*
19:4–6 *64, 122, 136, 180, 315*
19:5–6 *133, 516*
19–24 *112, 115, 135*
20 *18, 115*
20:1–17 *369*
20–31 *27*
22:22–24 *505*
24:4 *13, 89*
25:17 *459*
25–31 *117*
25–40 *112, 117*
32 *460*
32–33 *117, 206*
34:1 *28*
34:2 *24*
34:6–7 *118, 299*
34:27 *89*
35:10 *261*
35–40 *27, 117*
40:34–38 *369*

Leviticus
8–10 *122*
11:44 *516*
11–15 *122*
16 *121*
16:2 *459*
16:15 *459*
17–26 *123, 139*
19 *139, 140*
19:2 *122, 123, 139*
19:9–10 *186*
19:18 *96*
19:28 *137, 138, 139, 140, 141*
20:26 *123, 140*
23:39–44 *369*
26 *157, 316, 320*
26:19–20 *185*

Numbers
1 *125*
6:1–21 *179*
6:2 *362*
10 *126*
10:11 *125*
11:4 *460*

12 *126*
13–14 *165, 166*
14 *94, 460*
14:11 *126*
16–17 *126*
20 *126*
21:4–9 *369*
22–25 *126*
24:17 *85*
25 *127, 460*
25:6–8 *411*
26 *125, 128*
31 *128*
33:2 *89*

Deuteronomy
4:2 *42*
4:6–8 *119*
4:15–16 *525*
6:4 *94, 142, 147, 412*
6:4–5 *215*
6:4–9 *139*
6:4–15 *209*
6:5 *96, 130*
6:5–9 *249*
6:9 *25*
7:3 *185*
8 *166*
9:7–12 *209*
10:18–19 *209*
11:26–28 *209*
14:28–29 *209*
15:1–18 *209*
17 *211*
17:14–20 *190, 192, 209, 210, 215*
17:15 *220*
17:16 *211*
17:17 *211*
17:18 *31*
17:18–19 *211*
17:19–20 *25, 211*
18:15 *113*
18:15–22 *283*
18:18 *304*
21:23 *411*
24:14–15 *209*
25 *456*
25:4 *456*
25:5–10 *186*

28 *316*
28:15–68 *209*
28:38 *308*
30:15–20 *209*
31:1–8 *165*
31:2–8 *203*
31:9 *89*
32 *316*
32:21 *455*
34 *89, 154, 531*

Joshua
1 *165*
1:7–8 *165*
1:8 *271*
1–5 *165*
2 *166, 488, 500*
2:9–13 *166*
3 *167*
3:15 *167*
3:16 *167*
4:9 *159*
5:9 *159*
6 *167*
6:14–16:25 *488*
6–12 *165*
8:31–32 *89*
8:32 *31*
8–12 *167*
13–22 *165, 170*
21:45 *164*
23–24 *165, 171*
24 *171*
24:15 *172*
24:18 *171*
24:19 *171*
24:21 *171*
24:22 *171*
24:24 *171*
24:26 *158*
25–28 *171*

Judges
1 *171*
1:1–3:6 *175*
1:21–36 *175*
2:1–5 *175*
2:6–23 *175*
2:11 *173, 176*

2:11–13 *174*
2:14–15 *176*
2:15 *176*
2:16 *176*
2:16–18 *173*
2:19 *176*
3 *185*
3:1–6 *175*
3:7–11 *176*
3:7–16:31 *175*
3:9 *177*
3:12–30 *177*
3:31 *177*
4 *177, 488*
4:17–22 *238*
5 *177*
5:24–27 *238*
6 *488*
6:36–40 *177*
6–8 *177*
8:22–31 *177*
11 *178*
11:29–40 *178*
11:39 *178*
11–12 *488*
13 *488*
14:3 *180*
14:5 *180*
14:9 *180*
14:10–18 *180*
17–18 *180*
17–21 *175, 181*
18:30 *181*
19 *93, 186*
19:22 *182*
19:30 *182*
19–21 *155, 180, 181*
21:25 *155, 182, 189*

Ruth
1:1 *184*
1:5 *185*
1:6 *185*
1:14 *186*
1:16 *186*
2 *186*
2:3 *186*
3:9 *187*

3:11 *187*
4 *187*
4:13 *185*
4:17 *188*

1 Samuel
1 *189*
1:1–28:20 *488*
1:22 *189*
1–7 *189*
2:1–10 *189*
2:10 *220*
3 *283*
7:3–4 *190*
8 *155, 190*
8–15 *190*
16 *191, 220, 488*
17 *150, 190, 225*
25 *159*

2 Samuel
6 *191*
7 *135, 191, 211, 220, 225, 283*
7:8 *152*
7:8–16 *136*
7:8–17 *152, 156, 315*
7:10–13 *362*
7:14–15 *220*
8 *191*
8:13–14 *369*
24 *488*

1 Kings
1 *203, 488*
1:1 *194*
1:1–2:12 *202*
1–2 *202*
1–11 *154, 193*
2:3 *89*
8:10 *369*
9:1–9 *369*
10 *210, 211*
10:1–9 *369*
10:14–22 *210*
10:23 *210*
10–11 *210, 252*
11 *211*
11:3 *211*

11:33–38 *220*
11–12 *225, 283*
12 *154, 193*
13:2 *9*
14:8 *220*
15:3 *220*
17:1 *488, 502*
17–18 *502*
18 *283*
18:41–45 *502*
22 *283*

2 Kings
2:1–13:21 *488*
2:11 *488*
2:14 *488*
3:26–27 *120*
10:10 *283*
14:6 *89*
17 *197, 225, 288*
18 *197*
18:3 *220*
18–19 *197, 290*
19 *283*
20 *197, 198*
21 *198, 214, 217, 291*
21:1–18 *213*
21:3–5 *215*
21:6 *215, 217*
21:9 *216*
21:10–13 *217*
21:13 *216, 218*
21:15 *217*
21:16 *216*
21:17–18 *216*
22:1–11 *32*
23 *193*
23:28–30 *291*
24–25 *60, 193, 283*
25:18–21 *157*

1 Chronicles
2–3 *202*
21–29 *201*
23:1 *202*
23:2–27:34 *202*
23–29 *202*
28:10 *203*

28:20 *203*
29:23–25 *203*

2 Chronicles
2–7 *201*
9 *154*
9–36 *154*
13:10–12 *201*
20:7 *500*
32 *290*
33 *214, 216, 217*
33:1–20 *213*

Ezra
1:1–2 *158*
1:1–4 *225*
6:18 *89*
7:10 *205, 222, 225*
9:6–15 *205*

Nehemiah
1:4–11 *205*
1:5 *118*
2:8 *205*
2:18 *205*
4:15 *205*
6:16 *205*
8:1–8 *205*
8:1–12 *206*
8:5 *32*
8:13–18 *206*
9:1–37 *206*
9:38 *205*
13:1 *89*
13:10–11 *206*
13:15–17 *206*
13:23–24 *206*
13:31 *206*

Esther
4:14 *207*
9:1 *207*

Job
1:1 *244*
1:9 *244*
1–2 *234*
3:7–8 *244*

3:33 *244*
19:23–24 *28*
28:28 *261*
38–41 *244*
42 *234*
42:10–17 *501*
42:17 *243*

Psalms

1 *241, 242, 247, 268, 270, 271*
1:1 *270*
1:3 *236, 272*
1:6 *236*
1–24 *231*
1–41 *247*
2 *241, 258, 268, 270, 271, 369*
2:1–2 *271*
2:2 *220*
2:6 *236*
2:7 *397*
2:11–12 *271*
2:12 *270*
3 *230, 241*
6 *241*
8 *99, 241, 263, 266, 267*
8:1 *99*
8:3–4 *266*
8:4 *266*
8:5–8 *267*
8:9 *99*
12 *241*
13 *241*
15:1 *236*
16 *407*
18 *241*
19 *11, 241*
19:1 *10, 236*
19:7–8 *28*
19:7–9 *11*
19:7–10 *17*
20 *241*
21 *241*
22 *9, 69, 241, 258, 278*
22:7–8 *370*
23 *78, 278*
24:1 *236*
25–29 *231*
29 *241*
31 *231, 365*

31:5 *364*
32 *241*
33 *241*
35 *241*
36 *456*
36:1 *457*
38 *230, 241*
40:6–8 *121*
41 *247*
42 *247*
42–72 *247*
45 *241*
45:1 *29*
51 *230, 241*
51:4 *146*
69 *69, 241*
69:26 *391*
70 *230*
72 *230, 241*
73 *247*
73–89 *247*
74 *241*
74:9–10 *546*
88 *241*
89 *135, 241, 257, 315*
89:3 *323*
89:20 *220, 323*
90 *230*
90–106 *247*
92 *230*
93 *241*
95–99 *241*
100 *230*
102 *241*
104 *241*
107 *241, 367*
107:23–30 *366*
107–150 *247*
109 *241*
109:8 *391*
110 *9, 241, 258, 453*
110:1 *369, 453*
110:4 *258, 453*
116 *241*
117 *240*
119 *119, 241*
126 *230*
130 *241*
132:17 *220*

136 *241, 257*
137 *241*
137:7 *309*
143 *241*
146–150 *241*

Proverbs
1:3 *250*
1:7 *261, 262*
1:20–33 *250*
1:29 *262*
1–9 *239, 249, 250*
2:5 *262*
3:1–4 *249*
3:12 *491*
3:13–20 *250*
8:1–9:18 *250*
9:10 *236, 261, 262*
10:1–22:16 *249*
10:1–31:9 *250*
10:2 *236*
10:4 *236*
10:7 *236*
10–24 *239*
10–31 *249*
15:33 *261*
16:33 *208*
22:6 *239, 249*
22:17–24:22 *249*
24:23–34 *249*
25–29 *249*
26:4–5 *239*
30 *249*
31:1–9 *249*
31:10–31 *249, 250*
31:26 *250*

Ecclesiastes
1:1–11 *252*
1:3 *252*
1:14 *253*
1:15 *276*
1:17 *253*
2:11 *253*
2:17 *253*
2:26 *253, 276*
3:1–14 *276*
3:11 *252, 276*
3:14 *276*

3:16–18 *276*
3:20 *252*
7:13 *276*
8:12–13 *276*
9:1 *276*
9:10 *252*
9:12 *253*
11:1 *236*
11:5 *276*
11:9 *276*
12:7 *252*
12:8–14 *252*
12:13 *277*
12:13–14 *253, 257, 263*
12:14 *276*

Song of Songs
1:5 *242*
2:16 *256*
6:3 *256*
7:10 *256*

Isaiah
1 *295*
1:10–17 *121*
1–39 *301*
5:1–7 *295*
6 *113, 283, 301, 331*
7:14 *323, 355, 369*
9:1–7 *289*
9:2 *321*
9:6 *323*
9:6–7 *157, 220*
9:7 *213, 318*
11:1–2 *213*
11:2 *221*
11:5 *221*
11:10 *221*
11:11–15 *157*
11:53 *213*
20 *296*
26 *407*
28:16 *516*
30:8 *28*
35:5–6 *323*
36–39 *290, 301*
40 *326*
40:1 *301*
40:2 *326*

40:3 *326*
40:5 *326*
40:6 *326*
40:6–8 *326*
40:8 *11*
40–55 *323, 324*
42 *323*
42:1 *221*
42:6–7 *398*
44:24–45:7 *225*
44:28 *9*
45:22 *405*
49 *323*
49:1 *454*
49:6 *220, 405*
50 *323*
52:13–15 *324*
52:13–53:12 *322, 323, 455*
52:15 *455*
53 *9, 121, 301, 323, 324, 331, 363*
53:3 *324, 325*
53:4 *324*
53:5 *324, 363*
53:5–6 *318, 324*
53:6 *324*
53:7 *324*
53:8 *324*
53:10 *325*
53:10–12 *325*
53:12 *324*
61:1 *323, 402*
65–66 *547*

Jeremiah

1 *113, 283, 304*
1:5 *414, 454*
2 *134, 242*
3:1 *196*
4:1–2 *316*
4:23 *100*
5:14 *11, 283*
7 *305*
16:14–15 *112*
17:1 *29*
23:4–6 *321*
23:5–6 *157, 213, 221*
23:6 *318*
28 *283, 304*
31 *137, 331*

31:27–34 *135, 305, 315*
31:31–34 *157, 331*
31:33 *317*
33:14–17 *213*
33:26 *323*
36:2 *29*
36:18 *29*
37:2 *13, 282*
49:7–22 *309*

Lamentations

3 *61*
3:19–24 *59*
3:19–38 *305*
4:9–10 *60*
4:21–22 *309*

Ezekiel

1 *81*
1–3 *113, 283, 306*
1–24 *306*
8 *306*
11:22–23 *328*
14:14 *234*
14:21 *316*
15 *306*
16 *306*
21 *306*
23 *295*
24:15–26 *296*
25:12–14 *309*
25–32 *306*
34 *306*
34:11 *317*
34:20–24 *213*
34:23 *321, 323*
34:23–24 *157, 306, 315, 318*
34:25 *306, 317*
34:25–31 *321*
34:26 *316, 317*
34–48 *306*
35:5–6 *309*
36:22 *306*
36:24 *137*
36:26 *9, 306*
36:26–27 *317*
37 *199, 331*
37:1–14 *306*
37:24 *318*

37:24–25 *157*
37:24–28 *213, 306*
37:25 *323*
40–48 *306*

Daniel
1 *332*
1–6 *306, 307*
2 *9*
7 *9, 81, 323, 332*
7–12 *307*
7:13–14 *81, 369*
9:4 *118*
9:11 *89*
10 *81*
12:1–3 *307*

Hosea
1–2 *134*
1–3 *242*
2:7 *287*
2:14–23 *157*
2:17 *287*
3 *298*
4 *472*
4:4–9 *287*
4:7 *472*
11:1 *354, 369*
11:2 *287*
11:2–11 *354*
12:13 *283*

Joel
1 *289*
2:12–13 *308*
2:13 *118*
2:28–32 *308*

Amos
1:2 *62*
2:7–8 *287*
3:15 *287*
4:6–13 *317*
4:12 *288*
5:1–3 *295*
5:21–24 *297*
5:21–25 *121*
6:4 *287*
7 *113, 283*

7:10–17 *283, 369*
7:14 *297*
7:17 *288*
9:11 *213, 400*
9:11–15 *297*

Obadiah
1:15–16 *309*
1:21 *309*

Jonah
1:3 *299*
1:15 *299*
1:17 *299*
3:4 *298*
3:7 *299*
4 *299*
4:2 *118, 299*
4:11 *299*

Micah
1:2 *300*
3:1 *300*
3:2 *299*
3:2–3 *299*
3:9 *299*
3:10 *300*
3:11-12 *288*
5:1–5 *289*
5:2 *220, 300*
5:4 *220*
5:5 *300*
6:1 *300*
6:6–8 *121*

Nahum
1:2–3 *302*
1:7 *302*
1:8 *302*
2:3–4 *302*
3:2–3 *302*

Habakkuk
1:2–4 *291, 302*
1:5–7 *291*
1:5–11 *302*
1:12–17 *302*
2:1 *302*
2:2 *24*

2:4 *303*
2:4–20 *302*
3 *303*

Zephaniah
1:2–6 *304*
2:4–15 *304*
3:9–20 *304*
3:17 *304*

Haggai
1:1–11 *310*
1:4 *309*
1:12–15 *310*
2:23 *310*

Zechariah
1 *310*
1–6 *310*
1–8 *311*
2 *310*
3 *311*
3:8 *213, 323*
3:8–9 *312, 318*
4 *310*
5 *310*
6 *311*
9:9 *312, 330*
9–14 *311, 312*
11:4–17 *312*
13:7 *312*
13:9 *312*
14:4 *331*

Malachi
1:6–14 *312*
2:1–9 *312*
2:10–16 *312*
3:1 *312, 321*
3:7–15 *312*
3:10 *317*
3:12 *316*
4:2 *319, 320*
4:4 *89*
4:5 *312*
4:6 *206*

Matthew
1:1 *107, 188, 362*

1:1–17 *343*
1:5 *167*
1:18–2:23 *343*
1:21 *362, 372*
1:22 *14*
1:23 *355, 369, 372*
2 *218, 219, 221*
2:1 *221*
2:2 *220*
2:3 *221*
2:4 *219*
2:6 *220*
2:15 *354, 369*
2:23 361
2–7 *112*
4:4 *129*
4:7 *129*
4:10 *129*
4:17 *356*
5 *269*
5:3 *499*
5:5 *499*
5:8 *500*
5:11–12 *499, 500*
5:12 *370*
5:17–48 *369*
5:18 *15, 86*
5:22 *499*
5:29–30 *138*
5:33–37 *500*
5:48 *499*
5–7 *498, 499*
6:19–21 *254, 500*
6:24 *499*
7 *67*
7:1 *66*
7:1–6 *499*
7:7–11 *499*
7:16–18 *499*
7:24 *499*
7:26 *499*
11:28 *369*
12:3 *369*
12:6 *369*
12:40 *16*
12:42 *369*
18:15–22 *372*
18:20 *355*
19:4 *16*

19:8 *89*
21:5 *312*
22:1–14 *350*
22:31–32 *14*
22:37–38 *129*
22:45 *369*
23:35 *369*
24:37–38 *369*
25:9 *350*
25:35–46 *123*
28:15 *347*
28:16–20 *372*
28:20 *362, 372*

Mark

1:1 *356, 373*
1:1–11 *342*
1:12–13 *342*
1:14–15 *342*
1:16–20 *342*
1:21–8:22 *342*
1:23–28 *348*
1:29–31 *348*
1:32–34 *348*
4:1–42 *342*
4:10–12 *372*
4:11–12 *357*
4:35–41 *372*
6:3 *494, 528*
6:34 *364*
8:23–30 *342*
8:28 *364*
8:31–33 *342*
9:2–13 *342*
9:14–10:52 *342*
10:45 *325, 363*
10:48 *364*
11:1–10 *342*
11:11–26 *342*
11:27–12:44 *342*
13 *342*
14:43–72 *342*
14:58 *341*
14:62 *259, 369*
15 *342*
15:22 *356*
15:29–30 *370*
15:39 *343, 373*
16:1–8 *342*

16:5–7 *373*
16:8 *373*

Luke

1 *387, 404*
1:1–4 *67, 351, 381, 384*
1:4 *341, 406*
1:5–2:52 *343, 351*
1:5–23 *351*
1:6 *357*
1:24–38 *351*
1:39–56 *351*
1:46–55 *364*
1:54–55 *364*
1:57–80 *351*
1:67–79 *364*
1:69 *323*
2:1–7 *352*
2:8–20 *352*
2:14 *325*
2:21–40 *352*
2:25 *357*
2:41–52 *352*
3:1–20 *352*
3:1–22 *352*
3:21–22 *352*
3:22 *402, 403*
3:23–4:13 *352*
3:23–38 *343, 352*
3:38 *369*
4:1–13 *352*
4:14–9:50 *352*
4:14–30 *352*
4:18 *402*
4:18–19 *370*
4:31–9:17 *352*
8:23–25 *367*
9:18–50 *352*
9:22 *358*
9:51–19:27 *352*
9:51–62 *352*
10:1–12 *352*
10:13–19:27 *352*
10:21 *402*
10:33 *350*
10:36 *350*
11:13 *402*
11:51 *16, 369*
12:12 *402*

13:31–34 *369*
15 *350*
17:26 *16*
17:26–27 *369*
18:1–8 *350*
18:9 *378*
18:9–14 *350, 358, 376*
19:28–23:56 *353*
19:28–44 *353*
19:45–20:19 *353*
20:20–47 *353*
21:1–36 *353*
21:14–15 *387*
21:37–22:53 *353*
22:13–20 *369*
22:54–23:56 *353*
22:69 *385*
23:28 *334*
23:34 *365*
23:42 *376*
23:43 *369*
23:46 *364, 374*
23:47 *343, 358, 374*
24 *396*
24:1–12 *353*
24:1–53 *353*
24:13–35 *353*
24:27 *396, 398*
24:36–49 *353*
24:44 *21, 39, 335*
24:44–45 *396, 398*
24:45 *335*
24:46 *336*
24:50–53 *353*

John

1 *327*
1:1–5 *369*
1:1–18 *344, 367, 374*
1:3 *367*
1:14 *306, 330, 368, 369, 374, 376*
1:18 *344*
1:29 *114, 121*
2:1–11 *359*
2:13 *344*
2:18–22 *341*
3 *16*
3:14–15 *369*
3:16 *66, 78*

4:25–26 *360*
4:46–54 *359*
5:1 *344*
5:39 *361*
5:46 *89*
6:1–14 *359*
6:16–21 *359*
6:32 *365*
6:33 *366*
6:35 *365*
6:54–55 *365*
6–8 *112*
7:19 *89*
7:37–39 *369*
8:58 *360, 367*
10 *306*
10:22–23 *344*
10:27 *16*
10:35 *15*
11 *344*
11:38–57 *359*
12:15 *312*
12:41 *301, 323*
14:15 *271*
17:24 *367*
19:28 *67, 69*
20:1–29 *359*
20:30–3 *25*
20:30–31 *340, 359*
20:31 *67, 341*
21:24 *30*

Acts

1:1–2 *381*
1:1–11 *379*
1:6 *379*
1:7–8 *379, 385, 387, 390*
1:8 *384, 390, 404, 405*
1:9–11 *406*
1:12–8:4 *390*
1:16 *14, 391*
1:20 *391*
1:21–26 *391*
1–10 *390*
1–12 *380*
2:1–4 *384*
2:1–13 *385*
2:3 *403*
2:14–21 *308*

2:16–17 *387*
2:17 *388*
2:17–21 *401*
2:29–36 *389*
2:36 *385*
2:37 *392*
2:38 *392*
2:47 *123*
3:11–26 *405*
3:21 *391*
3:22 *89*
3:24–26 *405*
4:8 *404*
4:12 *358, 391*
5:29 *391*
6:10 *387*
7 *400, 478*
7:55 *380*
7:55–56 *389*
7:56 *385*
8:5–15:41 *390*
8:32–35 *400*
8:34–35 *319*
9:1 *409*
9:1–18 *409*
9:1–22 *406*
9:3 *413*
9:3–6 *409*
9:5 *412*
9:6 *391*
9:9 *410*
9:14 *401*
9:15 *455*
9:16 *391*
9:21 *401*
11:19 *495*
12:2 *494*
12:17 *494*
12:20–23 *393*
12:22 *393*
12:23 *393*
13:9 *404*
13:32–33 *397*
13:47 *400*
13–28 *380, 390*
14:22 *391*
15 *398*
15:8–11 *399*
15:13 *494*

15:13–18 *400*
16:1–28:31 *390*
16:10 *381*
16:16–40 *415*
16:30–31 *391*
17:3 *391*
17:4–10 *415*
18 *430*
21:18 *494*
21:27–28 *415*
22:1–30 *407*
22:3–21 *409*
22:6 *407*
22:16 *401*
23:6 *392, 411*
23:7–9 *392*
26 *395*
26:1–3 *395*
26:4–7 *395*
26:5 *411*
26:8 *395*
26:9–20 *395, 409*
26:16–18 *397*
26:21–23 *395*
26:24–32 *395*
26:27 *395*
28 *387*
28:16–31 *384*

Romans
1:1 *414*
1:2 *442*
1:3 *452*
1:11 *429*
1:15 *464*
1:16–17 *464, 469*
1:16–18 *429*
1:17 *303, 468*
1:20 *10*
2:25–29 *419*
3:4 *14*
3:8 *417*
3:9 *457*
3:10–18 *456*
3:18 *456*
3:21–26 *469*
3:23 *104*
3:25 *458*
3:27–4:25 *463*

3:27–31 *466*
4 *458*
4:1–8 *466*
4:2–5 *503*
4:3 *458*
4:9 *458*
4:23 *458*
4:23–25 *466*
5:1 *463*
5:5 *462, 467*
5:12 *104*
5:12–14 *457*
5:12–21 *457*
5:14 *457*
5:15–21 *466*
6:1–2 *417, 504*
6:1–11 *467*
6:3–4 *466*
6:23 *104*
7:7 *461*
7:7–25 *416, 429, 462*
8:11 *470*
8:17 *416, 467*
8:18–39 *429*
8:19–27 *417*
8:22 *104*
8:23 *470*
8:23–25 *473*
8:24 *419*
8:28–30 *467*
8:28–39 *466*
8:34 *453*
8:38–39 *468*
9:1–5 *416*
9:11 *467*
9–11 *429*
10:1–2 *416*
10:1–4 *469*
10:5 *89*
10:8–13 *465*
10:13 *468*
10:19 *455*
11:5 *467*
11:7 *467*
11:13 *455*
11:13–14 *455*
11:13–15 *418*
11:28 *467*
13:9–10 *462*
13:14 *468*

14:23 *461*
15:4 *76*
15:7–13 *455*
15:20–21 *455*
15:24 *416*
16:17–20 *429*
16:22 *31*

1 Corinthians
1:8–9 *468*
1:10–6:20 *430*
1:10–17 *430*
1:11 *430*
1:18 *431*
1:18–25 *221*
1:27–28 *152*
1:30 *431, 466, 470*
1:30–31 *461*
1:31 *431*
2:12–14 *72*
2:14 *16*
3:1–23 *430*
4 *430*
5 *430*
5:2 *431*
5:7 *453*
6 *430*
6:19–20 *140*
7 *430*
7:1 *430*
7:40 *26*
8 *430*
8:4 *412*
8:5–6 *144*
8:6 *468*
9 *431*
9:7–10 *456*
9:23 *413, 416*
10 *112, 431*
10:1–13 *460*
10:4 *451*
10:8 *460*
10:9–10 *460*
10:10 *460*
10:11–12 *460*
10:31 *141*
11:1 *419, 472*
11:1–17 *431*
11:18–34 *431*
12:3 *468*

12–14 *431*
13:9–10 *471, 527*
13:12 *471*
15 *431*
15:3–4 *413, 454*
15:9–10 *412*
15:20 *443*
15:35–55 *473*
15:45 *457*
15:50–54 *457*
15:55–57 *468*
16:1–3 *416*
16:17 *430*

2 Corinthians

1:3–7 *432*
1:8–10 *432*
1:20 *419, 442*
1–9 *432*
2:1 *432*
2:3–9 *432*
2:4 *432*
2:5–8 *432*
2:10 *432*
4:5 *468*
5 *112*
5:20–21 *466, 469*
6:14–18 *112*
6:16 *14*
6–7 *432*
7:2 *432*
7:8–12 *432*
10:10–12 *417*
10–13 *432*
11:5 *432*
11:5–6 *415*
11:24 *415*
11:25–28 *416*
11:28 *416*
12:7 *415*
12:10 *415*

Galatians

1:1 *414, 449*
1:1–5 *449*
1:2 *449*
1:3 *449*
1:3–5 *449*
1:4 *432, 433*
1:6–2:14 *448*

1:6–4:31 *450*
1:6–7 *433*
1:6–10 *417, 448*
1:8–9 *48*
1:11–12 *414*
1:14 *411*
1:15 *454*
1:15–16 *414*
1:19 *494*
2:8 *455*
2:11–14 *415*
2:15–21 *433, 448, 449, 466, 467*
2:16 *442*
2:17 *417*
2:19–20 *466*
2:21 *446*
3 *458*
3:1–6:10 *449*
3:6 *458*
3:6–9 *433*
3:8 *454*
3:10–14 *434*
3:11 *303*
3:13 *411*
3:15–18 *454, 458*
3:21–24 *461*
3:24 *461*
3:25–28 *467*
3:26–29 *433*
3:28 *145*
4 *147*
4:13–14 *415*
5:1–6:10 *450*
5:2–6 *433*
5:5 *466*
5:6 *504*
5:7–12 *415*
5:16 *461*
6:11–12 *415*
6:11–13 *433*
6:11–18 *449, 450*
6:15 *443*
6:17 *416*
6:18 *450*

Ephesians

1:3–14 *434, 467*
1:5 *467*
1:7 *470*
1:11 *467*

1:11–15 467
1:14 470
1:15–23 468
1:16–19 434
1:21 468
2:1–3 470
2:4 121
4:1 434
4:5 468
4:30 470
5:15 434
5:17 471
5:22–32 134, 242
6:10–20 434

Philippians
1:6 419, 440
1:12–18 426, 435
1:19–26 435
1:21–23 473
1:21–26 467
2:1–3 435
2:5–11 436, 443
2:9–11 468
2:14–16 435
2:22 439
3:2 44, 435
3:2–3 415
3:5 411
3:6 411
3:7–11 416, 466
3:7–20 436
3:17 473
3:17–21 472, 473
3:21 473
4:13 66

Colossians
1:14 470
1:15 104
1:19 437
2:8 48, 436
2:11–15 437, 467
3:1 466
3:1–4 467
3:16 248
4:10 436
4:14 381
4:16 35, 44

1 Thessalonians
1:4 467
1:5 437
2:14 438
2:18 415
3:1–13 438
4:3–8 438
4:9 438
4:13–17 438, 468
5:11 438
5:12–13 438
5:17 438

2 Thessalonians
1:3–10 438
2:1–2 438
3:11–12 438
3:13 438

1 Timothy
1:3 438
1:3–11 438
1:12–14 413
1:16 413
2:1–8 438
3 438
4 438
5:1–16 438
5:17–22 438
6:1–5 438
6:1–19 438
6:3–10 48
6:20–21 438

2 Timothy
1:6–7 439
1:8–18 439
2:1–7 439
2:8 452
2:9–10 467
2:14–4:5 439
2:15 52
3:1–9 439
3:12 222
3:16 13, 14, 80, 163, 229
3:16–17 17, 76
4:2 313
4:6 439
4:6–8 382

4:6–20 *424*
4:7–8 *418*
4:10–11 *382*
4:10–12 *439*
4:11 *381*
4:13 *30*
4:13–22 *439*

Titus
1:5 *438*
1:5–9 *439*
1:10–2:15 *439*
3 *439*

Philemon
10 *439*
10:12–14 *439*
10:13 *439*
10:15–16 *439*

Hebrews
1 *486*
1:1–2 *14, 481, 487*
1:1–4 *480, 482, 484, 486, 489*
1:2–3 *489*
1:5–9 *489*
1:5–14 *484*
2:1–4 *484*
2:3 *478*
2:5 *492*
2:5–3:11 *484*
2:10 *490*
2:10–13 *493*
2:14–18 *492, 493*
3:1–6 *481, 489*
3:6 *487, 492*
3:7–4:11 *489*
3:7–19 *128, 481, 487*
3:11–4:13 *486*
3:12 *480*
3:12–15 *484*
3:14 *492*
3:16–19 *484*
3:19 *487*
4:1–3 *484*
4:1–10 *481*
4:4–10 *484*
4:11–16 *484*
4:14 *487*

4:15 *490*
5:1–10 *481, 484*
5:7–9 *490*
5:9 *490*
5:11–6:17 *484*
6:18 *487*
6:18–10:18 *485*
6:19–7:28 *481*
6:20 *486*
7 *260*
7:1 *486*
7:1–19 *486*
7:25 *489*
8 *481*
9:1–10:31 *481*
10:1 *487, 490*
10:1–2 *479*
10:1–18 *121*
10:7 *490*
10:19–31 *485*
10:23 *487, 492*
10:31 *485*
10:32–11:40 *485*
10:36–39 *487*
11:4 *488*
11:5 *488*
11:6 *488*
11:7 *488*
11:8–10 *488*
11:11–12 *488*
11:12–16 *488*
11:14 *492*
11:17–19 *488*
11:20 *488*
11:21 *488*
11:22 *488*
11:23 *488*
11:24–29 *488*
11:30–31 *488*
11:32–38 *488*
11:39–40 *488, 490*
12:1–29 *485*
12:6 *491*
12:18–24 *481*
12:18–29 *490*
12:22 *491, 492*
12:23–25 *491*
13 *477, 478*
13:1–17 *485*

13:8 *489*
13:14 *492*
13:18–25 *483, 485*
13:23 *479*
13:24 *479*

James

1:1 *493, 494, 495, 509, 528*
1:1–8 *498*
1:2 *499*
1:2–4 *506*
1:4 *499*
1:5 *499*
1:9–11 *496, 498*
1:13–15 *498*
1:17 *499*
1:17–18 *498*
1:18 *497*
1:19–20 *498*
1:20 *499*
1:21 *497, 505*
1:22–23 *499*
1:26 *498*
1:27 *498*
2:1–13 *496*
2:5 *499*
2:13 *499*
2:14 *496, 500, 503*
2:14–26 *498, 500, 506*
2:21 *500*
2:23 *500*
2:23–24 *503*
2:25 *501*
3:1 *496*
3:1–12 *498*
3:12 *499*
3:15 *496*
4:1–10 *498*
4:2–3 *499*
4:4 *499*
4:8 *500*
4:13–17 *498*
5 *501*
5:1 *504*
5:1–3 *500*
5:1–12 *498*
5:4 *497, 505*
5:5–6 *505*
5:7 *498*

5:7–9 *501*
5:7–12 *505*
5:8 *505*
5:9 *496, 505*
5:10 *500*
5:11 *234, 501*
5:12 *500, 533*
5:13–20 *498, 502*
5:17 *502*
5:19–20 *505*

1 Peter

1:1 *495, 507, 509*
1:3–9 *509, 510*
1:3–10 *511*
1:3–11 *517*
1:3–12 *512*
1:6 *519*
1:7 *510*
1:8 *519*
1:13–17 *512*
1:15–16 *123*
1:16 *122, 510, 516, 517, 519*
1:16–21 *516*
1:17 *512*
1:18–3:22 *513*
1:18–20 *121*
1:18–21 *513*
1:22–25 *513*
2:1–10 *513*
2:5 *513, 516*
2:6 *516*
2:9 *133*
2:9–10 *66, 137*
2:11 *509, 513*
2:11–17 *513*
2:18–25 *513*
2:20 *509*
3:1–7 *513*
3:8–17 *513*
3:17 *509*
3:18 *513*
3:18–22 *513*
4:1–6 *513*
4:1–11 *510, 511*
4:1–19 *513*
4:3–4 *509*
4:7–11 *513*
4:17 *513, 518*

4:17–19 *510*
4:19 *519*
5:1–14 *514*
5:4 *510, 511, 514*
5:5 *514*
5:7 *514*

2 Peter

1:3–4 *517*
1:3–11 *510, 511, 514, 517*
1:5–11 *518*
1:12 *515*
1:12–15 *515*
1:12–21 *510*
1:14 *515*
1:16–21 *515*
1:19–21 *283*
1:21 *14*
2 *507, 511, 519, 528*
2:1 *507, 515, 517*
2:1–22 *515*
2:3 *517*
2:3–5 *510*
2:4 *510*
2:5 *510, 517*
2:6 *510*
2:12 *509*
2:17 *510*
2:19 *510*
3:1–13 *510, 511, 515, 533*
3:4 *518*
3:5–10 *518*
3:10–15 *519*
3:13 *510*
3:14 *515, 519*
3:14–16 *35*
3:14–18 *515*
3:15–16 *26, 44, 515*
3:16 *422*
3:17 *510*
3:18 *510, 515*

1 John

1:1–4 *522, 527*
1:5–10 *520, 523*
2:1–2 *523, 526*
2:3–4:21 *523*
2:18 *526, 527*
2:19 *520*

2:22 *526*
2:22–23 *520*
3:2 *527*
3:8 *521*
3:10 *524*
3:11–12 *521, 525*
3:12 *533*
3:23 *521*
3:24 *527*
4:1–3 *533*
4:2–3 *520*
4:3 *526*
4:6 *527*
4:8 *526*
4:9–11 *526*
4:10 *526*
4:16 *526*
5:1–21 *523*
5:4–5 *527*
5:21 *523, 525*

2 John

1:1 *520*
1:1–3 *523*
1:4–11 *523*
1:12 *30*
1:12–13 *524*
7 *526*

3 John

1:1 *520*
1:1–2 *524*
1:3–12 *524*
1:5–8 *524*
1:9 *521*
1:13–15 *524*
13 *31*

Jude

1:1 *528*
1:3 *528, 529, 532*
1:3–4 *529*
1:4 *528, 529*
1:5 *529, 530*
1:5–7 *529*
1:6 *528*
1:7 *528*
1:8–16 *529*
1:9 *531*

1:11 *528, 530*
1:14–15 *532*
1:17–18 *529*
1:17–19 *529*
1:20–25 *529*
3 *534*
11 *533*
14 *40*

Revelation
1 *81, 82*
1:1 *540*
1:1–2 *537*
1:1–8 *542*
1:3 *537, 540*
1:4 *540, 541*
1:8 *547*
1:9 *535, 537*
1:9–3:22 *542*
1:11 *26*
2:4 *537*
2:6 *537*
2:9–10 *537*
2:13 *537*
2:14–15 *537*
2:20–22 *537*
2–3 *537, 539, 541*
3 *312*
3:3 *537*
3:9 *537*
3:16 *537*
4:1–5:14 *542*
4–22 *539*
6:1–17 *542*
6:9–11 *546*

6:10 *546*
6–16 *541*
7:1–17 *542*
8:1–5 *542, 548*
8:6–9:21 *542*
10:1–11:14 *542*
11:15–19 *542*
11:19 *547*
12:1 *545*
12:1–6 *543*
12:1–13:18 *542*
12:11 *548*
14:1–20 *542*
15:1–16:21 *542*
17:1–18:24 *542*
19:1–10 *542*
19:11–21 *542*
19:16 *548*
20:1–2 *539*
20:1–10 *538, 539, 542*
20:3 *539*
20:4–6 *539*
20:7–10 *539*
20:11–15 *542*
21:1–8 *542*
21:2 *547*
21:6 *547*
21:9–27 *306, 542*
21:22 *547*
22:1–7 *542*
22:8–21 *542*
22:13 *547*
22:18–19 *541*
22:21 *541*